THE SOURCEBOOK OF ARTISTS
DESIGNER'S EDITION
10

::: THE GUILD®

Kraus Sikes Inc.
Madison, Wisconsin
USA

TABLE OF CONTENTS

FEATURES

THE GUILD at Ten   ix
by Jody Clowes
"THE GUILD is more than just a beautiful book," says the author, a specialist in the decorative arts. Her short history describes what else it is, and how it got to be that way.

Commission Profiles
Thumbnail sketches of projects by ten distinguished GUILD artists.

Marilyn Forth	x	Ulrika Leander	xiv
Thomas Masaryk	xi	John Clark	xv
Doug Weigel	xiii	Ira A. Keer	xv
Linda Perry	xiii	Jonathan Winfisky	xvi
Joan Schulze	xiv	Amanda Richardson	xvi

Reflections on the Commissioning Process
Short interviews with some long-time advertisers.

Barbara Grenell	9	Timothy and Andrea Biggs	121
Joyce Lopez	19	Glenn Elvig	143
B.J. Adams	27	Frank Colson	149
Elizabeth MacDonald	88	Nancy J. Young	157
Shawn Athari	93	J.E. Jasen	160
Beth Cunningham	111	Angelika Traylor	176

The Studio Furniture Movement   134
An overview of independent furniture makers in the last half-century.

Acknowledgements   207
Ten years of THE GUILD has meant over 200,000 beautiful books in print. Publisher Toni Sikes recalls the people who helped make it happen.

RESOURCES

Ten Great Ways to Use the Designer's Edition   1
A tour of the book's features and possibilities.

Gallery Listings   177
Our state-by-state directory of 1,500 galleries in the U.S. and Canada.

Organizations and Publications   210
Selected groups and periodicals focusing on the decorative arts.

Index of Artists By State   213

Index of Artists and Companies   214

TABLE OF CONTENTS

ARTISTS

Artists by Section
Turn the page for a listing of featured artists.

WORK FOR THE WALL

Tapestry 4

Art Quilts 10

Paper 20

Fiber 28

Ceramics 81

Glass 89

Other Media 94

Painted Finishes and Murals 112

FURNITURE

Wood 124

Metal 137

Other Media 144

ACCESSORIES

Lighting 152

Textiles and Floor Coverings 158

Sculpture and Objects 161

THE GUILD REGISTER®

Concise product and pricing information, as well as addresses and phones,
for artists working in two important areas.

THE GUILD REGISTER of Fiber Art for the Wall 45

THE GUILD REGISTER of Ceramic Art for the Wall 70

ARTISTS BY SECTION

WORK FOR THE WALL

Tapestry

Laura Militzer Bryant   4

Victor Jacoby   5

Ulrika Leander   6

Loretta Mossman   7

Sheila O'Hara   8

Art Quilts

Emma Allebes   10

Beth Cassidy   11

M.A. Klein   12

Verena Levine   13

Therese May   14

Jean Neblett   15

Linda S. Perry   16

Susan Sawyer   17

Kathleen Sharp   18

Paper

Karen Adachi   20

Elaine Albers Cohen   21

Martha Chatelain   22

Marlene Lenker   23

Keiko Nelson   24

Marjorie Tomchuk   25

Judith Uehling   26

Fiber

B.J. Adams   28

Sally Bailey   29

Susan Eileen Burnes   30

Barbara Cade   31

Phyllis 'Ceratto' Evans   32

Doris Finch   33

Marilyn Forth   34

Barbara Grenell   35

Bill Hio   36

Marie-Laure Ilie   37

Rachel Lindstrom   38

Joyce P. Lopez   39

Jewell Peterson   40

Mary Curtis Ratcliff   41

Amanda Richardson   42

Joan Schulze   43

Nancy Taylor Stonington   44

Ceramics

George Alexander   81

Art on Tiles   82

George F. Fishman   83

J. Louis Heithmar   84

Beverlee Lehr   85

Elizabeth MacDonald   86

William C. Richards   87

Glass

Shawn Athari   89

Stephen Brathwaite   90

Dale R. Eggert   91

Toby Mason   92

Other Media

Carolyn Blakeslee   94

Jeff Entner   95

Ted Box   95

Barbara Brotherton   96

Myra Burg   97

Deborah Carlson   98

Cloisonné Enamels by M. Slepian   99

Beth Cunningham   100

Alonzo Davis   101

Marsha Farley   102

Silja Lahtinen   103

Dianna Thornhill Miller   104

Jim Miller   104

Bernie Rowell   105

ARTISTS BY SECTION

WORK FOR THE WALL

Other Media

Kurt Shaw   106

Celia Soper   107

Martin Sturman   108

Susan Venable   109

Alice Van Leunen   110

Marjorie A. Atwood   112

Painted Finishes and Murals

Andrea M. Biggs   113

Timothy G. Biggs   113

Bill Gibbons Studio   114

Eyecon, Inc.   115

Dale B. Fehr   116

Yoshi Hayashi   117

Thomas Masaryk   118

Melissa A. Murphy   119

Vigini & Associates   120

FURNITURE

Wood

Jeff Entner   124

Ted Box   124

John Clark   125

Concepts By J, Inc.   126

Glenn Elvig   127

Off The Wall Design Studios, Inc.   128

Paul Reiber   129

Bill Rix   130

Ryerson Designs   131

Claude Terrell   132

Peter Tischler   133

Metal

Sean Calyer   137

Christopher Thomson Ironworks   138

Craig Kaviar   139

Paul Knoblauch   140

Konried Muench Designs   141

Doug Weigel   142

Other Media

Brigitte Benzakin   144

Lynn DiNino   145

FurnARTure etc.   146

Igor Naskalov   147

Toni Putnam   148

ACCESSORIES

Peter M. Fillerup   152

Lightspann Illumination Design   153

Pam Morris   154

William C. Richards   155

Angelika Traylor   156

Natalie Darmohraj   158

Diann Parrott   159

Shawn Athari   161

Frank Colson   162

Carole Alden Doubek   163

Mari Marks Fleming   164

Shuji Ikeda   165

Johanna Okovic Goodman   166

J.E. Jasen   167

Anne Mayer Meier   168

National Sculptors' Guild   169

Nourot Glass Studio   170

Charles Pearson   171

Timothy Roeder   171

Martin Sturman   172

Tim Walker   173

Jonathan Winfisky   174

Allen Young   175

Nancy J. Young   175

THE GUILD'S SUCCESS HAS DEPENDED ON THE ENERGY AND EFFORTS OF MANY PEOPLE.

Originally, Toni Sikes (creative director, market researcher and fire-under-the-feet) and Bill Kraus (company lawyer, accountant, business advisor, newsletter editor and moral support) were joined by a secretary and production manager in their New York apartment; four sales representatives worked in the field. Today, in Wisconsin, the company relies on eight administrative and production staff and seven sales representatives, each a specialist in their field. Kraus is no longer active in the business (other than listening to Sikes over dinner every night); as vice president of sales, Susan Evans is second-in-charge of the growing business.

From the very beginning, when the hours were long and the pay meager, people came to THE GUILD because they believed in its goals. And, according to Toni Sikes, each of these people has left a mark. "THE GUILD is what it is today because a great many smart and devoted people have cared about it and moved it forward. We've been very fortunate."

Photo: UPI / Bettmann

THE GUILD AT TEN

By Jody Clowes

> THE GUILD is more than just a beautiful book. It is a link between artists and the architects, designers, professional consultants and others who create our built environment, and it succeeds largely because it presents artists' work in a format which is readily understood in the design world.
>
> THE GUILD treats lamps and wall sconces as lighting, not wood or metal or glass. It embraces paper, fiber, mixed media and ceramic relief under the rubric "Work for the Wall." Its articles address pragmatic concerns about the durability and care of artwork, the nature of collaboration, and the logistics of the commissioning process.
>
> THE GUILD is based on the recognition that artists and design professionals operate in remarkably separate realms; even their literature is distinct. Architects who might consider using hand-forged banisters or custom woodwork aren't likely to reach for craft magazines. And most interior designers would order tile through a distributor, rather than from a nearby ceramist— not because of quality or expense, but because they don't have the time or the resources to locate an artist. As a bridge between these groups, THE GUILD provides ready access to artists as thousands of volumes are distributed directly to the design trades each year.
>
> During the last ten years, THE GUILD has evolved in step with the artists it represents, stretching to reach new audiences, struggling to define itself and its goals, and finding its place in the increasingly sophisticated market that has emerged to support the architectural and decorative arts.
>
> As a resource for design professionals, THE GUILD strives to be both inspirational and useful. Its longevity and consistent record of successful commissions demonstrate its effectiveness.
>
> — J.C.

I N 1985, Kraus Sikes Inc. was all concept and no product. It consisted quite literally of Bill Kraus and Toni Sikes working out of their New York apartment; they didn't have a book or even a color brochure to show prospective advertisers. One year later, *THE GUILD: A Sourcebook of American Craft Artists* was in the hands of 10,000 design professionals across the United States. Today, the company's bustling offices publish three glossy sourcebooks annually for distribution around the globe.

IN THE BEGINNING

AN IDEA is only as good as its time. Opulence and decoration were unquestionably in style again in the 1980s, in backlash against the sterile hegemony of Modernism. The Postmodern movement brought a concern for detail, wit and delight back from the architectural shadows, and interior design revelled in ever more eclectic, improbable compositions. As the art market reached new highs, interest in the studio crafts soared along with it.

This giddy atmosphere was at its peak when Toni Sikes began formulating her ideas for the fledgling GUILD. She was armed with a master's degree in market research and fueled by her passion for the architectural arts and a strong desire to help artists sell their work.

MISTAKES AND MENTORS

IRONICALLY, the spark that first ignited THE GUILD fizzled. A friend sent Sikes a book on architectural arts in the West, published by the Western States Arts Foundation, and she fell in love with it. Investing two years of work and a good deal of money (her own and a publisher's), Sikes developed a similar book with a Midwest focus. Then it all fell apart.

"My publisher fell upon hard times," Sikes explains. "Months after I'd delivered the book, they told me they'd decided not to publish it. It was devastating, but it was also a real turning point. That's when I decided I would never again do something that was not in my control."

At this critical juncture, Sikes discovered the illustration and photography sourcebook *American Showcase*. Ira Shapiro, the founder and owner, encouraged her idea of a crafts sourcebook and shared crucial information. "Even today, much of our business is modelled after his," Sikes says frankly.

Sikes and Kraus spent 1984 on market research and a business plan and "Kraus Sikes Inc." was incorporated in January

ARTIST: MARILYN FORTH
LIAISON: ED VAN FLEET (RECORDING ARTIST)
TYPE OF WORK: PAINTED SILK (REPRODUCTION)
TITLE: *PANSIES*
SITE: ALBUM COVER

Ironically, just as Marilyn Forth began to increase the scale of her silk paintings, she was asked permission use a tiny detail for a high-profile project. Ed Van Fleet, musician, composer and producer, saw Pansies in THE GUILD and chose a small section of the 4' X 5' original for the cover of an audio cassette album. Forth and Van Fleet share a delight in the beauty of the natural world; the composer often blends electronic and acoustic instruments with sounds from nature.

Photo: Anthony Potter Photography

EACH EDITION OF THE GUILD
CARRIES THE SEEDS OF
FUTURE COMMISSIONS.

IN THE FOLLOWING PAGES,
WE HIGHLIGHT TEN PROJECTS
GENERATED THROUGH
THE GUILD
IN THE LAST DECADE.

Photo: Craig Allen

ARTIST: THOMAS MASARYK
LIASON: BONNIE GABRYS (INTERIOR DESIGNER)
                  BONNIE GABRYS INTERIORS
TYPE OF WORK: TROMPE L'OEIL CEILING AND WALLS
SITE: PRIVATE RESIDENCE
                  GREENWICH, CT

Thomas Masaryk sought to create a "gentle quietness" in this
large hallway—nearly 12'H x 10'W x 60'L—through carefully
controlled layers of acrylic paints thinned with gels. According to
Masaryk, creating 'straight' lines on the arched ceiling was particularly challenging and exacting. Both the faux stone walls and the
trompe l'oeil coffered ceiling are top-coated with an overglaze,
enhancing the dreamy quality of the artist's illusion.

1985. By June, four sales reps were hard at work selling pages in THE GUILD.

Asking artists to pay for advertising was virtually unheard of at this time (see sidebar), and there were no precedents for sourcebooks in the architectural or decorative arts. Furthermore, a number of Sikes' colleagues in the nonprofit crafts community expressed skepticism. She was told that artists didn't have the money to buy pages, at least not on an annual basis, and that they'd never come through with good photographs. "I heard that more than anything else," she recalls. "Now good photography is a common indicator of an artist's professionalism."

'TRUST ME'

BUT the greatest hurdle for the business was very basic: establishing trust. With no product and no track record, this was no small feat. More critically, Kraus Sikes Inc. had to overcome fears raised by a recent scandal in California, where many artists had been conned into buying ads in someone else's book-to-be. The 'publisher' had simply disappeared with the money, and the craft community was abuzz with angry stories.

"I knew it was impossible to say 'Trust me' to a field that didn't know who I was," Sikes says. "So I didn't try." Instead, she threw a grand party for THE GUILD, hoping that goodwill and great dancing would communicate for her.

Sikes invited all 609 exhibitors at the 1985 American Craft Enterprises fair in West Springfield, Massachusetts to a 'coming out party' for THE GUILD. The party was held in a huge, renovated dance hall in a nearby town. There was a DJ from Studio 54, old black and white films projected on the wall, and a company of swing dancers. "I think it was the best party I've ever been to," Sikes recalls, "We danced all night. It was definitely the right way to begin."

▶

A REVIEW PROCESS

PAGE sales were off to a good start, but to develop THE GUILD's credibility Sikes knew they'd have to review each submission before accepting it for the book. She designed review committees to represent the concerns of THE GUILD's users; over the years, members have included architects, interior designers, art consultants and editors from the design trade.

Architects Malcolm Holzman and Robert Jensen and editor Beverly Russell, who comprised the first committee, struggled to define their role. Russell and Holzman were very selective, but Jensen, a pragmatist, argued for including the full spectrum of what artists had to offer.

Jensen's view prevailed, and over the years, quality and appropriateness for THE GUILD's distribution, rather than style, have become the most important review criteria. THE GUILD is designed to showcase artists' work for potential buyers, not to arbitrate taste, and its success is due in no small measure to the wide range of aesthetic concerns its advertisers represent.

HANGING TOUGH

KRAUS SIKES INC. struggled through its first year, and the failure of direct mail efforts for book sales was its worst disappointment. Gambling on an elaborate brochure, they hoped to sell 3,000 copies of *THE GUILD 1*. Instead, they sold fewer than 300.

To offset this loss, the staff redoubled its publicity efforts, arranging press coverage, public lectures and exhibitions at high-profile locations like Bloomingdale's. *Metropolitan Home* was particularly supportive, giving regular coverage to GUILD artists and co-sponsoring THE GUILD's first American Craft Awards. As Sikes had hoped, the awards generated great press coverage for both the award winners and THE GUILD. They continued for four years, but by 1990, the rapid expansion of the business precluded outside ventures.

BUILDING BRIDGES

Today it's hard to believe that Toni Sikes met with so much resistance when she first proposed selling pages in THE GUILD to artists. But even in the mid-1980s, as galleries and collectors in the field proliferated, the anachronistic idealism which had characterized the craft movement since the nineteenth century still exerted a major influence. Many early proponents of the crafts revival had seen the crafts as tools for reforming the evils of industrial capitalism, and part of their legacy is the generalized suspicion of business and marketing that has been pervasive in the field until recently.

To some artists, advertising still means selling out, and purists regard even gallery sale commissions with distrust. The romance of creative self-sufficiency, of making a simple living with one's hands, is sustained by the example of those few sculptors, weavers and smiths who do manage to support themselves through word-of-mouth, walk-in business and blessed free press. For most artists, however, local markets and outlets simply aren't enough.

In order to communicate their vision, artists must find their ideal audience. Before 1986, nothing like THE GUILD existed for artists in the architectural and decorative arts. Though some specialist galleries and enlightened art consultants were working to advance the crafts, few outlets addressed themselves to commissioned or architectural art.

What these outlets cannot offer is the integrative, collaborative spirit of art made for a certain place and person, designed to articulate both the special qualities of those surroundings and the client's needs. It's this spirit that THE GUILD has fostered over the past decade, by building a bridge across the strange chasm that all too often keeps artists, architects and designers apart.

— J.C.

Doug Weigel's steel sculptures and mixed-media furniture often incorporate images from the southwestern United States. This table features Kokopelli, the humpbacked flute player often seen in ancient pottery and rock carvings of the area. The table is part of a large private collection which includes several works by Weigel.

Paging through THE GUILD 5, art consultant Candy Morgan was struck by a quilt that reminded her of a stained glass window. Morgan asked the artist, Linda Perry, to create a piece with a similar feel for the chapel of a Shriner's Hospital. The small room is a place for patients and family to pray and meditate, says Perry, "the perfect place for a work that conveys hope and light."

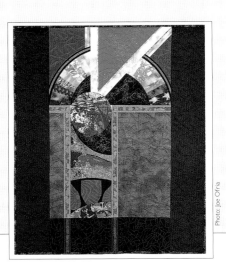

Photo: Joe Ofria

As the business stabilized, Sikes clarified and expanded her goals. THE GUILD's name suggests craftsmanship and professionalism, but it was also chosen because it implies membership. She wanted advertisers to feel they were joining a venture, not just sending money for ads. Artists received regular questionnaires and marketing tips, and THE GUILD offered them mailing lists and tearsheets at nominal rates.

In addition to his role as THE GUILD's legal and financial advisor, Kraus edited "The Guild Letter," a newsletter which guided advertisers through the foreign territory of the design professions. He focused on simple truths ("Normal people prefer photographs to slides," he once wrote), and his pithy, no-nonsense articles never strayed from the business at hand: exposing artists' work to their target audiences. Bridging the barriers of professional conduct continues to be a hallmark of THE GUILD.

GOOD THINGS HAPPEN SLOWLY

THESE efforts also helped to keep artists with THE GUILD during its first several years. Though occasionally artists receive a quick response from their advertising, sourcebooks rarely provide instant gratification.

"It's not so hard to sell pages the first time around, if you have a market artists are trying to reach. It's much harder to sell in the second year, because advertisers usually don't have sales right away," Sikes explains. "We actually did better the first year than the second, and I panicked."

This is a classic scenario for reference books, but Sikes and many of the artists didn't know that yet. By the third year, however, artists began calling to describe commissions they'd gotten through THE GUILD. Today, two-thirds of GUILD artists are repeat advertisers.

THE GUILD TRAVELS

DURING that difficult second year, Hearst Books International purchased 500 copies of *THE GUILD 2* to sell overseas. The books sold incredibly fast, especially in Japan. Due in large part to the success of international book sales, the business broke even for the first time with *THE GUILD 4*. Since then, through a continuing relationship with Rockport Publishers, international sales have outstripped domestic and now provide the financial stability that allows artists' advertising rates to be kept relatively low. They have also opened up new markets for artists, whose work is seen around the world through THE GUILD.

With worldwide distribution out of Kentucky and Massachusetts, advertisers throughout the United States and Canada, and printers in Japan and Hong Kong, it no longer seemed important that the company be headquartered in New York City. In 1990, Kraus and Sikes moved back home to Madison, Wisconsin.

REINVENTING THE GUILD

WITH room to breathe again, Sikes began reconsidering her approach to the business. In 1990, the company sold stock to Jim Black and Susan Evans, who became active partners. It was Black, with years of experience publishing directories, who helped her break free of some dearly-held assumptions.

Through the first five years, Sikes had concentrated her efforts on reaching out to artists and producing beautiful books. Black convinced her to turn her attention to THE GUILD's audience. "We had some huge fights," Sikes remembers. "He'd say, 'Pay attention to the users of your books. That's the most important thing you can do for advertisers.'"

Black also lobbied for free listings of artists, galleries and other resources. Sikes finally agreed to include these in *THE GUILD 7*. "It took me a while to understand that the more

ARTIST:	JOAN SCHULZE
LIASON:	BROTHER JOSEPH ASPELL, SM
TYPE OF WORK:	FREE HANGING FIBER AND PAPER CONSTRUCTION
TITLE:	*IN PRINCIPIO (IN THE BEGINNING)*
SITE:	SANCTUARY, QUEEN OF THE APOSTLES CATHOLIC CHURCH, SAN JOSE, CA

In 1983, Brother Joseph Aspell purchased a quilt from fiber artist Joan Schulze for the Marianist's retreat house in Cupertino, CA. Over the years, the two kept in touch through studio visits, GUILD reprints, shows and occasional conversations. Ten years later, working from drawings provided by Brother Joseph, Schulze began a piece that took her in a new direction. "The scale and complexity of this project challenged all my resources," says Schultz. "It's a long way from the studio to such a large and important space."

Photo: Sharon Risendorph

ARTIST:	ULRIKA LEANDER
LIASON:	KATHLEEN WERLE (INTERIOR DESIGNER) DESIGN CINCINNATI INT'L, INC.
TYPE OF WORK:	TAPESTRY
TITLE:	*LOVE OF CHRIST IMPELS US*
SITE:	ST. MARY'S HOSPITAL HUNTINGTON, WV

In 1980, after a decade of designing tapestries in her native Sweden, Ulrika Leander moved to the mountains of eastern Tennessee. "Everywhere one looks," she says, "nature is generous and inspiring." With her classical Scandinavian training, Leander has been warmly received in this country; this 4' x 7' tapestry was the outcome of the very first phone call she received through a display of her work in THE GUILD.

Photo: J.W. Nave Photography

ARTIST: JOHN CLARK
LIASON: KAREN LEAGUE (INTERIOR DESIGNER)
JOVA, DANIELS, BUSBY, INC.
TYPE OF WORK: HANDMADE FURNITURE
TITLE: *STELLA END TABLES*
SITE: HEADQUARTERS OF *SOUTHERN LIVING*
MAGAZINE, BIRMINGHAM, AL

Southern Living's new corporate headquarters boasts a fine collection of contemporary work by southern artists. John Clark, one of several furniture makers represented, took an unusual step in integrating his work with the surrounding architecture. With the help of designer Karen League, he obtained slabs of the same granite used for the building's walls and floors. Clark used the slabs to form the top surface of these end tables, named after his young daughter.

ARTIST: IRA A. KEER
LIASON: PRIVATE COLLECTOR
TYPE OF WORK: PORTRAIT MIRROR AND CLOTHES BAR
TITLE: *LIKE THE WIND*
SITE: PRIVATE RESIDENCE
MINNEAPOLIS, MN

The works of Ira Keer, an interior architect, explore the creative and artistic possibilities of furniture. Like the Wind, the first piece in his line of limited-edition portrait and dressing mirrors, is a whimsical collage about bicycling and swimming, and was a gift for a biathlete. The piece, fabricated by Jon Frost, contains quilted maple, purple-heart, ebonize walnut, dyed maple and various bicycle components.

Photo: Mike Parker, Minneapolis, MN

reasons people had to use the books, the more successful they'd be for the advertisers." Now these listings are among the books' fastest growing sections.

As a former art consultant, Susan Evans was convinced that sculpture belonged in the book; she got her way with *THE GUILD 6*. Each year since, the architectural arts and sculpture have filled more pages, making it plain that Sikes' original aims—and Evans' conviction—were on target. Because the book was becoming unwieldy (a sure mark of success), *THE GUILD 6* was published as two editions directed separately to architects and interior designers.

In the ninth year, the *Gallery Edition* was added, to serve potters, glassblowers and others who rarely seek architectural commissions. In this volume, artists have the option to purchase half-page displays. "It's really expanded what we can offer," says Sikes. "Advertisers can choose from a wide range of rates and audiences now, and the number of artists we work with each year has jumped."

SUCCESS STORIES

THE GUILD may not work for everyone, but there's no question that it has become a powerful resource for many artists and their clients. Increasingly, overseas sales are bringing in commissions from all over the world, especially Japan and Hong Kong. And THE GUILD reaches markets which few artists could otherwise target. Corporate offices, public buildings, churches, and private residences continue to be major sources for commissions, but quite a few advertisers have seen their work in less common settings, including catalogs, books, and cassette covers; even Disney has commissioned work through THE GUILD.

INTO THE NEXT MILLENNIUM

WHAT will the next ten years bring? First, Sikes would like to see the new *Gallery Edition* include artists from Europe and the Far East, and she hasn't ruled out creating a separate volume for sculpture and public art. Kraus Sikes Inc. may also expand its publishing someday, with new books for a general consumer audience.

But these are modest goals. Sikes likes to envision the day when *THE GUILD 20* is published, divided into enough editions to fill an entire shelf. "My model is *Sweet's*, the annual bible for architects. It's in eighteen volumes!"

And why not? In ten years, THE GUILD has overcome the field's ingrained resistance to marketing, along with the typical obstacles that threaten most new businesses. And for many users, reaching for THE GUILD has become an old habit, not the afterthought it once was.

More importantly, THE GUILD has nurtured the idea that art is basic to our lives, while generating hundreds of new commissions for artists. "There are wonderful works of art in the world today that wouldn't be there if it weren't for THE GUILD," Sikes says. "And I know for a fact that we help many artists continue to make a living through their art. That thought is very satisfying."

Jody Clowes writes about the decorative and architectural arts for American Craft and other publications.

ARTIST:	JONATHAN WINFISKY
LIASON:	PRIVATE COLLECTOR
TYPE OF WORK:	PERFUME VIALS
SITE:	KABUL, SAUDI ARABIA

Like most GUILD artists, Jonathan Winfisky is pleased to accept overseas commissions. This request for 16 perfume vials was no exception, but it came with an unusual condition. The Saudi Arabian businessman who hired Winfisky explained that the vials were to be gifts for his 16 wives. To avoid any suggestion of favoritism, he asked that the pieces be as nearly identical as possible.

ARTIST:	AMANDA RIGHARDSON
LIASON:	EVALYN DANIEL (ART CONSULTANT)
	DANIEL FINE ART
TYPE OF WORK:	LAYERED, HAND-DYED FABRIC
TITLE:	*CRESCENT SAND*
SITE:	SOUTH LAKE TAHOE EMBASSY SUITES
	LAKE TAHOE, CA

Although Amanda Richardson's commission for the South Lake Tahoe Embassy Suites did not specifically call for a local subject, Richardson chose to feature a combination of lake, mountains, shore and flowers in her 5' x 16' tapestry. The familiar, bold landscape offered a sense of drama well suited to the location. Richardson's goal, as with other projects, was to create artwork that seems "inevitable in the space, so that you just can't imagine the setting without it."

Photo: Patrick Kirby

10 *Great Ways*

1 QUALITY CONTROL. This book begins with an assurance that these artists are reliable and professional. Featured artists in THE GUILD have been juried in on the basis of experience, quality of work, and a solid reputation for working with designer professionals.

2 MOTIVATION. Taking your copy of THE GUILD to client meetings is highly recommended. Clients have been known to reach levels of extreme excitement upon viewing the artistic possibilities showcased here.

3 OLD ENOUGH TO HAVE A HISTORY. Curious about where we came from? Read "THE GUILD at Ten" by Jody Clowes, beginning on page ix. Jody, who writes about the decorative arts for national publications, immersed herself in our old files and newsletters, as well as our earlier volumes. She presents an entertaining story from an informed perspective.

4 GO AHEAD AND CALL. If something intrigues you while perusing the *Designer's Edition*—a shape, a form, an exotic use of the commonplace—please, give the artist a call. Serendipity often leads to a wonderful creation.

5 MORE ARTISTS ... AND MORE. THE GUILD REGISTERs of fiber and ceramic art for the wall list contact and pricing information for hundreds of artists working in these media. The ceramic register is new this year, and we think it will be very well used.

6 DESKTOP DIRECTORY. The *Designer's Edition 10* is organized for quick reference, as well as leisurely browsing. The "Index of Artists and Companies" includes all artists listed in THE GUILD REGISTERs, as well as those featured with full-color pages, so finding a current phone number or checking product information is easily done. The information in your rolodex may grow stale; the *Designer's Edition* is fresh each year.

7 INTERVIEWS. Throughout the book, you'll find interviews with 'devoted advertisers' who have been with THE GUILD from the very beginning. The interviews were conducted by Marcia Kraus and Molly Rose Teuke, both free-lance writers with a keen interest in the arts.

8 THE PROOF OF THE PUDDING. We always love to hear about commissions and purchases generated through THE GUILD. For this special anniversary edition, we highlight several for your enjoyment. Look for them beginning on page x.

9 DUST OFF THAT EARLY GUILD. We've published books for designers, architects and art consultants for ten years. Many of the artists whose work you see in this volume were also featured in earlier GUILD publications. Look for references on color-page displays.

10 OUR NEXT LANDMARK. THE GUILD will be 20 in the year 2005. We'd like to feature *your* project in that anniversary edition. Please take a minute and daydream about the artwork you'll commission in the next ten years!

WORK FOR THE WALL

Laura Militzer Bryant

2595 30th Avenue North
St. Petersburg, FL 33713
FAX 813-321-1905
TEL 813-327-3100

Art critic Joan Altabe states, "The mark of good art has always been its almightiness, its power to suggest, to stir. The more it does this, the greater the work. Witness Laura Militzer Bryant's collection of weavings."

Laura's hand-dyed, double-woven, highly charged and dynamic tapestries interpret time and space through geometry and the emotive power of color.

Recipient of both NEA and State of Florida individual artist grants, Laura has amassed an impressive resume of national museum, gallery and one-person shows, as well as awards and commissions.

A *Sanctuary*, 57" x 43¾"

B *Disclosure*, 22" x 74" x 2"

A

B

Victor Jacoby

1086 17th Street
Eureka, CA 95501
TEL 707-442-3809

Victor Jacoby has been creating and exhibiting hand-woven tapestries for 20 years. Since 1975 he has woven both corporate and residential commissions. Themes include landscape, floral, figurative, and those appropriate to individual client's needs. Clients include AT&T; Kaiser Permanente; Marriott Corporation; Shearson, Lehman, Hutton; and Yoshizama Hospital in Japan.

Further information available upon request.

A *From the Doorway*, 1993, 49" x 36"

B *End of the Street*, 1993, 48" x 36"

C *Garden Fuchsia*, 1994, 36" x 36"

A

B

C

Photos: Leonard Stevens

Ulrika Leander

Contemporary Tapestry Weaving
107 Westoverlook Drive
Oak Ridge, TN 37830
FAX 615-483-7911
TEL 615-482-6849

Ulrika Leander has established a reputation for superb craftsmanship and a remarkable range of creative and imaginative designs. With 25 years of experience in this field, Leander has installed more than 150 tapestries commissioned for public, private and commercial settings in the United States and in her native Scandinavia.

Using 100 percent natural fibers, she produces single pieces measuring up to 12' x 30'.

Resume, slides and a videotape are available upon request.

Also see these GUILD publications:
Designer's Edition: 8, 9

A *Our Duty—Our Bounty*, 1988, University of Tennessee College of Veterinary Medicine, Knoxville, TN, 12' x 15'

B *Early Morning*, 1986, private collection, 7' x 5'

A

B

Photos: J.R. Rodgers, Knoxville, TN

Loretta Mossman

2416 Aspen Street
Philadelphia, PA 19130
(215) 765-3248
FAX (215) 483-4864

Loretta Mossman's tapestries are artworks conceived and developed for individual spaces and design concepts. A colorist, she creates moods with her rich palette. Using traditional techniques, pure wools are colored with luxurious natural pigments and woven to form single panels or multi-dimensional constructions. Designs and textures are created and enhanced with eclectic accents such as appliquéd fabrics, buttons and found objects.

The artist welcomes the opportunity to collaborate with architects, designers and consultants and will scale designs to meet the specifications of private, corporate or architectural settings. Design portfolios are available for a fee, refundable with first commission.

Loretta Mossman's work has been exhibited widely and she is represented in public and private collections.

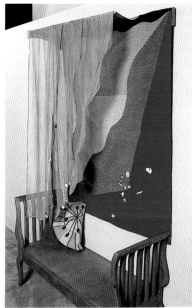

Sheila O'Hara

1318 Hale Drive
Concord, CA 94518
TEL 510-676-8767

Sheila O'Hara has been internationally recognized for her innovative tapestries for over 20 years. Her work has been featured in publications such as *American Craft*, *FIBERARTS*, *Metropolis*, and *The New York Times*.

Her weavings are included in the collections of the Smithsonian's Cooper-Hewitt Museum, the Fine Arts Museum of San Francisco, AT&T, the Oakland Federal Building, and BankAmerica Corporation.

A *Real Escape*, wool, 10' x 12½'

B *Telefun*, wool, 5' x 11½', commission for AT&T, San Francisco

A

B

Gary Sinick

Printed in Hong Kong ©1995 THE GUILD: Designer's Edition

BARBARA GRENELL
fiber

There's a contemplative, serene quality in the work of fiber artist Barbara Grenell. "I live in a beautiful mountainous region, where I can see a river from my window," she says. "Natural beauty is important to me."

Grenell uses a tapestry technique to create weavings that illustrate landscapes and natural earth forms. "I use a natural linen warp, keeping it visible in the piece," she says.

Photo: Diane Davis

"I'm always fighting the static element of weaving, trying to make my work look more spontaneous than most traditional methods allow."

Dyeing her own yarn is another way Grenell lends spontaneity to her work, and it gives her some variation on the colors available to other artists. "It's part of the painterly aspect of my work that I'm always trying to get back to," she explains. Grenell employs a variety of techniques—using a large tapestry fork rather than a beater, and sometimes wrapping the warp—to add texture and motion to her work.

A recent commission illustrates Grenell's adaptable approach. The client, a produce cooperative in a lush California valley, gave Grenell free reign, but liked the feeling of the Arts and Crafts movement. The result was a woven landscape rooted in those traditions yet reflecting the modern function of the business.

"The specific wishes of a client can push me to achieve a new way of approaching my work visually," she says. "I seldom feel constrained by the challenges inherent in a site. I used them as stepping stones to something else, as opportunities to stretch in new ways."

See these GUILD publications:
THE GUILD: 1, 2, 3, 4
Designer's Edition: 7, 8, 9, 10
Gallery Edition: 1

Emma Allebes

8398 Sunset Avenue
Fair Oaks, CA 95628
FAX 916-961-8653
TEL 916-961-8639

Emma, a fiber artist for over 30 years, describes her work as "Textiles—Comfort for the Eye." Her art quilts are often pictorial and tell a story, always positive and uplifting, and have a unique range of style. Inspirational themes can be serious to whimsical. The highest quality of materials and workmanship are utilized. She finds challenging sizes and shapes stimulating to her design process and project input is welcome on commissioned work.

Emma has received international recognition and awards. Her work has been placed in both private and museum collections and published both nationally and internationally.

A *Seeds Are His Promise*, 1993, quilt, 56"H x 72"W

B *Worldwide Brotherhood*, 1991, quilt, 108"H x 90"W

A

B

Printed in Hong Kong ©1995 THE GUILD: Designer's Edition

Beth Cassidy

2416 NW 60th Street
Seattle, WA 98107
FAX 206-706-0406
TEL 206-783-6226

Euphonious color. Vibrant texture. Works
are thoughtfully designed and durable. Beth
Cassidy's work is collected and commissioned
nationally by both private and corporate
clients. She works to ensure that her pieces suit
their environment as well as the aesthetics of
each individual client. This established artist has
placed her fiber and mixed-media collages on
many walls and over many beds and sofas. Call
for details.

A *Detritus IV*, 72" x 96"

B *Change*, 74" x 62"

A

B

Photos: Hal Gage

M.A. Klein

M.A. Klein Design
20 Arastradero Road
Portola Valley, CA 94028
TEL 415-854-7815
TEL 800-700-7815

M. A. Klein's current work can be called contemporary narrative mixed-media collage incorporating fabrics, papers and threads. Techniques include painting, dyeing, gluing, sewing, fabric manipulation and stitchery.

A professional artist for 30 years, M.A. is noted for her active groupings of people (children and adults), animals, birds and fish, She creates individual pieces and groupings of related works in a wide variety of sizes.

Prices for her unique, highly textured designs vary according to complexity and size of work. Contact artist for information regarding commissions and available work.

Also see these GUILD publications:
Designer's Edition: 8, 9
Gallery Edition: 1

A Most Unusual Watering Hole (detail)

A Most Unusual Watering Hole, 42" x 108", commission for the Library of Congress, Washington, DC, 1994

Joel Breger

Printed in Hong Kong ©1995 THE GUILD: Designer's Edition

Verena Levine

Verena Levine Pictorial and Narrative Quilts
4305 37th Street NW
Washington, DC 20008
TEL 202-537-0916

Verena Levine's quilts depict scenes of contemporary urban and rural American life. For 15 years, she has produced original works of all sizes for corporate and residential spaces in the U.S. and abroad.

Machine pieced and appliquéd from many different fabrics, her quilts are sturdy and easy to install. The time from contract to the completed work averages 6 to 12 weeks.

Slides, pricing and scheduling upon request.

Completed works also available.

A *Autumn,* 35" x 29"

B *Fish Market,* 46" x 31"

A

B

Photos: Mark Gulezian

Therese May

651 N. 4th Street
San Jose, CA 95112
TEL 408-292-3247

Therese May's quilts are made up of playful
fantasy animal and plant imagery and are
machine appliquéd using straight stitch and
satin stitch. Threads are left uncut to form a
network of texture across the surface. Acrylic
paint is added as a finishing touch. Her work is
widely published and exhibited throughout the
U.S., Europe and Japan.

Prices for finished pieces range from $1,000 to
$40,000. Commissions accepted; May will work
with clients via drawings and samples.

More information available upon request.

Also see these GUILD publications:
Designer's Edition: 6, 7, 8

Love the Child, 1993, embellished quilt, 27" x 29"   Pat Kirk

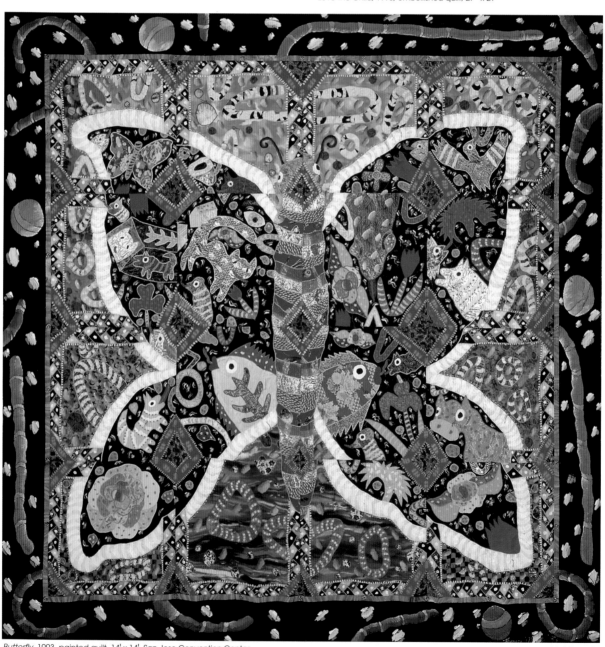

Butterfly, 1993, painted quilt, 14' x 14', San Jose Convention Center   Mert Carpenter

14   Work for the Wall: Art Quilts

Jean Neblett

628 Rhode Island Street
San Francisco, CA 94107-2628
FAX 415-821-2772
TEL 415-550-2613

Jean Neblett is a studio artist with a background in fiber arts and textiles. Composed of silk, linen, metal, and hand-dyed cotton, her work involves the layering, scrimming, folding, tearing and manipulating of fabric. An ongoing dialogue with form, color, placement and shape is explored. Rich, multi-planed work results, with many freely swinging surfaces.

Exhibited and published nationally, Neblett's work is featured in collections both private and corporate. Of varying sizes, it is easily shipped and mounted. A slide portfolio and price list are available. Commissioned work is encouraged.

Also see these GUILD publications:
Designer's Edition: 7, 9

A *Abstraction VIII: Red Scrim*, 41"H x 46"W

B *Abstraction VII: Green Meditation*, 60"H x 41"W

Printed in Hong Kong ©1995 THE GUILD: Designer's Edition

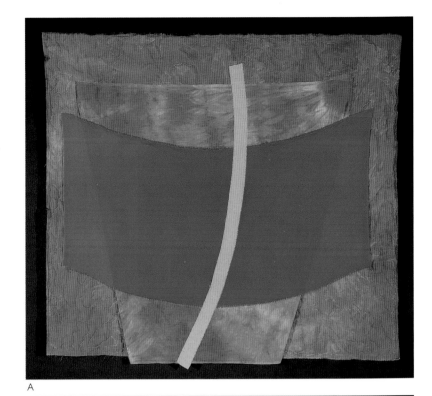

A

B

Photos: David Belda

Linda S. Perry

Art Quilts
96 Burlington Street
Lexington, MA 02173
TEL 617-863-1107

Linda Perry's award-winning quilts reflect her interest in Japanese design, Renaissance frescoes and classical mythology. She employs a wide range of fine fabrics including hand-dyed and hand-printed cottons and silks. Her works have been selected for numerous juried and museum shows throughout the United States.

Perry's corporate clients include Rhone Poulenc Rorer, the Hilton Hotels, New England Medical Center and the Shriner's Hospital.

Please contact the artist for additional information and slides.

A *Naos* (detail)

B *Naos* (full view), 48" x 30"

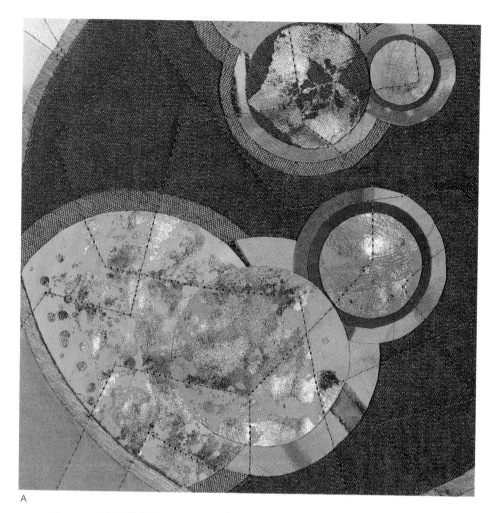

A

B

Printed in Hong Kong ©1995 THE GUILD: Designer's Edition

Susan Sawyer

RD 1, Box 107
East Calais, VT 05650
TEL 802-456-8836

Susan Sawyer has been making art quilts since 1971. Trained in fine arts (BA from New College, MFA from Vermont College), she produces work which combines a sophisticated use of color and pattern and a love and knowledge of nature with the warm accessibility of the quilt. She uses a widely varied palette in compositions evoking season, light, landscape and idea in luminous detail. Made of the finest printed and hand-dyed cottons, her work is both expressive and contemplative in spirit, celebrating the beauty of the world around us.

Sawyer's award-winning work is nationally exhibited and published, and can be found in both private and public collections. She welcomes selected commissions, enjoys working with clients and will design site-specific works. Slides, prices and further information are available upon request.

SHOWN: *Little Waterfall*, 1994, machine-pieced, hand-quilted cottons, 54" x 30"

Erik Borg

Kathleen Sharp

17360 Valley Oak
Monte Sereno, CA 95030
TEL 408-395-3014

The expertly crafted studio art quilts of Kathleen Sharp grace private and public spaces in the United States, Europe, and Australia.

A full-time and widely exhibited artist for 18 years, her work has been featured in such prestigious publications as *Fiberarts* and *Surface Design Journal.*

Known for their rich fabrics, her quilts frequently suggest three-dimensional space through references to architectural motifs.

Completed works available for sale range from 30" framed studies to wall hangings of more than 8'. Commissioned work reflecting her artistic vision is tailored to specific color/space requirements. Prices start at $250/square foot.

Inquiries welcome.

Also see these GUILD publications:
Designer's Edition: 6, 9

A *Summer House,* quilt triptych, 61"H x 86"W
    ©1994 Sharp

B *Theatre,* quilt, 42"H x 36"W, ©1994 Sharp

A

B

JOYCE LOPEZ *fiber*

Visual weight is a different concept altogether from physical weight, says Joyce Lopez, and it's a vital element in her large-scale works. Lopez's artistry involves wrapping chromed steel with a silk-like cotton thread. The design emerges from the juxtaposition of the vibrantly colored threads.

Lopez does a lot of lobby pieces, a kind of work, she says, that requires an awareness of space, traffic flow, visual unity and visual weight. To illustrate, she describes a commission shown on the cover of the *Designer's Edition 7.* The challenge was to create something for the lobby of an elegant apartment building that would both draw the eye from a distance, and unify the space at close proximity.

"I chose a pair of rectangular shapes," she says, "and in the areas closest to the elevator, created a suggestion of a curtain being drawn." Using close to 50 different colors, she added images that suggest fragments of brocade and oriental carpets, with hints of detail from Pompeii, a Frank Lloyd Wright window design, and other elegant images.

Lopez draws on the strength of both weaving and sculpture to create her images. "I wanted to marry these two forms in a unique way that would become known as my signature," she says. "My technique remains fairly constant; it's the design that is evolving and growing more complex. That's the joy of working on a large scale—it lets me grow as an artist."

See these GUILD publications:
THE GUILD: 2, 3, 4, 5
Designer's Edition: 6, 7, 8, 9, 10
Architect's Edition: 8

Karen Adachi

702 Monarch Way
Santa Cruz, CA 95060
TEL 408-429-6192

Karen Adachi creates her three-dimensional handmade paper pieces by using layers of irregularly shaped vacuumed-cast paper. She makes free-standing, two-sided sculptures and wall pieces for corporate, private and residential interiors. Her work is shown nationally through major galleries and representatives.

The pieces are richly textures and embellished with dyes, acrylics, metallics and pearlescents. Painted bamboo and sticks are used to create a dramatic statement of pattern and line. Three-dimensional sculptures are mounted on painted metal bases for stability and strength.

Custom work in any size, shape and color is available. Contact the artist for further information and slides.

Printed in Hong Kong ©1995 THE GUILD: Designer's Edition

Elaine Albers Cohen

32106 Lake Road
Avon Lake, OH 44012
TEL 216-661-1689
TEL 216-933-5979

Hand-cast paper reliefs combine sculpture and painting. Gallery wall pieces in acrylic-painted cast paper and collages of dyed and painted art papers are available. Most reliefs are framed in plexiglass boxes, others are adhered to canvas and protected with polymer. Commissions welcomed.

Collections: Metropolitan General Hospital, Cleveland, OH; West Shore Unitarian Church, Rocky River, OH; Akron General Hospital, Akron, OH

Also see this GUILD publication:
Designer's Edition: 9

A cast paper, 24" x 24"

B *Collage I* and *II*, each 24" x 32"

C cast paper, 30" x 42" x 3"

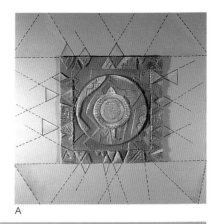

A

B

C

Martha Chatelain

Artfocus, Ltd.
PO Box 9855
San Diego, CA 92169-0855
FAX 619-581-6536
TEL 619-581-6410

Martha Chatelain creates richly textured three-dimensional handmade paper and mixed-media wall sculptures enhanced with fiber dyes and iridescent powders.

Call to discuss design specifications, client environment and/or site-specific commissions. Allow four to six weeks following design approval.

Prices, from $800 to $5,000, depend on size and complexity.

Selected collections: American Airlines, Bank of America, Champion Paper, IBM, International Paper, Potlatch, Upjohn and Xerox Corporations, Hilton and Sheraton Hotels, Nordstrom.

A *Finesse*, 45" x 53" x 6"

B *Waves Upon the Shore*, 48" x 70" x 5"

A

B

Marlene Lenker

Lenker Fine Arts
28 Northview Terrace
Cedar Grove, NJ 07009
FAX 201-239-8671 *51
TEL 201-239-8671
TEL 203-767-2098

Marlene Lenker is an internationally recognized painter. For 28 years she has been mastering her art. Marlene is listed in *Who's Who in American Art* and *American Women*. Her current series, *Mosaic Tile Fragments*, is created on 350-pound, 100%-rag paper, incorporating innovative multi-media techniques resulting in unique, iconic and elegant art. The tiles are adhered to board or canvas. Colors and patinas are light-fast and permanent.

Selected collections: Arthur Young, Union Carbide, Warner-Lambert, Ortho, Merrill Lynch, Hewlitt Packard, Pepsico, Prudential, Lever Bros., Johnson & Johnson, Sheraton, Kidder-Peabody.

Inquiries, studio visits, and commissions are welcomed.

A *Sub-Terrain* (detail), ©1994, 30" x 40"

B *Sunrise*, ©1994, 30" x 40"

C *Four Seasons*, each panel 24" x 48"

A

B

C

David Hollander

Keiko Nelson

Art Studio
2604 3rd Street
San Francisco, CA 94107
FAX 510-527-4822
TEL 415-824-1545

Keiko Nelson specializes in richly textured wall sculpture created from cast paper. Despite her flexibility in numerous other media, her 20-year commitment to cast paper has set her apart from other mixed-media artists. From small wall decorations to large-scale corporate installations, her works accommodate a wide variety of requirements for the client and the space.

Always abstract, her works range from refined organic forms to bold paintings or sculptures that cut into their environment and give that space a statement of its own. Also, cast paper has a unique quality of appearing delicate despite its durability.

International clients include: Hotel Nikko, Kaiser Hospital, Epcot Center, Cairo Opera House, and NTT International.

Ms Nelson is readily available to discuss design specifications for site-specific commissions.

Marjorie Tomchuk

44 Horton Lane
New Canaan, CT 06840
FAX 203-972-3182
TEL 203-972-0137

Known for her embossings on artist-made paper, Marjorie Tomchuk's recent work displays brilliant color and bold design. An artist for 30 years, she has placed art in more than 50 major corporations and many museums. Individual panels are as large as 4' x 6'. Please contact the artist for a color brochure packet or book.

Also see these GUILD publications:
THE GUILD: 5
Designer's Edition: 6, 7, 8, 9

A *Probe*, embossed multiple on artist-made paper, 25" x 36", edition of 100

B *Transmission*, embossed multiple on artist-made paper, 25" x 36", edition of 100

A

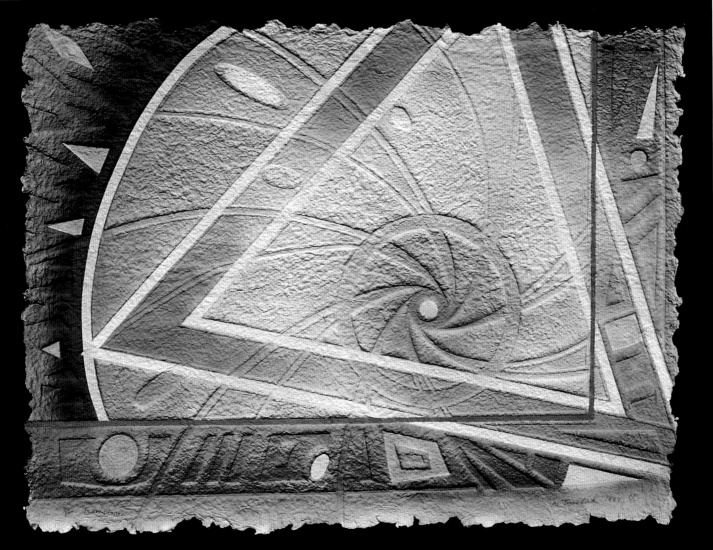

B

Judith Uehling

152 Wooster Street
New York, NY 10012
FAX 212-254-2075
TEL 212-254-2075

These compelling wall sculptures evolved after a decade of work, first in London, then Berlin. They continue the urban, architectural theme in Judith Uehling's work.

The window shown here was cast from a mold taken directly from the window of an 1830 East German schoolhouse and mayor's office. *Shutter* was cast from the iron fire-protective shutters outside Uehling's New York studio loft.

Finished works are lightweight and produced in editions. A dozen different versions exist in various pigmented colors and bronzes.

Uehling's work is found in over 30 permanent collections, including the Victoria & Albert Museum in London. She has 20 years' experience in commission work here and abroad.

A *Brandenburg Window*, bronze over cast paper, lace, 42"H x 30"W x 3"D

B *Shutter*, bronze over cast paper, 8'6"H x 43"W x 4"D

A

B

Photos: D. James Dee

Printed in Hong Kong ©1995 THE GUILD: Designer's Edition

fiber
B.J. ADAMS

When Corporate Annual Reports in New York asked B.J. Adams to create an image for the cover of a BELLSOUTH annual report, the client had a very specific concept in mind. "Their theme was 'Investing in the Fabric of Society,'" she says, "and they thought they wanted something woven."

The problem? Adams isn't a weaver. She paints on canvas and then covers the image with machine-stitched thread to get a variety of textures and effects, sometimes letting the painted canvas show through. But the work her client had seen in THE GUILD suggested the imagery of weaving, and they asked Adams to go ahead anyway.

Adams' work is generally abstract, and BELLSOUTH wanted several specific elements—including a house, a telephone, and a globe—woven together into one unified piece. "It seemed like an impossible task, but it challenged me in a lot of ways," she says, "and that was very satisfying."

Photo: Andrea Uravitch

The constraints of the commission required that Adams develop new techniques. "They wanted cut edges, but they also wanted some of the fiber to extend off the edge. So I developed a technique for going off the edge without sewing, and now I find myself cutting off edges in other pieces, just like I did for them," she says. "I like being forced to go in new directions. Commissioned work makes me change in ways that help me grow as an artist."

The finished piece proved so popular with the client that they bought not just the image, but the piece itself. Reproductions now appear in a corporate video, on folders distributed to stockholders, and on the covers of several BELLSOUTH telephone books.

See these GUILD publications:
THE GUILD: 1, 2, 3, 5
Designer's Edition: 6, 7, 8, 10

B.J. Adams

Art in Fiber
2821 Arizona Terrace NW
Washington, DC 20016
FAX 202-686-1042
TEL   202-364-8404

B.J. Adams has collaborated with clients on artwork for business, hotel, banking, medical and government buildings, as well as residential settings. Using flexible materials, fabrics, threads and paint, she creates wall hangings designed to enhance their surroundings. Designs can be illustrative with innovative free-hand machine drawing, geometric, or flowing abstractions. Pieces may have flat-stitched or textured, manipulated fabric surfaces. A complete range of colors is available.

For more information call or write.

Also see these GUILD publications:
THE GUILD: 1, 2, 3, 5
Designer's Edition: 6, 7, 8

A *Limits of Reality*, 11" x 13", machine stitching on painted canvas

B *Art Tour of Washington, DC* (detail)

C *Art Tour of Washington, DC*, machine drawing on pieced fabrics, 27" x 38"

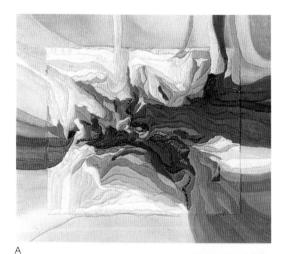

A

B

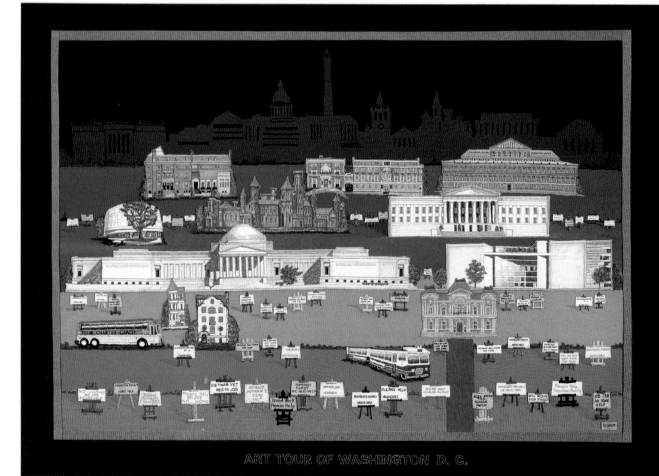

C

Photos: Joel Breger

Sally Bailey

Hooked on Art
PO Box 60204
Santa Barbara, CA 93160
TEL 805-967-3350

Recycled wool clothing is used to produce traditional hand-hooked 'rugs' and wall hangings. All designs are original, based on primary drawings and photographs, and an extensive collection of folk and multi-cultural images.

Work can be commissioned. Available for loan are photos and prices of works in stock. Sizes range from 1.7 to 9.8 square feet.

A *Lizard*, 19.5" x 20.5"

B *No More Lost Marbles*, 37.5" x 37.5"

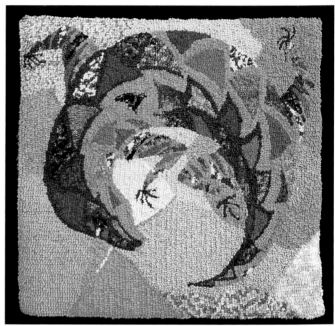

A

B

Wayne McCall

Susan Eileen Burnes

6980 Mill Road
Brecksville, OH 44141
FAX 216-526-0874
TEL 216-838-5955

Susan Eileen Burnes creates needle-made fiber art with fine wool, silk and cotton fibers. Row upon row of color-filled stitches capture light and form appealing textures. These award-winning designs utilize bold colors and strong images ranging from the simple whimsy of folk art to elegant expressions of cultural motifs.

Susan enjoys collaborating with clients to produce creations reflecting their interests, visions and preferred color schemes. Recent commissions include a series of images inspired by the land and nature forms of the Grand Tetons.

Miniaturized versions (two to three inches) of the standard wall pieces may be framed or worn as personal adornment.

Completed works available and commissions welcome.

A *Goldenrod*, 1994, embroidery and fabric construction, 10"H x 10"W

B *Visions of Cornwall*, 1993, embroidery, 24"H x 18"W

B

Photos: Ronald Matye

Barbara Cade

262 Hideaway Hills Drive
Hot Springs, AR 71901
TEL 501-262-4065

Luscious vegetation.
One flower or one whole bouquet.
For people who are not afraid of getting back to nature.
For people who like making dramatic statements.
For people who like being different.

Working in age-old primitive methods, Barbara Cade creates one-of-a-kind, hand-felted wool flowers. Her work has been exhibited in museum juried shows for 25 years, is represented in many corporation collections and is part of the permanent collection of the Tacoma Art Museum.

Easy to install. Arrangeable.

Care: dust with hose-type spray vacuum; use insect spray labeled for fabrics, only if necessary. No weeding required.

For slides of other species and varieties, send $20 (refundable). Commissions welcome.

Also see these GUILD publications:
Designer's Edition: 8, 9

SHOWN: *Pansy Bouquet*, 1994, felt sculpture, approximate size 18'L x 10'H x 1'D

Cindy Momchilov

Phyllis 'Ceratto' Evans

6969 Island Center Road NE
Bainbridge Island, WA 98110
TEL 206-842-5042

Phyllis 'Ceratto' Evans creates her compelling images by fusing aged Japanese kimono silk to canvas. The natural iridescence of silk is retained in the process of fusing she has developed. Each piece is beautifully crafted and stunningly conveys the artist's passion for her subjects of European architecture and the natural environment. A protective coating ensures easy maintenance and longevity without altering the textural qualities of the works.

Phyllis' creativity and skill with textiles spans many years. Her award-winning work resides in both corporate and private collections.

Commissions are welcomed.

Also see this GUILD publication:
Designer's Edition: 9

A *fuori mia porta* (detail)

B *il barco rifiuto*, 31" x 23"

C *fuori mia porta*, 23" x 18"

A

B

C

Photos: Wally Hampton Photography, Inc.

Doris Finch

Doris Finch Fabric Art
2144 Crescent Drive
Altadena, CA 91001
TEL 818-797-6172

Using rich fabrics, including silks, brocades and metallics, the artist creates unique scroll-form wall hangings for private and commercial interiors. Images range from abstract through architectural to organic; work may be flat or three-dimensional.

Ms. Finch works closely with the client to see that commissioned work will harmonize with the site while making its own evocative statement. Dense machine satin stitching assures great durability. Pieces come complete with hand-finished wood poles for hanging.

Prices range from $1,500 to $4,000 depending on size and complexity; multi-panel pieces are generally higher. Design fee is 10%. Resume, slides and references on request.

A *Trunk VI*, 1994, 56"W x 31"L

B *Star*, 1992, 38"W x 48"L

C *Trunk VI*, installed on the yacht Amante

A

B

C

© Neil Rabinowitz, 1994

Marilyn Forth

416 David Drive
North Syracuse, NY 13212
FAX 315-458-0913
TEL 315-458-3786

Marilyn Forth's vibrant floral paintings on silk contain intricate drawings created with hot wax. These batiks promote a garden atmosphere and are especially pleasing with natural foliage. Soft lighting enhances the ambiance. Pillows can be ordered to complete the look. Colors are matched and designs coordinated.

Paintings may be ordered stretched and framed or unstretched for easier shipping.

Marilyn Forth has taught textile arts courses at Syracuse University. Her work has been collected for 20 years. Marilyn's paintings are in major collections, museums and galleries throughout the United States.

Limited edition or one-of-a-kind.

Price lists, slides and references.

Also see these GUILD publications:
Designer's Edition: 6, 7 , 8

A *Moonlit Blossoms*, 42" x 45"

B *Mermaids Garden*, 20" x 45"

A

B

Barbara Grenell

1132 Hall's Chapel Road
Burnsville, NC 28714
FAX 704-675-4073
TEL 704-675-4073

Barbara Grenell's unique partial wrap-faced technique and rich fiber palette create a more painterly control of line and composition than traditional tapestry. Her multiple-panel tapestries and dimensional constructions are internationally collected and commissioned for corporate, private and public sites. Awarded an N.E.A. Fellowship, Barbara Grenell creates landscapes which are widely exhibited and unlimited in size and format.

Clients include: Association of American Medical Colleges, Washington, DC; Bankers Trust, New York, NY; Duke University, Durham, NC; Ernst & Young, Washington, DC; Merck & Co., Rahway, NJ; Nations Bank, Charlotte, NC; Sheraton Hotel, Burlingame, CA; Southern Bell, Atlanta, GA; West Allis Memorial Hospital, Milwaukee, WI.

Highland Autumn, 60"H x 48"W

Zenith, 36"H x 72"W

Bill Hio

34 Cypress Drive
Scotia, NY 12302
TEL 518-399-7404

Wool's gentle strength and capacity to carry color makes these cross stitch wall hangings powerful in their initial impact and comforting in their allotted space. They tend to seize the attention of the casual observer as he passes by and attract a more extended interest than most wall art. Their unusual visual strength has a powerful and pleasant impact on the observer.

Works may be commissioned. Also available are photos and prices of completed works. Sizes range from 36" x 36" to 72" x 108". Prices begin at $400 and reach over $4,000 for mural-size pieces.

A *Grid*, 36" x 72"

B *Connections*, 58" x 80"

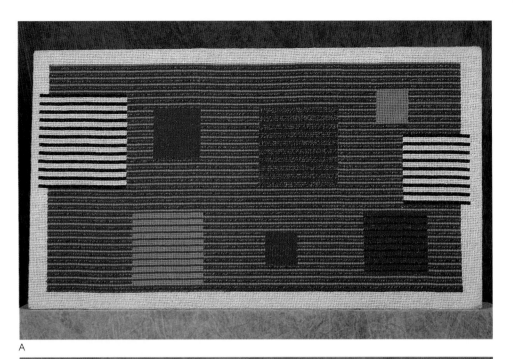

A

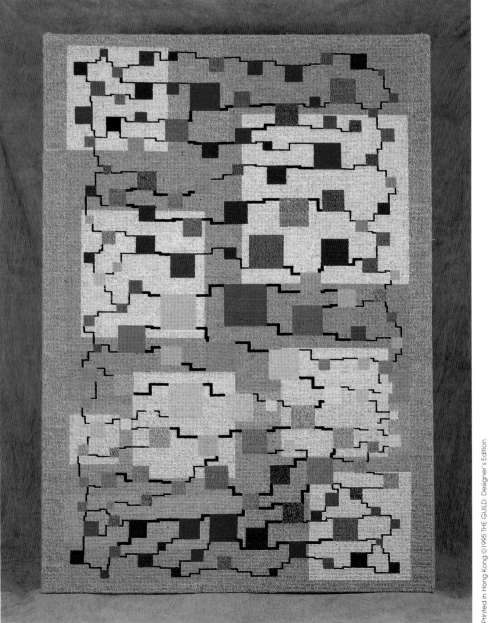

B

Photos: Brian R. Burt

Printed in Hong Kong ©1995 THE GUILD: Designer's Edition

Marie-Laure Ilie

Marilor Art Studio
106 Via Sevilla
Redondo Beach, CA 90277
FAX 310-375-4977
TEL 310-375-4977

For the past 20 years, Ilie has created hand-painted silk wall hangings in two styles with equal success and guaranteed quality for innumerable private and corporate collections.

The top image is typical of her 'traditional' paintings, inspired by ancient art. See *THE GUILD 8*, page 42; *THE GUILD 9*, page 45.

Below, her abstract compositions, whether free hanging, or hanging on a wall like tapestry, combine several layers of hand-painted silk with cut-out transparent veils. See *THE GUILD 8*, page 43; *THE GUILD 9*, page 46.

Call collect for prices, photos, slides, samples or proposal designs. Also see *THE GUILD 4, 5, 7*.

Please note new address and phone number.

A *Medieval Tapestry Scene*, 50" x 57"

B *Melody*, hand-painted nylon, mesh-fused, 72" x 24" x 12"

C *Ragtime*, wall hanging, 50" x 64"

A

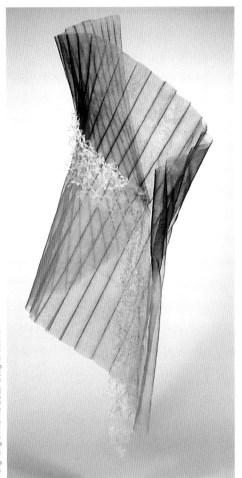

B

C

Rachel Lindstrom

24231 North 41 Avenue
Glendale, AZ 85310
TEL 602-780-0861

In her mixed-fiber collages, Rachel Lindstrom incorporates diverse archival fiber processes: papermaking and basketry using native desert plant fibers; hand-dyeing, hand-spinning and felting of luxury fibers; dyeing, discharging and distressing fine fabrics. Her abstract imagery is drawn from ancient and contemporary birth and transformation mythology.

A *Bag Lady's Augury*, discharged, painted satin laminate on silk noil, 36"H x 48"W

B *Placentation*, handmade paper, acrylics, acid dyes, hand-spun wool and silk on silk/linen, 36"H x 24"W

A

B

Photos: Dan Delaney

Printed in Hong Kong ©1995 THE GUILD: Designer's Edition

Joyce P. Lopez

Joyce Lopez Studio
1147 West Ohio Street #304
Chicago, IL 60622-5874
FAX 312-243-5033
TEL 312-243-5033

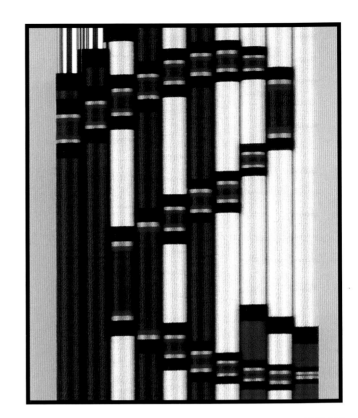

Joyce Lopez, a sculptor for 20 years, meticulously creates her sculpture out of thread and metal, resulting in beautifully designed, dramatic artwork enhancing corporate, public and private interiors. With over 300 fiber colors to choose from, designers', architects' and consultants' color specifications are always met.

Included in major collections and nationally exhibited; publications include four book covers for Harper Collins and the cover of *THE GUILD 7*.

Easily maintained, commissioned sculptures take two to four months to complete. Price range: $2,800 to $80,000. Call, FAX or write for a brochure.

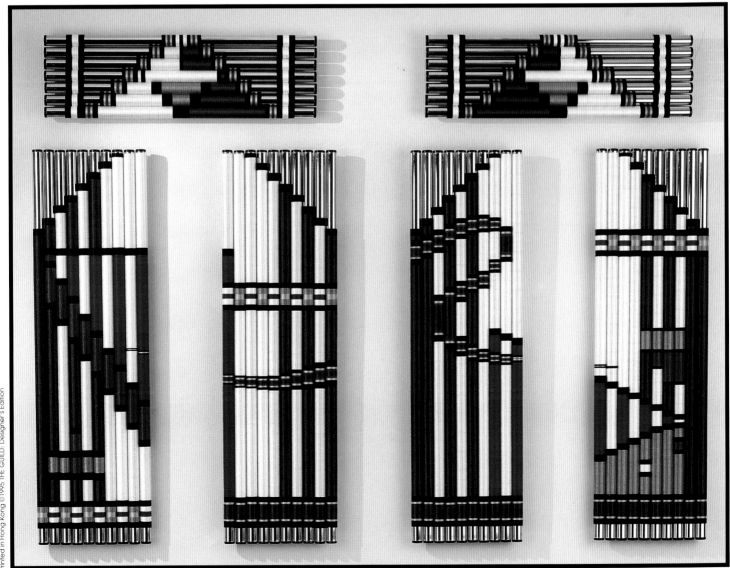

W.C. Graustein Memorial Fund commission, sculpture, chromed steel and thread, 40" x 60"

Jewell Peterson

Tactile Impressions
PO Box 64657
Tucson, AZ 85728-4657
TEL 520-324-0327

Jewell Peterson has been creating felted wool constructions for 25 years. Her vivid landscapes and still lifes are inspired by her love of color and natural themes. After creating the basic composition, she stitches details with a sewing machine, adding dimension to the work.

The dyes are colorfast and the artwork can be vacuumed when dusty. Wool naturally resists moisture and soil and can be washed or dry cleaned if needed.

Jewell's *Tactile Impressions* contain both the softness of fiber and the clarity of fine art. Displayed on stretched canvas or free floated on the wall, *Tactile Impressions* are included in many private and corporate collections.

Commissions are welcome and completed works may also be available.

Sizes range from 25"W x 30"H to 70"W x 76"H. Prices range from $1,200 to $4,000.

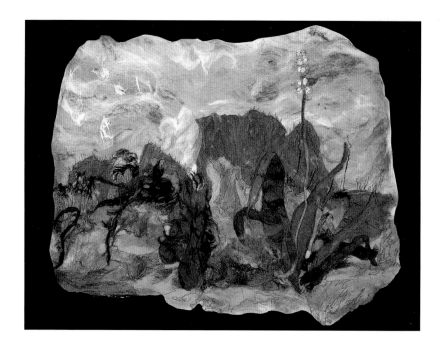

Printed in Hong Kong ©1995 THE GUILD: Designer's Edition

Mary Curtis Ratcliff

630 Neilson Street
Berkeley, CA 94707
TEL 510-526-8472

Mary Curtis Ratcliff, a graduate of the Rhode Island School of Design, has been working in a variety of sculptural media for over 20 years. Her designs range from sensuous and elegant ribbon pieces to more recent works incorporating industrial materials—including nylon and painted vinyl—which are woven through metal screens shaped in abstract forms. Her work has been placed in private residences, corporate offices and restaurants; it has been featured in more than 50 exhibitions and publications.

Ratcliff's wall sculptures are lightweight, easy to ship and maintain, durable, and lightfast. Prices range from $750 to $3,500 retail. Lead-time averages two to three months for completed work. Call or write for current scheduling, prices, slides, and literature.

A *Hussy*, 1990, plastic, stainless steel, 49" x 41" x 8"

B *Aureola*, 1991, acrylic on vinyl, steel, 50" x 50" x 7"

A

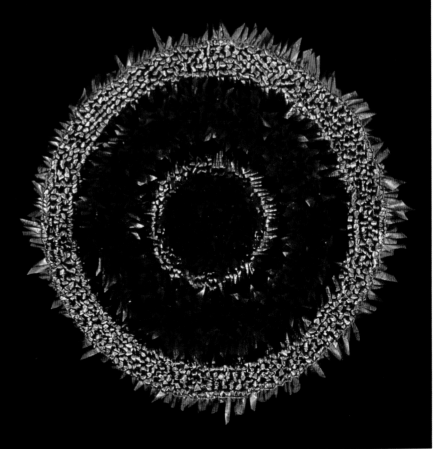

B

Photos: Dennis Galloway

Amanda Richardson

PO Box 2147
Friday Harbor, WA 98250
TEL 360-378-4359

The rich, light-reflective tapestries of Amanda Richardson respond to their environment, the image varying with the angle and intensity of light, allowing the viewer to become actively involved in the artistic experience.

The artist developed the technique of Richardson Tapestry, in which fabrics are hand dyed, cut into intricate forms, and bonded together, layer on layer, to build up a rich, complex final image. These images give the impression of great spatial depth, with a visual impact few art mediums can equal.

A professional artist for 17 years, Richardson has had numerous shows in America and Europe. Recent clients include BASF, Embassy Suites Hotels, Marriott Hotels, Hilton Hotels, The Rouse Co., The Oliver Carr Co. and the University of Alaska.

Pricing, scheduling and commission details are available upon request.

Also see these GUILD publications:
Designer's Edition: 6, 7, 8, 9

Woodland Cascade, Richardson Tapestry, BASF, NJ, 10'4" x 9'5"

Joan Schulze

808 Piper Avenue
Sunnyvale, CA 94087
FAX 408-736-7833
TEL 408-736-7833

Joan Schulze has pioneered silk and paper layered constructions. Fresh and new in their expressive qualities, these two-sided works function as traditional wall quilts or exciting free-standing screens; they may also be hung in architectural installations. Textures combine the elegance of painted silk with paper surfaces reminiscent of peeling frescoes. Back lighted, they glow.

Lightfast and durable; easily installed.

Commissions accepted.

SHOWN: *in principio (In The Beginning)*, eight hangings, painted paper, silk, mixed media, stitched and quilted, largest 8'6" x 6'6", for the sanctuary of Queen of Apostles Church, San Jose, CA

Printed in Hong Kong ©1995 THE GUILD: Designer's Edition

Photos: Sharon Risedorph

Nancy Taylor Stonington

N. Taylor Stonington, Inc.
P.O. Box 2269
Vashon, WA 98070
(206) 463-2860
FAX (206) 463-6598

Nationally known for 25 years for her watercolors, Stonington produced her first fiber mural in 1983. Since then, she has created many of these large-scale, painting-based murals in response to growing demand for representational work to brighten public spaces.

The murals are constructed from hundreds of shades/textures of top quality, plush carpet—cut, pieced, glued onto wood panels, and wall-mounted to form a continuous image. They create a soft warmth, absorb sound and resist damage.

Inquiries welcome!

Dutch Harbor View, 1993, Grand Aleutian Hotel, Dutch Harbor, Alaska, fiber mural, 20'W x 18'H

THE GUILD REGISTER™
of Fiber Art for the Wall

Welcome to **THE GUILD REGISTER of Fiber Art for the Wall**, a tool for interior designers, art consultants, architects, hospitality designers, resource librarians and others who purchase or commission artwork for projects they oversee. In the last three years, this register has become a major source of relevant information about artists and artisans working in fiber art for the wall. The listing format includes basic contact information as well as details about products, techniques, sizes and pricing.

This glossary of fiber terms may be useful as you read about—and contact—the artists listed in THE GUILD REGISTER.

GLOSSARY OF FIBER ART TERMS

AIRBRUSH: a method of spraying dyes or paints onto a surface using a brush device driven by an air compressor.

APPLIQUÉ: a quilting technique whereby pieces of fabric are layered on top of one another and joined with decorative stitches.

BEADING: the process whereby decorative beads are sewn, glued or otherwise attached to a surface.

CASTING: a process of pouring paper pulp into or onto a mold to make a three-dimensional piece.

DYEING: a method whereby fibers or fabrics are colored, using either synthetic or natural dye substances.

EMBROIDERY: a form of needlework using decorative threads to embellish a piece of cloth or other fiber object.

FELTING: the process whereby natural fibers (most commonly wools) are subjected to heat, water and pressure to form a nonwoven fabric.

LAMINATING: the process whereby two or more layers of fabric, felt or paper pulps are pressed or glued together in some fashion to make a stronger, one-layer piece.

PAINTING: a process whereby fabrics or other fiber art are decorated by hand with dyes or pigments.

QUILTING: sewing two layers of fabrics together, usually in a decorative pattern, with an inner layer of batting "sandwiched" between.

SILKSCREEN: the process whereby paints or dyes are forced with a squeegee through a piece of fabric stretched onto a frame. A film or resist of some type is used to block out a portion of the screen, creating a stencil design.

STAMPING/PRINTING: the process whereby fabrics or other fiber art are decorated with rubber stamps or other objects and ink or dyes.

WEAVING: the process of joining fibers, threads or yarns at right angles on a loom to form a piece of cloth. Various patterns in the cloth are formed depending on the way these fibers are interwoven with one another.

WRAPPING: the process whereby fibers, yarns or other materials are wrapped around a core material.

FIBER ART FOR THE WALL

★ **KAREN ADACHI**
702 MONARCH WAY
SANTA CRUZ, CA 95060-3091
TEL 408-429-6192
Established: 1972
Products: paper
Techniques: airbush, casting, dyeing
Size Range: 27" × 29" to 7' × 9'
Price Range: $100 to $2,000/piece

See page 20 for photographs and additional information.

SANDY ADAIR
FIBRE DESIGN
RR 3 BOX 912
BOONE, NC 28607-9544
TEL 704-264-0259
Established: 1978
Products: tapestries, macramé
Techniques: weaving, embroidery, off-loom weaving
Size Range: 1' × 3' to 6' × 10'
Price Range: $100 to $125/sq. ft.

★ **B.J. ADAMS**
ART IN FIBER
2821 ARIZONA TER NW
WASHINGTON, DC 20016-2642
FAX 202-686-1042
TEL 202-364-8404
Established: 1970
Products: fabric constructions
Techniques: painting, appliqué, machine embroidery
Size Range: 12" × 12" to unlimited (modular)
Price Range: $100 to $400/sq. ft.

See page 28 for photographs and additional information.

DONNA ALBERT
PO BOX 7743
LANCASTER, PA 17604-7743
TEL 717-399-9880
Established: 1969
Products: art quilts, pictorial quilts
Techniques: embroidery, quilting, heat-fusion appliqué
Size Range: 12" × 18" to 10' × 10'
Price Range: $400 to $8,000/piece

ROBERT W. ALEXANDER (BILL)
INDUSTRIAL STRENGTH ART
PO BOX 599
11907 MORGANTON HWY
MORGANTON, GA 30560-0599
TEL 706-374-5792
Established: 1978
Products: fiber installations
Techniques: wrapping
Size Range: 8" × 10" to 40' × 65'
Price Range: $40 to $400/sq. ft.

★ **EMMA ALLEBES**
8398 SUNSET AVE
FAIR OAKS, CA 95628
FAX 916-961-8653
TEL 916-961-8639
Established: 1980
Products: art quilts
Techniques: quilting, embroidery, beading, hand manipulation
Size Range: 48" × 48" to 9' × 9'
Price Range: $2,000 to $15,000/piece

See page 10 for photographs and additional information.

MARTA AMUNDSON
GOOSE KNOB GLASS AND FIBER
HC36-85 GOOSE KNOB DR
RIVERTON, WY 82501
FAX 307-856-5176
TEL 307-856-3373
Established: 1976
Products: art quilts
Techniques: appliqué, embroidery, quilting
Size Range: 2' × 2' to 12' × 12'
Price Range: $500 to $18,000/piece

ANANSA-PURUO DESIGNS
ROBYN DAUGHTRY
PO BOX 1215
SILVER SPRING, MD 20910
FAX 301-585-0367
TEL 301-585-2665
Established: 1980
Products: paper
Techniques: painting, dyeing, collage
Size Range: 8" × 14" to 6' × 8'
Price Range: $150 to $225/sq. ft.

CAROL ARMSTRONG
CAROL ARMSTRONG QUILTS
STAR SIDING RD HC 01 BOX 125
SHINGLETON, MI 49884
TEL 906-452-6469
Established: 1980
Products: art quilts
Techniques: appliqué, embroidery, quilting
Size Range: 8" × 8" to 100" × 100"
Price Range: $50 to $5,000/piece

SANDY ASKEW
50951 EXPRESSWAY
BELLEVILLE, MI 48111
TEL 313-483-5529
Established: 1975
Products: fiber installations
Techniques: contemporary coil weaving
Size Range: 12" × 36" to 6' × 12'
Price Range: $100 to $5,000/piece

CATHY PHILLIPS ATEN
CATHY ATEN TEXTILES
RR 2 BOX 154
SANTA FE, NM 87505-8659
TEL 505-983-7753
Established: 1978
Products: painted wool tapestries
Techniques: painting, stamping or printing
Size Range: 4' × 6' to 10' × 20'
Price Range: $1,800 to $8,000/piece

ELLEN ATHENS
PO BOX 1386
MENDOCINO, CA 95460-1386
TEL 707-937-2642
Established: 1982
Products: tapestries
Techniques: weaving
Size Range: 2' × 2' to 5' × 15'
Price Range: $400 to $18,000/piece

CAROL ATLESON
FIBER ART STUDIO
465 RUSKIN RD
AMHERST, NY 14226-4235
TEL 716-834-9384
Established: 1979
Products: tapestries
Techniques: weaving
Size Range: 2' × 3' to 7' × 7'
Price Range: $1,200 to $10,000/piece

★ **MARJORIE ATWOOD**
1509 S ELWOOD
TULSA, OK 74119
FAX 918-583-0886
TEL 918-583-0886
Established: 1987
Products: mixed media installations
Techniques: painting, gilding
Size Range: 12" × 6" to 12' × 16'
Price Range: $40 to $200/sq. ft.

See page 112 for photographs and additional information.

JOANN BACHELDER
RIVERTOWN TEXTILES
1001 S HENRY ST
BAY CITY, MI 48706-5007
TEL 517-892-3013
Established: 1978
Products: wall hangings
Techniques: dyeing, weaving
Size Range: 20" × 20" to 9' × 12'
Price Range: $350 to $2,500/piece

SHIRLEY ROESE BAHNSEN
413½ 21ST PLACE CT
CLINTON, IA 52732-6137
TEL 319-243-5863
Established: 1966
Products: paper
Techniques: laminating, painting, weaving
Size Range: 24" × 36" to 42" × 72"
Price Range: $600 to $2,000/piece

★ **SALLY BAILEY**
HOOKED ON ART
PO BOX 60204
SANTA BARBARA, CA 93160-0204
TEL 805-967-3350
Established: 1969
Products: hooked art hangings
Techniques: traditional hooking
Size Range: 12" × 18" to 30" × 72"
Price Range: $75 to $200/sq. ft.

See page 29 for photographs and additional information.

MARTIN K. BAKER
ARTESANOS TIPICOS/COYOTE DESIGNS
715 CLEVELAND ST
MISSOULA, MT 59801-3738
FAX 406-728-3668
TEL 406-728-2789
Established: 1974
Products: tapestries
Techniques: painting, silkscreen, weaving
Size Range: 24" × 24" to 22' × 36'
Price Range: $20 to $100/sq. ft.

DORIS BALLY
420 N CRAIG ST
PITTSBURGH, PA 15213-1105
FAX 412-621-9030
TEL 412-621-3709
Established: 1963
Products: tapestries
Techniques: weaving
Size Range: 20" × 20" to 94" × 20'
Price Range: $150 to $155/sq. ft.

BARBARA FARRELL ARTS
BARBARA FARRELL
PO BOX 2944
SANFORD, FL 32772-2944
FAX 407-321-8666
TEL 407-321-0100
Established: 1973
Products: mixed media installations
Techniques: painting, stitchery, fresco
Size Range: 4' × 5' to 10' × 12'
Price Range: $100 minimum/sq. ft.

BARKER-SCHWARTZ DESIGNS
915 SPRING GARDEN ST FL 3
PHILADELPHIA, PA 19123-2605
TEL 215-236-0745
Established: 1980
Products: woven floorcloths
Techniques: appliqué, weaving, hand stitching
Size Range: 3' × 4' to 8' × 11'
Price Range: $100 to $125/sq. ft.

TERESA BARKLEY
2440 27TH ST
ASTORIA, NY 11102-2312
TEL 718-545-4281
Established: 1978
Products: art quilts
Techniques: appliqué, painting, quilting
Size Range: 16" × 20" to 103" × 110"
Price Range: $500 to $20,000/piece

SONYA LEE BARRINGTON

837 47TH AVE
SAN FRANCISCO, CA 94121-3207
TEL 415-221-6510
Established: 1972
Products: art quilts
Techniques: dyeing, quilting, marble printing
Size Range: 2' × 2' to 5' × 7'
Price Range: $125 to $225/sq. ft.

BARBARA, RUTH & STEVEN BARRON

BARRON DESIGNS
1943 NEW YORK AVE
HUNTINGTON STATION, NY
  11746-2909
FAX 516-549-9122
TEL 516-549-4242
Established: 1972
Products: fiber installations
Techniques: embroidery, weaving, wrapping
Size Range: up to 24' × 24'
Price Range: $400 to $24,000/piece

DOREEN BECK
DINK SIEGEL

100 W 57TH ST #10G
NEW YORK, NY 10019-3327
TEL 212-246-9757
Established: 1974
Products: art quilts
Techniques: appliqué, quilting
Size Range: 2' × 3' to 4' × 5'
Price Range: $1,500 to $10,000/piece

JUDY BECKER

27 ALBION ST
NEWTON, MA 02159-2119
TEL 617-332-6778
Established: 1981
Products: art quilts
Techniques: appliqué, dyeing, quilting
Size Range: 3' × 3' to 10' × 15'
Price Range: $900 to $8,000/piece
Price Range: $50 to $100/sq. ft.

PAMELA E. BECKER

5 HENDRICK RD
FLEMINGTON, NJ 08822-7155
TEL 908-806-4911
Established: 1978
Products: fabric constructions
Techniques: appliqué, painting, piecing
Size Range: 28" × 32" to 8' × 16'
Price Range: $3,000 to $15,000/piece

SUE BENNER

8517 SAN FERNANDO WAY
DALLAS, TX 75218-4306
TEL 214-324-3550
Established: 1980
Products: art quilts
Techniques: dyeing, painting, quilting
Size Range: 15" × 15" to 12' × 15'
Price Range: $375 to $20,000/piece

ASTRID HILGER BENNETT

909 WEBSTER ST
IOWA CITY, IA 52240-4738
TEL 319-338-9176
Established: 1978
Products: fabric constructions
Techniques: dyeing, painting, silkscreen
Size Range: 18" × 24" to 8' × 10'
Price Range: $250 to $8,000/piece

CHRISTINA BENSON-VOS

126 MADISON ST #1
HOBOKEN, NJ 07030-1858
TEL 201-656-7441
TEL 212-982-5960
Established: 1986
Products: tapestries
Techniques: weaving
Size Range: 4' × 6' to 6' × 8'
Price Range: $5,000 to $15,000/piece

LYNN BERKOWITZ

PO BOX 121
SLATEDALE, PA 18079-0121
TEL 610-767-8072
Established: 1978
Products: fabric constructions
Techniques: dyeing, weaving
Size Range: 10" × 10" to 8' × 8'
Price Range: $400 to $5,000/piece

JULIE BERNER

29953 FOX HOLLOW RD
EUGENE, OR 97405-9436
TEL 503-484-9220
Established: 1981
Products: art quilts
Techniques: embroidery, silkscreen, patchwork
Size Range: 36" × 36" to 2' × 25'
Price Range: $1,000 to $10,000/piece
Price Range: $75 to $175/sq. ft.

LOUISE LEMIEUX BÉRUBÉ

CENTRE DES METIERS D'ART
1751 RUE RICHARDSON
BUREAU 5530
MONTREAL, QC H3K 1G6
CANADA
FAX 514-933-6305
TEL 514-933-3728
Established: 1979
Products: fabric constructions
Techniques: weaving with metal wires
Size Range: 8" × 8" to 6' × 6'
Price Range: $300 to $15,000/piece

BIG SUR HANDWOVENS

LAVERNE MCLEOD
THE VILLAGE SHOP #7
BIG SUR, CA 93920
TEL 408-667-2589
Established: 1986
Products: fiber installations
Techniques: weaving
Size Range: 12" × 12" to 60" × 100"
Price Range: $200 to $3,000/piece

ELIZABETH BILLINGS

EP BILLINGS, WEAVER
PO BOX 124
WOODSTOCK, VT 05091-0124
TEL 802-457-2576
Established: 1987
Products: tapestries
Techniques: weaving, natural-dyed ikat
Size Range: 24" × 24" to 20' × 30'
Price Range: $400 to $20,000/piece

REBECCA BLUESTONE

PO BOX 1704
SANTA FE, NM 87504-1704
FAX 505-986-3412
TEL 505-989-9599
Established: 1984
Products: tapestries
Techniques: weaving, dyeing, embroidery
Size Range: 5' × 3' to 20' × 6'
Price Range: $80 to $175/sq. ft.

CHRIS BOBIN

FABRIC EFFECTS
20 W 20TH ST FL 5
NEW YORK, NY 10011-4213
FAX 212-255-3077
TEL 212-255-5225
Established: 1980
Products: art quilts
Techniques: appliqué, embroidery, quilting
Size Range: 3' × 4' to 7' × 9'
Price Range: $500 to $4,500/piece

NANCY BONEY

97 KING ST
FANWOOD, NJ 07023-1517
TEL 908-889-8219
Established: 1973
Products: fabric constructions
Techniques: appliqué, fabric sculpture
Size Range: 24" × 36" to 5' × 8'
Price Range: $65 to $85/sq. ft.

DANA BOUSSARD

2 HEART CREEK RRT #1
ARLEE, MT 59821
FAX 406-726-4136
TEL 406-726-3357
Established: 1966
Products: fiber installations
Techniques: airbush, appliqué, painting
Size Range: 3' × 4' to 10' × 100'
Price Range: $150 to $300/sq. ft.

GEORGE-ANN BOWERS

1199 CORNELL AVE
BERKELEY, CA 94706-2305
TEL 501-524-3611
Products: tapestries
Techniques: weaving, painting, dyeing
Size Range: 23" × 27" to 38" × 108"
Price Range: $150 to $250/sq. ft.

ODETTE BRABEC

1107 GOLF AVE
HIGHLAND PARK, IL 60035-3637
TEL 708-432-2704
Established: 1977
Products: tapestries
Techniques: weaving
Size Range: 24" × 24" to 5' × 10'
Price Range: $1,000 to $13,000/piece

Mary Balzer Buskirk, *New Mexico Sky* ©, from the *Gods at Play* series, 44" × 44"

FIBER ART FOR THE WALL

JEANNE BRAEN
14 LEVESQUE LN
MONT VERNON, NH 03057-1420
TEL 603-672-7822
Established: 1975
Products: tapestries
Techniques: weaving
Size Range: 3' x 5' to 9' x 12'
Price Range: $80 to $100/sq. ft.

ANN BRAUER
PO BOX 164 282 EMMET RD
ASHFIELD, MA 01330-0164
TEL 413-628-4014
Established: 1981
Products: art quilts
Techniques: quilting, appliqué
Size Range: 4" x 4" to 8' x 12'
Price Range: $200 to $10,000/piece

ANN SHERWIN BROMBERG
44 WASHINGTON ST #1017
BROOKLINE, MA 02146-7106
TEL 617-731-2545
Established: 1960
Products: woven watercolor paintings
Techniques: painting, weaving
Size Range: 12" x 12" to 5' x 80'
Price Range: $500 to $80,000/piece

LYNDA BROTHERS
4255 HITCH BLVD
MOORPARK, CA 93021-9731
TEL 805-523-3101
Established: 1969
Products: tapestries
Techniques: painting, weaving, marbling
Size Range: unlimited
Price Range: $35 to $400/sq. ft.

TAFI BROWN
TY BRYN DESIGN STUDIOS
PO BOX 319
ALSTEAD, NH 03602-0319
TEL 603-756-3412
Established: 1975
Products: tapestries
Techniques: quilting, cyanotype
Size Range: 12" x 12" to 96" x 96"
Price Range: $250 to $18,000/piece

LOIS BRYANT
503 S 8TH ST
LINDENHURST, NY 11757-4616
TEL 516-226-7819
Established: 1979
Products: fiber installations
Techniques: weaving
Size Range: 1' x 1' to 8' x 17'
Price Range: $175 to $250/sq. ft.

★ LAURA BRYANT
2595 30TH AVE N
SAINT PETERSBURG, FL 33713
FAX 813-321-1905
TEL 813-327-3100
Established: 1979
Products: double-woven tapestries
Techniques: weaving, dyeing, warp
painting
Size Range: 20" x 20" to 10' x 30'
Price Range: $9.80 to $20,000/piece
Price Range: $200/sq. ft.

See page 4 for photographs and additional information.

★ MYRA BURG
2913 3RD ST #201
SANTA MONICA, CA 90405
FAX 310-399-0623
TEL 310-399-5040
Established: 1977
Products: mixed media installations,
rare wood, metals
Techniques: wrapping, assemblies
Size Range: 1' x 1' to 100' x 200'
Price Range: $600 to $60,000/piece
Price Range: $150 to $450/sq. ft.

See page 97 for photographs and additional information.

PATRICIA BURLING
WILLOWWEAVE
17 FRESH MEADOW RD
WESTON, CT 06883-2604
TEL 203-454-2742
Established: 1979
Products: wall hangings
Techniques: dyeing, weaving
Size Range: panels up to any size
Price Range: $45 to $47/sq. ft.

★ SUSAN EILEEN BURNES
6980 MILL RD
BRECKSVILLE, OH 44141-1812
FAX 216-526-0874
TEL 216-838-5955
Established: 1991
Products: fabric constructions
Techniques: embroidery, painting, fiber
bonding
Size Range: 4" x 6" to 36" x 48"
Price Range: $200 to $4,000/piece

See page 30 for photographs and additional information.

★ MARY BALZER BUSKIRK
BUSKIRK STUDIOS
53 VIA VENTURA
MONTEREY, CA 93940-4340
TEL 408-375-6165
Established: 1956
Products: tapestries
Techniques: painting, weaving, gold and
silver leaf
Size Range: 1' x 1' to 20' x 20'
Price Range: $100 to $175/sq. ft.

See photograph on page 47.

★ BARBARA CADE
262 HIDEAWAY HILLS DR
HOT SPRINGS, AR 71901-8841
TEL 501-262-4065
Established: 1978
Products: sculpture
Techniques: felting, weaving, wrapping
Size Range: 24" x 24" to 60" x 78"
Price Range: $600 to $8,000/piece

See page 31 for photographs and additional information.

MONECA CALVERT
6104 BROOKSIDE CIR
ROCKLIN, CA 95677
TEL 916-783-1189
Established: 1983
Products: art quilts
Techniques: appliqué, embroidery,
quilting
Size Range: 2' x 2' to 8' x 8'
Price Range: $1,800 to $20,000/piece

LUCINDA CARLSTROM
LUCINDA CARLSTROM STUDIO
1075 STANDARD DR NE
ATLANTA, GA 30319-3357
TEL 404-231-0227
Established: 1974
Products: mixed media installations
Techniques: quilting, gold leaf piece work
with paper, silk
Size Range: 20" x 20" to 80" x 120"
Price Range: $160 to $250/sq. ft.

ERIKA CARTER
2440 KILLARNEY WAY SE
BELLEVUE, WA 98004-7038
TEL 206-451-9712
Established: 1984
Products: art quilts
Techniques: appliqué, painting, quilting
Size Range: 26" x 36" to 60" x 66"
Price Range: $125 to $175/sq. ft.

Pat Dozier, Nightflashing, 1993, tapestry, 80" x 24"

★ BETH CASSIDY

2416 NW 60TH ST
SEATTLE, WA 98107
FAX 206-706-0406
TEL 206-783-6226

Established: 1980
Products: fabric constructions
Techniques: quilting, laminating, beading
Size Range: 12" × 12" to 144" × 144"
Price Range: $300 to $5,000/piece
Price Range: $10 to $75/sq. ft.

See page 11 for photographs and additional information.

MARY ALLEN CHAISSON

ALLEN POINT STUDIO
ALLEN POINT RD RR1 BOX 285
S HARPSWELL, ME 04079
FAX 207-833-6820
TEL 207-833-6842
Established: 1972
Products: art quilts
Techniques: appliqué, painting, quilting
Size Range: 2' × 2' to 7' × 7'
Price Range: $400 to $5,000/piece

★ MARTHA CHATELAIN

ARTFOCUS, LTD.
PO BOX 9855
SAN DIEGO, CA 92169-0855
TEL 619-581-6410

Established: 1982
Products: paper
Techniques: casting, dyeing, embossing
Size Range: 10" × 10" to 4' × 14'
Price Range: $300 to $8,500/piece

See page 22 for photographs and additional information.

JILL NORDFORS CLARK

JILL NORDFORS CLARK FIBER ART &
   INTERIOR DESIGN
3419 N ADAMS ST
TACOMA, WA 98407-6038
TEL 206-759-6158
Established: 1974
Products: mixed media installations
Techniques: appliqué, embroidery, painting
Size Range: 16" × 20" to 30" × 40"
Price Range: $750 to $1,200/piece

SUSANNE CLAWSON

5093 VELDA DAIRY RD
TALLAHASSEE, FL 32308-6801
TEL 904-893-5656
Established: 1985
Products: high-relief wall art
Techniques: casting, dyeing, handmade paper
Size Range: 20" × 20" to 8' × 10'
Price Range: $500 to $14,000/piece

ANTONIO COCILOVO

LIFEFORMS
2600 PINE DR
PRESCOTT, AZ 86301-4098
TEL 602-445-1643
Established: 1974
Products: paint on custom fabrics
Techniques: painting, airbrush
Size Range: 2' × 2' and up
Price Range: $200 to $5,000/piece
Price Range: $30 to $50/sq. ft.

★ ELAINE ALBERS COHEN

32106 LAKE RD
AVON LAKE, OH 44012-1808
TEL 216-933-5979

Established: 1965
Products: cast paper reliefs
Techniques: casting, dyeing, painting
Size Range: 18" × 24" to 6' × 6'
Price Range: $100 to $150/sq. ft.

See page 21 for photographs and additional information.

JUDITH CONTENT

JUDITH CONTENT TEXTILES AND
   DESIGNS
827 MATADERO AVE
PALO ALTO, CA 94306-2606
TEL 415-857-0289
Established: 1979
Products: art quilts
Techniques: dyeing, quilting
Size Range: 2' × 5' to 18' × 22'
Price Range: $250 to $30,000/piece

DEBBI COOPER

DEBBI COOPER STUDIOS
3450 PINE HAVEN RD
COMMERCE TWP, MI 48382-2161
TEL 810-363-0165
Established: 1982
Products: fabric constructions
Techniques: weaving, dyeing, surface design
Size Range: 1' × 1' to 5' × 7'
Price Range: $100 to $2,000/piece

STEPHANIE RANDALL COOPER

2911 YORK RD
EVERETT, WA 98204-5407
FAX 205-745-2115
TEL 206-745-2115
Established: 1987
Products: art quilts
Techniques: painting, dyeing, rip and tear assembly
Size Range: 48" × 60" to 84" × 84"
Price Range: $1,000 to $4,000/piece

BARBARA CORNETT

FIBERSTRUCTIONS
1101 JEFFERSON ST
LYNCHBURG, VA 24504-1709
TEL 804-528-3136
Established: 1976
Products: mixed media installations
Techniques: painting, felting, fiber sculpture
Size Range: 2' × 3' to 12' × 20'
Price Range: $500 to $50,000/piece

JOYCE CRAIN

2901 BENTON BLVD
MINNEAPOLIS, MN 55416-4328
TEL 612-377-0042
Established: 1970
Products: mixed media installations
Techniques: interlacing
Size Range: 12" × 12" to 9' × 15'
Price Range: $500 to $40,000/piece

BARBARA LYDECKER CRANE

18 HILL ST
LEXINGTON, MA 02173-4318
TEL 617-862-1579
Established: 1985
Products: art quilts
Techniques: dyeing, painting, quilting
Size Range: 2' × 2' to 6' × 6'
Price Range: $200 to $8,000/piece

GLORIA E. CROUSE

FIBER ART
4325 JOHN LUHR RD NE
OLYMPIA, WA 98516-2320
TEL 206-491-1980
Established: 1970
Products: fabric constructions
Techniques: beading, embroidery, rug hooking
Size Range: 5" × 5" to 20' × 20'
Price Range: $50 to $150/sq. ft.

Alexandra Friedman, *Three Graces*, wool tapestry, 50" × 59"

FIBER ART FOR THE WALL

★ BETH CUNNINGHAM
32 SWEETCAKE MOUNTAIN RD
NEW FAIRFIELD, CT 06812-4107
TEL 203-746-5160
Established: 1976
Products: mixed media installations
Techniques: airbush, painting, layering
Size Range: 1' x 1' to 6' x 12'
Price Range: $150 to $10,000/sq. ft.

See page 100 for photographs and additional information.

MARGARET CUSACK
124 HOYT ST
BROOKLYN, NY 11217-2215
FAX 718-237-0145
TEL 718-237-0145
Established: 1972
Products: fiber installations, marketing materials
Techniques: appliqué, airbrush, dyeing
Size Range: 18" x 24" to 72" x 144"
Price Range: $180 to $500/sq. ft.

DIANA DABINETT
BOX 254
TORBAY, NF A1K 1E3
CANADA
TEL 709-335-2637
Established: 1966
Products: fiber installations
Techniques: dyeing, painting, quilting
Size Range: 4" to 6" to 9' x 21'
Price Range: $100 to $4,500/piece

JUDY B. DALES
JUDY DALES, QUILTMAKER
129 HOLLY LN
BOONTON, NJ 07005-1624
TEL 201-334-1563
Established: 1980
Products: art quilts
Techniques: quilting, curved piecing
Size Range: 30" x 40" to 90" x 90"
Price Range: $500 to $10,000/piece

SUZANNE DALTON
DALTON & FOLES DESIGN
12387 SCOTT RD
ELLSWORTH, MI 49729
FAX 616-599-2496
TEL 616-599-2496
Established: 1977
Products: fiber installations
Techniques: weaving
Size Range: 2' x 6' to 30' x 40'
Price Range: $1,200 to $40,000/piece

★ NATALIE DARMOHRAJ
NATALKA DESIGNS
PO BOX 40309
PROVIDENCE, RI 02940-0309
FAX 401-351-2685
TEL 401-351-8841
Products: woven wall pieces
Techniques: dyeing, weaving
Size Range: 40" x 40" to 60" x 90"
Price Range: $500 to $5,000/piece

See page 158 for photographs and additional information.

Joan Griffin, *Releasing Boundaries*, tapestry, wool, silk, 3' x 4'

HEIDI DARR-HOPE
3718 TOMAKA RD
COLUMBIA, SC 29205-1558
FAX 803-771-4140
TEL 803-782-5341
Established: 1982
Products: mixed media constructions
Techniques: embroidery, painting, collage
Size Range: 10" x 14" to 6' x 12'
Price Range: $300 to $8,000/piece

KAREN DAVIDSON
PO BOX 637
HANA, HI 96713-0637
TEL 808-248-7094
Established: 1980
Products: paper
Techniques: casting, dyeing, painting
Size Range: 24" x 24" to 8' x 15'
Price Range: $300 to $10,000/piece

D. JOYCE DAVIES
D. JOYCE
185 ROBINSON ST PH2
OAKVILLE, ON L6J 7N9
CANADA
FAX 905-845-6823
TEL 905-845-6823
Established: 1980
Products: art quilts
Techniques: appliqué, quilting, embellishments
Size Range: 36" x 36" to 70" x 70"
Price Range: $800 to $3,500/piece

★ ALONZO DAVIS
PO BOX 12248
MEMPHIS, TN 38182-0248
FAX 901-276-0660
TEL 901-276-9070
Established: 1973
Products: paper
Techniques: painting, weaving
Size Range: 30" x 22" to 8' x 10'
Price Range: $1,500 to $15,000/piece

See page 101 for photographs and additional information.

ARDYTH DAVIS
11436 HOLLOW TIMBER CT
RESTON, VA 22094-1980
TEL 703-904-8027
Established: 1975
Products: fabric constructions
Techniques: dyeing, painting, pleating
Size Range: 12" x 12" to 80" x 80"
Price Range: $150 to $10,000/piece

LENORE DAVIS
LENORE DAVIS SOFT OBJECTS
655 NELSON PL
NEWPORT, KY 41071-1742
TEL 606-261-4523
Established: 1969
Products: art quilts
Techniques: dyeing, quilting, stamping/printing
Size Range: 12" x 12" to 100" x 100
Price Range: $100 to $300/sq. ft.

NANCY STANFORD DAVIS
26 AUSTIN RD
WILMINGTON, DE 19810-2203
TEL 302-478-7529
Established: 1992
Products: art quilts
Techniques: dyeing, quilting, weaving
Size Range: 2' x 2' to 8' x 8'
Price Range: $75 to $125/sq. ft.

NANETTE DAVIS-SHAKLHO
1289 E GRAND AVE #318
ESCONDIDO, CA 92027-3063
TEL 619-745-6091
Established: 1986
Products: fabric constructions
Techniques: dyeing, painting, pleating
Size Range: 18" x 18" to 6' x 12'
Price Range: $1,100 to $12,000/piece

DECONSTRUCTED DESIGNS LTD
JULIA A. WALSH
PO BOX 6503
HUNTSVILLE, TX 77342-6503
TEL 409-291-0195
Established: 1987
Products: fabric constructions
Techniques: quilting, slashing
Size Range: 16" x 20" to 65" x 55"
Price Range: $250 to $12,500/piece

JEAN DEEMER
1537 BRIARWOOD CIR
CUYAHOGA FALLS, OH 44221-3623
TEL 216-929-1995
Established: 1975
Products: paper constructions
Techniques: painting, collage
Size Range: 18" x 24" to 5' x 6'
Price Range: $375 to $3,500/piece

ANDREA DEIMEL
82 E HILLCREST AVE
CHALFONT, PA 18914
TEL 215-997-7964
Established: 1977
Products: mixed media installations
Techniques: embroidery, sculptural wood frames
Size Range: 12" x 10" to 24" x 30"
Price Range: $400 to $1,000/piece

E. DELZOPPO
GREY SEAL WEAVING STUDIO
#3886 POINT MICHAUD
CAPE BRETON ISLAND, NS B0E 1W0
CANADA
TEL 902-587-2494
Established: 1984
Products: damask compositions
Techniques: weaving, drawloom damask
Size Range: 6" x 6" to 45" x 72"
Price Range: $150 to $3,000/piece

LINDA DENIER

DENIER TAPESTRY STUDIO
745 EDENWOOD DR
ROSELLE, IL 60172-2824
TEL 708-893-5854
Established: 1990
Products: tapestries
Techniques: weaving
Size Range: 3" x 5" to 5' x 6'
Price Range: $150 to $175/sq. ft.

NANCY DeYOUNG

PO BOX 17423
BOULDER, CO 80308-0423
TEL 303-442-0229
Established: 1990
Products: paper
Techniques: casting, dyeing, painting
Size Range: 8" x 10" to 4' x 5'
Price Range: $100 to $3,000/piece

SALLY DILLON

7123 DALEWOOD LN
DALLAS, TX 75214-1812
TEL 214-821-1018
Established: 1970
Products: art quilts
Techniques: dyeing, painting, quilting
Size Range: 12" X 12" to 72" X 96"
Price Range: $100 to $10,000/piece
Price Range: $75 to $200/sq. ft.

JUDITH DINGLE

JUDITH DINGLE DESIGN
140 EVELYN AVE
TORONTO, ON M6P 2Z7
CANADA
TEL 416-766-9411
Established: 1978
Products: fabric constructions, textile,
mixed media constructions
Techniques: laminating, quilting, pieced
and constructed
Size Range: 48" x 48" to 20' x 40'
Price Range: $125 to $250/sq. ft.

JUDY DIOSZEGI

JUDY DIOSZEGI, DESIGNER
2628 ROSLYN CIR
HIGHLAND PARK, IL 60035-1910
TEL 708-433-2585
Established: 1976
Products: tapestries
Techniques: appliqué, embroidery,
quilting
Size Range: 18" x 36" to 12' x 24'
Price Range: $200 to $30,000/piece

SEENA DONNESON

SEENA DONNESON STUDIO
4349 10TH ST
LONG ISLAND CITY, NY 11101-6926
TEL 718-706-1342
Established: 1968
Products: tapestries, mixed media
installations, paper
Techniques: painting, molding
Size Range: 20" x 20" to 60" x 60"
Price Range: $1,000 to $15,000/piece

★ CAROLE ALDEN DOUBEK

2020 S 300TH E
SALT LAKE CITY, UT 84115-2234
TEL 801-487-1410
Established: 1980
Products: art quilts
Techniques: painting, appliqué, airbrush
Size Range: 1' x 1' to 6' x 12'
Price Range: $195 to $5,000/piece

**See page 163 for photographs and
additional information.**

ARNELLE A. DOW

THE BATIK LADY
448 MILTON ST
CINCINNATI, OH 45210-1428
TEL 606-261-4523
Established: 1973
Products: fiber installations
Techniques: appliqué, painting, batik,
oriental rug restoration
Size Range: 2" x 2" to 10' x 65'
Price Range: $65 to $15,000/piece

★ PAT DOZIER

PO BOX 76
MEDANALES, NM 87548-0076
TEL 505-685-4776
Established: 1992
Products: tapestries
Techniques: weaving
Size Range: 24" x 24" to 80" x 32"
Price Range: $95 to $125/piece

See photograph on page 48.

DRAWN THREAD DESIGNS

JULIA A. WALSH
PO BOX 6503
HUNTSVILLE, TX 77342-6503
TEL 409-291-0195
Established: 1987
Products: tapestries
Size Range: $200 - $10500 sq. ft.

SUSAN DUNSHEE

986 ACEQUIA MADRE ST
SANTA FE, NM 87501-2819
TEL 505-982-0988
Products: fiber constructions
Techniques: dyeing, laminating, machine
stitching
Size Range: 10" x 18" to 12' x 12'
Price Range: $95 to $210/sq. ft.

DONNA DURBIN

4034 WOODCRAFT ST
HOUSTON, TX 77025-5709
TEL 713-664-4764
Established: 1987
Products: tapestries
Techniques: painting, appliqué, weaving
Size Range: 8" x 8" to 8' x 20'
Price Range: $400 to $10,000/piece

EATON DESIGNS

1522 E VICTORY ST #5
PHOENIX, AZ 85040-1306
FAX 602-276-7276
TEL 800-276-6806
Established: 1986
Products: wool wall hangings
Techniques: hand tufting
Size Range: 1' x 1' to 14' x 14'
Price Range: $70 - $250/sq. ft.

Katherine Holzknecht, *Dynamic Concurrence*, 1994, mixed-media, 3'H x 8'W x 4"D

FIBER ART FOR THE WALL

MARGIT ECHOLS
ROWHOUSE PRESS
PO BOX 20531
NEW YORK, NY 10025-1514
FAX 212-662-7828
TEL 212-662-9604
Established: 1972
Products: art and traditional quilts
Techniques: appliqué, quilting, piecing
Size Range: 24" × 24" to 12' × 12'
Price Range: $1,000 to $10,000/piece

LORE EDZARD
815 RUNNING DEER
NASHVILLE, TN 37221-2234
TEL 615-662-2583
Established: 1967
Products: tapestries
Techniques: dyeing, embroidery, weaving, knotting
Size Range: 2' × 3' to 8' × 10'
Price Range: $100 to $150/sq. ft.

EFREM WEITZMAN ART WORKS
EFREM WEITZMAN
PO BOX 1092
SOUTH FALLSBURG, NY 12779-1092
FAX 914-434-2408
TEL 914-434-2408
Established: 1960
Products: tapestries
Techniques: appliqué, weaving, quilting, arraiolos, hand-tufting
Size Range: 4' × 7' to 90' × 20'
Price Range: $175 to $400/sq. ft.

SU EGEN
SU EGEN, HANDWEAVER/DESIGNER
2233 E HAWTHORNE ST
TUCSON, AZ 85719-4941
FAX 520-325-0009
TEL 520-325-0009
Established: 1970
Products: tapestries
Techniques: weaving
Size Range: unlimited
Price Range: $125 to $300/sq. ft.

SYLVIA H. EINSTEIN
11 OAK AVE
BELMONT, MA 02178-2751
TEL 617-484-9541
Established: 1980
Products: art quilts
Techniques: quilting
Size Range: 8" × 8" to 60" × 90"
Price Range: $150 to $3,000/piece

NANCY N. ERICKSON
DANCING RABBIT STUDIOS
3250 PATTEE CANYON RD
MISSOULA, MT 59803-1703
TEL 406-549-4671
Established: 1963
Products: art quilts, oil paintstick works
Techniques: appliqué, painting, quilting
Size Range: 16" × 24" to 9' × 10'
Price Range: $400 to $8,200/piece

KAREN EUBEL
150 1ST AVE #404
NEW YORK, NY 10009-5704
TEL 212-995-9624
Established: 1970
Products: paper
Techniques: painting, weaving, stenciling
Size Range: 1' × 1' to 3' × 4'
Price Range: $400 to $1,200/piece

★ PHYLLIS 'CERATTO' EVANS
6969 ISLAND CENTER RD NE
BAINBRIDGE ISLAND, WA
98110-1681
TEL 206-842-5042
Established: 1987
Products: fiber collage
Techniques: laminating
Size Range: unlimited
Price Range: $400 to $10,000/piece
Price Range: $150 to $350/sq. ft.

See page 32 for photographs and additional information.

CARYL BRYER FALLERT
2031 COLLINS RD
OSWEGO, IL 60543-9670
TEL 708-554-1177
Established: 1983
Products: art quilts
Techniques: dyeing, painting, quilting
Size Range: 1' × 1' to 10' × 15'
Price Range: $125 to $300/sq. ft.

JUDITH POXSON FAWKES
C/O LAURA RUSSO GALLERY
805 NW 21ST AVE
PORTLAND, OR 97209-1408
TEL 503-226-2754
Established: 1970
Products: tapestries
Techniques: weaving
Size Range: 3' × 3' to 8' × 20'
Price Range: $150 minimum/sq. ft.

★ DORIS FINCH
DORIS FINCH FABRIC ART
2144 CRESCENT DR
ALTADENA, CA 91001-2112
TEL 818-797-6172
Established: 1987
Products: embellished appliquéd hangings
Techniques: appliqué, dyeing, stuffing
Size Range: 20" × 30" to 72" × 36"
Price Range: $1,000 to $7,000/piece

See page 33 for photographs and additional information.

PAMELA FLANDERS
FLANDERS FINE ART
6820 ROYALWOOD WAY
SAN JOSE, CA 95120-2228
TEL 408-997-8438
Established: 1983
Products: paper
Techniques: laminating, painting, collage
Size Range: 8" × 8" to 40" × 60"
Price Range: $200 to $500/piece

MARTI FLEISCHER
128 MONTICELLO RD
OAK RIDGE, TN 37830-8258
TEL 615-483-0772
Established: 1990
Products: tapestries
Techniques: weaving
Size Range: 4" × 3" to 2½' × 7'
Price Range: $200 to $1,000/piece

★ MARI MARKS FLEMING
1431 GLENDALE AVE
BERKELEY, CA 94708-2027
TEL 510-548-3121
Established: 1989
Products: mixed media installations
Techniques: laminating, painting, fiber constructions
Size Range: 18" × 12" to 10' × 15'
Price Range: $500 to $15,000/piece

See page 164 for photographs and additional information.

BARBARA FLETCHER
88 BEALS ST
BROOKLINE, MA 02146-3011
TEL 617-277-3019
Established: 1987
Products: paper
Techniques: airbush, casting, dyeing
Size Range: 3" × 4" to 30" × 40"
Price Range: $25 to $1,000/piece

ROBERT FORMAN
412 GRAND ST
HOBOKEN, NJ 07030-2703
TEL 201-659-7069
Established: 1975
Products: yarn painting
Techniques: yarn glued to board
Size Range: 24" × 30" to 60" × 96"
Price Range: $3,000 to $15,000/piece

★ MARILYN FORTH
416 DAVID DR
N SYRACUSE, NY 13212-1929
FAX 315-458-0913
TEL 315-458-3786
Established: 1974
Products: framed batiks
Techniques: painting, wax drawn line
Size Range: 1' × 1' to 4' × 6'
Price Range: $180 to $2,500/piece

See page 34 for photographs and additional information.

Janet M. Hutchinson, *Spring*, 1993, hand-painted silk, 46" × 76", photo: Jerry Anthony

ROBERTA A. FOUNTAIN

PO BOX 2324
AMHERST, MA 01004-2324
TEL 413-256-1794
Established: 1975
Products: paper
Techniques: dyeing, laminating, quilting
Size Range: 1' x 1' to 3' x 5'
Price Range: $150 to $1,500/piece

FOWLER AND THELEN STUDIO

201 FAIRBROOK ST
NORTHVILLE, MI 48167-1503
TEL 313-348-6654
Established: 1972
Products: mixed media installations
Techniques: weaving
Size Range: 2' x 3' to 50' x 50'
Price Range: $500 to $5,000/piece

★ ALEXANDRA FRIEDMAN

56 ARBOR ST
HARTFORD, CT 06106-1201
FAX 203-232-9362
TEL 203-236-3311
Established: 1972
Products: tapestries
Techniques: weaving, embroidery
Size Range: open and flexible
Price Range: $125 to $250/sq. ft.

See photograph on page 49.

JAN FRIEDMAN

1409 E DAVENPORT ST
IOWA CITY, IA 52245-3021
Established: 1979
Products: tapestries
Techniques: appliqué, dyeing, weaving
Size Range: 20" x 24" to 10' x 15'
Price Range: $95/sq. ft.

WAYNE A.O. FUERST

ORCHID STUDIO
40 WOODLAND RD
ASHLAND, MA 01721-1417
TEL 508-881-2525
Established: 1979
Products: handmade paper paintings
Techniques: layers of paper fiber
Size Range: 13" x 20" to 33" x 79"
Price Range: $150/sq. ft.

SUSAN GARDELS

1316 ARTHUR AVE
DES MOINES, IA 50316-1961
TEL 515-265-2361
Products: paper
Techniques: painting, weaving, sewing
Size Range: 12" x 9" to 40" x 60"
Price Range: $95 to $2,500 framed/piece

JUDITH GEIGER

JUDITH GEIGER GALLERY
10 W FIGUEROA ST
SANTA BARBARA, CA 93101-3104
TEL 805-564-1881
Established: 1982
Products: hand-painted silk
Techniques: dyeing, painting, gutta resist
Size Range: 4" x 6" to 33" x 44"
Price Range: $20 to $450/piece

CAROL H. GERSEN

STUDIO ART QUILTS
18839 MANOR CHURCH RD
BOONSBORO, MD 21713-2511
TEL 301-432-6484
Established: 1981
Products: art quilts
Techniques: dyeing, quilting
Size Range: 3' x 3' to 5' x 8'
Price Range: $900 to $6,000/piece

JAMES R. GILBERT

WOVEN STRUCTURES
PO BOX 474
BLOOMFIELD HILLS, MI 48303-0474
TEL 810-772-7087
Established: 1970
Products: fiber installations
Techniques: dyeing, silkscreen, weaving
Size Range: 3' x 3' to 6' x 90'
Price Range: $350 to $7,000/piece

SUSAN GILMOUR

71 GREENWOOD WAY
MILL VALLEY, CA 94941-1122
TEL 415-383-0108
Established: 1970
Products: tapestries
Techniques: painting, wrapping, corded raw silk
Size Range: 1' x 3' to 8' x 40'
Price Range: $1,200 to $50,000/piece

SUELLEN GLASHAUSSER

202 S 2ND AVE
HIGHLAND PARK, NJ 08904-2225
TEL 908-545-6928
Established: 1971
Products: mixed media installations
Techniques: embroidery, laminating, painting
Size Range: 3" x 6" to 85" x 120"
Price Range: $400 to $1,500/piece

LAYNE GOLDSMITH

PO BOX 563
SNOHOMISH, WA 98291-0563
FAX 206-334-5569
TEL 206-334-5569
Established: 1972
Products: felted wall constructions
Techniques: dyeing, felting, mixed textile media
Size Range: 4' x 5' to 12' x 60'
Price Range: $500 to $45,000/piece
Price Range: $100 to $300/sq. ft.

INA GOLUB

366 ROLLING ROCK RD
MOUNTAINSIDE, NJ 07092-2120
FAX 908-232-7981
TEL 908-232-5376
Established: 1963
Products: tapestries
Techniques: appliqué, beading, weaving
Size Range: 2' x 2' to 10' x 12'
Price Range: $2,000 to $25,000/piece

RUTH GOWELL

7010 ARONOW DR
FALLS CHURCH, VA 22042-1805
TEL 703-532-8645
Established: 1978
Products: wall hangings
Techniques: dyeing, weaving
Size Range: 16" x 16" to 5' x 10'
Price Range: $250 to $4,000/piece

CHARLES GRAY

PO BOX 707
WEST POINT, GA 31833-0707
FAX 800-658-4198
TEL 800-658-4198
Established: 1973
Products: Kinetic Canvas™
Techniques: weaving
Size Range: 1' x 1' to 40' x 60'
Price Range: $47 to $69/sq. ft.

LAURA ELIZABETH GREEN

5523 HIGHLAND ST S
ST PETERSBURG, FL 33705-5135
TEL 813-867-1204
Established: 1973
Products: art quilts
Techniques: appliqué, dyeing, quilting
Size Range: 4" x 4" to 8' x 8'
Price Range: $250 to $2,500/piece

★ BARBARA GRENELL

1132 HALLS CHAPPEL RD
BURNSVILLE, NC 28714-9760
TEL 704-675-4073
Established: 1972
Products: fiber installations
Techniques: dyeing, weaving
Size Range: all sizes
Price Range: $100 to $175/sq. ft.

See page 35 for photographs and additional information.

DON GRIFFIN

3306 KENJAC RD
BALTIMORE, MD 21244-1322
TEL 410-655-8755
Established: 1973
Products: mixed media installations
Techniques: painting, collage
Size Range: 36" x 30" to 6' x 10'
Price Range: $500 to $3,500/piece

Carrie Jacobson-May, *Sobranes Ridge*, 1994, tufted wool tapestry, 50" x 64"

FIBER ART FOR THE WALL

★ JOAN GRIFFIN

FIBER DESIGN STUDIO
67 LAKE ST
HAMMONDSPORT, NY 14840-0541
FAX 607-569-3340
TEL 607-569-2256
Established: 1980
Products: tapestries
Techniques: weaving
Size Range: 12" x 12" to 5' x 10'
Price Range: $180 to $9,500/piece

See photograph on page 50.

MARILYN GRISHAM

315 POST RD
EL DORADO, KS 67042-4059
Established: 1970
Products: tapestries
Techniques: weaving, embroidery,
weft-face brocade
Size Range: 3' x 5' to 12' x 24'
Price Range: $2,500 to $55,000/piece

CLAIRE FAY HABERFELD

QUILTVISION
10762 MOORE WAY
BROOMFIELD, CO 80021-3629
TEL 303-469-1403
Established: 1981
Products: art quilts
Techniques: appliqué, painting, quilting
Size Range: 1' x 1' to 10' x 10'
Price Range: $75 to $95/sq. ft.

MARCIA HAMMOND

RR 1 BOX 898
PUTNEY, VT 05346-9746
TEL 802-387-2202
Established: 1977
Products: fiber installations
Techniques: weaving
Size Range: 48" x 18" to 12' x 6'
Price Range: $40 to $80/piece

HARRIET HANSON

THE STUDIOSPACE
1732 W HUBBARD ST
CHICAGO, IL 60622-6271
TEL 312-243-4144
Established: 1970
Products: handmade paper
Techniques: dimensional sculpture
Size Range: 18" x 24" to 36" to 48"
Price Range: $600 to $3,000/piece

TIM HARDING

HARDING DESIGN STUDIO
402 N MAIN ST
STILLWATER, MN 55082-5051
TEL 612-351-0383
Established: 1974
Products: fiber installations
Techniques: dyeing, quilting, slashing and
fraying
Size Range: 50" x 70" to 10' x 18'
Price Range: $50 to $100/sq. ft.

PETER HARRIS

TAPESTRY AND DESIGN
RR 2
AYTON, ON N0G 1C0
CANADA
TEL 519-665-2245
Established: 1973
Products: tapestries
Techniques: weaving
Size Range: 36" x 48" to 60" x 96"
Price Range: $2,500 to $10,000/piece

RENEE HARRIS

RENEE HARRIS STUDIO
642 CLEMMER AVE
CINCINNATI, OH 45219-1038
TEL 513-241-5909
Established: 1985
Products: fiber installations
Techniques: embroidery, felting
Size Range: 16" x 20" to 3' x 4'
Price Range: $300 to $1,200/piece

ANN L. HARTLEY

TREE HOUSE STUDIO
13515 SEA ISLAND DR
HOUSTON, TX 77069-2436
TEL 713-444-1118
Established: 1975
Products: mixed media installations
Techniques: painting, stamping/printing,
wrapping
Price Range: $300 to $1,500/piece

SARAH D. HASKELL

30 N MAIN ST
NEWMARKET, NH 03857-1210
TEL 603-659-5250
Established: 1976
Products: wall pieces
Techniques: weaving, painting
Size Range: 12" x 12" to 15' x 20'
Price Range: $100 to $200/sq. ft.

SHARON HEIDINGSFELDER

8010 DAN THOMAS RD
LITTLE ROCK, AR 72206-4148
FAX 501-671-2251
TEL 501-490-0405
Established: 1973
Products: art quilts
Techniques: dyeing, quilting, silkscreen
Size Range: 72" x 72" to 78" x 84"
Price Range: $4,000 to $6,500/piece

MARTHA HEINE

7 HAGGIS CT
DURHAM, NC 27705-2166
TEL 919-479-3270
Established: 1980
Products: tapestries
Techniques: weaving
Size Range: 36" x 48" to 6' x 7'
Price Range: $2,200 to $7,600/piece

SHEILA A. HELD

2762 MAYFAIR CT
WAUWATOSA, WI 53222-4105
TEL 414-475-6479
Established: 1975
Products: tapestries
Techniques: weaving
Size Range: 36" x 36" to 80" x 50"
Price Range: $1,000 to $6,000/piece
Price Range: $200 to $300/sq. ft.

HELIO GRAPHICS

DAWN WILKINS
PO BOX 6213
KEY WEST, FL 33041-6213
TEL 305-294-7901
Established: 1980
Products: mixed media installations,
painted canvas and prints
Techniques: painting, silkscreen, hand
painting
Size Range: 20" x 20" to 50" x 60"
Price Range: $200 to $2,000/piece

BARBARA HELLER

TAPESTRYARTS
4796 W SEVENTH AVE
VANCOUVER, BC V6T 1C6
CANADA
TEL 604-224-2060
Established: 1975
Products: tapestries
Techniques: weaving
Size Range: 12" x 12" to 4' x 6'
Price Range: $100 to $10,000/piece

SUSAN HART HENEGAR

5449 BELLEVUE AVE
LA JOLLA, CA 92037-7625
FAX 619-459-5693
TEL 619-459-5681
Established: 1978
Products: tapestries
Techniques: weaving, Aubusson tapestry
Size Range: 8" x 8" to 8' x 24'
Price Range: $150 to $300/sq. ft.

MARILYN HENRION

505 LAGUARDIA PL #23D
NEW YORK, NY 10012-2005
TEL 212-982-8949
Established: 1978
Products: art quilts
Techniques: hand quilting
Size Range: 24" x 24" to 80" x 80"
Price Range: $500 to $7,500/piece

HELENA HERNMARCK

HELENA HERNMARCK
TAPESTRIES, INC.
879 N SALEM RD
RIDGEFIELD, CT 06877-1714
FAX 203-431-9570
TEL 203-438-9220
Established: 1964
Products: tapestries
Techniques: weaving
Size Range: 10 sq. ft. to 400 sq. ft.
Price Range: $600 to $1,200/sq. ft.

Susan Kimber, *Cow at the Bridgewater Fair*, 54"H x 41"W

JANE HERRICK

4219 MEADOW LN
EAU CLAIRE, WI 54701-7487
TEL 715-833-9745

Established: 1982
Products: fabric constructions
Techniques: laminating, painting, stamping/printing
Size Range: 17" × 18" to 4'6" × 7'
Price Range: $300 to $3,600/piece

PAMELA HILL

PO BOX 800 8500 LAFAYETTE
MOKELUMNE HILL, CA 95245-0800
FAX 209-286-1001
TEL 209-286-1217

Established: 1975
Products: art quilts
Techniques: quilting, piecing
Size Range: 40" × 40" to 10' × 24'
Price Range: $600 to $5,000/piece

★ BILL HIO

34 CYPRESS DR
SCOTIA, NY 12302-4325
TEL 518-399-7404

Established: 1990
Products: tapestries
Techniques: needle stitch
Size Range: 32" × 32" to 64" × 128"
Price Range: $400 to $4,000/piece

See page 36 for photographs and additional information.

DOROTHY HOLDEN

301 KENT RD
CHARLOTTESVILLE, VA 22903-2409
TEL 804-971-5803

Established: 1977
Products: art quilts
Techniques: quilting
Size Range: 2' × 2' to 6' × 7'
Price Range: $850 to $6,500/piece

BONNIE LEE HOLLAND

6407 LANDON LN
BETHESDA, MD 20817-5603
TEL 301-229-4388

Established: 1982
Products: atrium and wall pieces
Techniques: appliqué, stamping/printing, dye painting
Size Range: 5" × 8" to 30' × 35'
Price Range: $200 to $30,000/piece

ELIZABETH HOLSTER

PAPER BY HOLSTER
727 E A ST
IRON MOUNTAIN, MI 49801-3505
TEL 906-779-2592

Established: 1974
Products: paper
Techniques: casting, painting, drawing/collagraph
Size Range: 24" × 24" to 60" × 60"
Price Range: $500 to $5,000/piece

★ KATHERINE HOLZKNECHT

22828 57TH AVE SE
WOODINVILLE, WA 98072-8660
TEL 206-481-7788

Established: 1976
Products: mixed media installations
Techniques: dyeing, laminating, lashing
Size Range: 2' × 2' to 20' × 60'
Price Range: $200/sq. ft.

See photograph on page 51.

DORA HSIUNG

HSIUNG DESIGN
95 WARREN ST
NEWTON, MA 02159-2334
TEL 617-969-4630

Established: 1978
Products: wall hangings
Techniques: wrapping, original off-loom weaving
Size Range: 12" × 12" to 16' × 21'
Price Range: $200 to $30,000/piece

JOHN D. HUBBARD

53 STONEGATE HTS
MARQUETTE, MI 49855-9449
TEL 906-249-1188

Established: 1968
Products: paper
Techniques: casting, airbrush, paper assemblage
Size Range: 18" × 20" to 48" × 60"
Price Range: $500 to $4,500/piece

DOROTHY HUGHES

DOROTHY HUGHES STUDIO
850 N MILWAUKEE AVE
CHICAGO, IL 60622-4143
FAX 312-563-1456
TEL 312-421-7045

Established: 1970
Products: fiber sculpture
Techniques: dyeing, weaving
Size Range: 12" × 12" to 22' × 33'
Price Range: $500 to $90,000/piece

WENDY C. HUHN

81763 LOST CREEK RD
DEXTER, OR 97431-9735
TEL 503-937-3147

Established: 1983
Products: art quilts
Techniques: airbrush, stamping/printing, stencils
Size Range: 36" × 36" to 90" × 90"
Price Range: $100 to $150/sq. ft.

CONSTANCE HUNT

1270 SANCHEZ ST
SAN FRANCISCO, CA 94114-3833
TEL 415-282-5170

Established: 1980
Products: tapestries
Techniques: weaving
Size Range: 6" × 9" to 72" × 80"
Price Range: $400 to $20,000/piece

★ JANET M. HUTCHINSON

ISLAND SILK
LAUREL RUN FARM HC-82
BOX 253A
MARLINTON, WV 24954
FAX 304-799-7158
TEL 304-799-7158

Established: 1986
Products: fiber installations
Techniques: painting, dyeing
Size Range: 30" × 20" to 8' × 4'
Price Range: $250 to $3,000/piece

See photograph on page 52.

★ MARIE-LAURE ILIE

MARILOR ART STUDIO
106 VIA SEVILLA
REDONDO BEACH, CA 90277-6749
FAX 310-375-4977
TEL 310-375-4977

Established: 1975
Products: fiber installations
Techniques: appliqué, painting, layering
Size Range: 2' × 3' to 8' × 12'
Price Range: $500 to $10,000/piece
Price Range: $60 to $120/sq. ft.

See page 37 for photographs and additional information.

IRA ONO DESIGNS

PO BOX 112
VOLCANO, HI 96785
TEL 808-967-7261

Products: fabric constructions, Japanese-paste paper screens
Techniques: painting, Japanese-paste paper
Size Range: 16" × 24" to 7' × 15'
Price Range: $400 to $4,000/piece

ELAINE IRELAND

711 HAMPSHIRE ST
SAN FRANCISCO, CA 94110-2129
TEL 415-648-8813

Established: 1972
Products: tapestries
Techniques: weaving combined w/mixed mediums
Size Range: miniatures to unlimited
Price Range: $500 to $1,000/sq. ft.

Chris King, *Sky Tower* (detail), pieced patchwork in artist-dyed raw silk, 8½"H × 12"W

FIBER ART FOR THE WALL

IRENE R. DE GAIR TAPESTRIES

IRENE R. DE GAIR
8415 OVERLOOK ST
VIENNA, VA 22182-5145
FAX 703-698-9208
TEL 703-698-9281
Established: 1978
Products: tapestries
Techniques: weaving
Size Range: 2' x 2' to 7' and up
Price Range: $45 to $90/sq. ft.

PEG IRISH

114 METOXIT RD
WAQUOIT, MA 02536-7723
TEL 508-548-3230
Established: 1988
Products: fiber installations
Techniques: dyeing, embroidery, rug hooking
Size Range: 8" x 8" to 4' x 8'
Price Range: $150 to $300/sq. ft.

CAROL KASMER IRVING

THE WEAVER'S WEB
1204 8TH AVE S
ESCANABA, MI 49829-3217
TEL 906-786-0331
Established: 1977
Products: fiber installations
Techniques: weaving
Size Range: 2' x 3' to 6' x 12'
Price Range: $120 to $1,500/piece

SUSAN IVERSON

SUSAN IVERSON - TAPESTRIES
904 BUFORD OAKS CIR
RICHMOND, VA 23235-4680
TEL 804-272-0225
Established: 1975
Products: tapestries
Techniques: dyeing, weaving
Size Range: 3' x 7' to 8' x 12'
Price Range: $125 to $200/sq. ft.

JK DESIGN

JOYCE KLIMAN
34 LASALLE PKWY
VICTOR, NY 14564
TEL 716-381-3259
Established: 1980
Products: fabric constructions utilizing ethnic fabrics, motifs
Techniques: appliqué, quilting, embroidery, stamping or printing
Size Range: 52" x 48" and larger
Price Range: $400 to $1,000/piece

★ CARRIE JACOBSON-MAY

504 PACHECO AVE
SANTA CRUZ, CA 95062
TEL 408-459-9559
Established: 1974
Products: tufted wall hangings
Techniques: dyeing, wrapping, tufting
Size Range: 30" x 30" to 10' x 12'
Price Range: $65 to $100/sq. ft.

See photograph on page 53.

★ VICTOR JACOBY

1086 17TH ST
EUREKA, CA 95501-2623
TEL 707-442-3809
Established: 1975
Products: tapestries
Techniques: weaving
Size Range: 2' x 2' to 8' x 24'
Price Range: $400 to $48,000/piece

See page 5 for photographs and additional information.

LUCY A. JAHNS

12 AUBURN CT
VERNON HILLS, IL 60061-2030
TEL 708-362-2144
Established: 1982
Products: fabric constructions
Techniques: appliqué, embroidery, painting
Size Range: 24" x 36" to 6' x 10'
Price Range: $600 to $5,800/piece

LOIS JAMES

1233 VIA LANDETA
PALOS VERDES, CA 90274
TEL 310-373-0342
Established: 1980
Products: mixed media installations
Techniques: painting, papermaking
Size Range: 16" x 20" to 6' x 12'
Price Range: $400 to $3,600/piece

MICHAEL JAMES

STUDIO QUILTS
258 OLD COLONY AVE
SOMERSET, MA 02726-5930
FAX 508-672-1370
TEL 508-672-1370
Established: 1973
Products: art quilts
Techniques: quilting, piecing
Size Range: 39" x 39" to 72" x 144"
Price Range: $3,500 to $16,000/piece

CATHERINE JANSEN

152 HEACOCK LN
WYNCOTE, PA 19095-1517
TEL 215-884-3174
Established: 1976
Products: art quilts
Techniques: photo process on cloth
Size Range: 8" x 10" to room sized
Price Range: $225 to $20,000/piece

JOCELYN STUDIO

JOCELYN GOLDMAN
39 OLD TOWN RD
EAST HADDAM, CT 06423-1453
FAX 203-526-2205
TEL 203-526-1581
Established: 1988
Products: art quilts
Techniques: weaving, appliqué, quilting
Size Range: 12" x 18" to 5' x 3'
Price Range: $200 to $875/piece

JOELL MILEO - PAPERMAKER

JOELL MILEO
PO BOX 8
MENDON, NY 14506-0008
TEL 716-624-9152
Established: 1988
Products: paper
Techniques: airbush, casting, dyeing
Size Range: 11" x 14" to 2' x 3'
Price Range: $125 to $1,500/piece

ROSITA JOHANSON

657 WOODBINE AVE
TORONTO, ON M4E 2J3
CANADA
TEL 416-699-4881
Established: 1984
Products: miniature fiber art
Techniques: appliqué, embroidery
Size Range: 6" x 6" to 8" x 9"
Price Range: $900 to $10,000/piece

VICKI L. JOHNSON

V&T GRAPHICS
225 MUIR DR
SOQUEL, CA 95073-9523
FAX 408-476-7567
TEL 408-476-7567
Established: 1970
Products: art quilts
Techniques: appliqué, painting, quilting
Size Range: 2' x 2' to 6' x 8'
Price Range: $400 to $10,000/piece

ANN JOHNSTON

910 YORK RD
LAKE OSWEGO, OR 97034-1742
TEL 503-635-1173
Established: 1981
Products: art quilts
Techniques: dyeing, quilting
Size Range: 8" x 8" to 9' x 9'
Price Range: $250 to $8,000/piece

OLGALYN JOLLY

O. JOLLY
63 GREENE ST
NEW YORK, NY 10012-4310
TEL 212-966-0185
Established: 1984
Products: fiber installations
Techniques: dyeing, loom knitting and dyeing
Size Range: 8" x 10" to 8' x 10'
Price Range: $125 to $200/sq. ft.

JOYCE HULBERT TAPESTRY & TEXTILE RESTORATION

JOYCE HULBERT
2339 3RD ST STE 31
SAN FRANCISCO, CA 94107-3137
TEL 415-255-4560
Established: 1981
Products: textile restorations
Techniques: dyeing, weaving, sewing
Size Range: miniature to 10' x 12'
Price Range: project estimate based on hourly fee/piece

Nancy Koenigsberg, *Landscape #5*, 1994, polynylon-coated copper wire, 3½' x 3½' x 14", photo: D. James Dee

JUDITH H. PERRY DESIGNS

JUDITH H. PERRY
969 WILLOW RD
WINNETKA, IL 60093-3634
TEL 708-441-6746
Established: 1978
Products: art quilts
Techniques: dyeing, painting, quilting
Size Range: 16" x 20" to 60" x 90"
Price Range: $150 to $6,000/piece

KAIDA ORIGINALS

CATHERINE FERRO
3405 HONEYWOOD DR
JOHNSON CITY, TN 37604-1478
FAX 615-282-6821
TEL 615-282-5847
Established: 1973
Products: paper, mixed collage
Techniques: painting, collage
Size Range: 8" x 10" to 4' x 5'
Price Range: $150 to $4,000/piece

HENDRIKA KAMSTRA

GINKGO STUDIO
1825 W COTTAGE ST
STEVENS POINT, WI 54481-3414
TEL 715-341-8277
Established: 1984
Products: mixed media/paper
installations
Techniques: airbush, casting, dyeing
Size Range: 12" x 15" to 30" x 40"
Price Range: $235 to $1,350/piece

JANIS KANTER

FANTASY FIBER
1923 W DICKENS AVE
CHICAGO, IL 60614-3935
FAX 312-862-0440
TEL 312-252-2119
Established: 1988
Products: tapestries with neon
Techniques: weaving
Size Range: 4' x 4' to 5' x 8'
Price Range: $3,000 to $10,000/piece

ANNA KARESH

ART STUDIO WEST
PO BOX 900528
SAN DIEGO, CA 92190-0528
FAX 619-565-1161
TEL 619-258-0766
Established: 1970
Products: mixed media installations
Techniques: casting, painting
Size Range: any size
Price Range: $800 to $4,000/piece

MARCIA KARLIN

45 KINGS CROSS DR
LINCOLNSHIRE, IL 60069-3342
TEL 708-940-4930
Established: 1985
Products: art quilts
Techniques: dyeing, painting, quilting
Size Range: 15" x 20" to 7' x 8'
Price Range: $500 to $10,000/piece

MARY LUCE KASPER

MK HANDWEAVING
106 HIGH ST
FLORENCE, MA 01060-1415
TEL 413-584-6667
Established: 1980
Products: hand-woven wall hangings
Techniques: dyeing, weaving
Size Range: 36" x 60" to 60" x 90" or
larger
Price Range: $60 to $90/sq. ft.

DONNA J. KATZ

2970 N LAKE SHORE DR #11E
CHICAGO, IL 60657-5643
TEL 312-525-3390
Established: 1975
Products: art quilts
Techniques: painting, quilting
Size Range: 18" x 24" to 8' x 8'
Price Range: $350 to $10,000/piece

JUDI KEEN

923 20TH ST
SACRAMENTO, CA 95814-3115
TEL 916-446-4777
Established: 1976
Products: tapestries
Techniques: embroidery
Size Range: 2" x 2" to 10" x 10"
Price Range: $500 to $4,500/piece

★ KEIKO NELSON ART STUDIO

KEIKO NELSON
2604 3RD ST
SAN FRANCISCO, CA 94107
FAX 510-527-4822
TEL 415-824-1545
Established: 1972
Products: mixed media installations, cast
paper constructions
Techniques: dyeing, casting, airbrush, cast
paper constructions
Size Range: 10" x 10" to 6' x 4'
Price Range: $300 to $8,500/piece

**See page 24 for photographs and
additional information.**

JANET KENNEDY

KENNEDY TAPESTRIES
41 NEWBURG ST
SAN FRANCISCO, CA 94131-1844
TEL 415-647-1844
Established: 1981
Products: tapestries
Techniques: weaving
Size Range: 5' x 7' to 10' x 20'
Price Range: $20,000 to $100,000/piece

ANNE MARIE KENNY

INDUSTRIAL QUILT STUDIO
1465 HOOKSETT RD #109
HOOKSETT, NH 03106-1862
TEL 603-268-0336
Established: 1982
Products: industrial quilts
Techniques: painting, stitching
Size Range: 3' x 3' to 12' x 12'
Price Range: $1,500 to $25,000/piece

★ SUSAN KIMBER

61 WARREN ST
NEW YORK, NY 10007-1016
TEL 212-766-3714
Established: 1973
Products: mixed media tapestry
Techniques: weaving, painting,
photography
Size Range: 12" x 12" to 54" x 120"
Price Range: $350 to $5,000/piece
Price Range: $175 to $300/sq. ft.

See photograph on page 54.

★ CHRIS KING

RR 1
BADDECK, NS B0E 1B0
CANADA
FAX 902-295-3141
TEL 902-295-3141
Established: 1989
Products: art quilts
Techniques: dyeing, piecing
Size Range: 9" x 12" to 10' x 10'
Price Range: $150 to $2,000/piece

See photograph on page 55.

GLENDA KING

845 25TH AVE
SAN FRANCISCO, CA 94121-3630
FAX 415-752-4932
TEL 415-752-4932
Established: 1989
Products: art quilts
Techniques: dyeing, embroidery, quilting,
shibori
Size Range: 2' x 2' to 6' x 6'
Price Range: $600 to $7,000/piece

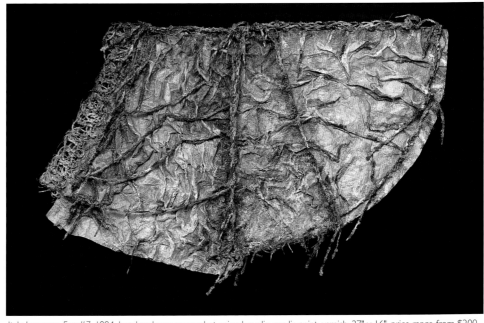

Itala Langmar, *Fan #7*, 1994, handmade paper, crochet, mixed media, acrylic paint, varnish, 27" x 16", price range from $200 to $500, photo: Deborah Fletcher, Chicago

FIBER ART FOR THE WALL

SARA NEWBERG KING
KING'S KREATIONS
6950 100TH ST NW
PINE ISLAND, MN 55963-9659
TEL 507-356-8839
Established: 1984
Products: art quilts
Techniques: quilting, embroidery,
discharge shibori
Size Range: 6" x 6" to 9' x 12'
Price Range: $50 to $125/sq. ft.

KIMBERLY HALDEMAN KLEIN
K. H. KLEIN
925 GRANDVIEW BLVD
LANCASTER, PA 17601-5105
TEL 717-293-9453
Established: 1976
Products: art quilts
Techniques: quilting, piecing
Size Range: 40" x 40" to 60" x 60"
Price Range: $400 to $1,200/piece

★ M.A. KLEIN
M.A. KLEIN DESIGN
20 ARASTRADERO RD
PORTOLA VALLEY, CA 94028-8013
TEL 415-854-4989
Established: 1962
Products: mixed media installations
Techniques: painting, embroidery, collage
Size Range: 12" x 15" to 8' x 24'
Price Range: $225 to $25,000/piece

**See page 12 for photographs and
additional information.**

ELLEN KOCHANSKY
EKO
1237 MILE CREEK RD
PICKENS, SC 29671-8703
FAX 803-868-4250
TEL 803-868-9749
Established: 1978
Products: art quilts
Techniques: embroidery, painting,
quilting
Size Range: 2' x 3' to 10' x 20'
Price Range: $90 to $150/sq. ft.

★ NANCY KOENIGSBERG
435 E 57TH ST
NEW YORK, NY 10022
FAX 212-980-6642
TEL 212-644-2398
Products: fabric constructions, fiber
installations
Techniques: weaving, wrapping
Size Range: 1' x 1' to 8' x 16'
Price Range: $75 to $200/sq. ft.

See photograph on page 56.

JOAN KOPCHIK
1335 STEPHEN WAY
SOUTHAMPTON, PA 18966-4349
TEL 215-322-1862
Established: 1976
Products: paper
Techniques: casting, painting, weaving
Size Range: 24" x 30" to 40" x 60"
Price Range: $600 to $2,500/piece

LAURENCE KORWIN
KORWIN DESIGN
333 N MICHIGAN AVE
CHICAGO, IL 60601-3901
TEL 312-372-8687
Established: 1980
Products: tapestries
Techniques: appliqué
Size Range: 6' x 6' to 50' x 12'
Price Range: $10,000 to $25,000/piece

LIBBY KOWALSKI
41 UNION SQ W
NEW YORK, NY 10003-3208
FAX 212-989-9702
TEL 212-627-5770
Established: 1981
Products: tapestries
Techniques: weaving
Size Range: 14" x 27" to 96" x 120"
Price Range: $500 to $6,000/piece

GRACE KRAFT
STONE SCHOOL HOUSE
MADRID, NM 87010
TEL 505-471-8062
Established: 1970
Products: fabric constructions, mixed
media installations
Techniques: silkscreen, painting, quilting,
embroidery, stamping
Size Range: 32" x 32" to 15' x 45'
Price Range: $600 to 36,000/piece

CANDACE KREITLOW
PO BOX 113
MAZOMANIE, WI 53560-0113
TEL 608-795-4680
Established: 1976
Products: woven wall constructions
Techniques: weaving, painting, sculpted
over frame
Size Range: 36" x 24" to 48" x 76" and
larger
Price Range: $600 to $6,000/piece

LIALIA KUCHMA
2423 W SUPERIOR ST
CHICAGO, IL 60612-1213
TEL 312-227-5445
Established: 1973
Products: tapestries
Techniques: weaving
Size Range: 36" x 48" to 96" x 240"
Price Range: $2,000 to $32,000/piece
Price Range: $150 to $350/sq. ft.

JANET KUEMMERLEIN
7701 CANTERBURY ST
PRAIRIE VILLAGE, KS 66208-3946
TEL 816-842-7049
Established: 1960
Products: fiber installations
Techniques: appliqué, embroidery,
wrapping, braiding, collage
Size Range: 2' x 3' to 5' x 50'
Price Range: $150 to $300/sq. ft.

★ SILJA (TALIKKA) LAHTINEN
SILJA'S FINE ART STUDIO
5220 SUNSET TRL
MARIETTA, GA 30068-4740
FAX 404-992-0350
TEL 404-992-8380
Established: 1978
Products: fiber material with wood
Techniques: beading, painting, screen
printing, photo etching
Size Range: 19" x 23" to 72" x 65"
Price Range: $250 to $29,000 per
group/piece
Price Range: $3.03 to $292.50/sq. ft.

**See page 103 for photographs and
additional information.**

COLETTE LAICO
968C HERITAGE HILLS DR
SOMERS, NY 10589-1913
TEL 914-276-2591
Products: mixed media installations
Techniques: casting, dyeing, embossing
Size Range: 9" x 12" to 4' x 6'
Price Range: $250 to $2,000/piece

MARY LANE
703 N FOOTE ST
OLYMPIA, WA 98502
TEL 360-956-9173
Established: 1982
Products: tapestries
Techniques: weaving
Size Range: 8' x 8" to 10' x 20'
Price Range: $300 to $10,000/piece

★ ITALA LANGMAR
604 EXMOOR RD
KENILWORTH, IL 60043-1021
TEL 708-251-0427
Established: 1984
Products: fiber installations, papier
mâché vessels
Techniques: painting, crochet
Size Range: 16" x 25" to 26" x 45"
Price Range: $150 to $450/piece

See photograph on page 57.

GAIL LARNED
LARNED MARLOW STUDIOS
144 S MONROE AVE
COLUMBUS, OH 43205-1084
TEL 614-258-7239
Established: 1974
Products: fiber installations
Techniques: dyeing, wrapping, knotting
Size Range: 2' x 4' to 5' x 15'
Price Range: $300 to $15,000/piece
Price Range: $35 to $200/sq. ft.

Cal Ling, *The Hinterlands*, 1992, handmade paper tiles, 10' x 15', State Department commission for the United
States Embassy in South Africa

KAREN LARSEN

CACOPHONY
7 AUSTIN PARK
CAMBRIDGE, MA 02139-2509
TEL 617-491-4025
Established: 1975
Products: art quilts
Techniques: appliqué, quilting, weaving
Size Range: 22" × 22" to 10' × 15'
Price Range: $60 to $100/sq. ft.

SUZANNE LARSEN

4901 COMMONWEALTH DR
SIESTA KEY
SARASOTA, FL 34242
TEL 813-349-2785
Established: 1952
Products: fabric surface design
Techniques: dyeing, painting, collage
Size Range: 2' × 3' to 5' × 5'
Price Range: $250 to $1,000/piece

JUDITH LARZELERE

CORPORARE FIBER ART
226 BEECH ST
BELMONT, MA 02178-1945
TEL 617-484-6091
Established: 1974
Products: art quilts
Techniques: quilting, strip piecing
Size Range: 20" × 20" to 112" × 144"
Price Range: $200 to $375/sq. ft.

IRAN LAWRENCE

IRAN LAWRENCE & CO.
30 KENSINGTON LN
NEWARK, DE 19713-3722
TEL 302-453-1682
Established: 1981
Products: fiber installations
Techniques: dyeing, painting, quilting
Size Range: 4' × 5' to 6' × 14'
Price Range: $150 to $500/sq. ft.

★ ULRIKA LEANDER

**CONTEMPORARY TAPESTRY
   WEAVING
107 WESTOVERLOOK DR
OAK RIDGE, TN 37830-3825
FAX 615-483-7911
TEL 615-482-6849**
Established: 1971
Products: tapestries
Techniques: weaving
Size Range: 4' × 4' to 12' × 30'
Price Range: $150 to $500/sq. ft.

**See page 6 for photographs and
additional information.**

SUSAN WEBB LEE

963 WOODS LOOP RD
WEDDINGTON, NC 28173-9376
TEL 704-843-1323
Established: 1979
Products: art quilts
Techniques: appliqué, painting, dyeing
Size Range: 25" × 25" to 6' × 8'
Price Range: $300 to $8,000/piece

CONNIE LEHMAN

PO BOX 281
ELIZABETH, CO 80107-0281
FAX 303-646-4638
TEL 303-646-4638
Established: 1975
Products: tapestries
Techniques: appliqué, beading,
embroidery
Size Range: 1.5" × 2" to 5" × 8"
Price Range: $500 to $1,500/piece

★ LENKER FINE ARTS

**MARLENE LENKER
28 NORTHVIEW TER
CEDAR GROVE, NJ 07009
FAX 201-239-8671
TEL 201-239-8671
TEL 203-767-2098**
Established: 1966
Products: paper
Techniques: painting, appliqué, burning
Size Range: 10" × 10" to 30" × 90"
Price Range: $200 to $3,000/piece

**See page 23 for photographs and
additional information.**

MICHELLE LESTER

MICHELLE LESTER STUDIO
15 W 17TH ST FL 9
NEW YORK, NY 10011-5506
FAX 212-627-8553
TEL 212-989-1411
Established: 1967
Products: tapestries, children's rugs
Techniques: weaving
Size Range: unlimited
Price Range: $250 to $550/sq. ft.

JUDY ZOELZER LEVINE

9415 N FAIRWAY DR
MILWAUKEE, WI 53217-1322
TEL 414-351-2631
Established: 1991
Products: art quilts
Techniques: appliqué, beading, quilting
Size Range: 30" × 30" to 60" × 80"
Price Range: $400 to $4,000/piece

★ VERENA LEVINE

**VERENA LEVINE PICTORIAL AND
   NARRATIVE QUILTS
4305 37TH ST NW
WASHINGTON, DC 20008
TEL 202-537-0916**
Established: 1982
Products: art quilts
Techniques: appliqué, quilting,
embroidery
Size Range: 18" × 16" to 120" × 120"
Price Range: $200 to $15,000/piece

**See page 13 for photographs and
additional information.**

BONNY LHOTKA

5658 CASCADE PL
BOULDER, CO 80303-2950
FAX 303-494-3472
TEL 303-494-5631
Established: 1972
Products: tapestries
Techniques: laminating, painting,
stamping/printing
Size Range: 24" × 36" to 10' × 30'
Price Range: $66 to $110/sq. ft.

WENDY LILIENTHAL

740 BUTTERFIELD RD
SAN ANSELMO, CA 94960-1105
TEL 415-453-1019
Established: 1978
Products: hand-cast paper
Techniques: airbush, casting, laminating
Size Range: 18" × 24" to 4' × 9'
Price Range: $500 to $4,500/piece

★ RACHEL LINDSTROM

**24231 N 41ST AVE
GLENDALE, AZ 85310-3235
TEL 602-780-0861**
Products: mixed fiber collages
Techniques: painting, dyeing, laminating
Size Range: 20" × 20" to 72" × 72"
Price Range: $200 to $500/sq. ft.

**See page 38 for photographs and
additional information.**

★ CAL LING

**CAL LING PAPERWORKS
441 CHERRY ST
CHICO, CA 95928-5114
TEL 916-893-0882**
Established: 1983
Products: paper
Techniques: painting, dyeing, casting
Size Range: 11½" × 16" to 10' × 15'
Price Range: $300 to $15,000/piece
Price Range: $80 to $250/sq. ft.

See photograph on page 58.

M. JOAN LINTAULT

306 N SPRINGER ST
CARBONDALE, IL 62901-1428
TEL 618-457-7815
Established: 1965
Products: art quilts
Techniques: dyeing, quilting, silkscreen
Size Range: 14" × 15" to 12' × 24'
Price Range: $1,000 to $30,000/piece

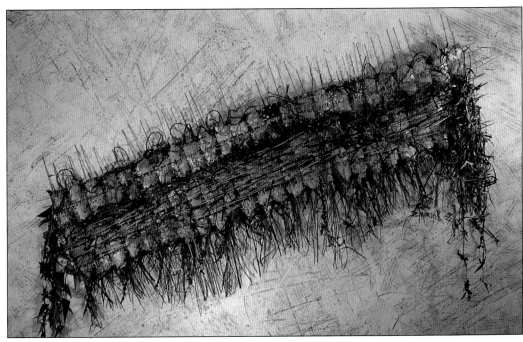

Edward Mordak, non-figurative weave, 88" × 56¼" × 8¼"

FIBER ART FOR THE WALL

★ **JOYCE P. LOPEZ**

JOYCE LOPEZ STUDIO
1147 W OHIO ST #304
CHICAGO, IL 60622-5874
FAX 312-243-5033
TEL 312-243-5033
Established: 1979
Products: sculpture/fiber
Techniques: wrapping
Size Range: 24" x 24" to 20' x 30'
Price Range: $2,800 to $75,000/piece

**See page 39 for photographs and
additional information.**

ANTONIA LOWDEN

ANTONIA LOWDEN DESIGN
155 S ARLINGTON AVE
RENO, NV 89501-1701
TEL 702-826-3655
Established: 1970
Products: tapestries
Techniques: weaving, mixed media
Size Range: 2' x 2' to 6' x 12'
Price Range: $500 to $20,000/piece

PEGGY CLARK LUMPKINS

RR 1 BOX 4650
BROWNVILLE, ME 04414-9720
TEL 207-965-8526
Established: 1979
Products: transparent tapestry
Techniques: weaving
Size Range: 2' x 1'6" to 8' x 14'
Price Range: $90 to $250/sq. ft.

YAEL LURIE
JEAN PIERRE LAROCHETTE

LURIE-LAROCHETTE
2216 GRANT ST
BERKELEY, CA 94703-1714
TEL 510-548-5744
Established: 1966
Products: tapestries
Techniques: weaving
Size Range: 8" x 12" to 6' x 16'
Price Range: $600 to $35,000/piece

NANCY LYON

102 SHAKER RD
NEW LONDON, NH 03257-5014
TEL 603-526-6754
Established: 1971
Products: hand-painted wall pieces
Techniques: painting, stamping or
printing
Size Range: 24" x 24" to unlimited
Price Range: $30 to $50/sq. ft.

MARGO MacDONALD

5814 CRESCENT BEACH RD
VAUGHN, WA 98394
TEL 206-884-2955
Established: 1980
Products: tapestries
Techniques: weaving
Size Range: 13" x 20" to 4'6" to 4'6"
Price Range: $500 to $2,000/piece

ANN MacEACHERN

MACEACHERN HANDWEAVING
& BASKETRY
PO BOX 80
ACTON, ME 04001-0080
TEL 207-636-2539
Established: 1970
Products: fiber installations
Techniques: embroidery, weaving,
wrapping, knotting, twining
Size Range: 8" x 12" to 2' x 8'
Price Range: $30 to $500/piece

JACKIE MacKAY

HANDWOVEN COUNTRY
   INTERIORS
RR 5
Berwick, NS B0P 1E0
CANADA
TEL 902-538-3315
Established: 1984
Products: tapestries
Techniques: dyeing, weaving
Size Range: 3' x 5' to 5' x 5'
Price Range: $300 to $2,000/piece

IRENE MAGINNISS

770 ANDOVER RD S
MANSFIELD, OH 44907-1511
TEL 419-756-2841
Established: 1970
Products: paper
Techniques: pulp painting, stitching,
embossing
Size Range: 6" x 6" to 6' x 8'
Price Range: $125 to $175/sq. ft.

JAN MAHER

817 GREENWOOD DR
GREENSBORO, NC 27410-4719
FAX 910-855-5746
TEL 910-855-5746
Established: 1982
Products: art quilts
Techniques: appliqué, silkscreen, beading
Size Range: 38" x 38" to 120" x 192"
Price Range: $125/sq. ft.

PATRICIA MALARCHER

93 IVY LN
ENGLEWOOD, NJ 07631
FAX 201-567-3709
TEL 201-568-1084
Established: 1963
Products: fabric constructions
Techniques: appliqué, painting, stamping
or printing
Size Range: 6" x 6" and up
Price Range: $200 to $400/sq. ft.

RUTH MANNING

177 ROGERS PKY
ROCHESTER, NY 14617-4205
TEL 716-467-6250
Established: 1980
Products: tapestries
Techniques: dyeing, weaving
Size Range: 1' x 1' to 4' x 6'
Price Range: $100 to $200/sq. ft.

SHARON MARCUS

TAPESTRY
4145 SW CORBETT AVE
PORTLAND, OR 97201-4201
FAX 503-796-1234
TEL 503-796-1234
Established: 1975
Products: tapestries
Techniques: weaving
Size Range: 3' x 3' to 9'6" x 15'
Price Range: $350/sq. ft.

JANE GOLDING MARIE

620 CHICAGO AVE
HASTINGS, NE 68901-5831
TEL 402-463-2669
Established: 1973
Products: fabric constructions
Techniques: painting, embroidery,
wrapping
Size Range: 12" x 12" to 8' x 12'
Price Range: $100 to $150/sq. ft.

MARY KAY COLLING
CONTEMPORARY PAPER ART

VILLAGE GATE SQ 274
N GOODMAN ST
ROCHESTER, NY 14607
TEL 716-442-8946
Established: 1988
Products: paper
Techniques: appliqué, casting, painting
Size Range: 5" x 7" to 4' x 4'
Price Range: $100 to $125/sq. ft.

Carol Owen, *Dawn Reflections*, handmade paper, 35" x 29"

PAMELA MATIOSIAN

MATIOSIAN STUDIO
1808 CENTRAL ST
EVANSTON, IL 60201-1510
TEL 708-475-5132
Established: 1980
Products: mixed media installations
Techniques: dyeing, painting, quilting
Size Range: 30" x 40" to 20' x 60'
Price Range: $2,500 to $65,000/piece

MARTHA MATTHEWS

7200 TERRACE DR
CHARLOTTE, NC 28211-6143
TEL 704-364-3435
Established: 1973
Products: tapestries
Techniques: weaving
Size Range: 2' x 3' to 8' x 20'
Price Range: $1,200 to $48,000/piece
Price Range: $200 to $300/sq. ft.

★ THERESE MAY

651 N 4TH ST
SAN JOSE, CA 95112-5143
TEL 408-292-3247
Established: 1965
Products: art quilts
Techniques: appliqué, embroidery,
painting
Size Range: 1' x 1' to 14' x 14'
Price Range: $500 to $41,000/piece

**See page 14 for photographs and
additional information.**

PHOEBE McAFEE

6 MONTEZUMA ST
SAN FRANCISCO, CA 94110-5109
TEL 415-282-3448
Established: 1967
Products: tapestries
Techniques: weaving, appliqué,
embroidery
Size Range: 1' x 2' to 8' x 24'
Price Range: $200 to $50,000/piece

JULIE McGINNIS

515 E ROCK ST
FAYETTEVILLE, AR 72701-4323
TEL 501-582-3707
Established: 1988
Products: art quilts
Techniques: dyeing, quilting, piecing
Size Range: 30" x 40" to 120" x 120"
Price Range: $300 to $2,000/piece

DIANNE McKENZIE

COMET STUDIOS
PO BOX 337
THE SEA RANCH, CA 95497-0337
FAX 707-785-2567
TEL 707-785-2567
Established: 1974
Products: tapestries
Techniques: dyeing, weaving
Size Range: 6' x 8' to 12' x 20'
Price Range: $250 to $500/sq. ft.

★ JIM MILLER
★ DIANNA THORNHILL MILLER

OMNI ART DESIGN
1716 W MAIN ST
FT WAYNE, IN 46808
TEL 219-422-3677
Established: 1965
Products: mixed media fabric
constructions
Techniques: weaving, wrapping, shaping
Size Range: 5' x 5' to 40' x 10'
Price Range: $5,000 to $50,000/piece

**See page 104 for photographs and
additional information.**

GERALDINE MILLHAM

GERALDINE MILLHAM
   TAPESTRIES
672 DRIFT RD
WESTPORT, MA 02790-1232
TEL 508-636-5437
Established: 1970
Products: tapestries
Techniques: weaving
Size Range: 2' x 2' to 10' x 20'
Price Range: $100 to $150/sq. ft.

BETH MINEAR

171 MONUMENT RD
ORLEANS, MA 02653-3507
TEL 508-255-3430
Established: 1978
Products: rugs, floor or wall
Techniques: weaving
Size Range: 24" x 24" and up
Price Range: $225 to $5,000/sq. ft.

NORMA MINKOWITZ

25 BROADVIEW RD
WESTPORT, CT 06880-2303
TEL 203-227-4497
Established: 1960
Products: mixed media installations
Techniques: painting, fiber construction
Size Range: 12" x 23" to 50" x 63"
Price Range: $3,000 to $10,000/piece

JULIA MITCHELL

JULIA MITCHELL TAPESTRY
   DESIGNER & WEAVER
PO BOX 1512
VINEYARD HAVEN, MA 02568-1512
TEL 508-693-6837
Established: 1978
Products: tapestries
Techniques: weaving
Size Range: 12" x 12" to 11' x any width
Price Range: $500 to $1,000/sq. ft.

KATHLEEN MOLLOHAN

524 S ROBERTS ST
HELENA, MT 59601-5435
TEL 406-442-9028
Established: 1983
Products: tapestries
Techniques: beading, painting, weaving
Size Range: 4' x 5' to 6' x 9'
Price Range: $130 to $150/sq. ft.

DOTTIE MOORE

1134 CHARLOTTE AVE
ROCK HILL, SC 29732-2452
TEL 803-327-5088
Established: 1976
Products: art quilts
Techniques: appliqué, embroidery,
quilting
Size Range: 24" x 24" to 72" x 72"
Price Range: $150 to $250/sq. ft.

★ EDWARD MORDAK

801 SUTTER ST #305
SAN FRANCISCO, CA 94109-6108
TEL 415-621-7121
Established: 1985
Products: mixed media installations,
paper
Techniques: beading, painting, weaving
Size Range: 20" x 30" to 5' x 10'
Price Range: $900 to $2,000/piece

See photograph on page 59.

★ LORETTA MOSSMAN

2416 ASPEN ST
PHILADELPHIA, PA 19130-2504
FAX 215-483-4864
TEL 215-765-3248
Established: 1980
Products: tapestries
Techniques: appliqué, embroidery,
painting
Size Range: unlimited
Price Range: $150 to $6,000/piece
Price Range: $100 to $200/sq. ft.

**See page 7 for photographs and
additional information.**

Kathryn Alison Pellman, *Gang Bait*, 118" x 90"

FIBER ART FOR THE WALL

STEPHANIE NADOLSKI

NADOLSKI FINE ART & DESIGN
25287 BARSUMIAN DR
BARRINGTON, IL 60010
FAX 708-526-5208
TEL 708-526-5208
Established: 1975
Products: mixed media installations,
handmade paper
Techniques: painting, casting, stamping
or printing
Size Range: 20" x 20" to 60" x 84"
Price Range: $250 to $6,000/piece

DOMINIE NASH

8612 RAYBURN RD
BETHESDA, MD 20817-3630
TEL 202-722-1407
Established: 1972
Products: art quilts
Techniques: dyeing, quilting, silkscreen
Size Range: 18" x 14" to 84" x 72"
Price Range: $400 to $4,000/piece
Price Range: $150 to $200/sq. ft.

MIRIAM NATHAN-ROBERTS

1351 ACTON ST
BERKELEY, CA 94706-2501
TEL 510-525-5432
Established: 1982
Products: art quilts
Techniques: airbush, appliqué, quilting
Size Range: 30" x 30" to 96" x 108"
Price Range: $100 to $200/sq. ft.

★ JEAN NEBLETT

628 RHODE ISLAND ST
SAN FRANCISCO, CA 94107-2628
FAX 415-821-2772
TEL 415-550-2613
Established: 1977
Products: art quilts
Techniques: appliqué, painting, quilting
Size Range: 4" x 5" to 5' x 6'
Price Range: $200 to $9,600/piece

**See page 15 for photographs and
additional information.**

DANA H. NELSON

155 FAIRVIEW RD
STOCKBRIDGE, GA 30281-1045
FAX 404-474-8720
TEL 404-474-8720
Established: 1980
Products: tapestries
Techniques: dyeing, embroidery, weaving
Size Range: 18" x 18" to 12'6" x 14'
Price Range: $50 to $10,000/piece

ANNA NESBITT

ROSE CREATIONS
823 CANE CREEK RD
PARIS, AR 72855
TEL 501-934-4610
Established: 1989
Products: 'home portraits' on canvas
panels
Techniques: painting
Size Range: 11" x 14" to 18" x 24"
Price Range: $150 to $420/piece

ROCHELLE NEWMAN

PYTHAGOREAN PRESS
PO BOX 5162
BRADFORD, MA 01835-0162
TEL 508-372-3129
Established: 1963
Products: tapestries
Techniques: weaving, wrapping,
crocheting
Size Range: 2' x 3' to 8' x 8'
Price Range: $100 to $150/sq. ft.

VELDA E. NEWMAN

102 WOODS CT
NEVADA CITY, CA 95959-3276
TEL 916-478-1518
Established: 1985
Products: art quilts
Techniques: appliqué, painting, quilting
Size Range: 1' x 1' to 6' x 17'
Price Range: $300 to $50,000/piece

ANNE MCKENZIE NICKOLSON

5020 N ILLINOIS ST
INDIANAPOLIS, IN 46208-2612
TEL 317-257-8929
Established: 1978
Products: art quilts
Techniques: appliqué, embroidery, piecing
Size Range: 15" x 15" to 14' x 14'
Price Range: $200 to $250/sq. ft.

CYNTHIA NIXON

CYNTHIA NIXON STUDIO
427 S NIXON RD
STATE COLLEGE, PA 16801-2318
TEL 814-238-4811
Established: 1978
Products: art quilts
Techniques: appliqué, embroidery,
painting
Size Range: 1' x 1' to 10' x 20'
Price Range: $200 to $15,000/piece

ELIZABETH NORDGREN

6 RYAN WAY
DURHAM, NH 03824-2916
TEL 603-868-2873
Established: 1973
Products: fiber installations
Techniques: dyeing, painting, weaving
Size Range: 3" x 5" to 6' x 12'
Price Range: $100 to $5,000/piece

INGE NØRGAARD

907 PIERCE ST
PORT TOWNSEND, WA 98368-8046
TEL 206-385-0637
Established: 1972
Products: tapestries
Techniques: weaving
Size Range: 3" x 3" to 10' x 15'
Price Range: $100 to $50,000/piece

SUSAN M. OAKS

6581 FOX RUN
SAN ANTONIO, TX 78233-4706
TEL 210-656-8440
Established: 1979
Products: framed fiber collage
Techniques: dyeing, painting,
stamping/printing
Size Range: 8" x 10" to 3'6" x 4'6"
Price Range: $200 to $850/piece

★ SHEILA O'HARA

7101 THORNDALE DR
OAKLAND, CA 94611-1031
TEL 510-339-3014
Established: 1977
Products: tapestries
Techniques: weaving
Size Range: 12" x 20" to 20' x 30'
Price Range: trade discount available
Price Range: $250 to $1,000/sq. ft.

**See page 8 for photographs and
additional information.**

ELLEN OPPENHEIMER

448 CLIFTON ST
OAKLAND, CA 94618-1163
TEL 510-658-9877
Established: 1970
Products: art quilts
Techniques: dyeing, quilting, silkscreen
Size Range: 30" x 30" to 96" x 96"
Price Range: $2,000 to $6,000/piece

Karen Perrine, *Red Forest*, 49"H x 70"W

★ **CAROL OWEN**

54 FEARRINGTON POST
PITTSBORO, NC 27312-8549
TEL 919-542-0616

Established: 1970
Products: paper
Techniques: laminating, painting, assemblage
Size Range: 16" × 16" to 4' × 8'
Price Range: $100 to $150/sq. ft.

See photograph on page 60.

KAREN S. PAGE

2910 DARLINGTON RD #1203
BEAVER FALLS, PA 15010-9603
TEL 412-846-0286

Established: 1986
Products: wall installations, rugs
Techniques: dyeing, felting, cutting (own technique)
Size Range: 1' × 1' to 8' × 12' or larger
Price Range: $200 to $20,000/piece

SOYOO HYUNJOO PARK

SOYOO ART STUDIO
193 CLOSTER DOCK RD
CLOSTER, NJ 07624-1907
FAX 201-767-0497
TEL 201-767-8766

Established: 1978
Products: tapestries
Techniques: painting, Gobelin tapestry weaving
Size Range: 7" × 7" to 10' × 10'
Price Range: $250 to $50,000/piece

SHARRON PARKER

ARTSPACE STUDIO 217
201 E DAVIE ST
RALEIGH, NC 27601-1869
TEL 919-828-4533

Products: wall hangings
Techniques: felting, stitching
Size Range: 10" × 12" to 5' × 10'
Price Range: $200 to $6,000/piece

★ **DIANN PARROTT**

DIANN PARROTT - YARDAGE
  ART
875 ST CLAIR AVE #4
ST PAUL, MN 55105-3278
FAX 612-222-4149
TEL 612-222-4149

Established: 1984
Products: pieced installations
Techniques: yardage printing, sewing, hand fringing
Size Range: 3' × 3' to 25' × 25'
Price Range: $150 to $250/sq. ft.

See page 159 for photographs and additional information.

JACQUE PARSLEY

2005 INDIAN CHUTE
LOUISVILLE, KY 40207-1184
TEL 502-893-2092

Established: 1976
Products: fabric constructions
Techniques: appliqué, embroidery, collage/assemblage
Size Range: 12" × 12" to 4' × 6'
Price Range: $800 to $2,000/piece

EVE S. PEARCE

RR 1 BOX 3880
BENNINGTON, VT 05201-9604
TEL 802-823-5580

Established: 1980
Products: tapestries
Techniques: weaving
Size Range: 2' × 2' to 4' × 8'
Price Range: $150 to $250/sq. ft.

★ **KATHRYN ALISON PELLMAN**

7149 WOODROW WILSON DR
LOS ANGELES CA 90068-1726
TEL 213-851-9320

Established: 1987
Products: art quilts
Techniques: appliqué, quilting
Size Range: 1' × 1' to 12' × 12'
Price Range: $200 to $10,000/piece

See photograph on page 61.

★ **KAREN PERRINE**

512 N K ST
TACOMA, WA 98403-1621
TEL 206-627-0449

Established: 1977
Products: fiber installations
Techniques: dyeing, painting, quilting
Size Range: 8" × 8" to 8' × 16'
Price Range: $100 to $300/sq. ft.

See photograph on page 62.

★ **LINDA S. PERRY**

ART QUILTS
96 BURLINGTON ST
LEXINGTON, MA 02173-1708
TEL 617-863-1107

Established: 1972
Products: art quilts
Techniques: dyeing, printing, metallic leaf
Size Range: 2' × 3' to 5' × 8'
Price Range: $125/sq. ft.

See page 16 for photographs and additional information.

★ **JEWELL PETERSON**

TACTILE IMPRESSIONS
3226 E PATRICIA ST
TUCSON, AZ 85716-4657
TEL 602-324-0327

Established: 1982
Products: fiber installations
Techniques: dyeing, felting, stitching
Size Range: 25" × 30" to 75" × 95"
Price Range: $600 to $3,000/piece

See page 40 for photographs and additional information.

SUE PIERCE

PIERCEWORKS
14414 WOODCREST DR
ROCKVILLE, MD 20853-2335
TEL 301-460-8111

Established: 1978
Products: art quilts
Techniques: appliqué, painting, quilting
Size Range: 15" × 15" to 6' × 12'
Price Range: $200 to $10,000/piece

PIPSISSEWA

FRANCES PUSCH
HC 68 BOX 46F
CUSHING, ME 04563-9505
TEL 207-354-0148

Established: 1992
Products: pieced-fabric pictures
Techniques: sewing
Size Range: 2½" × 3½" (8" × 10" framed)
Price Range: $36/piece

★ **JUDITH PLOTNER**

JUDITH PLOTNER ART
  QUILTS/L'ATELIER PLOTNER
214 GOAT FARM RD
GLOVERSVILLE, NY 12078-7315
TEL 518-725-3222
TEL 718-548-0581

Established: 1962
Products: art quilts
Techniques: painting, quilting, piecing
Size Range: 15" × 15" to 6' × 7' (panels)
Price Range: $400 to $6,000/piece

See photograph below.

Judith Plotner, *Shrine Series V,* pieced and quilted cotton and satin, 20"H × 16"W

JUNCO SATO POLLACK

11 POLO DR NE
ATLANTA, GA 30309-2745
FAX 404-892-2155
TEL 404-892-2155

Established: 1980
Products: fabric constructions, light-reflective art
Techniques: embroidery, airbrush, shibori, gold leaf, heat transfer
Size Range: 15" × 15" to 6' × 10'
Price Range: $2,000 - $8,000/piece

JASON POLLEN

4348 LOCUST ST
KANSAS CITY, MO 64110-1531
FAX 816-561-6404
TEL 816-561-6261

Established: 1976
Products: fabric constructions
Techniques: appliqué, dyeing, stamping/printing
Size Range: 14" × 27" to 20" × 48"
Price Range: $2,000 to $10,000/piece

SUZANNE PRETTY

SUZANNE PRETTY TAPESTRY
  STUDIO
4 ELM ST
FARMINGTON, NH 03835-1508
TEL 603-755-3964

Established: 1969
Products: tapestries
Techniques: weaving
Size Range: 30" × 30" to 5' × 15'
Price Range: $250 to $450/sq. ft.

FIBER ART FOR THE WALL

NANCY PRICHARD
2604 W CHUBB LAKE AVE
VIRGINIA BEACH, VA 23455-1322
TEL 804-363-9272
Established: 1980
Products: paper
Techniques: collage
Size Range: 16" × 18" to 36" × 36"
Price Range: $275 to $450/piece

QUINT-ROSE
PO BOX 54
TENANTS HARBOR, ME 04860
Established: 1975
Products: paper
Techniques: painting, wrapping
Size Range: 8" × 3" to 8" × 20"
Price Range: $800 to $6,000/piece

★ MARY CURTIS RATCLIFF
630 WEILSON ST
BERKELEY, CA 94707
TEL 510-526-8472
Established: 1972
Products: mixed media installations
Techniques: painting, weaving, knotting
Size Range: 31" × 38" to 41" × 94"
Price Range: $700 to $3,200/piece

**See page 41 for photographs and
additional information.**

COLLINS REDMAN
14981 HILL RD
SEDALIA, CO 80135-9755
TEL 303-647-2250
Established: 1988
Products: tapestries
Techniques: weaving, dyeing
Size Range: 22" × 22" to 60" × 80"
Price Range: $75 to $100/sq. ft.

FRAN REED
FREED FIBERS
2424 SPRUCEWOOD ST
ANCHORAGE, AK 99508-3975
FAX 907-279-8195
TEL 907-276-7717
Established: 1975
Products: fiber installations, fish skin and
gut forms
Techniques: airbush, weaving, surface
design
Size Range: 40" × 40" to 5' × 20'
Price Range: $1,000 to $25,000/piece
Price Range: $100 to $1,000/sq. ft.

MYRA REICHEL
121 E SIXTH ST
MEDIA, PA 19063-2503
TEL 610-565-5028
Established: 1973
Products: tapestries
Techniques: weaving, inlaid weaving,
tapestry
Size Range: 6" × 6" to 30' × 40'
Price Range: $50 to $500/sq. ft.

ROBIN REIDER
WEAVINGS BY ROBIN
PO BOX 687
CHIMAYO, NM 87522-0687
TEL 505-351-4474
Established: 1980
Products: tapestries
Techniques: dyeing, weaving
Size Range: 45" × 16" to 8' × 5'
Price Range: $180 to $4,000/piece

SISTER REMY REVOR
MOUNT MARY COLLEGE
2900 N MENOMONEE RIVER PKY
MILWAUKEE, WI 53222-4545
TEL 414-258-4810
Products: screen printed panels
Techniques: dyeing, silkscreen,
stamping/printing
Size Range: 36" × 24" to 48" × 96"
Price Range: $200 to $600/piece

★ AMANDA RICHARDSON
PO BOX 2147
FRIDAY HARBOR, WA 98250-2147
TEL 360-378-3224
Established: 1978
Products: fiber installations
Techniques: dyeing, laminating,
Richardson Tapestry
Size Range: 3' × 4' to unlimited
Price Range: $500/sq. ft.

**See page 42 for photographs and
additional information.**

NANILEE S. ROBARGE
1260 HAIGHT ST #4
SAN FRANCISCO, CA 94117-3040
TEL 415-241-9182
Established: 1991
Products: weavings
Techniques: dyeing, silkscreen, weaving
Size Range: 12" × 15" to 6' × 6'
Price Range: $100 to $7,000/piece

EVA R. ROBBINS
EVA R WORKS & YARN, INC.
109 TOWNE RD
OAK RIDGE, TN 37830-5476
TEL 615-483-7492
Established: 1970
Products: fiber wall hangings
Techniques: rug knotting
Size Range: 1' × 3'6" to 3'6" × 5'
Price Range: $250 to $1,000/piece

**ROCOCO STUDIO OF
FIBER, COLOR & DESIGN**
ANN MCCOLLUM
18 HORSESHOE RIDGE
BARNARDSVILLE, NC 28709
TEL 704-626-3777
Established: 1993
Products: fiber installations, kimono floats
Techniques: weaving, dyeing, design
patterns
Size Range: 10" × 4" to 25' × 30'
Price Range: $145 to $3,000/piece

GRETCHEN ROMEY-TANZER
TANZER'S FIBERWORK
33 MONUMENT RD
ORLEANS, MA 02653-3511
TEL 508-255-9022
Established: 1987
Products: tapestries
Techniques: dyeing, silkscreen, weaving
Size Range: 18" × 18" to 36" × 48"
Price Range: $200 to $1,200/piece

GLORIA F. ROSS
GLORIA F. ROSS TAPESTRIES
21 E 87 ST
NEW YORK, NY 10128-0506
TEL 212-369-3337
Established: 1965
Products: tapestries
Techniques: weaving
Size Range: 5' × 2½' to 18' × 45'
Price Range: $2,000 to $200,000/piece
Price Range: $55 to $500/sq. ft.

★ BERNIE ROWELL
BERNIE ROWELL STUDIO
1525 BRANSON AVE
KNOXVILLE, TN 37917-3843
TEL 615-523-5244
Established: 1975
Products: fiber installations
Techniques: appliqué, embroidery,
painting
Size Range: 30" × 40" to 6' × 24'
Price Range: $80 to $90/sq. ft.

**See page 105 for photographs and
additional information.**

JOAN RUSSELL
DIMENSIONAL TAPESTRY
2509 HILL CT
BERKELEY, CA 94708-1910
TEL 510-849-0459
Established: 1970
Products: tapestries
Techniques: weaving, painting, paper
Size Range: 12" × 12" to 12' × 40"
Price Range: $100 to $150/sq. ft.

JUDE RUSSELL
733 NW EVERETT ST #17
PORTLAND, OR 97209-3517
FAX 503-223-1437
TEL 503-295-0417
Established: 1979
Products: art quilts
Techniques: airbush, appliqué, painting
Size Range: 2' × 3' to 7' × 24'
Price Range: $1,850 to $24,000/piece

ARTURO ALONZO SANDOVAL
HIGH-TECH ART FORMS
PO BOX 237
LEXINGTON, KY 40584-0237
TEL 606-273-8898
Established: 1969
Products: fabric constructions
Techniques: weaving, machine stitching,
interlacing collage
Size Range: 8" × 8" to 30' × 40'
Price Range: $250 to $30,000/piece

STEPHANIE SANTMYERS
QUILT ART
7 PIPERS GLEN CT
GREENSBORO, NC 27406-5500
TEL 910-852-6439
Established: 1985
Products: art quilts
Techniques: quilting
Size Range: 40" × 40" to 73" × 73"
Price Range: $300 to $22,000/piece

JOY SAVILLE
244 DODDS LN
PRINCETON, NJ 08540-4108
TEL 609-924-6824
Established: 1976
Products: fabric constructions
Techniques: piecing
Size Range: 28 × 28 to unlimited
Price Range: $400 to $600/sq. ft.

★ SUSAN SAWYER
RR 1 BOX 107
EAST CALAIS, VT 05650-9506
TEL 802-456-8836
Established: 1971
Products: art quilts
Techniques: appliqué, quilting, piecing
Size Range: 8" × 8" to 84" × 84"
Price Range: $100 to $7,000/piece

**See page 17 for photographs and
additional information.**

DEIDRE SCHERER
PO BOX 156
WILLIAMSVILLE, VT 05362-0156
FAX 802-348-7136
TEL 802-348-7807
Established: 1970
Products: fabric constructions
Techniques: appliqué, machine-stitching,
piecing, layering
Size Range: 8" × 6" to 6' × 15'
Price Range: $500 to $25,000/piece

JULIA SCHLOSS
HANDWOVEN ORIGINALS
RR 1 BOX 5053
BAR HARBOR, ME 04609-9748
TEL 207-288-9882
Established: 1976
Products: tapestries
Techniques: weaving
Size Range: 36" × 55" to 56" × 120"
Price Range: $1,000 to $10,000/piece
Price Range: $100 to $150/sq. ft.

★ JOAN SCHULZE
808 PIPER AVE
SUNNYVALE, CA 94087-1245
FAX 408-736-7833
TEL 408-736-7833
Established: 1970
Products: art quilts
Techniques: laminating, painting, quilting
Size Range: 16" × 20" to 10' × 20'
Price Range: $800 to $30,000/piece

**See page 43 for photographs and
additional information.**

AMANDA SEARS

PO BOX 244
SANTA CRUZ, CA 95061-0244
TEL 408-457-1630
Established: 1983
Products: raffia rugs
Techniques: dyeing, tufting
Size Range: 2' x 3' x 9' x 12'
Price Range: $85 to $100/sq. ft.

SALLY A. SELLERS

3919 WAUNA VISTA DR
VANCOUVER, WA 98661-6031
TEL 206-693-4160
Established: 1989
Products: art quilts
Techniques: appliqué, painting, quilting
Size Range: 2' x 2' to 6' x 6'
Price Range: $450 to $4,000/piece

★ KATHLEEN SHARP

17360 VALLEY OAK DR
MONTE SERENO, CA 95030-2217
TEL 408-395-3014
Established: 1978
Products: art quilts
Techniques: appliqué, quilting, piecing
Size Range: 14" x 14" to 75" x 100"
Price Range: $300 to $9,000/piece

See page 18 for photographs and additional information.

BARBARA SHAWCROFT

4 ANCHOR DR #243
EMERYVILLE, CA 94608-1564
TEL 510-486-0354
Established: 1967
Products: mixed media installations,
3D-sculptural wall installations
Techniques: hand constructed, 3D
Size Range: 2" x 2" to 50' x 20'
Price Range: $1,500 to $50,000/piece

SUSAN SHIE
JAMES ACORD

TURTLE MOON STUDIOS
2612 ARMSTRONG DR
WOOSTER, OH 44691-1806
TEL 216-345-5778
Established: 1977
Products: art quilts
Techniques: appliqué, embroidery,
painting
Size Range: 6" x 8" to 100" x 100"
Price Range: $200 to $25,000/piece

SALLY SHORE

SALLY SHORE/WEAVER
LUDLAM LANE
LOCUST VALLEY, NY 11560
TEL 516-671-7276
Established: 1971
Products: fiber installations
Techniques: weaving
Size Range: 9" x 9" to 7' x 15'
Price Range: $150 to $10,000/piece

ANE SHUSTA

PO BOX 18
SNOQUALMIE PASS, WA 98068-0018
TEL 206-434-6115
Established: 1983
Products: tapestries
Techniques: weaving
Size Range: 3' x 5' to 5' x 8'
Price Range: $1,000 to $10,000/piece

LAURA LAZAR SIEGEL

10 CROSSWAY
SCARSDALE, NY 10583-7118
FAX 212-808-0406
TEL 914-723-9392
Established: 1960
Products: fiber installations, marriage
canopies
Techniques: painting, dyeing, layering
Size Range: 20" x 28" to 7' x 5'
Price Range: $800 to $2,000/piece

LOUISE SILK

CITY QUILT
210 CONOVER RD
PITTSBURGH, PA 15208-2604
TEL 412-361-1158
Established: 1978
Products: art quilts
Techniques: appliqué, quilting,
stamping/printing
Size Range: 8" x 8" to 18' x 18'
Price Range: $50 to $5,500/piece

MARY JO SINCLAIR

BARKING DOG STUDIO
10 MILTON ST
ST. AUGUSTINE, FL 32095-2114
FAX 904-824-1441
TEL 904-824-1441
Established: 1978
Products: mixed media installations
Techniques: weaving, airbrush, laminating
Size Range: 2' x 3' to 10' x 17'
Price Range: $200 to $230/sq. ft.

SUSAN SINGLETON

AZO INC.
1101 E PIKE ST
SEATTLE, WA 98122-3915
FAX 206-322-5062
TEL 206-322-0390
Established: 1971
Products: paper
Techniques: painting, dyeing, gold leafing
Size Range: 15 x 15" to 12' x 12'
Price Range: $100 to $150/sq. ft.

JULIE SLOANE

245 SCOTT ST #1
SAN FRANCISCO, CA 94117-3233
TEL 415-861-0779
Established: 1992
Products: fabric constructions
Techniques: embroidery, painting,
quilting
Size Range: miniature to unlimited
Price Range: $50 to $1,000/piece

MARY E. SLY

SAN JUAN SILK
PO BOX 1925
FRIDAY HARBOR, WA 98250-1925
TEL 206-378-7110
Established: 1980
Products: silk, floral wall hangings
Techniques: resist, hand painted with
dyes
Size Range: 15" x 65" to 60" x 60"
Price Range: $95 - $2,500/piece

C. ELIZABETH SMATHERS

3002 SIMMONS AVE
NASHVILLE, TN 37211-2425
TEL 615-331-4619
Established: 1985
Products: tapestries
Techniques: weaving
Size Range: 18" x 18" to unlimited
Price Range: $100 to $225/sq. ft.

BARBARA LEE SMITH

BARBARA LEE SMITH INC.
PO BOX 365 7349 MADISON ST
FOREST PARK, IL 60130-0365
FAX 708-383-3349
TEL 708-771-9697
Established: 1975
Products: mixed media installations
Techniques: painting, embroidery, fusing
Size Range: 3' x 5' to 15' x 15'
Price Range: $500 to $40,000/piece

Joan Stubbins, *Cosmic Strings*, ©1993, weaving, 40" x 51", photo: Albin Dearing

ELLY SMITH

PO BOX 523
MEDINA, WA 98039-0523
Established: 1974
Products: framed stitcheries, family samplers
Techniques: embroidery
Size Range: 9" x 8" to 74" x 74"
Price Range: $300 to $4,000/piece
Price Range: $250 to $300/sq. ft.

GLORIA ZMOLEK SMITH

ZPAPERSMITH
384 21ST ST SE
CEDAR RAPIDS, IA 52403-4255
TEL 319-366-0273
Established: 1983
Products: handmade paper quilts
Techniques: embroidery, wrapping, origami
Size Range: 6" x 6" to 4' x 4'
Price Range: $100 to $3,750/piece

LYN SOUTHWORTH

LYN SOUTHWORTH SURFACE
    DESIGN
821 14TH ST #4
SANTA MONICA, CA 90403
FAX 310-395-2537
TEL 310-395-2537
Established: 1985
Products: mixed media installations
Techniques: weaving, painting, dyeing
Size Range: 12" x 12" to 60" x 48"
Price Range: $200 to $4,000/piece

KATHY SPOERING

KATHY SPOERING, TAPESTRIES
2306 DOGWOOD CT
GRAND JUNCTION, CO 81506-8473
TEL 303-242-9081
Established: 1989
Products: tapestries
Techniques: weaving
Size Range: 18" x 18" to 48" x 48"
Price Range: $1,100 to $6,000/piece

SPRINGFLOWER

PO BOX 54
GAYS MILLS, WI 54631-0054
TEL 608-735-4595
Established: 1986
Products: tapestries, belts, scarves, bags, bracelets
Techniques: embroidery, weaving
Size Range: 12" x 36" to 6' x 3'
Price Range: $10 to $60/piece

CARE STANDLEY

1040 TALBOT AVE
ALBANY, CA 94706-2332
TEL 510-525-8609
Established: 1982
Products: tapestries
Techniques: weaving
Size Range: 1' x 1' to 4' x 6'
Price Range: $650 to $10,000/piece

HILLARY STEEL

HILLARY L. STEEL - HANDWEAVER
9409 BILTMORE DR
SILVER SPRING, MD 20901
TEL 301-587-8373
Established: 1981
Products: resist dyed, woven wall pieces
Techniques: weaving, dyeing, resist dyeing
Size Range: 14" x 14" to 10' x 10'
Price Range: $250 to $15,000/piece

ELINOR STEELE

61 WEYBRIDGE ST
MIDDLEBURY, VT 05753-1024
TEL 802-388-6546
Established: 1974
Products: tapestries
Techniques: weaving
Size Range: 2' x 3' to 8' x 12'
Price Range: $200 to $300/sq. ft.

JOY STOCKSDALE

2145 OREGON ST
BERKELEY, CA 94705-1004
FAX 707-829-3285
TEL 510-841-2008
Established: 1981
Products: fiber installations
Techniques: painting, quilting, silkscreen
Size Range: 3' x 4' to 8' x 10'
Price Range: $250 to $1,000/piece

GLENNE STOLL

900 S GENEVA
AURORA, CO 80231
FAX 303-355-2401
TEL 303-364-3927
Established: 1970
Products: art quilts
Techniques: quilting, piecing
Size Range: 2' x 2' to 12' x 12'
Price Range: $200 - $10,000 sq. ft./piece
Price Range: $50 to $150/sq. ft.

★ NANCY TAYLOR STONINGTON

22735 CAREY RD SW
VASHON, WA 98070-6809
FAX 206-463-6598
TEL 206-463-2860
Established: 1970
Products: fiber installations
Techniques: construction
Size Range: 4' x 9' to 20' x 20'
Price Range: $10,000 to $60,000/piece

See page 44 for photographs and additional information.

★ JOAN STUBBINS

2616 S MAHONING AVE
ALLIANCE, OH 44601-8212
TEL 216-823-7328
Established: 1988
Products: tapestries
Techniques: dyeing, embroidery, weaving
Size Range: 20" x 30" to 40" x 55"
Price Range: $200/sq. ft.

See photograph on page 65.

Daniele Todaro, *Rapunzel*, ©1993, machine pieced and quilted, cottons, triptych, each panel 56"H x 33"W

JANICE M. SULLIVAN
4166A 20TH ST
SAN FRANCISCO, CA 94114-2850
TEL 415-431-6835
Established: 1984
Products: fabric constructions
Techniques: weaving, painting, airbrush
Size Range: 20" × 20" to 96" × 108"
Price Range: $200 to $300/sq. ft.

SUSAN STARR & CO.
SUSAN STARR
1580 JONES RD
ROSWELL, GA 30075-2726
FAX 404-993-3980
TEL 404-993-3980
Established: 1974
Products: tapestries, fiber installations, constructions
Techniques: dyeing, painting, weaving
Size Range: any size
Price Range: $125 to $200/sq. ft.

LYNNE SWARD
625 BISHOP DR
VIRGINIA BEACH, VA 23455-6543
TEL 804-497-7917
Established: 1974
Products: fabric constructions, marketing materials
Techniques: appliqué, beading, embroidery
Size Range: 8" × 8" to 3' × 6'
Price Range: $150 to $4,000/piece

TERRY TAUBE
73-1100 ALIHILANI DR
KAILUA-KONA, HI 96740
TEL 808-325-5496
Established: 1985
Products: paper
Techniques: casting, dyeing, weaving
Size Range: all sizes
Price Range: $100 to $200/sq. ft.

CAMERON TAYLOR-BROWN
418 S MANSFIELD AVE
LOS ANGELES, CA 90036-3516
FAX 213-938-0088
TEL 213-938-0088
Established: 1982
Products: fiber installations
Techniques: embroidery, painting, weaving
Size Range: 24" × 24" to 8' × 120'
Price Range: $100 to $150/sq. ft.

★ DANIELE TODARO
TODARO & ASSOCIATES
4920 W 63RD ST
LOS ANGELES, CA 90056
FAX 213-299-9394
TEL 213-299-9393
Established: 1974
Products: art quilts
Techniques: appliqué, quilting, stamping or printing
Size Range: 1' × 1' to 6' × 9'
Price Range: $100 to $150/piece

See photograph on page 66.

CAROLYN & VINCENT TOLPO
PO BOX 134
SHAWNEE, CO 80475-0134
TEL 303-670-1733
Established: 1979
Products: fiber installations
Techniques: painting, wrapping
Size Range: 30" × 36" to 10' × 30'
Price Range: $600 to $12,000/piece

RAYMOND D. TOMASSO
INTER-OCEAN CURIOSITY STUDIO
2998 S BANNOCK ST
ENGLEWOOD, CO 80110-1519
TEL 303-789-0282
Established: 1978
Products: paper
Techniques: airbrush, casting, painting
Size Range: 9" × 11" to 4' × 6'
Price Range: $400 to $3,500/piece

★ MARJORIE TOMCHUK
44 HORTON LN
NEW CANAAN, CT 06840-6824
FAX 203-972-3182
TEL 203-972-0137
Established: 1965
Products: paper
Techniques: airbrush, casting, painting, embossings
Size Range: 10" × 13" to 4' × 6'
Price Range: $175 to $3,000/piece

See page 25 for photographs and additional information.

PAMELA TOPHAM
LANDSCAPE TAPESTRIES
PO BOX 1057
WAINSCOTT, NY 11975-1057
TEL 516-537-2871
Established: 1976
Products: landscape tapestries
Techniques: weaving
Size Range: 22" × 25" to 6' × 12' and up
Price Range: $800 to $25,000/piece

MICHELE TUEGEL
MICHELE TUEGEL PAPERWORKS
433 MONTE CRISTO BLVD
TIERRA VERDE, FL 33715-1840
TEL 813-821-7391
Established: 1977
Products: paper
Techniques: casting, laminating
Size Range: 8" × 10" to 40" × 60"
Price Range: $75 to $1,500/piece

TWINROCKER HANDMADE PAPER
KATHRYN CLARK - ARTIST
PO BOX 413
BROOKSTON, IN 47923-0413
TEL 317-563-3119
Established: 1971
Products: paper
Techniques: laminating, embedding, collage
Size Range: 18" × 24" to 48" × 72" or larger
Price Range: $250 to $3,000/piece

KAIJA TYNI-RAUTIAINEN
5390 GORDON AVE
BURNABY, BC V5E 3L8
CANADA
TEL 604-524-2455
Established: 1974
Products: tapestries
Techniques: weaving
Size Range: 16" × 16" to 60" × 90"
Price Range: $300 to $350/sq. ft.

★ JUDITH UEHLING
152 WOOSTER ST
NEW YORK, NY 10012-5331
FAX 212-254-2075
TEL 212-254-2075
Established: 1970
Products: paper
Techniques: painting, casting, bronze
Size Range: 23" × 28" to 8'4" × 44'
Price Range: $750 to $5,000/piece

See page 26 for photographs and additional information.

CONNIE UTTERBACK
3641 MIDVALE AVE #204
LOS ANGELES, CA 90034-6600
TEL 310-841-6675
Established: 1981
Products: fabric constructions
Techniques: construction technique
Size Range: 2' × 3' to 7' × 12'
Price Range: $700 to $9,500/piece

LYDIA VAN GELDER
FIBER ARTS
758 SUCHER LN
SANTA ROSA, CA 95401-3623
TEL 707-546-4139
Established: 1950
Products: fiber constructions
Techniques: weaving, ikat, shifu
Size Range: 12" × 12" to 4'6" × 9'
Price Range: $100 to $2,000/piece

★ ALICE VAN LEUNEN
PO BOX 408
LAKE OSWEGO, OR 97034-0408
FAX 503-636-0787
TEL 503-636-0787
Established: 1968
Products: mixed media installations
Techniques: painting, weaving, metallic foil work
Size Range: 24" × 30" to 10' × 12'
Price Range: $500 to $30,000/piece

See page 110 for photographs and additional information.

AASE VASLOW
100 ORCHARD LN
OAK RIDGE, TN 37830-3803
TEL 615-483-3650
Established: 1976
Products: tapestries
Techniques: beading, painting, weaving
Size Range: 30" × 30" to 5' × 10'
Price Range: $120 to $240/sq. ft.

Anita Joan Whatley, *Another River Sunset*, 1993, silk-screened China Silk, 73" × 47½".

★ SUSAN VENABLE

VENABLE STUDIO
214 S VENICE BLVD
VENICE, CA 90291-4537
FAX 310-822-0050
TEL 310-827-7233
Established: 1975
Products: mixed media installations
Techniques: painting, copper wire
constructions
Size Range: 24" to 48" minimum; no
upper limit
Price Range: $2,000 to $75,000/piece

**See page 109 for photographs and
additional information.**

BETTY VERA

41 UNION SQ W #531
NEW YORK, NY 10003-3208
TEL 212-924-2478
Products: tapestries
Techniques: weaving, warp painting,
embroidery
Size Range: 1' x 1' to 8' x 10'
Price Range: $400 to $30,000/piece

JUDITH VIEROW

803 GILBERT ST
COLUMBUS, OH 43206-1518
TEL 614-444-4568
Established: 1974
Products: art quilts
Techniques: appliqué, painting, quilting,
piecing, stitching
Size Range: 16" x 20" to 96" x 96"
Price Range: $500 to $10,000/piece

BARBARA ALLEN WAGNER

THE CROW'S NEST
7 SKYLINE PL
ASTORIA, OR 97103-6439
TEL 503-325-5548
Established: 1955
Products: tapestries
Techniques: embroidery, weaving,
needlepoint
Size Range: 1'6" x 3' to 5' x 8'
Price Range: $200 to $400/sq. ft.

DAVID WALKER

2905 PROBASCO CT
CINCINNATI, OH 45220-2712
TEL 513-961-9065
Established: 1987
Products: art quilts
Techniques: appliqué, quilting,
embellishment
Size Range: 19" x 19" to 80" x 80"
Price Range: $400 to $5,000/piece

★ TIM WALKER

POP CAT STUDIO
28277 TOWNLEY
MADISON HTS, MI 48071-2846
TEL 810-543-1942
Established: 1986
Products: mixed media installations
Techniques: painting, casting, laminating
Size Range: 28½" x 15½" to 8'8" x 6'8"
Price Range: $1,600 to $25,000/piece

**See page 173 for photographs and
additional information.**

JULIA WALSH

HISTORIC DESIGNS, LTD.
1905 NORMAL PARK #201
PO BOX 6503
HUNTSVILLE, TX 77342
TEL 409-291-0195
Established: 1987
Products: tapestries
Techniques: weaving, embroidery,
knotting
Size Range: 3' x 2' to 8' x 5'
Price Range: $1,500 to $35,000/piece

GRACEANN WARN

GRACEANN WARN STUDIO
1524 STRIETER RD
ANN ARBOR, MI 48103
TEL 313-665-2374
Established: 1985
Products: mixed media installations
Techniques: painting, collage
Size Range: 12" x 18" to 36" x 48"
Price Range: $300 to $2,500/piece

LAURA WASILOWSKI

324 VINCENT PL
ELGIN, IL 60123
TEL 708-931-7684
Established: 1986
Products: art quilts
Techniques: dyeing, quilting, stamping
or printing
Size Range: 1' x 1' to 5' x 6'
Price Range: $100 to $200/sq. ft.

WEAVING/SOUTHWEST

216 B PUEBLO NORTE
TAOS, NM 87571
TEL 505-758-0433
Established: 1962
Products: tapestries
Techniques: weaving
Size Range: 24" x 36" to 60" x 96"
Price Range: $21 to $400/sq. ft.

Harriet Zeitlin, *Tumbling Kimonos*, machine pieced, hand quilted and appliquéd, 108" x 84"

HELEN WEBBER

HELEN WEBBER DESIGNS
555 PACIFIC AVE
SAN FRANCISCO, CA 94133-4609
FAX 415-989-5746
TEL 415-989-5521
Established: 1973
Products: tapestries
Techniques: appliqué, painting, collage
Size Range: 3' x 4' to 10' x 65'
Price Range: $150 to $300/sq. ft.

LEANNE WEISSLER

28 LINCOLN CIR
CRESTWOOD, NY 11937
TEL 914-935-9342
Established: 1975
Products: mixed media installations,
painting
Techniques: painting, handmade paper,
printing, collage
Size Range: 12" x 12" to 40" x 50"
Price Range: $150 to $1,500/piece

CAROL D. WESTFALL

162 WHITFORD AVE
NUTLEY, NJ 07110
FAX 201-235-0218
TEL 201-235-0813
Established: 1972
Products: fiber art
Techniques: weaving, quilting, computer
collage
Size Range: 2" x 2" to 3' x 2'
Price Range: $350 to $3,000/piece

★ ANITA JOAN WHATLEY

1395 MELROSE COVE
MEMPHIS, TN 38106-5002
TEL 901-774-1000
TEL 901-774-2773
Established: 1982
Products: screen printed silk paintings
Techniques: silkscreen
Size Range: 3' x 3.5' to 9' x 48' per
panel
Price Range: $17.50 to $3,600/piece

See photograph on page 67.

JUDI MAUREEN WHITE

RENAISSANCE FIBRES
2062 E MALIBU DR
TEMPE, AZ 85282-5966
TEL 602-838-0416
Established: 1970
Products: mixed media installations
Techniques: painting, weaving, sculpting
Size Range: 45" x 99" to 96" x 240"
Price Range: $3,200 to $25,000/piece

NANCY WHITTINGTON

105 WATTERS RD
CARRBORO, NC 27510
FAX 919-933-0631
TEL 919-933-0624
Established: 1975
Products: art quilts
Techniques: appliqué, dyeing, silkscreen
Size Range: 32" x 22" to 9' x 8'
Price Range: $375 to $8,000/piece

ELIZABETH WILEY

E W WEAVES
1481 BUCKHORN RD PO BOX 1181
WILLITS, CA 95490-1181
TEL 707-459-9293
Established: 1982
Products: woven wall pieces
Techniques: embroidery, weaving
Size Range: 18" x 18" to 45" x 108"
Price Range: $12 to $54/sq. ft.

JODY WILLIAMS

FLYING PAPER
3953 16TH AVE S
MINNEAPOLIS, MN 55407-2828
TEL 612-721-2891
Established: 1982
Products: handmade paper
Techniques: casting, stamping/printing,
collage
Size Range: 6" x 8" to 36" x 60"
Price Range: $250 to $3,000/piece

JAY WILSON

WILSON & YAMADA ART STUDIO
3155 NAHENAHE PL
KIHEI, HI 96753-9314
TEL 808-874-3597
Established: 1976
Products: tapestries
Techniques: dyeing, weaving
Size Range: 6' x 4' to 8' x 12'
Price Range: $15,000 to $75,000/piece

WINDLINES

SYLVIA GENTILE
1450 23RD ST
SANTA MONICA, CA 90404-2902
FAX 310-828-5830
TEL 310-828-1938
Established: 1982
Products: fabric constructions
Techniques: appliqué, quilting, weaving
Size Range: 3' x 5' to 20' x 40'
Price Range: $1,000 to $40,000/piece

NANCY WINES-DeWAN

CONTEMPORARY MAINE TEXTILES
PO BOX 861
YARMOUTH, ME 04096-0861
TEL 207-846-6058
Established: 1970
Products: tapestries
Techniques: weaving
Size Range: 10" x 10" to 120" x 144"
Price Range: $150 to $200/sq. ft.

MAUREEN ZALE

481 MELINDA CR
WHITE LAKE, MI 48686
TEL 810-698-1748
Established: 1993
Products: fabric constructions
Techniques: painting, wrapping, fabric
manipulation
Size Range: 16" x 20" to 40" x 60"
Price Range: $95 to $1,000/piece

★ HARRIET ZEITLIN

202 S SALTAIR AVE
LOS ANGELES, CA 90049-4127
TEL 310-472-0534
Established: 1950
Products: art quilts, mixed media
installations
Techniques: appliqué, quilting, found
objects
Size Range: 36" x 30" to 11' x 7'
Price Range: $1,000 to $10,000/piece

See photograph on page 68.

ZEN AGAIN PRODUCTIONS

KIMBYL EDWARDS
1459 18TH ST # 193
SAN FRANCISCO, CA 94107-2801
FAX 415-647-6478
TEL 415-621-4433
Established: 1989
Products: lighted, handmade paper
sculptures
Techniques: wrapping, hand building
Size Range: 4" x 9" to 36" x 45"
Price Range: $75 to $1,500/piece

MARY ZICAFOOSE

4371 SW TERWILLIGER BLVD
PORTLAND, OR 97201-2874
TEL 503-241-0202
Established: 1979
Products: tapestries
Techniques: dyeing, weaving,
weft-faced ikat
Size Range: 2' x 2' to 20' x 15'
Price Range: $65 to $350/sq. ft.

CHARLOTTE ZIEBARTH

CHARLOTTE ZIEBARTH TAPESTRIES
3070 ASH AVE
BOULDER, CO 80303-3419
TEL 303-494-2601
Established: 1978
Products: tapestries
Techniques: dyeing, weaving
Size Range: 24" x 30" to 5' x 10'
Price Range: $400 to $10,000/piece

BHAKTI ZIEK

5225 GREENE ST
PHILADELPHIA, PA 19144-2927
TEL 215-844-4402
Established: 1980
Products: tapestries
Techniques: dyeing, painting, weaving
Size Range: 4" x 8" to 9' x 20'
Price Range: $100 to $300/sq. ft.

◆

THE GUILD REGISTER™
of Ceramic Art for the Wall

Welcome to **THE GUILD REGISTER** of Ceramic Art for the Wall, a new reference section within the *Designer's Edition*.

Why this new resource?

The design community has rediscovered the beauty and value of custom ceramics for wall applications. Many of today's freshest designs feature this work: murals and mosaics, relief sculpture and tile panels, columns and screens, mirrors and platters. The work is very strong and wonderfully varied.

We invite you to use **THE GUILD REGISTER** of Ceramic Art for the Wall to identify experienced, professional artists for the projects you oversee.

MARY LOU ALBERETTI

ALBERETTI ARTS
16 POSSUM DR
NEW FAIRFIELD, CT 06812
TEL 203-746-1321

Established: 1973
Products: wall reliefs
Media: stoneware, earthenware
Techniques: constructed
Finishes: glazed, unglazed
Installation: interior, permanent, movable
Size Range: 18" x 18" to 6' x 6'
Price Range: $600 to $5,000 for architectural wall sculptures

★ GEORGE ALEXANDER

1261 CERRO GORDO RD
SANTA FE, NM 87501
TEL 505-983-8003

Products: panels or screens, columns, wall reliefs
Media: stoneware
Techniques: constructed, molded, wheel thrown
Finishes: glazed, unglazed
Installation: interior, exterior, permanent, movable, site specific
Size Range: 12" x 12" to 8' x 8'
Price Range: $500 to $700/sq. ft.

See page 81 for photographs and additional information.

ALFREDO RATINOFF STUDIO

ALFREDO RATINOFF
11908 WINTERTHUR LN #106
RESTON, VA 22091-1956
TEL 703-716-2931

Established: 1984
Products: tiles, murals, platters
Media: stoneware, porcelain, earthenware
Techniques: cast, constructed, wheel thrown
Finishes: glazed, raku fired, inlaid colored clays
Installation: interior, exterior, permanent, movable, site specific
Size Range: 4" x 4" to 10' x 30'
Price Range: $40 to $280/sq. ft.
Price Range: $150 to $1,500 for platters and small murals

ANDREW LEICESTER & ASSOCIATES

ANDREW LEICESTER
1500 JACKSON ST NE
MINNEAPOLIS, MN 55413-1561
TEL 612-781-7422
FAX 612-781-7422

Established: 1970
Products: mosaics, columns, wall reliefs
Media: stoneware, glass, brick
Techniques: cast, constructed, molded
Finishes: glazed, unglazed
Installation: interior, exterior, permanent, site specific
Size Range: 2' x 2' to 25' x 100'
Price Range: $100 to $250/sq. ft.
Price Range: $25,00 to $250,000 for wall reliefs, mosaics

ANTICHITÀ MODERNA

BARBARA PETRARCA
655 UTICA AVE
BOULDER, CO 80304
TEL 303-444-3626
FAX 303-449-8870

Established: 1993
Products: tiles, wall reliefs, entryway surrounds
Media: stoneware, earthenware, terra cotta
Techniques: cast, constructed, hand-sculpted
Finishes: unglazed, salt or sodium fired, raku fired
Installation: interior, permanent, site specific
Size Range: 4" x 4" to 16" x 12"
Price Range: $150 to $300/sq. ft.
Price Range: $50 to $150 for each tile/module

ARCHITECTURAL CERAMICS

ELIZABETH GRAJALES
667 CARROLL ST
BROOKLYN, NY 11215
TEL 718-857-0729
FAX 718-857-0729

Established: 1978
Products: tiles, mosaics, wall reliefs
Media: stoneware, earthenware, brick
Techniques: cast, constructed, molded
Finishes: glazed, unglazed
Installation: interior, exterior, site specific, ceramic frieze
Size Range: 8" x 8" to 15' x 13'
Price Range: $250 to $400/sq. ft.
Price Range: $250 to $400 for tiles

★ ART ON TILES

RITA PAUL
32 WASHINGTON SQ W
NEW YORK, NY 10011-9194
TEL 212-674-6388
FAX 212-979-8373

Established: 1970
Products: tiles, panels or screens, murals
Media: stoneware, 6" x 6" bisque tiles
Techniques: constructed
Finishes: glazed
Installation: interior, exterior, permanent, movable, site specific, w/marble or granite tiles
Size Range: 4' x 2' to 8½' x 6'
Price Range: $500 to $10,000 for murals

See page 82 for photographs and additional information.

ARTISTIC LICENSE

GINIA CLEEVES
1551 16 ST
SANTA MONICA, CA 90404-3308
TEL 310-453-0932
FAX 310-453-0804

Established: 1980
Products: tiles, murals
Finishes: glazed, unglazed
Installation: interior, exterior, permanent, movable, site specific
Price Range: $50 to $150/sq. ft.
Price Range: $7 to $15 for 6" x 6" or 8" x 8" tiles

MIMI ASATO

MIMI'S STUDIO
3120 COLFAX AVE S
MINNEAPOLIS, MN 55408
TEL 612-823-6589
FAX 612-798-4814
Established: 1989
Products: tiles, murals, platters
Media: stoneware, earthenware, mirror
Techniques: constructed
Finishes: glazed, underglaze painted
Installation: interior, exterior
Size Range: 1' x 1' to 2' x 2'
Price Range: $200 to $800 for murals, platters and art tiles

MELINDA ASHLEY

ASHLEY ART STUDIO
144 MOODY ST BLDG 18
WALTHAM, MA 02154
TEL 617-891-8811
FAX 617-891-8811
Established: 1976
Products: tiles, murals, platters
Media: stoneware, porcelain, earthenware
Techniques: cast, molded, wheel thrown
Finishes: glazed, unglazed, inlaid colored clays
Installation: interior, exterior, permanent, movable, site specific
Size Range: 2' x 2' to 4' x 11'
Price Range: $150 to $300/sq. ft.
Price Range: $600 to $12,000 for murals

MARVIN BARTEL

1708 LINCOLNWAY E
GOSHEN, IN 46526-5022
TEL 219-533-0171
FAX 219-535-7660
Established: 1965
Products: tiles, wall reliefs, fireplace surfaces
Media: stoneware, porcelain
Techniques: constructed, wheel thrown, unique tile patterns
Finishes: glazed, unglazed, reliefs and photos
Installation: interior, exterior, permanent, movable, site specific
Size Range: 4' x 4' to 8' x 10'
Price Range: $70 to $130/sq. ft.
Price Range: $1,400 to $14,000 for various tile projects

MARLO BARTELS

MARLO BARTELS ARCHITECTURAL CERAMICS
2307 #7 LAGUNA CANYON RD
LAGUNA BEACH, CA 92651
TEL 714-494-4408
FAX 714-497-0400
Established: 1979
Products: tiles, mosaics, murals
Installation: interior, exterior, permanent, movable, site specific
Size Range: 3" x 3" to 130' x 130'
Price Range: $1 to $20/sq. ft.

BARBARA BEDESSEM

NORTHVIEW DESIGNS
544 STORLE AVE
BURLINGTON, WI 53105
TEL 414-763-6545
Established: 1970
Products: tiles, murals
Media: commercial tile
Techniques: custom painting
Finishes: glazed
Installation: interior, exterior, permanent, movable, site specific
Size Range: 4" x 4" to 4' x 4'
Price Range: $30 to $75/sq. ft.
Price Range: $3 to $20 for single tiles

BENEDIKT STREBEL CERAMICS

BENEDIKT STREBEL
978 GUERRERO ST
SAN FRANCISCO, CA 94110
TEL 415-824-7949
Established: 1982
Products: tiles, platters, tiles for floor and walls
Media: stoneware, porcelain, earthenware
Techniques: cast, molded, wheel thrown
Finishes: glazed, unglazed, colored slips
Installation: interior, exterior, permanent, site specific
Size Range: 20 sq ft x 20,000 sq ft
Price Range: $15 to $40/sq. ft.

SIMI BERMAN

PO BOX 58
CHESTERFIELD, NH 03443-0058
TEL 603-256-8477
FAX 802-257-5119
Established: 1982
Products: wall reliefs
Media: earthenware
Techniques: constructed
Finishes: painted with gouaches
Installation: interior, movable
Size Range: 12" x 10" to 22" x 18"
Price Range: $110 to $400 for wall sculpture

SUSAN O. BLISS

JOPPA CLAYWORKS
PO BOX 281 RFD1
WARNER, NH 03278
TEL 603-456-3276
Established: 1979
Products: tiles, wall reliefs, mirrors, doorways
Media: earthenware
Techniques: constructed, free form cut-out slabs
Finishes: glazed, unglazed, burnished, incised line
Installation: interior, permanent, movable, site specific
Size Range: 12" x 6" to 60" x 28"
Price Range: $100 to $300/sq. ft.
Price Range: $300 to $1,000 for cut-out wall tile

MARGARET BOOZER

BOOZER CERAMICS
1803 BILTMORE ST NW #614
WASHINGTON, DC 20009
TEL 202-588-9830
Established: 1992
Products: tiles, wall reliefs
Media: stoneware, earthenware, wood
Techniques: constructed, molded
Finishes: glazed, unglazed, saggar fired
Installation: interior, exterior, permanent, movable, site specific
Size Range: 6" x 6" to 6' x 6'
Price Range: $50 to $1,500 for wall reliefs

BRUCE BRECKENRIDGE

1715 REGENT ST
MADISON, WI 53705
TEL 608-262-6546
Established: 1954
Products: tiles, murals, platters, wall reliefs
Media: porcelain, earthenware
Finishes: glazed
Installation: interior, exterior, permanent, movable, site specific
Size Range: 48" x 24" to 12' x 30'
Price Range: $180 to $250/sq. ft. for majolica tile murals

CYNTHIA BRINGLE

BRINGLE POTTERY STUDIO
PENLAND SCHOOL RD
PENLAND, NC 28765-9999
TEL 704-765-0240
FAX 704-765-0240
Established: 1965
Products: murals, platters, wall reliefs
Media: stoneware, raku fired
Techniques: constructed, wheel thrown
Finishes: glazed, wood fired, raku fired
Installation: interior, permanent, movable, site specific
Size Range: 1' x 3' to 8' x 10'
Price Range: $250 to $600/sq. ft.
Price Range: $500 to $1,000 for platters

BRISSON STUDIO

HARRIET E. BRISSON
PO BOX 85
REHOBOTH, MA 02769
TEL 401-456-8054
FAX 401-456-8379
Established: 1966
Products: tiles, lighted panels
Media: earthenware, mirror
Techniques: cast, constructed, molded
Finishes: glazed, unglazed, raku fired
Installation: interior, permanent, movable
Size Range: 12" x 15" to 8' x 32'
Price Range: $100 to $1,000 for wall hanging

KAREN CARD

1407 SEABRIGHT AVE
SANTA CRUZ, CA 95062-2526
TEL 408-426-2181
Established: 1987
Products: wall reliefs, torso, callipygians
Media: earthenware, raku and patina
Techniques: cast, slab construction
Finishes: raku fired, patina
Installation: interior, exterior, movable
Size Range: 16" x 14" to 30" x 24"
Price Range: $500 to $800 for torso, callipygian

ROBERT CARLSON
MARILEE HALL

PRIMUS STUDIO
2350 BROWN'S MILL RD
COOKEVILLE, TN 38506
TEL 615-526-6649
Established: 1971
Products: platters, wall reliefs, dimensional tile murals
Media: stoneware, earthenware, raku, pit fire
Techniques: cast, constructed, wheel thrown
Finishes: glazed, salt or sodium fired, raku fired
Installation: interior, permanent, movable, site specific
Size Range: 10" x 10" to 20' x 30'
Price Range: $200/sq. ft.
Price Range: $450 for platters (23" to 24"Dia)

CLAYMANIA

MEG ETSEN
31123 VIA COLINAS #1108
WESTLAKE VILLAGE, CA 91362-4503
TEL 818-889-3013
Established: 1982
Products: tiles, murals, wall reliefs, fireplace designs
Media: stoneware, earthenware
Techniques: molded
Finishes: glazed, unglazed
Installation: interior, exterior, permanent custom designed
Size Range: 4" x 4" to 10' x 5'
Price Range: $4 to $20/sq. ft.
Price Range: $400 to $5,000 for architectural ceramics

COELHO STUDIOS

JACK NEULIST-COELHO
PO BOX 620
6135 W EVANS CREEK RD
ROGUE RIVER, OR 97537
TEL 503-582-0216
Established: 1970
Products: murals, columns, wall reliefs, door surrounds
Media: stoneware, porcelain, earthenware
Techniques: constructed, molded, wheel thrown
Finishes: glazed, unglazed, inlaid colored clays
Installation: interior, exterior, permanent, movable, site specific
Size Range: 18" x 16" to unlimited scale
Price Range: $500 to $10,000 for small wall pieces to large murals

CERAMIC ART FOR THE WALL

★ **FRANK COLSON**
COLSON STUDIO
COLSON SCHOOL OF ART
1666 HILLVIEW ST
SARASOTA, FL 34239
TEL 813-953-5892
FAX 813-953-5892
Established: 1963
Products: tiles, murals
Media: stoneware, earthenware
Techniques: cast, constructed, molded
Finishes: glazed, unglazed, raku fired
Installation: interior, exterior, permanent, movable
Size Range: 10" × 10" to 20' × 16'
Price Range: $35 to $60/sq. ft.
Price Range: $25 to $60 for mural composites

See page 162 for photographs and additional information.

DIANA CRAIN

DIANA CRAIN PORCELAINS
173 LIVE OAK DR
PETALUMA, CA 94952
TEL 707-795-2451
FAX 707-795-2451
Established: 1973
Products: porcelain wall vases
Media: porcelain
Techniques: constructed
Finishes: glazed, unglazed, inlaid colored clays
Installation: interior, exterior, movable
Size Range: 8" × 5" to 22" × 20"
Price Range: $40 to $220 for a wall vase

LYNDA CURTIS

L. CURTIS DESIGNS
145 HUDSON ST
NEW YORK, NY 10013-2103
TEL 212-966-1720
FAX 212-966-1720
Established: 1989
Products: tiles, murals, wall reliefs
Media: stoneware, earthenware
Techniques: cast, constructed, molded
Finishes: glazed, unglazed
Installation: interior, exterior, permanent, site specific
Size Range: 4" × 4" to 120" × 120"
Price Range: $15 to $300/sq. ft.
Price Range: $10 to $10,000 for individual tiles, wall murals

DABBERT STUDIO

DAVE & PAT DABBERT
3009 MAYFIELD WY
MICHIGAN CITY, IN 46360
TEL 219-879-7201
TEL 813-925-9929
Established: 1968
Products: tiles, panels or screens, platters, wall reliefs
Media: porcelain
Techniques: constructed, wheel thrown
Finishes: glazed, unglazed, inlaid colored clays
Installation: interior, permanent, movable
Size Range: 3½" × 10" to 10' × 5'
Price Range: $175 to $400/sq. ft.
Price Range: $50 to $5,000 for wall sculptures

DALE ALLISON-HARTLEY STUDIO/GALLERY

DALE ALLISON-HARTLEY
RTS BOX 83A
EMPORIA, KS 66801
TEL 316-279-4543
Established: 1976
Products: platters
Media: porcelain, earthenware
Techniques: constructed
Finishes: glazed, salt or sodium fired, raku fired
Installation: interior, movable
Size Range: 7" × 7" to 20" × 20"
Price Range: $100 to $500 for platters

PHILLIP DAUZIG

GET CRACKING
86 EDGEMONT RD
UPPER MONTCLAIR, NJ 07043
TEL 201-746-0709
Established: 1970
Products: tiles, mosaics, murals
Media: stoneware, porcelain, mirror
Techniques: constructed, shaped, cemented
Finishes: glazed
Installation: interior, exterior, permanent, site specific
Size Range: 2' × 2' to 20' × 40'
Price Range: $90 to $180/sq. ft.

DAVIS TILE TECHNIQUES, INC.

DOROTHY A. DAVIS
827 EXPOSITION AVE
DALLAS, TX 75226-1743
TEL 214-826-5130
FAX 214-826-5130
Established: 1975
Products: tiles, panels or screens, murals, embossed tile
Media: earthenware
Techniques: constructed, molded
Finishes: glazed, unglazed
Installation: interior, exterior, permanent, movable, site specific
Size Range: 2' × 2' to 100' × 100'
Price Range: $18 to $150/sq. ft.
Price Range: $35 to $50 for tiles

LYNN B. DENTON

607 S 9 ST
PHILADELPHIA, PA 19147
TEL 215-923-6192
Established: 1964
Products: tiles, mosaics, murals
Media: stoneware, porcelain, earthenware
Techniques: constructed
Finishes: glazed, unglazed
Installation: interior, exterior, permanent, movable, site specific
Size Range: 2' × 2' to 10' × 30'
Price Range: $25 to $100/sq. ft.
Price Range: $100 to $30,000 for murals

DESIGN TILES OF MIFFLINBURG

JOANNAH SKUCEK
508 CHESTNUT ST
MIFFLINBURG, PA 17844
TEL 717-966-3373
FAX 717-966-3128
Established: 1983
Products: tiles, murals
Media: stoneware, porcelain, earthenware
Techniques: molded
Finishes: glazed, unglazed
Installation: interior, exterior, permanent
Size Range: 2" × 2" to 11' × 5'
Price Range: $20 to $25/sq. ft.
Price Range: $5 to $30 for hand-painted 6" tiles

NELL DEVITT

NELL DEVITT POTTERY
RR3 BOX 84
BLOOMFIELD, IN 47424
TEL 812-384-3012
Established: 1985
Products: tiles, murals, wall reliefs
Media: earthenware
Techniques: constructed
Finishes: unglazed, raku fired
Installation: interior, movable
Size Range: 8" × 8" to 7' × 9'
Price Range: $200 to $6,000 for clay tiles, murals

DIMENSION DESIGNS

RUTH CRANMER
709 MOORESTOWN-
  CENTERTON RD
MT LAUREL, NJ 08054
TEL 609-234-6156
Established: 1990
Products: tiles
Media: porcelain
Finishes: glazed, unglazed
Installation: interior, exterior, permanent, movable, site specific
Size Range: 4" × 4" to 14" × 14"
Price Range: $80 to $120/sq. ft.

ERIC DOCTORS

ERIC DOCTORS CERAMIC
  SCULPTURE AND VESSELS
2759 EASTWOOD AVE
EVANSTON, IL 60201
TEL 708-864-8481
FAX 708-864-6157
Established: 1984
Products: panels or screens, murals, Islamic patterns
Media: stoneware
Techniques: constructed, carved
Finishes: glazed
Installation: interior, permanent, movable, site specific, modular
Size Range: 1' × 1' to 6' × 18'
Price Range: $50 to $150/sq. ft.

STEVEN DONEGAN

915 SPRING GARDEN ST
PHILADELPHIA, PA 19123-2605
TEL 215-232-5459
FAX 215-232-5664
Established: 1976
Products: tiles, murals
Media: earthenware
Techniques: constructed
Finishes: glazed
Installation: interior, permanent, movable
Size Range: 31" × 22" to 11' × 12'
Price Range: $250/sq. ft.

NANCY WEEKS DUDCHENKO

DUDCHENKO STUDIOS
3815 RIDGE PIKE
COLLEGEVILLE, PA 19426-3121
TEL 610-489-7231
FAX 610-489-7233
Established: 1969
Products: wall reliefs, free-standing panels
Media: stoneware
Techniques: constructed, layered, folded, stamped
Finishes: glazed, oil paint, stains
Installation: interior, exterior, permanent, movable, site specific, ready-made works
Size Range: 2' × 2' to 3' × 10'
Price Range: $150 to $250/sq. ft.
Price Range: $600 to $7,500 for multi-sectional wall sculptures

ANDRA ELLIS

221 PELHAM RD
PHILADELPHIA, PA 19119
TEL 215-849-2667
Established: 1976
Products: murals, wall reliefs
Media: stoneware, porcelain, earthenware
Techniques: constructed
Finishes: glazed, unglazed, inlaid colored clays
Installation: interior, exterior, permanent, movable, site specific
Size Range: 24" × 30" to 10' × 20'
Price Range: $2,000 to $20,000 for wall reliefs, murals

MAUREEN ELLIS

ELLIS CERAMICS
3070 KERNER BLVD #N
SAN RAFAEL, CA 94901-5419
TEL 415-453-2116
FAX 415-485-4305
Established: 1980
Products: tiles, murals, platters
Media: earthenware
Techniques: constructed, molded
Finishes: airbrushed acrylics
Installation: interior, permanent, movable, site specific
Size Range: 4' × 4" to 30' × 500'
Price Range: $50 to $500/sq. ft.

ELEANOR J. EVART

EVART WOODS
22628 VALLEY VIEW DR
HAYWARD, CA 94541-3537
TEL 510-582-7038
Established: 1977
Products: tiles, mosaics, wall reliefs
Media: earthenware, brick
Techniques: cast, constructed, molded
Finishes: glazed, unglazed, raku fired
inlaid colored clays
Installation: interior, exterior, permanent,
movable, site specific
Size Range: 6" × 6" to 12' × 12'
Price Range: $100 to $150/sq. ft.

RANDY FEIN

MOUNTAIN STUDIO
4163 YOUNGSTOWN RD
LINCOLNVILLE, ME 04849
TEL 207-763-3433
Established: 1975
Products: murals, columns, wall reliefs
Media: earthenware, glass, brick
Techniques: constructed
Finishes: glazed, unglazed, raku fired
Installation: interior, exterior, permanent,
site specific
Size Range: 24" × 24" to unlimited
Price Range: $200 to $500/sq. ft.
Price Range: $500 to $50,000 for one-
of-a-kind relief sculpture mural

FIRECLAY TILE

PAUL BURNS
495 W JULIAN ST
SAN JOSE, CA 95110-2337
TEL 408-275-1182
FAX 408-275-1187
Established: 1986
Products: tiles, murals, wall reliefs
Media: stoneware, earthenware
Techniques: molded
Finishes: glazed, unglazed
Installation: interior, exterior
Price Range: $7.40 to $12/sq. ft.
Price Range: $3 to $6 for crown
moldings

CAROL FLEMING

TERRA NOVA
914 CONCORDIA LN
ST LOUIS, MO 63105-3049
TEL 314-721-5841
FAX 314-721-9868
Established: 1989
Products: columns, wall reliefs
Media: stoneware
Techniques: constructed, modeled
Finishes: glazed, unglazed, inlaid colored
clays
Installation: interior, exterior, permanent,
site specific
Size Range: 8" × 8" to 9' × 4'
Price Range: $100 to $3,000 , for
columns

PENELOPE FLEMING

7740 WASHINGTON LN
ELKINS PARK, PA 19027
TEL 215-576-6830
Established: 1972
Products: wall reliefs
Media: earthenware, slate
Techniques: constructed
Finishes: glazed, unglazed, raku fired
Installation: interior, permanent, site
specific
Size Range: 12" × 12" to 96" × 170"
Price Range: $400 to $20,000 for
sculptural wall reliefs

STEVEN FORBES-DESOULE

FORBES-DESOULE STUDIO
143 DAVID BIDDLE TR
WEAVERVILLE, NC 28787
TEL 704-645-9065
Established: 1980
Products: murals, platters, wall reliefs
Media: raku
Techniques: constructed, slabs
Finishes: glazed, raku fired, acrylics
Installation: interior, permanent, movable
Size Range: 15" × 15" to 6' × 8'
Price Range: $165 to $185/sq. ft.
Price Range: $500 to $700 for platters

MARK W. FORMAN

2851 SW 71ST TER #1112
DAVIE, FL 33314-1122
Established: 1965
Products: wall reliefs
Media: stoneware
Techniques: constructed
Finishes: raku fired
Installation: interior, exterior, permanent,
movable
Size Range: 53" × 23" and up
Price Range: $2,000 and up for wall
forms

JIM FOSTER

10315 N COUNTY RD
FT COLLINS, CO 80524
TEL 303-568-7768
Established: 1963
Products: tiles, panels or screens,
mosaics, murals, platters
Media: porcelain, clay to bronze
Techniques: cast, constructed, molded,
wheel thrown
Finishes: glazed, lusters
Installation: interior, exterior, permanent,
movable, site specific, art in public places
Size Range: 4" × 4" to 20' × 20'
Price Range: $500 to $1,200 for
sculptures

SARAH FREDERICK

SARAH FREDERICK STUDIO
   POTTERY
2735 FIELD AVE
LOUISVILLE, KY 40206
TEL 502-897-1298
Established: 1980
Products: platters, wall reliefs, soft
sculpture
Media: porcelain, earthenware
Techniques: hand built
Finishes: glazed, unglazed, high and low-
fire color
Installation: interior, exterior, movable
Size Range: 12" × 12" to 24" × 24"
Price Range: $300 to $1,000

FULPER TILE

ANNE FULPER
BOX 373
YARDLEY, PA 19067
TEL 2157368512
Established: 1987
Products: tiles, lamps
Media: stoneware
Techniques: cast, molded, extruded
Finishes: glazed
Installation: interior, permanent, site
specific
Size Range: 2" × 2" to 1' × 1'
Price Range: $64.71 to $97.41/sq. ft.
Price Range: $2.71 to $100 for mirror,
matte, crystalline

GOOSENECK DESIGNS

JACKIE & CHRIS SMITH
2020 HUGHES SHOP RD
WESTMINSTER, MD 21158-2963
TEL 410-848-5663
Products: tiles, murals, columns, wall
reliefs
Media: stoneware, porcelain, earthen-
ware
Techniques: constructed, molded, wheel
thrown
Finishes: glazed, unglazed, wood fired
Installation: interior, exterior, permanent,
movable, site specific
Size Range: 32" × 40" to 8' × 24'
Price Range: $45 to $110/sq. ft.
Price Range: $2,200 to $5,600 for
fireplace surrounds, fountains, murals

ELISE GRAY

1483 OGLETHORPE ST
MACON, GA 31201
TEL 912-738-0438
Established: 1972
Products: wall reliefs
Media: stoneware
Techniques: constructed, molded, hand
built
Finishes: glazed, unglazed
Installation: interior, permanent, movable,
site specific
Size Range: 24" × 33" to 6½' × 18'
Price Range: $200 to $300/sq. ft.
Price Range: $1,000 to $22,000 for wall
reliefs

MARION GREBOW

123 PICKETTS RIDGE RD
W REDDING, CT 06896-1101
TEL 203-938-4188
Established: 1974
Products: tiles, murals, fund raising
murals
Media: earthenware
Techniques: cast, realistic painting
Finishes: glazed
Installation: interior, permanent, site
specific
Size Range: 12" × 12" to 8' × 14'
Price Range: $25 to $150/sq. ft.
Price Range: $1,500 to $10,000 for
kitchen and baths, fireplaces, murals

MICHELLE GREGOR

PALM
965 CAPP ST #5
SAN FRANCISCO, CA 94606
TEL 510-834-1324
Established: 1984
Products: murals, platters, wall reliefs
Media: stoneware, porcelain
Techniques: constructed, molded, wheel
thrown
Finishes: glazed, colored slips
Installation: interior, exterior, permanent,
movable, site specific
Size Range: 12" × 12" to unlimited
Price Range: $200 to $350/sq. ft.
Price Range: $100 to $300, for platters,
approx. 18" diameter

KAREN M. GUNDERMAN

11618 N COUNTRY LN
MEQUON, WI 53092
TEL 414-229-6351
FAX 414-229-6154
Established: 1975
Products: mosaics, murals, wall reliefs
Media: earthenware, glass
Techniques: constructed
Finishes: glazed
Installation: interior, movable
Size Range: 30" × 48" to 9' × 15'
Price Range: $2,800 to $18,000 for
murals

LARRY HALVORSEN

LARRY HALVORSEN/CERAMICS
335 NW 51
SEATTLE, WA 98107
TEL 206-781-1434
Established: 1981
Products: tiles, platters, wall reliefs
Media: stoneware
Techniques: constructed
Finishes: glazed, unglazed
Installation: interior, exterior, permanent,
movable, site specific
Size Range: 14" × 14" to unlimited
Price Range: $75 to $125/sq. ft.

CERAMIC ART FOR THE WALL

LISA HARRIS
CLASSIC ELEMENTS
1021 W LILL
CHICAGO, IL 60614
TEL 312-525-7863
Established: 1979
Products: tiles, platters, wall reliefs
Media: earthenware
Techniques: constructed, molded, stamping, incising
Finishes: glazed, hand painted, aged look
Installation: interior, permanent, movable, site specific
Size Range: 8" × 8" to 4' × 4'
Price Range: $32 to $108/sq. ft.
Price Range: $175 to $400 for platters, wall relief

DEBORAH HECHT
CUSTOM DESIGN ON TILE
1865 HARVEST LN
BLOOMFIELD HILLS, MI 48302
TEL 810-333-2168
Established: 1975
Products: tiles, murals, table tops
Media: stoneware, earthenware
Techniques: constructed, molded, glazed on commercial tile
Finishes: glazed
Installation: interior, exterior, permanent, movable, site specific
Size Range: 10" × 8" to 4' × 8'
Price Range: $150 to $400/sq. ft.

MARK HEIMANN
LOST MOUNTAIN CLAYWORKS
22009 S LOST MOUNTAIN RD
ESTACADA, OR 97023
TEL 503-631-8686
Established: 1975
Products: tiles, platters, masks, shields
Media: stoneware, fiber, found objects
Techniques: constructed, molded, wheel thrown
Finishes: glazed, unglazed, carved, embossed
Installation: interior, exterior, permanent, movable, site specific
Size Range: 18" × 10" to 7' × 4'
Price Range: $4 to $22/sq. ft.
Price Range: $100 to $500 for platters, masks, medicine shields

★ JEFF HEITHMAR
INTAGLIA
484 W 43 ST #25Q
NEW YORK, NY 10036
TEL 212-268-0012
Established: 1980
Products: tiles, murals, inlaid ceramics
Media: inlaid ceramic tile
Techniques: constructed, inlayed
Finishes: glazed, unglazed
Installation: interior, exterior, permanent, movable, site specific
Size Range: 2" × 2" to 50' × 20'
Price Range: $5 to $200/sq. ft.
Price Range: $75 to $5,000 for murals

See page 84 for photographs and additional information.

MARION E. HELD
71 N FULLERTON AVE
MONTCLAIR, NJ 07042
TEL 201-783-7428
Established: 1977
Products: tiles, wall reliefs
Media: stoneware
Techniques: cast, constructed, molded
Finishes: glazed, unglazed
Installation: interior, exterior, permanent, movable, site specific
Price Range: $100 to $125/sq. ft.

HOGAN YOUNG
PO BOX 1314
IDYLLWILD, CA 92549-1314
TEL 909-659-3224
FAX 909-659-3224
Established: 1970
Products: tiles, murals
Media: stoneware, porcelain, earthenware
Techniques: constructed, molded
Finishes: glazed, unglazed
Installation: interior, exterior, permanent, movable, site specific
Size Range: 11" × 11" to 10' × 70'
Price Range: $50 to $125/sq. ft.
Price Range: $90 to $220, for wall hangings

CLAUDIA HOLLISTER
1314 NW IRVING ST #206
PORTLAND, OR 97209-2722
TEL 503-228-7648
FAX 503-226-0429
Established: 1980
Products: tiles, murals, wall reliefs
Media: stoneware, porcelain
Techniques: constructed, molded
Finishes: glazed, unglazed, inlaid colored clays
Installation: interior, exterior, permanent, movable, site specific
Size Range: 24" × 18" to 20' × 30'
Price Range: $100 to $250/sq. ft.

JERI HOLLISTER
801 AMHERST AVE
ANN ARBOR, MI 48105-1652
TEL 313-761-1971
FAX 313-747-4121
Established: 1987
Products: panels or screens, wall reliefs
Media: earthenware
Techniques: constructed
Finishes: glazed, unglazed
Installation: interior, permanent, movable, site specific
Size Range: 18" × 12" to 60" × 72"
Price Range: $500 to $5,000 for wall reliefs and free-standing panels

RICHARD HOUSTON
PO BOX 1356
ASHLAND, OR 97520-0046
TEL 503-482-7323
Established: 1986
Products: panels or screens, murals
Media: drywall
Techniques: constructed
Finishes: painted
Installation: interior, exterior, permanent, movable, site specific, ceilings
Size Range: 12" × 12" to 32' × 160'
Price Range: $1,200 to $50,000 for murals

HUNT KEISER STUDIO TILE
CAROL KEISER & BILL HUNT
RR4 BOX 260
PUTNEY, VT 05546
Established: 1960
Products: tiles, panels or screens, murals
Media: porcelain
Techniques: molded
Finishes: glazed
Installation: interior, permanent, movable
Price Range: $100 to $150/sq. ft.

JEFF IRWIN
JEFF IRWIN CERAMIC ART
(STUDIO 1)
3594 3 AVE
SAN DIEGO, CA 92103
TEL 619-544-6420
Established: 1982
Products: tiles, platters, wall reliefs
Media: stoneware, porcelain, earthenware
Techniques: constructed, molded
Finishes: glazed
Installation: interior, exterior, permanent, movable, site specific
Size Range: 1' × 1' to 8' × 10'
Price Range: $200 to $300/sq. ft.
Price Range: $400 to $600 for 22" platter, hand drawn tiles

★ J.E. JASEN
JUNE JASEN
36 E 10TH ST
NEW YORK, NY 10003-6219
TEL 212-674-6113
FAX 212-777-6375
Established: 1979
Products: tiles, murals, wall reliefs
Media: glass, glass on metal
Finishes: glazed, gloss and matte
Installation: interior, exterior, permanent, site specific
Size Range: 6" × 6" to unlimited
Price Range: $200 to $450/sq. ft.

See page 167 for photographs and additional information.

SHELLIE JACOBSON
RD2 GRANDVIEW RD
SKILLMAN, NJ 08558
TEL 609-466-3612
Established: 1978
Products: tiles, platters, wall reliefs
Media: porcelain
Techniques: constructed, hand built
Finishes: glazed, unglazed, sawdust fired
Installation: interior, movable
Size Range: 15½" × 12¾" to 4'2" × 4'2"
Price Range: $150 to $1,500 for wall reliefs, wall platters

AMANDA JAFFE
CERAMIC TILE MURALS
NMSU ART DEPT 3572 BOX 30001
LAS CRUCES, NM 88003
TEL 505-646-1225
FAX 505-646-8036
Established: 1978
Products: tiles, murals, wall reliefs
Media: stoneware, vitreous white clay
Techniques: molded, cast and carved
Finishes: glazed, glossy and dry surfaces
Installation: interior, exterior, permanent, movable, site specific
Size Range: 12" × 12" to 8' × 22'
Price Range: $2,500 to $40,000 for tile murals

B.J. JENSEN
B. JENSEN TILE
22017 NW BECK RD
PORTLAND, OR 97231
TEL 503-621-3487
FAX 503-621-3297
Established: 1972
Products: tiles, panels or screens, murals
Media: stoneware, porcelain, earthenware
Techniques: constructed, extruded
Finishes: glazed, unglazed, hand painted
Installation: interior, permanent, movable, site specific
Size Range: 6" × 6" to 12' × 20'
Price Range: $100 to $250/sq. ft.
Price Range: $20 to $50 for individual tiles

ANTHONY J. JEROSKI
A.J. DESIGNS INC.
PO BOX 576
MUNCIE, IN 47308-0576
TEL 317-287-1647
Established: 1988
Products: tiles, panels or screens, murals
Media: stoneware, porcelain, mixed media
Techniques: constructed, molded
Finishes: glazed, mixed media
Installation: interior, permanent, movable
Size Range: 18" × 10" to 10' × 18'
Price Range: $150 to $25,000 for sculptural forms/murals

JOCELYN STUDIO
JOCELYN GOLDMAN
39 OLD TOWN ST
EAST HADDAM, CT 06423
TEL 203-526-1581
FAX 203-526-2205
Established: 1988
Products: wall reliefs
Media: stoneware, earthenware
Techniques: constructed, molded, wheel
thrown
Finishes: glazed, raku fired, inlaid colored
clays
Installation: interior, permanent, movable,
site specific, individual objects
Size Range: 4" × 4" to 4' × 4'
Price Range: $35 to $175/sq. ft.
Price Range: $150 to $300 for sculptural
murals per square foot

TOVE B. JOHANSEN
6613 BRAWNER ST
MCLEAN, VA 22101
TEL 703-893-6728
Established: 1952
Products: tiles, panels or screens,
mosaics, requests from architects
Media: brick, refractory clay, marble
Techniques: cast, constructed, molded
Finishes: glazed, unglazed
Installation: interior, exterior, permanent,
movable, site specific, insured, warranted
Size Range: 2' × 3' to 12' × 54'
Price Range: $100/sq. ft.

JUNIPER TREE TILEWORKS
WILLIAM DISBRO
ANDREA BENNER DISBRO
75 CAMBELL AVE
JAMESTOWN, NY 14701
TEL 716-665-3320
Established: 1972
Products: tiles
Media: porcelain, earthenware
Techniques: molded
Finishes: glazed
Installation: interior, exterior, permanent,
movable
Size Range: 4" × 4" to 8" × 8"
Price Range: $18 for 4" × 4" tile; $90 for
8" × 8" tile, all ½" thick

DIANE KATSIAFICAS
165 WESTERN AVE N #300
ST PAUL, MN 55102-4611
TEL 612-222-6926
FAX 612-625-8096
Established: 1976
Products: mosaics, columns, wall reliefs
Media: earthenware, brick, mixed
Techniques: constructed
Finishes: glazed, unglazed
Installation: interior, exterior, permanent,
site specific
Size Range: variable
Price Range: $1,000 to $50,000 for site
specific wall reliefs, columns

STEVEN & SUSAN KEMENYFFY
4570 OLD STATE RD
MCKEAN, PA 16426-2239
TEL 814-734-4421
FAX 814-734-4421
Established: 1967
Products: tiles, murals, wall reliefs
Media: raku
Techniques: constructed
Finishes: raku fired
Installation: interior, permanent, site
specific
Size Range: 32" × 36" to 11' × 12'
Price Range: $1,500 to $7,500 for wall
reliefs, sculpture

DOUGLAS KENNEY
DOUGLAS KENNEY CERAMICS
102 W NORWOOD CT
SAN ANTONIO, TX 78212
TEL 210-822-7917
Established: 1989
Products: tiles, platters, wall reliefs
Media: stoneware, porcelain, earthen-
ware
Techniques: constructed, molded, wheel
thrown
Finishes: glazed, unglazed
Installation: interior, movable, site specific
Size Range: 20" × 20" to 42" × 42"
Price Range: $40 to $100/sq. ft.
Price Range: $480 to $1,400 for platters
23" to 34"Dia

STEPHEN KNAPP
74 COMMODORE RD
WORCESTER, MA 01602-2727
TEL 508-757-2507
FAX 508-797-3228
Established: 1972
Products: mosaics, murals
Media: porcelain, glass
Techniques: constructed
Finishes: glazed
Installation: interior, exterior, permanent,
site specific
Size Range: 4' × 6' to 9' × 62'
Price Range: $100 to $500/sq. ft.

KAREN KOBLITZ
2919 TILDEN AVE
LOS ANGELES, CA 90064
TEL 310-477-1937
FAX 310-477-1160
Established: 1976
Products: tiles, columns, wall reliefs
Media: earthenware
Techniques: cast, molded, wheel thrown
Finishes: glazed, unglazed
Installation: interior, exterior, permanent,
movable, site specific
Size Range: 9" × 9" to 5' × 5'
Price Range: $150 to $250/sq. ft.
Price Range: $1,900 to $20,000 for wall
reliefs

KRYSIA
KRYSIA STRONSKI
1360 LUCERNE
MONTREAL, PB H3R 2H9
CANADA
TEL 514-731-0234
Established: 1985
Products: panels or screens, murals, wall
reliefs
Media: stoneware, earthenware, paper
clay
Techniques: cast, constructed
Finishes: glazed, terra sigillata
Installation: interior, permanent, movable,
site specific
Size Range: 2' × 1' to 8' × 12"
Price Range: $30 to $100/sq. ft.
Price Range: $150 to $1,500 for panel

PETER LADOCHY
COMPANY OF ANGELS
17 OCEAN FRONT AVE
CAYUCOS, CA 93430-1642
TEL 805-995-3579
Established: 1977
Products: mosaics, murals, wall reliefs
Media: earthenware, glass
Techniques: constructed
Finishes: inlaid colored clays
Installation: interior, exterior, permanent
Size Range: 2' × 3' to 26' × 46'
Price Range: $60 to $600 for murals/
sq. ft.

LALUZ CANYON STUDIO TILES
JERRY WELLMAN
NINA MASTRANGELO
PO 10627
ALAMEDA, MN 87184
TEL 505-899-9977
FAX 505-898-8819
Established: 1982
Products: tiles, murals
Media: porcelain
Techniques: handpainted, glazed
Finishes: glazed
Installation: interior, permanent, site
specific
Size Range: 4.25" × 4.25" to 120" × 120"
Price Range: $30 to $270/sq. ft.
Price Range: $3.50 to $30 for individual
tiles

LATKA STUDIOS
TOM & JEAN LATKA
229 MIDWAY AVE
PUEBLO, CO 81004-1912
TEL 710-543-0720
Established: 1965
Products: tiles, mosaics, murals, custom
extruded clay
Media: stoneware, earthenware, brick,
bronze
Techniques: constructed, molded, wheel
thrown, extruded molding
Finishes: glazed, unglazed, raku fired
Installation: interior, exterior, permanent,
movable, site specific
Size Range: 1' × 1' to 8' × 8'
Price Range: $100 to $300 for murals/
sq. ft.
Price Range: $100 to $300, for wall
work

PATRICIA LAY
77 GRAND ST
JERSEY CITY, NJ 07302-4521
TEL 201-333-5437
Established: 1968
Products: tiles, murals, wall reliefs
Media: stoneware, earthenware
Techniques: cast, constructed, molded
Finishes: glazed, unglazed, inlaid colored
clays
Installation: interior, exterior, permanent,
movable, site specific
Size Range: 12" × 12" to 12' × 40'
Price Range: $500 to $1,000/sq. ft.

DEIRDRE LEE
URBAN JUNGLE ART AND DESIGN
244 W BROOKES AVE
SAN DIEGO, CA 92103-4810
TEL 619-299-1644
FAX 619-296-1570
Established: 1971
Products: tiles, murals
Media: earthenware
Techniques: constructed, molded
Finishes: glazed, bold colors and designs
Installation: interior, exterior, permanent,
movable, site specific
Size Range: 6" × 18" and up
Price Range: $40 to $75/sq. ft.
Price Range: $100 and up for murals and
borders

★ BEVERLEE LEHR
RT 2 BOX 112
PALMYRA, PA 17078
TEL 7178384937
Established: 1973
Products: panels or screens, wall reliefs,
hollow 3D tiles
Media: stoneware
Techniques: constructed, press molded
Finishes: glazed, multicolored
Installation: interior, exterior, permanent,
movable, site specific
Size Range: 24" × 36" to 60 sq.ft.
Price Range: $300 to $350/sq. ft.
Price Range: $400 and up for murals;
$100 for 11" × 16" platter

**See page 85 for photographs and
additional information.**

THOMAS W. LOLLAR
50 W 106TH ST #2A
NEW YORK, NY 10025-3888
TEL 212-864-7973
Established: 1979
Products: tiles, panels or screens, murals
Media: stoneware, earthenware
Techniques: constructed, slab, bas-relief
Finishes: glazed, unglazed, painted
Installation: interior, exterior, permanent,
movable, site specific
Size Range: 24" × 22" to 10' × 10'
Price Range: $300 to $500/sq. ft.
Price Range: $10,000 to $15,000 for
5' × 12' murals

CERAMIC ART FOR THE WALL

LORART CERAMICS

LORA SUMMERVILLE
RR3 BOX 249
CASEY, IL 62420-9219
TEL 217-923-5594

Established: 1990
Products: wall reliefs, containers, music boxes
Media: stoneware
Techniques: constructed, hand built
Finishes: glazed
Installation: interior, exterior, movable
Size Range: 10" × 8" to 23" × 23"
Price Range: $50 to $300 for wall reliefs, containers, music boxes

JERE LYKINS

UNDERLAND EXPLORATIONS
387 BERRY COLLEGE
MT BERRY, GA 30149-0387
TEL 706-232-5374
FAX 706-236-9004

Established: 1967
Products: wall reliefs
Media: earthenware, raku
Techniques: cast, constructed, wheel thrown
Finishes: glazed, unglazed, raku fired
Installation: interior, movable
Size Range: 16" × 20" to 48" × 96"
Price Range: $750 to $5,000 for wall reliefs

★ ELIZABETH MACDONALD

BOX 186
BRIDGEWATER, CT 06752
TEL 203-354-0594

Established: 1972
Products: tiles, murals, columns
Media: stoneware
Techniques: constructed
Finishes: powdered pigment
Installation: interior, exterior, permanent, movable, site specific
Size Range: 6" × 6" to 16' × 16'
Price Range: $200 to $300/sq. ft.
Price Range: $150 to $100,000 for wall constuctions

See below and page 86 for photographs and additional information.

THOMAS MALTBIE

CHRISTIAN ART WORKS
PO BOX 21
DILLSBORO, IN 47018
TEL 812-432-3126

Established: 1980
Products: panels or screens, platters, scriptural themes
Media: earthenware, wood, paper
Techniques: constructed, wheel thrown
Finishes: unglazed, raku fired
Installation: interior, permanent, movable, site specific
Size Range: 18" × 18" to 3' × 21'
Price Range: $50 to $100/sq. ft.
Price Range: $450 to $600 for 18" platters, 6 sq. ft. panels

MAUREEN R. WEISS

PO BOX 8615
RANCHO SANTA FE, CA 92067-8615
TEL 619-756-1460

Established: 1991
Products: tiles, wall reliefs, towers
Media: ceramic/metals
Techniques: constructed, molded, carved
Finishes: glazed, metal/wood mounted
Installation: interior, exterior, permanent, movable, site specific
Size Range: 3" × 1" to 6' × 6'
Price Range: $25 to $5,000 for towers, wall or floor sculptures

DONNA MCGEE

47 EAST ST
HADLEY, MA 01035
TEL 413-584-0508

Established: 1978
Products: tiles, murals, platters
Media: earthenware
Techniques: constructed
Finishes: glazed
Installation: interior, exterior, permanent, movable, site specific
Size Range: 19" × 12" to unlimited
Price Range: $85 and up for plaques, platters, murals

CHRISTINE MERRIMAN

MERRYWOMAN STUDIOS
PO BOX 18
BRIDGEWATER, VT 05034
TEL 802-672-5141

Established: 1970
Products: tiles, panels or screens, murals, fireplace screens
Media: raku talc-ware
Techniques: constructed, molded, arc welded metal frames
Finishes: salt or sodium fired, wood fired, raku fired
Installation: interior, exterior, permanent, movable, site specific
Size Range: 12" × 12" to 8' × 10'
Price Range: $75 to $300/sq. ft.
Price Range: $185 to $675 for framed tiles

BRENDA MINISA

STUDIO DEL PINETO
PANTRY RD BOX 85
N HATFIELD, MA 01066
TEL 413-247-5262

Established: 1961
Products: panels, murals, wall reliefs
Media: stoneware, porcelain, earthenware, cold-cast porcelain
Techniques: cast, constructed, molded
Finishes: glazed, unglazed, acrylic patinas
Installation: interior, exterior, permanent, movable, site specific
Size Range: no limits
Price Range: $150 to $500/sq. ft.
Price Range: $350 and up for panels, etc.

Elizabeth MacDonald, *Landscape*, 1994, clay, commissioned by Sinauer Associates, Sunderland, MA, 6½' × 9'

MONTANA ART WORKS

MARTIN HOLT
567 3 ST
HELENA, MT 59601-5364
TEL 406-442-6331
FAX 406-444-7536

Established: 1968
Products: tiles, platters, wall reliefs
Media: porcelain, earthenware, brick
Techniques: constructed, wheel thrown
Finishes: glazed, unglazed, inlaid colored clays
Installation: interior, exterior, permanent, movable, site specific
Size Range: 14" × 14" to 4' × 6'
Price Range: $800 to $1,500 for platters

JUDY MOONELIS

JUDY MOONELIS STUDIO
63 ORCHARD ST FL 5
NEW YORK, NY 10002
TEL 212-925-7667

Established: 1980
Products: wall installations
Media: ceramic, mixed media
Techniques: constructed hand formed
Finishes: unglazed, terra sigilatta
Installation: interior, permanent, movable, site specific
Size Range: 4" × 3" to 12' × 20'
Price Range: $2,500 to $25,000 for wall installations

JUAN & PATRICIA NAVARRETE

NAVARRETE STUDIO
PO BOX 2251
TAOS, NM 87571
TEL 505-776-2942

Established: 1980
Products: murals, wall reliefs
Media: plaster
Techniques: cast, constructed, created on site
Finishes: textural to smooth
Installation: interior, exterior, permanent, site specific
Size Range: 6' × 9' to 10' × 76'
Price Range: $60 to $175/sq. ft.

PATRICIA NAYLOR

PO BOX 2701
SANTA FE, NM 87504
TEL 505-473-9414

Established: 1981
Products: wall reliefs, modular collage
Media: earthenware, copper
Techniques: constructed
Finishes: painted, smoke fired
Installation: interior, movable, site specific
Size Range: 12" × 12" to unlimited
Price Range: $200 to $400/sq. ft.

★ LAUREL NEFF

PO BOX 3341
MADISON, WI 53704
TEL 608-255-0056

Established: 1991
Products: mosaics
Media: glass, mirror, tile, mixed media
Techniques: constructed
Installation: interior, exterior, permanent, movable, site specific
Size Range: 12" × 12" to 12' × 12' or larger
Price Range: $10 to $50/sq. ft. for permanent mosaics
Price Range: $50 to $1,000 for portable mosaics

See photograph below.

LEON NIGROSH

LEON NIGROSH/CERAMIC DESIGNER
11 CHATANIKA AVE
WORCESTER, MA 01602-1109
TEL 508-757-0401

Established: 1963
Products: murals, custom designs
Media: stoneware, porcelain, earthenware
Techniques: constructed, molded, hand built
Finishes: glazed, unglazed, luster glaze
Installation: interior, exterior, permanent, movable, site specific
Size Range: 4" × 6" to 5' × 20'
Price Range: $100 to $300/sq. ft.

SUSAN NOWOGRODZKI

RD1 BOX 46 ELLIOT RD
E GREENBUSH, NY 12061
TEL 518-477-7780

Established: 1974
Products: tiles, murals
Media: stoneware, porcelain, earthenware
Techniques: constructed
Finishes: glazed, unglazed, raku fired
Installation: interior, exterior, permanent, movable, site specific
Size Range: 8" × 12" to 4' × 6'
Price Range: $125 to $2,500 per piece for tile mural

ONE OFF STUDIO

CAROL SMERALDO
SITELL COMP 27, SS#2
EAST PRESTON, NS B2W 3Y5
CANADA
TEL 902-434-1336
FAX 902-434-1336

Established: 1972
Products: murals, platters, wall reliefs
Media: stoneware, porcelain
Techniques: constructed, molded, wheel thrown
Finishes: glazed, unglazed, inlaid colored clays
Installation: interior, movable
Size Range: 12" × 30" to 5' × 10'
Price Range: $150 to $6,000 for platters, murals, wall reliefs

ALENA ORT

ALENA ORT CERAMICS
4 WASHINGTON SQ VILLAGE #15M
NEW YORK, NY 10012-1936
TEL 212-254-6123

Established: 1982
Products: tiles, lighted panels, platters, wall reliefs
Media: stoneware, neon, stone
Techniques: hand built
Finishes: glazed, unglazed, low fire, textured
Installation: interior, exterior, site specific
Size Range: 8" × 10" to 10' × 36'
Price Range: $50 to $200/sq. ft.
Price Range: $50 to $2,000 for platters, tile and neon wall pieces

CAROLYN PAYNE

PAYNE CREATIONS TILE
4829 N ANTIOCH
KANSAS CITY, MO 64119
TEL 816-452-8660
FAX 816-452-0070

Established: 1985
Products: tiles, murals
Media: earthenware
Techniques: molded
Finishes: glazed
Installation: interior, exterior
Size Range: 6" × 6" to 6' × 6'
Price Range: $75 to $250/sq. ft.
Price Range: $8 to $16 for trivets

PEACE VALLEY TILE

64 BEULAH RD
NEW BRITAIN, PA 18901
TEL 215-340-0888
Products: tiles, mosaics, murals
Media: stoneware, earthenware
Techniques: constructed, molded, wheel thrown
Finishes: glazed, unglazed, inlaid colored clays
Installation: interior, exterior, site specific
Size Range: 1" × 1" to unlimited
Price Range: $8 to $50/sq. ft.
Price Range: $100 and up for murals

DONALD C. PENNY

DON'S POTTERY
2005 BAYTREE RD
VALDOSTA, GA 31602-3503
TEL 912-247-0289
FAX 912-244-1443

Established: 1960
Products: tiles, murals, waterfalls with pools
Media: stoneware, porcelain, earthenware
Techniques: constructed, molded, carved
Finishes: glazed, unglazed, inlaid colored clays
Installation: interior, exterior, permanent, movable, site specific, waterfalls with pools
Size Range: 4" × 4" to 68" × 212"
Price Range: $65 to $100/sq. ft.

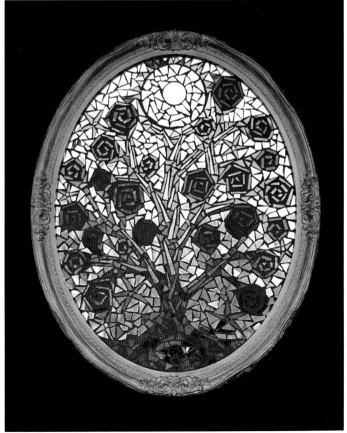

Laurel Neff, *Sarah's Rosebush*, 1995, colored mirror, iridized glass mosaic with rose-colored grout on found frame, 30" × 24"

CERAMIC ART FOR THE WALL

GAIL PIEPENBURG
24723 WESTMORELAND DR
FARMINGTON HILLS, MI 48336-1963
TEL 810-478-5720
Established: 1987
Products: platters, wall reliefs
Media: earthenware
Techniques: constructed, molded
Finishes: glazed, unglazed, raku fired
Installation: interior, movable, sectional pieces
Size Range: 16" × 12" and up
Price Range: $150 to $6,000 for wall reliefs and platters

KRISTIN & STEPHEN POWERS
TRIKEENAN TILEWORKS
9 FOREST RD
HANCOCK, NH 03449-6111
TEL 603-525-4245
FAX 603-525-4245
Established: 1986
Products: tiles, mosaics, murals
Media: stoneware, earthenware
Techniques: cast, constructed, molded
Finishes: glazed, unglazed
Installation: interior, exterior, permanent, movable, site specific
Size Range: 2" × 2" to 15' × 25'
Price Range: $75 to $500/sq. ft.
Price Range: $10 to $400 for single handcarved tiles

POWNING DESIGNS LTD.
PETER W. POWNING
R.R. #5
SUSSEX, NB
CANANDA
TEL 506-433-1188
FAX 506-433-6979
Established: 1972
Products: tiles, murals, fireplace surrounds
Media: glass, raku
Techniques: constructed, molded, wheel thrown
Finishes: glazed, raku fired, inlaid colored clays
Installation: interior, permanent, site specific
Size Range: 18" × 24" to 10' × 20'
Price Range: $150 to $250/sq. ft.

JUD RANDALL
IMPRESSIONS IN CLAY
8705 GARDNER RD #14
TAMPA, FL 33625-3714
TEL 813-920-2410
Established: 1981
Products: tiles, fountains
Media: stoneware, earthenware, raku
Techniques: constructed, molded, wheel thrown
Finishes: glazed, unglazed, raku fired
Installation: interior, exterior, permanent, movable, site specific
Size Range: 2" × 1" to 10' × 5'
Price Range: $15 to $40/sq. ft.
Price Range: $500 to $20,000 for fountains/relief

PAULA RICE
SCULPTURE AND WALL RELIEFS
3210 W MOUNTAIN DR
FLAGSTAFF, AZ 86001-1054
TEL 602-774-4044
Established: 1965
Products: murals, wall reliefs
Media: stoneware, porcelain, earthenware
Techniques: constructed
Finishes: glazed, unglazed, raku fired
Installation: interior, permanent, movable, site specific
Size Range: 18" × 18" to 6' × 20'
Price Range: $100 to $200/sq. ft.
Price Range: $1,600 to $2,000 for wall reliefs

★ WILLIAM C. RICHARDS
CLAY CANVAS DESIGNS
PO BOX 361
UNDERWOOD, WA 98651
TEL 509-493-3928
FAX 509-493-2732
Established: 1980
Products: platters, wall reliefs
Media: stoneware
Techniques: constructed, wheel thrown
Finishes: stains
Installation: interior, movable, site specific, custom available
Size Range: 11" × 11" to 3' × 6'
Price Range: $130 to $3,000 for plates and panels
See pages 87 and 155 for photographs and additional information.

JOHN WINSTON ROGERS
JOHN ROGERS DESIGNS
14928 NW MILL RD
PORTLAND, OR 97231
TEL 503-239-4181
FAX 503-239-4181
Established: 1972
Products: murals, columns, wall reliefs
Media: stoneware, porcelain, glass
Techniques: cast, constructed, molded
Finishes: glazed, unglazed
Installation: interior, exterior, permanent, movable, site specific
Size Range: 48" × 48" to 12' × 60'
Price Range: $20 to $250/sq. ft.

LOIS S. SATTLER
LOIS SATTLER CERAMICS
3620 PACIFIC AVE
VENICE, CA 90292-5724
TEL 310-821-7055
Established: 1974
Products: platters, wall reliefs
Media: stoneware, porcelain, metal
Techniques: constructed
Finishes: glazed, unglazed
Installation: interior, exterior, movable
Size Range: 14" × 16" to 4' × 6'
Price Range: $220 to $2,000 for platters, wall pieces

LOREN SCHERBAK
5718 WAINWRIGHT AVE
ROCKVILLE, MD 20851
TEL 301-468-0159
Established: 1985
Products: tiles, platters, wall reliefs
Media: stoneware, earthenware
Techniques: cast, constructed, molded
Finishes: glazed, unglazed, raku fired
Installation: interior, movable
Size Range: 6" × 6" to 16" × 35"
Price Range: $75 for 12" × 12" platters; $300 for triptych wall reliefs

BARBARA SEBASTIAN
BARBARA SEBASTIAN CLAYWORKS
  & MURALS
1777 YOSEMITE AVE #4B1
SAN FRANCISCO, CA 94124
TEL 415-822-3243
Established: 1976
Products: panels or screens, murals, wall reliefs
Media: low fired clay and canvas
Techniques: constructed
Finishes: glazed, unglazed, painted
Installation: interior, exterior, permanent, movable, site specific
Size Range: 12" × 12" to 20' × 100'
Price Range: $75 to $150/sq. ft.
Price Range: $10 to $25 per square foot for painted murals

ERICKA CLARK SHAW
451 EUREKA ST
SAN FRANCISCO, CA 94114-2714
TEL 800-484-9955 × 8271
Established: 1974
Products: wall reliefs
Media: earthenware
Techniques: constructed, molded, airbrushed
Finishes: inlaid colored clays, airbrushed underglazes
Installation: interior, permanent, movable, site specific
Size Range: 12" × 12" to 60' to 40'
Price Range: $180 to $250/sq. ft.

MICHAEL SHEBA
140 EVELYN AVE
TORONTO, ON M6P 2Z7
CANADA
TEL 416-766-9411
Established: 1974
Products: murals, platters, wall reliefs
Media: earthenware, raku
Techniques: constructed, molded, wheel thrown
Finishes: glazed, raku fired, smoked/sawdust fired
Installation: interior, permanent, movable, site specific
Size Range: 14" × 14" to 6' × 10'
Price Range: $150 to $250/sq. ft.
Price Range: $250 to $750 for platters, wall reliefs

J. PAUL SIRES
CENTER OF THE EARTH
3204 N DAVIDSON ST
CHARLOTTE, NC 28205-1034
TEL 704-375-5756
FAX 704-375-5756
Established: 1983
Products: murals, platters, wall reliefs
Media: stoneware, earthenware, brick
Techniques: constructed, molded, carved
Finishes: glazed, unglazed
Installation: interior, exterior, permanent, movable, site specific
Size Range: 19" × 19" to 24' × 24'
Price Range: $25 to $150/sq. ft.
Price Range: $450 for large platters

SKARL CERAMICS
DALE SKARL
1447 MEADOW RD
COLUMBUS, OH 43212-3009
TEL 614-486-8700
Established: 1982
Products: tiles, mosaics, murals
Media: earthenware
Techniques: cast, constructed, molded
Finishes: glazed, unglazed
Installation: interior, permanent
Size Range: 4" × 4" to 10' × 20'
Price Range: $100 to $200/sq. ft.

PAT SMITH
90 GREENE ST
NEW YORK, NY 10012-3855
TEL 212-219-8519
Established: 1975
Products: panels or screens, wall reliefs, assemblages
Media: porcelain, slate, copper, steel
Techniques: cast, constructed
Finishes: unglazed
Installation: interior, exterior, movable, site specific
Size Range: 12" × 12" to 8' × 6'
Price Range: $750 to $9,000 for wall reliefs

MARGARET SORIERO
RT 9 BOX 72-SB
SANTA FE, NM 87505
TEL 505-986-8658
FAX 505-989-7884
Established: 1965
Products: tiles, murals, wall reliefs
Media: stoneware, earthenware
Techniques: cast, constructed, molded
Finishes: glazed
Installation: interior, exterior, permanent, movable
Size Range: 12" × 12" to 4½' × 3½'
Price Range: $100 to $600/sq. ft.
Price Range: $300 to $10,000 for murals

ALAN STEINBERG

BRATTLEBORO CLAYWORKS
RD 5 BOX 250 PUTNEY RD
BRATTLEBORO, VT 05301-9190
TEL 802-254-9174
Established: 1976
Products: murals, platters, wall reliefs
Media: stoneware, porcelain
Techniques: constructed
Finishes: glazed, unglazed, inlaid colored
clays
Installation: interior, exterior, permanent,
movable, site specific
Size Range: 4" × 12" to 48" × 120"
Price Range: $100 to $200/sq. ft.
Price Range: $28 to $5,000 for murals

HARRIET STORY

STORY POTTERY
9 FOUNTAIN ST
MINERAL POINT, WI 53565
TEL 608-987-2903
Established: 1975
Products: tiles, platters wall hangings
Media: stoneware
Techniques: constructed, wheel thrown
Finishes: glazed, unglazed
Installation: interior, permanent, movable,
site specific
Size Range: 18" × 6" to 10' × 14'
Price Range: $50 to $70/sq. ft.
Price Range: $500 to $1,200 for platters,
wall hangings

NATALIE & RICHARD SURVING

SURVING STUDIO
RD4 BOX 449
MIDDLETOWN, NY 10940
TEL 914-355-1430
FAX 914-355-1517
Established: 1971
Products: tiles, murals, wall reliefs
Media: porcelain
Techniques: constructed, molded
Finishes: glazed
Installation: interior, exterior, permanent,
movable
Size Range: 4" × 4" to 6' × 8'
Price Range: $30 for 4" tile sculpture

LAURIE SYLWESTER

RAKU BY L. SYLWESTER
18363 YOSEMITE RD
TUOLUMNE, CA 95379
TEL 209-928-3423
Established: 1971
Products: platters, wall reliefs, raku
vessels
Media: raku
Techniques: constructed, wheel thrown
Finishes: glazed, raku fired
Installation: interior, permanent, movable
Size Range: 6" × 6" to 40" × 64"
Price Range: $100 to $300 for platters;
$1,000 to $4,000 for wall murals

DENISE S. TENNEN

CLAY CONSTRUCTIONS
895 FRONT AVE
ST PAUL, MN 55103
TEL 612-489-4374
FAX 612-489-4374
Established: 1988
Products: wall reliefs
Media: sculpture clay
Techniques: coil and slab built
Finishes: unglazed, oxide washes
Installation: interior, exterior, permanent,
movable, site specific
Size Range: 12" × 12" to 18" × 8'
Price Range: $200 to $750/sq. ft.
Price Range: $500 to $6,000 for wall
sculpture, relief

TERRA DESIGNS

ANNA SALIBELLO
241 E BLACKWELL ST
DOVER, NJ 07801-4140
TEL 201-539-2999
FAX 201-328-3624
Established: 1969
Products: tiles, mosaics, murals
Media: stoneware, porcelain, earthen-
ware
Techniques: constructed, molded,
extruded
Finishes: glazed, unglazed
Installation: interior, exterior, permanent,
restoration mosaics
Size Range: ½" × ½" to 12' × 35'
Price Range: $14 to $500/sq. ft.

NEIL TETKOWSKI

365 W 20 ST #9A
NEW YORK, NY 10011
TEL 212-255-1850
Established: 1987
Products: wall reliefs, disks sculpture
Media: earthenware
Techniques: constructed, wheel thrown
Finishes: glazed, unglazed, salt or sodium
fired
Installation: interior, exterior, permanent,
movable, site specific
Size Range: 18" × 18" to 12' × 24'
Price Range: $150 to $200/sq. ft.
Price Range: $1,000 to $6,000 for disks

★ AMA TORRANCE

PLEUR AIR STUDIOS
143 TUNNEL RD
BERKELEY, CA 94705
TEL 510-644-0727
FAX 510-704-9784
Established: 1988
Products: wall reliefs, figures
Media: stoneware, porcelain
Techniques: constructed
Finishes: glazed
Installation: interior, exterior, permanent,
movable, site specific
Size Range: 13" × 14" to 78" × 38"
Price Range: $300 to $500/sq. ft.
Price Range: $500 to $2,500 for a partial
or whole figure

See photograph this page.

KATHERYN M. TRENSHAW

PO BOX 51132
KALAMAZOO, MI 49005
TEL 616-385-2649
Established: 1982
Products: wall reliefs, masks
Media: stoneware
Techniques: sculpted
Finishes: unglazed, raku fired
Installation: interior, exterior, permanent,
movable
Size Range: 10" × 10" to 6' × 20'
Price Range: $500 to $2,000 for wall
sculptures

SUSAN TUNICK

771 WEST END AVE #10E
NEW YORK, NY 10025
TEL 212-962-1750
TEL 212-962-1864
Established: 1968
Products: mosaics, murals, wall reliefs
Media: stoneware, porcelain, earthen-
ware
Techniques: constructed, ceramic mosaic
Finishes: glazed, mosaic shards
Installation: interior, exterior, permanent,
movable, site specific
Size Range: 7" × 7" to 16'L × 1'W
Price Range: $600 to $18,000 for murals,
wall reliefs

GAYLE L. TUSTIN

3842 EDGEWOOD RD
WILMINGTON, NC 28403
TEL 910-392-4408
Established: 1982
Products: tiles, murals, wall reliefs
Media: stoneware, earthenware, brick
Techniques: cast, constructed, molded
Finishes: glazed, unglazed, luster, photo
transfer
Installation: interior, exterior, permanent,
movable, site specific
Size Range: 1" × 1" to 22' × 13'
Price Range: $100 to $400/sq. ft.
Price Range: $400 to $3,000 for original
wall relief panels

VACCARO STUDIO

LOUIS VACCARO
531 SPRINGTOWN RD
NEW PALTZ, NY 12561-3028
TEL 914-658-9859
Products: wall reliefs
Media: earthenware
Techniques: constructed
Finishes: unglazed
Installation: interior, site specific
Size Range: 2' × 2' to 4' × 5'
Price Range: $800 to $2,000 for wall
reliefs

Ama Torrance, *David*, 1992, glazed ceramic, 38" × 15" × 8", photo: Lee Fatherree

CERAMIC ART FOR THE WALL

JOAN WEISSMAN

3710 SILVER SE
ALBUQUERQUE, NM 87108
TEL 505-265-0144
FAX 505-268-9665
Established: 1970
Products: tiles, murals, platters
Media: stoneware, porcelain, earthenware
Techniques: constructed
Finishes: glazed, inlaid colored clays, relief and carved
Installation: interior, exterior, permanent, site specific
Size Range: 15" x 15" to 10' x 40'
Price Range: $100 to $150/sq. ft.
Price Range: $300 to $500 for sconces, platters

PAULA WINOKUR

WINOKUR POTTERY
435 NORRISTOWN RD
HORSHAM, PA 19044
TEL 215-675-7708
Established: 1966
Products: wall reliefs, fireplace surrounds
Media: porcelain
Techniques: constructed
Finishes: unglazed
Installation: interior, exterior, permanent, movable, site specific
Size Range: 8" x 12" to 36" x 120"
Price Range: $800 to $15,000 for small wall piece, large fireplace

NINA YANKOWITZ

106 SPRING ST
NEW YORK, NY 10012
TEL 212-226-4375
FAX 212-343-1877
Established: 1969
Products: tiles, murals, columns, mosaic, ceramic reliefs
Techniques: cast
Finishes: glazed
Installation: interior, exterior, permanent, site specific
Size Range: 2' x 12' to 2,000 sq. ft.
Price Range: $25 to $200/sq. ft.

DALE ZHEUTLIN

55 WEBSTER AVE
NEW ROCHELLE, NY 10801
TEL 914-576-0082
FAX 914-738-8373
Products: tiles, murals, wall reliefs
Media: porcelain
Techniques: constructed
Finishes: glazed
Installation: interior, exterior, permanent, movable, site specific
Size Range: 13" x 13" to 20' x 20'
Price Range: $250 to $350/sq. ft.

A. JEFFREY ZIGULIS

2259 SCHAEFFER RD
SEBASTOPOL, CA 95472-5500
TEL 707-829-5636
FAX 707-823-2137
Established: 1976
Products: tiles, platters, wall reliefs, masks
Media: stoneware, porcelain
Techniques: constructed, molded
Finishes: unglazed, salt or sodium fired, raku fired
Installation: interior, exterior, permanent, movable
Size Range: 6" x 6" to unlimited
Price Range: $60 to $100/sq. ft.
Price Range: $100 to $1,000 for tiles, platters

ARNOLD ZIMMERMAN

76 AINSLIE ST
BROOKLYN, NY 11211
TEL 718-388-4914
FAX 212-242-3703
Established: 1979
Products: tiles, murals, platters
Media: stoneware, porcelain, earthenware
Techniques: cast, constructed, molded
Finishes: glazed, unglazed
Installation: interior, exterior, permanent, movable, site specific
Size Range: 4½" x 4½" to 120" x 240"
Price Range: $100 to $150/sq. ft.
Price Range: $500 to $2,500 for platters, tiles, murals

◆

For more ceramic art for the wall, see the Architectural Ceramics, Mosaics and Wall Reliefs section of *The Sourcebook of Artists: Architect's Edition.*

Call 1-800-969-1556 for order information.

George Alexander

Handsel Gallery
306 Camino Del Monte Sol
Santa Fe, NM 87501
TEL 800-821-1261
TEL 505-988-4030

George Alexander's ceramics are unique artistic expressions rooted in the tradition of Italian majolica. Richly glazed and exuberantly decorated with fruits, vegetables, flowers and foliage, Alexander's vases, bowls, mirrors and architectural elements are imbued with intrigue and whimsy. Crafted in a cone 5 stoneware, they belie their implied fragility. It is his stunning contrasts of forms, colors and textures which delight the senses.

George Alexander is uniquely adept in translating the constraints of specifications into highly original work. Commissions are welcome, and additional information is available upon request.

Also see these GUILD publications:
Designer's Edition: 8, 9

A installation, 1994, 76"H x 106"W x 7"D

B *Sunflower and Poppy Mirror*, 1994,
54"H x 33"W x 4"D

C *Tapestry Series: Poppies*, 1994, 52"H x 38"W x 7"D

A

B

C

Art on Tiles

Rita Paul
32 Washington Square West
New York, NY 10011
FAX 212-979-8373
TEL 212-674-6388

Rita Paul creates sensuous paintings on tile. Her solid experience working with large-scale figural paintings, both in watercolor and oil, has given her the technical mastery with which to transmute any great painting onto tile. She has equal facility with abstract, contemporary or realistic subjects. Fitting the subject to the space involved is a challenge she prefers to resolve by working closely with the architect or designer on a conceptual level.

A bathroom, 32 Washington Square West, NY, 42"H x 77"W

B elevator landing, Washington Square Hotel, NY, 60"H x 36"W

C C3 Restaurant, Washington Square Hotel, NY, based on Klimt, 43"H x 122"W

A

B

C

George F. Fishman

103 NE 99th Street
Miami Shores, FL 33138
FAX 305-751-1770
TEL 305-758-1141

George Fishman's mosaics combine glass, porcelain and glazed tiles. Pictorial and abstract images can be incorporated into walls, floors or fountain design. Classical or contemporary style to suit project needs.

Swimmer and *Passion Vine* floor medallions are shown premounted for shipment. *Deco Rugs* were inserted into travertine floor.

Artist collaborates with designers on concept and theme development. Meticulous attention is given to details of expediting any scale project through installation.

Durable, easily maintained materials are especially suited for exterior and high-traffic settings.

J. Louis Heithmar

Intaglia
484 West 43 Street, Apt. #25Q
New York, NY 10036
TEL 212-268-0012

Intaglia…beautiful, sensuous lines, inlaid in ceramic tile, rendered like Matisse or Erté. This clearly describes the vision and old-world-craftsmanship of J. Louis Heithmar. His style, developed over 15 years, runs classical to contemporary. Imagine any subject, original designs or interpretations of paintings or photos, custom cut in any size tile. Mr. Heithmar's tile works have been installed on floors, walls and ceilings, and may be framed as breathtaking art. They require no special care and last a lifetime. These personalized works have been commissioned by collectors, architects, interior designers and home owners.

Recent commissions in New York City include corporate logos and murals for restaurants, cafes and malls: *White Saxaphone*, 4' x 12' and *Keyboard*, 1' x 25', inlaid in a black floor of Rudy's Blues Bar, 9th Avenue and 44th Street; *Woman Diving into a Cup of Cappuccino*, 3' x 6', entrance wall of Soho Cafe, Broome Street and West Broadway; *Three Fish* (logo), 3' x 5', foyer of Mika Bistro, 349 West Broadway; *Sixteen Angels*, surrounding two sides of building of mini-mall at 179 Grand Street; *RMI Logo*, 8' x 8' foyer floor at Spring and Hudson.

Beverlee Lehr

Route 2, Box 112
Palmyra, PA 17078
FAX 717-838-6428
TEL 717-838-4937

Beverlee Lehr produces sculptural paintings in glazed stoneware for specific public, corporate and residential sites. Hand-building with clay slabs, she draws inspiration from landscapes, plants, and human anatomy for her abstract, three-dimensional constructions.

Deep sculptural relief is created by the hollow construction of each modular section. The durable and easily maintained glazed surfaces are available in a broad range of colors and are suitable for both interior and exterior applications. The modules are easily shipped via UPS. On-site installation on the plywood backplate supplied with each work is a simple follow-the-numbers procedure.

Ms. Lehr's sculptures have been exhibited in major shows nationally and internationally and are represented in both civic and corporate collections. Her work was recently acquired for the ceramic art collection of Monarch Tile. Commissions are welcome. Further information is available upon request

Also see this GUILD publication:
Designer's Edition: 9

A *Fields* (glaze detail)

B *Fields* (sculptural detail)

C *Fields*, 1994, handbuilt stoneware, 48" x 27" x 3"

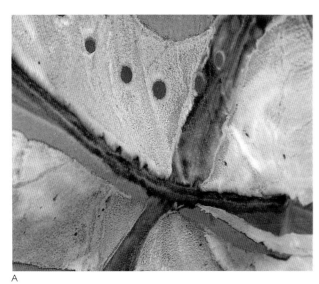

A

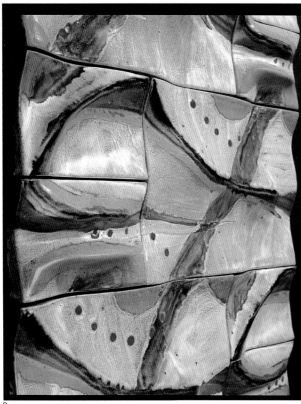

B

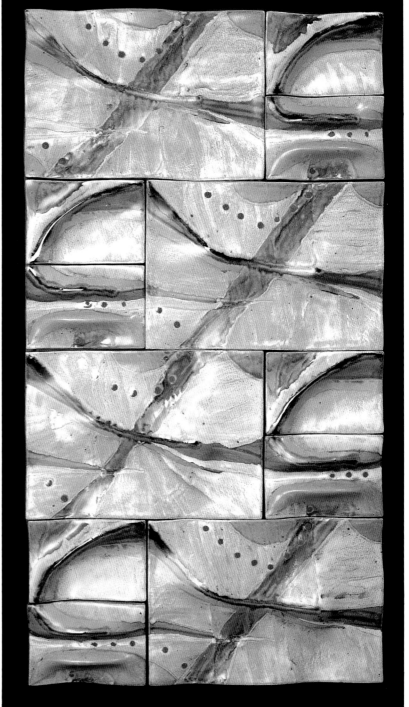

C

Photos: Carl Socolow

Elizabeth MacDonald

Box 186
Bridgewater, CT 06752
FAX 203-350-4052
TEL 203-354-0594

Elizabeth MacDonald produces tile paintings by layering color onto thin, textured stoneware, achieving a surface that combines the subtlety of nature with the formality of a grid. Compositions, including free-standing columns, wall panels, and architectural installations, may be large- or small-scale and are suitable for interior and exterior settings. Tiles are light weight and durable, and require little maintenance. Imagery can vary from formal patterning to reflections of the sky and land.

Recent commissions include Nobu Restaurant, New York, NY; University of Maryland Medical Center, Baltimore, MD; Northwest Asset Management, Walnut Creek, CA; Norelco and U.S. Trust, Stamford, CT.

Also see these GUILD publications:
THE GUILD: 1, 2, 3, 4, 5
The Designer's Edition: 6, 8, 9
Architect's Edition: 6, 7, 8, 9, 10

SHOWN: Landscape, 1994, clay, commissioned by Sinauer Associates, Sunderland, MA, 6½' x 9'

Photos: Chris Small

Printed in Hong Kong ©1995 THE GUILD: Designer's Edition

William C. Richards

Clay Canvas Designs
P.O. Box 361
Underwood, WA 98651
(509) 493-3928
FAX (509) 493-2732

Will Richards received his BFA in ceramics and glass from the University of Minnesota in 1978, and an MFA from the University of Washington in 1981.

His ceramic work can be found in numerous corporate collections, as well as residential environments (see Accessories: Lighting). His stoneware plates and panels are unique creations, combining textural surfaces and dimensional materials. The surfaces are colored with multiple layers of stain and sealed for longevity. Each plate and panel piece is wired for wall mount.

He welcomes commissions and custom orders. Plates are sized 11" to 45" diameter; panels are 6' x 3' overall. Professional profile and detailed information available.

Top: ceramic plates, 25" diameter
Bottom: ceramic panels, 6' x 3' overall

ELIZABETH MACDONALD
ceramics

When asked to talk about a favorite commission, ceramist Elizabeth MacDonald throws up her hands. "I can't single out just one," she says. "Each project is such a different experience and together they combine to build up a wonderful kind of technical repertoire."

Still, Elizabeth does mention one residential project as being particularly fulfilling. In this case, she created an 18-foot tile fireplace surround beside an indoor swimming pool. The satisfaction, she believes, came from the unique combination of people and elements. "Everyone was so enthusiastic; I felt like part of a cooperative, collaborative adventure. And it was artistically satisfying, too, with elements of sculpture and painting within an architectural framework."

While private commissions are often exciting for artistic reasons, Elizabeth says, public projects can be thrilling because they're so visible. "My largest public project was 700 square feet of tile on the exterior of a building in Hartford. The architects allowed me the freedom of choice in color and imagery. It was a real pleasure to do that project—and now it's there for all the world to see!"

Photo: Eric Luden

Elizabeth has also derived tremendous pleasure from the many commissions she's done for hospitals. "In fact, I got a letter recently from someone who was visiting a sick relative late at night. You know how tired and awful you can feel in a hospital—even as a visitor. This person said she suddenly saw a piece of mine and was lifted by that experience. How satisfying it was to hear that!"

See these GUILD publications:
THE GUILD: 1, 2, 3, 4, 5
Architect's Edition: 6, 7, 8, 9, 10
Designer's Edition: 6, 8, 9, 10

Shawn Athari

Shawn Athari's, Inc.
14332 Mulholland Drive
Los Angeles, CA 90077
FAX 818-787-MASK
TEL 310-476-0066

Shawn Athari's 20 years of experience has given her the opportunity to perfect a variety of glass techniques. The combination of these techniques results in glass sculptures unique in her field. Athari has created a chronology of work depicting an ever-changing evolution of both her skills and techniques. Shawn uses hot-glass methods of reforming glass, then layers the individual pieces, melts them together and shapes them. Most pieces are inspired by images from history.

Galleries include:
The Art of Disney, Walt Disney World, FL
Little Switzerland, AK and Caribbean
Symmetry, Saratoga Springs, NY
Mindscape, Evanston, IL

Also see these GUILD publications:
THE GUILD: 5
Designer's Edition: 6, 7, 8, 9
Gallery Edition: 1

A *Bedu, Africa,* 15" x 33" x 5"

B *Puppy Love,* contemporary, 24" x 39" x 2"

A

B

Photos: Robert Baumbach

Stephen Brathwaite

R.R. #1
Pakenham, ON K0A 2X0
Canada
FAX 613-256-4816
TEL 613-256-4816

Commissioned portraits, panels or furniture. Brathwaite's work is owned by every level of government and represented Canada at Expo '92.

"(Brathwaite) works at the intersection point of art, design, and architecture while handling the demands of each with equal charm ... a quality all too rare in today's art ....

"Though sophisticated in concept and design, their charm, honesty and even humor give his pieces an immediacy and accessibility....

"(The portraits) and his mixture of materials always have a degree of magic in them, almost a kind of artistic alchemy.

"We definitely need more magic like this in our lives."

—Donald Brackett, Art Critic CJRC, CBC
Azure Magazine

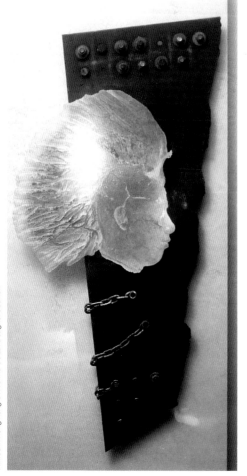

Dale R. Eggert

Eggert Glass
1918 East Beverly Road
Shorewood, WI 53211
TEL 414-962-0808

Glass and metal combine in dramatic wall sculptures for residential and business interiors.

By sandblast etching and painting on half-inch or thicker plate-glass panels mounted in simple and elegant wrought iron frameworks, Dale Eggert creates distinctive contemporary sculpture. His work has been exhibited in galleries and juried exhibitions in both the United States and Japan.

These one-of-a-kind pieces are also available in floor-standing and tabletop designs. Delivery in 30 to 90 days for custom commissions.

Also see these GUILD publications:
Designer's Edition: 7, 8

A wall sculpture, 24"Dia

B wall sculpture, 31"L x 28"W

A

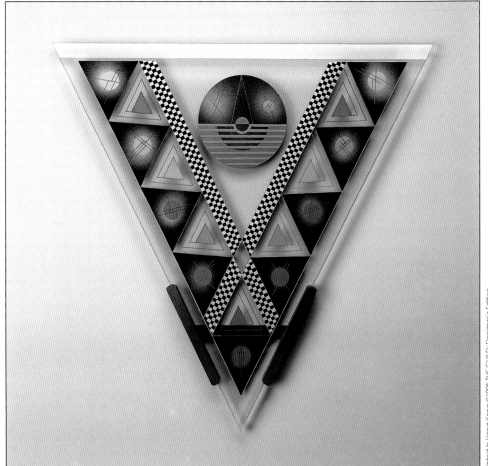

B

Printed in Hong Kong ©1995 THE GUILD: Designer's Edition

Photos: William Lemke

Toby Mason

Reflective Glass Mosaics
911 Country Club Drive NE
Vienna, VA 22180-3621
FAX 703-242-1231
TEL 703-242-2223

Toby Mason started making colored mirror mosaics in 1972. The process he developed now yields highly reflective works that are unique and architecturally versatile. Mirror mosaics do not require back-lit openings, making them suitable for any wall. They are durable and smooth and can be used where traditional art glass cannot.

Mirror mosaics change their appearance according to the light in the foreground, the surroundings, and the position of the observer. They are luminescent in dim light and will brighten dark spaces by reflecting ambient light brilliantly, or subtly, depending on the hue, value and texture of the glass.

Mr. Mason's work is in the homes of royalty.

Early collaboration is encouraged.

Also see this GUILD publication:
Architect's Edition: 10

A *Before the Wind*, 17" x 28"

B *Triumph of Light*, 35" x 29"

SHAWN ATHARI
glass

Glass artist Shawn Athari sees her art as a matter of interpretation forming a bridge from one world to another.

A recent commission by a gallery in Alaska led her to interpret a variety of traditional Northwest images in a non-traditional medium. "I'm inspired by historical artifacts," Athari says, "in this case, the tools and images of the Aleutian and Pacific Northwest Indian traditions ."

Photo: Robert Baumbach

Athari works by fusing glass, layer on layer, color on color, to achieve a design or a figure. "I love working with hot glass," she says, "because it moves and you don't know just how it's going to turn out."

Another recent commission illustrates how Athari bridges worlds—in this case the world of fantasy characters with the world of fine art. Designers at the Walt Disney company had been watching her work through THE GUILD for some time, and asked her to create several pieces for a one-of-a-kind gallery at Disney World's Village Marketplace. Athari browsed through the Disney archives in Burbank and selected several images she might work from. Ultimately she created bowls and stand-up figures representing Minnie, Mickey, Donald and Pluto.

The challenge, says Athari, was to take these familiar characters and interpret them in new ways that would add dimension to the buyer's appreciation. But that wasn't the only challenge. "I had to please not only myself," she says, "but the art department, the legal department, the copyright department, and a series of other people in the various chains of command. In that way, this was a very challenging job—but I'm thrilled with the results."

See these GUILD publications:
THE GUILD: 4, 5
Designer's Edition: 6, 7, 8, 9, 10
Gallery Edition: 1

93

Carolyn Blakeslee

Tangier Sound Studios
PO Box 320-G
Upper Fairmount, MD 21867
FAX 410-651-5313
TEL 410-651-9150

Carolyn Blakeslee works realistically in oils. Her smooth luminous paintings are Pro-Life in nature. "My passion is to celebrate the preciousness, the beauty, the ineffable *is*ness of life, like the silence of new-fallen snow, in my paintings of water, roses, and other growing and fluid things. In expressing these things, I play with composition. I want drama, force, and interest—I want each silent subject to tell a huge dynamic, nearly abstract story."

Commissions are welcome; some existing works may be available. All work documented and guaranteed. The artist offers a trade-up option. Further information upon request.

A   *Newborn*, 1994, oil on canvas, 30" x 19"

B   *Quadruplets*, 1994, oil on canvas, 30" x 36"

C   *Emerging*, 1994, oil on canvas, 12" x 16"

D   *Celebrate Life: Safe and Warm*, 1994, oil on canvas, 30" x 22"

A

B

C

D

Ted Box
Jeff Entner

Ocean Art
PO Box 1764
Edgartown, MA 02539
TEL 508-696-6126

The wall hangings of Ted Box are composed of driftwood objects collected from the beaches of Martha's Vineyard.

The scale, proportion and texture of these pieces capture the harmony of the sea, sun, wind and sand.

In private or corporate collections, these sculptures—ranging in height from 3 to 20 feet, and in price from $1,000 to $15,000 and up—produce a visual and experiencial pleasure that is akin to a day at the shore.

The subtle color artistry of Entner enhances these pieces with color and natural light as soothing and powerful as the sea itself.

Printed in Hong Kong ©1995 THE GUILD: Designer's Edition

Photos: Bob Schellhammer

Barbara Brotherton

Barbro Designs
56 Canyon Road
Fairfax, CA 94930
FAX 415-485-0242
TEL 415-485-0242

Barbara Brotherton's unique wall sculptures are inspired by crusty, faded and peeling wall, door and ancient building surfaces seen in her travels to Italy, Cypress, Turkey, Egypt, China and Japan.

She combines materials such as distressed wood, earthy pigments, gold, silver, copper leaf, cast stone, and patinas to create contemporary wall pieces that reflect her deep appreciation of Middle Eastern and Far Eastern culture, design and architecture.

Her exhibits are widely represented in private and corporate collections.

Slides, price lists and color samples available. Site-specific commissions welcomed.

Allende Flying Wall, 21" x 42" x 1"

The Tao of Dow, 48" x 36" x 1"

Myra Burg

2913 3rd Street #201
Santa Monica, CA 90405
FAX 310-399-0623
TEL 310-399-5040

Myra Burg blends her 20-year weaving and tapestry-making background with architecture, producing pieces limitless in color and boundless in size, due to simple expressed installation systems.

Natural fibers, rare hardwoods, and metals create obelisk, aerial, free-standing, door-panel, wall-mounted, gates, exterior, never-been-done-before, and other custom installations. Pieces may be subtle, with colors quietly fitting the context, or vibrant and lively. A practicing architect, she devotes particular concern to installation details, which comprise the structure of the art. Her works are included in university, government, corporate, commercial and private collections. Collaboration welcome. Sizes: tabletop to airplane hangar.

Myra works personally with all clients. Installation available. Schedule: 30 to 120 days.

A *Your red is so nice, your blue is so nice*

B *Gibbous Moon*

C untitled, Holiday Inn

D *Miro's Dream* series

E *The Tulip Screen*

A

B

C

D

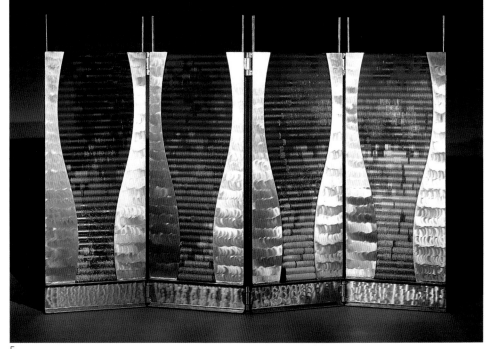

E

Deborah Carlson

29770 Denali Lane
Evergreen, CO 80439
FAX 303-674-2818
TEL 303- 670-8934

Deborah creates original images that are a reaction to the architectural spaces, edges, cracks and crevices in the world around her.

Deborah's two-dimensional framed wall pieces are her own creation of patinaed copper, leafing and paint. These individual abstract paintings contain sensuous metal surfaces that are covered with a variety of textures and layers of color. With a near-monochromatic palette, gold leaf is applied and scraped in places to reveal underlying strata, creating an almost archeological impression.

The artist has 20 years experience in corporate design, allowing her to create art that is both rich and unique in quality.

Deborah's work is nationally represented in corporate and private collections.

Commissions accepted. More information available upon request.

Printed in Hong Kong ©1995 THE GUILD: Designer's Edition

Cloisonné Enamels
by M. Slepian

Marian Slepian
5 Overlook Drive
Bridgewater, NJ 08807
FAX 908-231-6667
TEL 908-526-5856

Marian Slepian is a recognized master in cloisonné enamel. For 30 years, she has created brilliant contemporary works of art in this ancient, virtually indestructible medium. Shown in museums, galleries and exhibitions internationally, her work is in the permanent collections of Merck and Company, AT&T and American Standard. She accepts commissions for site-specific installations in corporate and public spaces.

Slepian's works for sacred settings are particularly inspired. Her large donor walls, Ark doors and cloisonné paintings infuse the environment with warmth, color and spiritual meaning. Her unique sacramental wine cups, Torah shields and other ritual objects are dramatically contemporary, yet retain the richness of their Byzantine heritage.

A Ark: *Twelve Tribes*, horizontally sliding doors

B Painting: *Skeins*, 20" x 43" x 2"

A

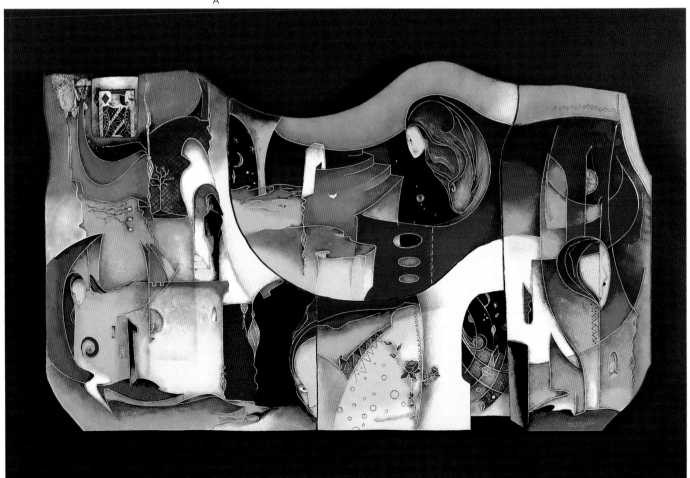

B

Photos: Armen Photographers

Beth Cunningham

32 Sweetcake Mountain Road
New Fairfield, CT 06812
TEL 203-746-5160

Known for her one-of-a-kind collage paintings, Beth Cunningham exhibits an elegant, understated use of materials and a meticulous level of craftsmanship. Wall pieces are scaled to accommodate large corporate areas, as well as small residential spaces; paintings are commissioned by collectors, as well as business, medical, banking and hotel facilities. Completed works are also available. Gallery inquiries and exhibition opportunities are welcome.

Also see these GUILD publications:
THE GUILD: 1, 2, 3, 4, 5
The Designer's Reference: 6, 7, 8, 9

A *Flying Free...*, private commission, 22" x 34"

B *Dreamtime: Landscape*, 24" x 36"

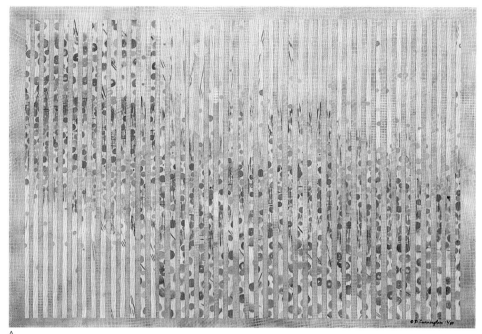

A

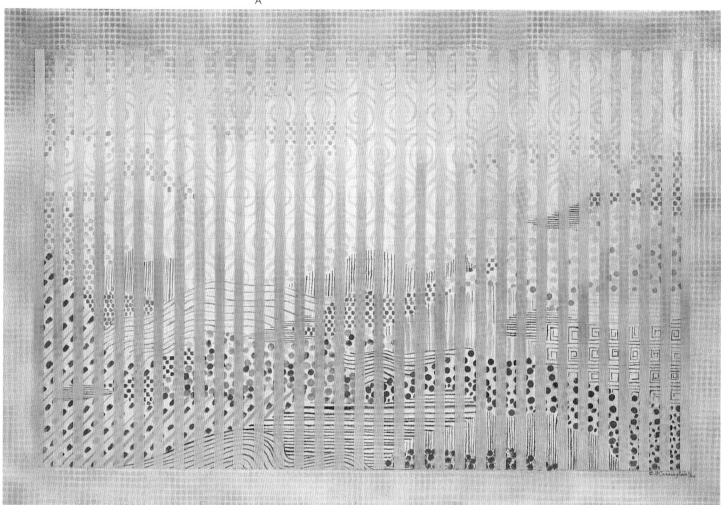

B

Photos: Michael Partenio Productions

Alonzo Davis

TEL 901-276-9070

Mary Lynn Perry, Representative
2222 Francisco Drive #510-136
El Dorado Hills, CA 95762-3762
FAX 916-939-9124
TEL 916-933-4004

"My art is on the edge of abstract expression-
ism. As with jazz, a painting or print often starts
out with a basic theme which I improvise on
and return to."

Commissions welcomed, slides available.

A *Talk That Walk*, 1994, acrylic on carved tar
  paper, 10"H x 12"W

B *Oregon Plateau I*, 1994, acrylic on woven paper,
  22"H x 30"W

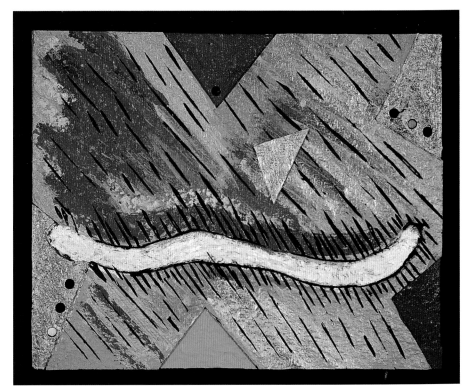

A

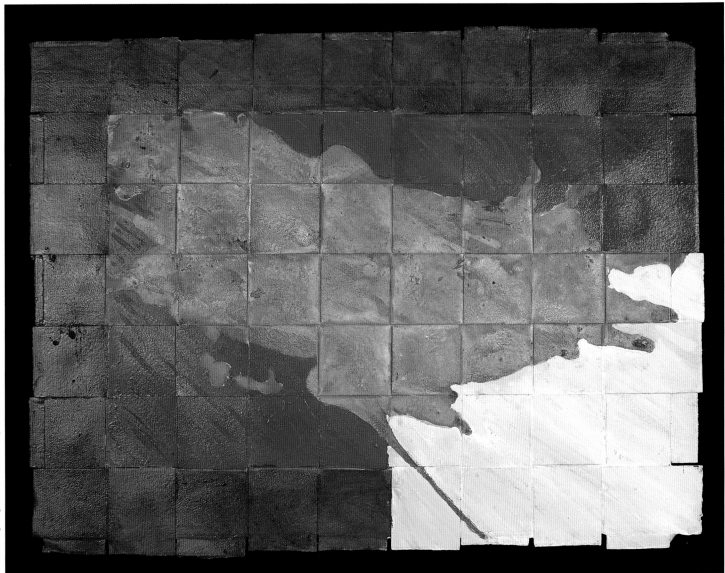

B

Marsha Farley

Mark Lawrence Associates
1081 High Falls Road
Catskill, NY 12414
FAX 800-583-0030
TEL   800-583-0010

A 50-year veteran of the art world, Marsha Farley creates wall reliefs from a unique variety of industrial materials. Bright color, rhythmic patterns and geometric simplicity characterize her sculpture.

Farley's work is included in numerous corporate and public collections, including Lincoln Center, the Allan Brady Company and the Smithsonian Institution. Her career includes three museum exhibits and over a dozen solo shows.

Slides, photos and a retrospective catalog are available. Commissions focus on client needs, budget and timeline. A modest design fee covers drawings and 3D pattern samples.

A *Calliope*, painted wood, auto parts,
   4"D x 48"Dia

B *Optic #1018*, painted wood, aluminum,
   laminate, 48"H x 84"W x 4"D

C *Undulating Canes*, bamboo, wire, rubber,
   36"H x 144"L x 12"D

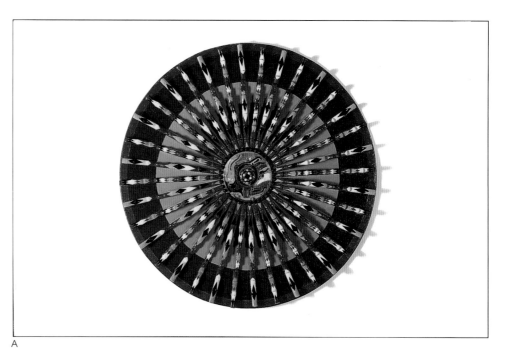

A

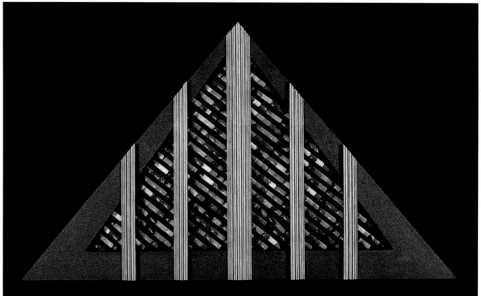

B

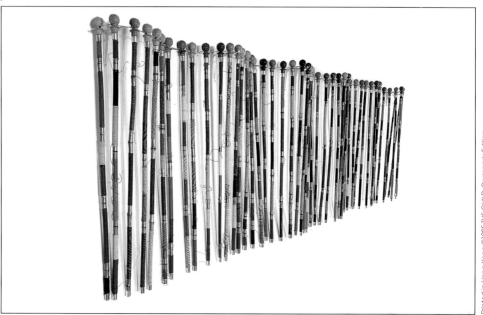

C

Printed in Hong Kong © 1995 THE GUILD: Designer's Edition

Silja Lahtinen

Silja's Fine Art Studio
5220 Sunset Trail
Marietta, Ga 30068
(404) 992-8380
FAX (404) 992-8380

Silja Talikka Lahtinen uses images from the myths and landscapes of her native Finland in her large wall panels. With striking combinations of colors and materials, her collages address the "poetry and spirituality that are missing from our modern life."

Lahtinen's other work—paintings of acrylic and oil on canvas, and drums of wood, rope, plywood and fiber—are well known to collectors in the United States and Europe. She exhibits regularly in New York and other U.S. cities, as well as in Paris, France and Helsinki, Finland.

Commissions are accepted. For more information, please contact the artist.

Top: collage on canvas, silkscreen, paper, fiber, etc., 72" x 65"
Bottom: *Eternity Has Ten Dimensions*, collage on canvas, fiber, handmade paper, silkscreen, 72" x 65"

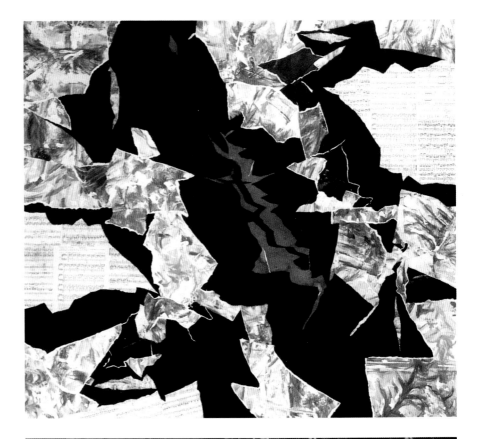

Dianna Thornhill Miller
Jim Miller

Omni Art Design
1716 West Main Street
Fort Wayne, IN 46808
FAX 219-422-3677
TEL 219-422-3677

Jim and Dianna Thornhill Miller's combined backgrounds in architecture and art have produced creative collaborations for specific environments since 1976. Working with clients and design professionals, they utilize a variety of media and techniques to create art that is original and responsive.

Leather Mosaic™ murals, a Miller innovation, provide rich color and texture in a durable, quality material. In formal geometric designs or thematic narratives, these works enhance more than 300 private and business environments in the United States and abroad.

Clients include: GTE, Lincoln Life, IBM, Blue Cross, G.E., Baxter, I.T.T., Glenbrook Mall, V.A.

Also see these GUILD publications:
Architect's Edition: 8, 9

A *Tri Kaleidoscope*, Magnavox, 4½'H x 11½'W

B *Laguna*, private residence, 3'H x 6'W

C *Stiles Coat of Arms*, Yale University, 5'H x 4'W

D *Justice* (detail), Baker & Daniels, 3½'H x 7½'W

E *Northern Territory*, NIPSCO, 6'H x 16'W

A

B

C

D

E

Bernie Rowell

Bernie Rowell Studio
1525 Branson Avenue
Knoxville, TN 37917
TEL 423-523-5244

Bernie Rowell's eclectic canvas constructions grace corporate, hospitality, and health care facilities throughout the United States. She has 15 years of experience producing site-specific commissions.

The visual beauty of electronic circuitry inspired Rowell's *Techno-Relic Series*. Ceramic semi-conductors, resistors and circuit boards embellish formal compositions. These modern *Urban Icons* salute the religion of technology.

Heavyweight canvas painted with saturated acrylic colors form the base. Metallic fabrics, beads, and layered appliquéd construction adds lush detail to these three-dimensional artworks.

Available in custom colors with shadow box presentations.

Site-specific commissions welcome.

Also see these GUILD publications:
THE GUILD: 2, 3
Designer's Edition: 7

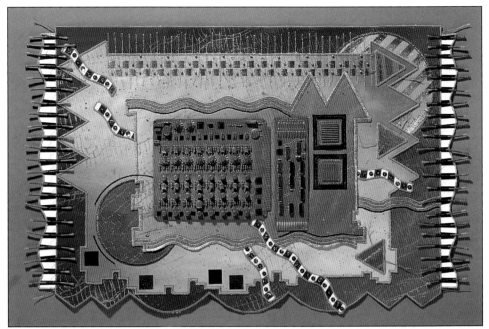

Ode to the Religion of Technology, 1994, 20" x 31"

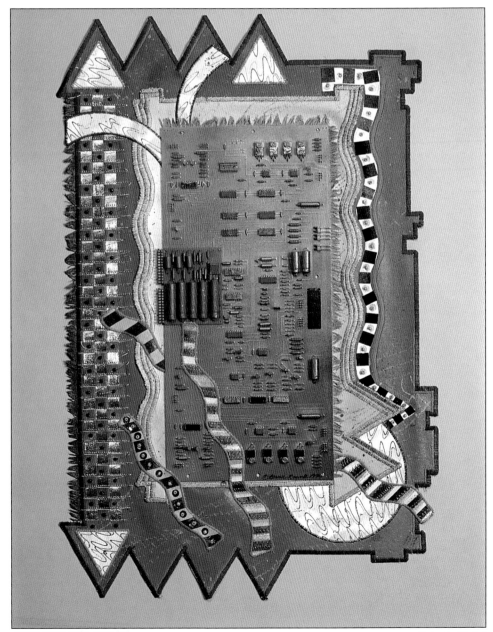

Future Fossil, 1994, 26" x 17"

Photos: David Luttrell

Kurt Shaw

12 Coulter Street
Pittsburgh, PA 15205
FAX 412-922-5818
TEL 412-922-5818

Kurt Shaw's intriguing works, made from painted sheet metal, are unique in color, depth and impact. Wall-hung sculptures make an impressive focal point in airy spaces; framed, one-of-a-kind paintings fit any space and budget.

Lightweight and easy to hang, Shaw's works require only occasional dusting. Sizes range from small to architectural scale. The artist offers site-specific solutions for unusual spaces and special design needs.

Also see this GUILD publication:
Designer's Edition: 9

A *Hallux,* 36"H x 72"W

B *Peppo Morula,* 96"H x 108"W

A

B

Photos: Richard Kelly

Celia Soper

214 Stephens Street
Lafayette, LA 70506
TEL 318-233-1635

Celia Soper specializes in bas-relief sculpture, custom tailored to suit the client's needs. Her work, whether in bronze or cast stone, artfully captures the likeness of a portrait subject, can embody the spirit of an individual or corporation, as in her montage pieces, or can depict any image of the client's choosing.

She works directly with individuals or firms, utilizing photographic references or shaded renderings.

Her distinctive sculptures can lend the perfect corporate touch to a board room or lobby, or serve as a lasting tribute at special commemorative events.

A bronze double portrait, life-size

B commemorative bronze, 30" x 40"

A

B

Photos: Ron Guidry

Martin Sturman

M. Sturman Steel Sculptures
20412 Roca Chica Drive
Malibu, CA 90265
FAX 818-905-7173
TEL 310-456-5716

Martin Sturman creates original steel sculptures in floral, figurative and abstract designs.

His sculptures range from tabletop to free-standing indoor and outdoor pieces, including sculpted tables and entry gates. These beautiful sculptures are executed in stainless steel, weathered (rusted) steel, powder-coated carbon steel and acrylic-painted carbon steel.

Martin frequently has sculptures available for immediate delivery, but encourages site-specific and collaborative efforts. Depending upon complexity, most sculptures can be shipped within 10 to 12 weeks of commission.

Sizes range from 12 inches to 10 feet high. Prices upon request.

Also see these GUILD publications:
Designer's Edition: 7, 8, 9

A *Repose*, 1994, stainless steel, 47" x 44" x 2"

B *Hanging Flowers*, acrylic on steel, 46" x 42" x 2"

A

B

Photos: Barry Michlin

Susan Venable

Venable Studio
214 South Venice Boulevard
Venice, CA 90291
FAX 310-822-0050
TEL 310-827-7233

Susan Venable's work is non-objective — an exploration of structure and surface. The reliefs are constructed of steel grids and twisted copper wire. The paintings are encaustic and oil on panel. In both, transparent layers are stacked to create a rich and complex surface, maximizing the physicality of the materials.

Venable's wall reliefs have been installed in public spaces, as well as private homes and museums. Commissions involving collaboration with architects are welcome, and have included Xerox, Bank of America, Hotel Nikko, IBM, and Western Digital, as well as corporations in Europe, Australia and Asia. The materials are durable and low maintenance, and suitable to installation in public areas.

Also see this GUILD publication:
Designer's Edition: 9

A *Crossroads*, one panel of diptych shown,
  3½' x 7½'

B *Giverny*, 5' x 10'

A

B   Photos: William Nettles

Alice Van Leunen

PO Box 408
Lake Oswego, OR 97034
FAX 503-636-0787
TEL 503-636-0787

Van Leunen specializes in mixed-media wall treatments and aerial installations. Many of the artworks are client- and site-specific, and the artist has extensive experience collaborating with designers as well as other artists. Works range in size from small, intimate pieces up to major architectural installations. Materials include paper; fabric; fibers; paint; metals and metallic foils; and glass, especially dichroic glass. Commissions are welcome, and the artist is available to supervise installations of major works.

The artist is represented in numerous private, corporate and public collections. Prices, slides and further information furnished on request.

SHOWN: *Cantang Balung*, 1994, commissioned for the P.T. Mulia Group, Djakarta, Indonesia, woven paper with paint, metallic foil, metallic fabric, acrylic, and wire, 52" x 108" x 4"

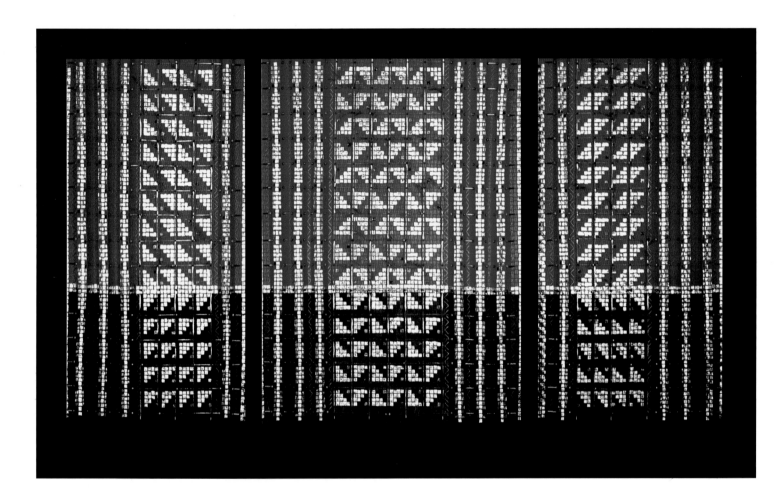

BETH CUNNINGHAM
mixed media

"I want people to walk away from my work with a sense of surprise," says multi-media artist Beth Cunningham," a feeling that they've found something unexpected. That feeling can be one more little thing that draws them in and lets them experience the work at another level."

Cunningham's work is made of two separate paintings. One, on stretched canvas, has an airbrushed background. The other, of stretched muslin, is painted by hand, covered with silk tissue, glossed with a polymer, cut into strips or squares, layered over the canvas, and glazed. Her work is evocative of landscapes, but is often more a reflection than an actual representation of terrain.

"I want people to have a sense of catching a glimpse, rather than seeing the whole thing," she says. "When you ride a motorcycle, which I love to do, you just catch fragments of the landscape you're passing through. Or you could think of it as peering through a venetian blind."

Cunningham comes to her art as a weaver who turned to other methods to create something more permanent. "I was always troubled by how vulnerable a weaving is," she says. "When I layer the strips or squares in a grid-like fashion and then gloss them, I retain the texture of a weaving, but I have something that is nearly impossible to destroy."

Her method also gives her an unusual flexibility, she says, recalling a recent commission. "The client had measured the space incorrectly, and my piece didn't fit," she remembers with a wry smile. "Someone suggested turning it on its side, and it worked! It looks like it was made that way."

Photo: Steve Siegel

See these GUILD publications:
THE GUILD: 1, 2, 3, 4, 5
Designer's Edition: 6, 7, 8, 9, 10

Marjorie A. Atwood

1509 South Elwood
Tulsa, OK 74109
FAX 918-583-0886
TEL 918-583-0886
TEL 800-484-9174 pin# 5096

Marjorie Atwood is a decorative artist with a background from Sarah Lawrence College and Parson's, as well as formal training in faux finishes, gilding and fresco in New York, San Francisco and London.

Atwood enhances residential and commercial environments by utilizing trompe l'oeil effects, murals, metallic finishes and specialized painting techniques on walls, floors, furniture, picture frames and decorative accessories. Floor cloths with coordinating tabletop accessories are another beautiful and unique way to accent an interior.

Work is site specific or studio produced, delivered and installed. Experienced at managing crews, budgets and schedules, she enjoys collaboration with architects and designers. Fees for design and execution of most projects range between $2,000 and $25,000.

Andrea M. Biggs
Timothy G. Biggs

279 Sterling Place
Brooklyn, NY 11238
(718) 857-9034

Andrea and Timothy Biggs are muralists collaborating to produce site-specific, custom works of art for residential and commercial sites.

On this page are shown two different bedrooms: A series of Fragonard figures cavorts around the domed ceiling in one; for the other, the client had a fantasy of living in a crumbling castle with a view. For this project, the Biggses painted four walls, the ceiling and the furniture, creating a medieval environment.

The Biggses have been commissioned to paint murals—and specialized finishes—for apartments and hotel lobbies, restaurants in New York and Asia, fashion showrooms and private residences. Their clients range from architects and interior designers to connoisseurs and home owners.

Also see these GUILD publications:
THE GUILD: 2, 3, 4, 5
The Architect's Source: 6, 7, 8, 9
The Designer's Reference: 7, 9

Bill Gibbons Studio

368 Broadway #203
New York, NY 10013
(212) 227-0039
FAX (212) 227-0039

Bill Gibbons is a mural painter with over ten years of experience designing and painting murals in a wide range of styles. The paintings shown here are varied because each was designed to harmonize with the architecture of its setting. His murals are painted on canvas and can be installed on site as easily as wallpaper.

Detail of a mural in Asian style

Detail of a mural based on Poussin landscapes

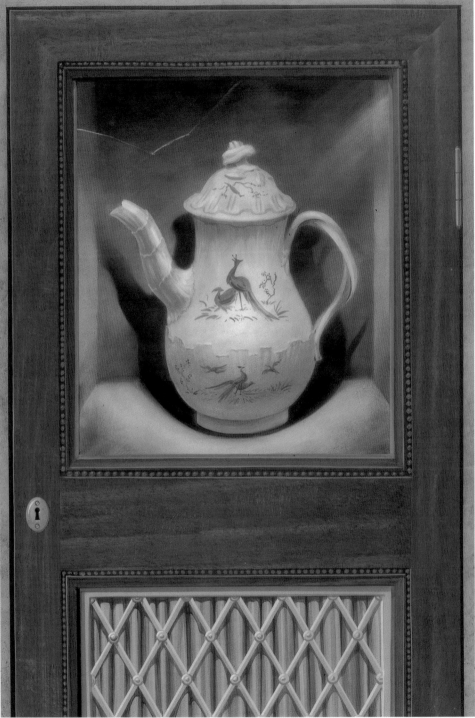

Detail of a trompe l'oeil china cabinet

EYECON, Inc.

Chris Arnold
Jeff Garrison
1915 West Colorado Boulevard
Dallas, TX 75208
TEL 214-871-3535

EYECON is a custom murals and design firm founded by artists Chris Arnold and Jeff Garrison. Both have worked with architects, designers and individuals to produce site-specific works of art for the corporate, public and private sector. They have the unique ability to translate conceptual ideas into monumental-scale creations, making a profound impact on their audience.

Additional creations not shown include *Children of the World*, a 60' x 8' interior mural for a group of internationally renowned neurosurgeons at Children's Medical Center, Dallas. Portfolio and complete client list available upon request.

A & C *Mass Transit*, Dallas, 214' x 121', outdoor mural for the Downtown Improvement District

B *The Office*, The Big One Restaurant, Dallas, 20' x 5', interior mural for Shannon Wynne

A   Lee Dirksen

B   Thom Wilson

C   Lee Dirksen

Dale B. Fehr

D. Benjamin Fehr Design
1140 Maggie Street Southeast
Calgary, AB T2G 4M1
Canada
FAX 403-266-3924
TEL   403-266-3924

Canadian D. Benjamin Fehr creates mural environments using time-honored themes in fresh context, noted for impact, well-researched detail, and transparent natural palette.

Multi-talented, with 27 art-years experience, he collaborates to ingeniously transform private spaces and public places into evocative habitats for the human spirit.

Interiors illuminate myth, psychology and practicality into breathtaking vision. Commissions welcome, hand-painted on site or shipped for installation.

A sunroom (detail), Grant residence

B ceiling, Canadian Children's Foundation, 9' x 11'

A

B

Photos: A Hi-tech Photography

Yoshi Hayashi

San Francisco, CA
TEL 415-552-0755

Yoshi Hayashi's designs range from very traditional 17th century Japanese lacquer art themes that are delicate with intricate detail, to those that are boldly geometric and contemporary. By skillfully applying metallic leaf and bronzing powders, he adds illumination and contrast to the network of color, pattern and texture. His original designs include screens, wall panels, furniture and decorative objects.

Hayashi's pieces have been commissioned for private collections, hotels, restaurants and offices in the United States and Japan. Prices upon request.

Photos: Ira D. Schrank

Thomas Masaryk

Trompe L'Oeil and Painted Finishes
99 Reeds Lane
Stratford, CT 06497
TEL 203-375-8645

Thomas Masaryk is a contemporary painter of illusions who brings his artistry and master craftsmanship to the home and commercial industry. He specializes in trompe l'oeil, faux marble and woodgraining. Artistic services include murals, faux bois intarsia, faux pietra dura, all types of special finishes, restoration painting and architectural gilding (interior/exterior).

Masaryk is well known for his meticulous and loving approach to the creative process, and for his technical knowledge and passion for painting. He designs alone or in collaboration with architects, designers, art consultants and clients. On-site services, as well as studio-produced works, are available.

The artist's work has been featured in individual and group exhibitions and numerous publications in the United States and overseas.

Also see these GUILD publications:
THE GUILD: 3, 4, 5
Architect's Edition: 6, 7, 8

SHOWN: counter-top screen dividing a kitchen and dining room (both views shown), hinged for center opening, private residence, 2¾'H x 3¼'L

Melissa A. Murphy

Specially For Children
PO Box 772927
Houston, TX 77215-2927
TEL 713-995-5646

Specializing in children's environments, Melissa Murphy transforms walls into windows and rooms into worlds. Collaborations with designers and architects create custom solutions for commercial and residential spaces, accented with dimensional figures and hand-painted furniture.

An accomplished illustrator, Melissa integrates her creations into videos, books and coloring books to heighten the children's involvement; her creations come alive and can be taken home. Brochure available upon request.

A St. Joseph Hospital, Sports Care Facility Hydrotherapy Room, pointillism, 3 walls, 2,000 sq. ft.

B UTMB Galveston, Children's Hospital, whimsical circus design, dimensional animals, columns, mural, collaboration with Falick/Klein Partnership, Inc., Houston, TX

C Memorial Southeast Hospital, Emergency Room, scary high-tech becomes reassuring, comforting surroundings

A

Bob Graham

B

C

Bob Graham

Vigini & Associates

Nicola Vigini
619 Western Avenue
Box 15
Seattle, WA 98104
(206) 682-4868

Nicola Vigini, born in Italy, is a fine and decorative artist. In Rome, he studied classical drawing and painting; later he apprenticed in restoration of 15th and 16th century frescoes. He completed his formal study in decorative art and design at the *Institut Supérieur de Peinture Décorative* in Paris, where he specialized in the traditional European techniques of mural painting, *trompe l'oeil, faux bois* and *faux marbre.* Brochure available by written request.

Inset: hand-painted, three-panel screen in style known as *grottesca,* 80" x 60"
Bottom: trompe l'oeil creating three-dimensional illusion of door with vintner's tools and wine casks, 8½' x 5'

TIMOTHY & ANDREA BIGGS
murals

"What makes a commission memorable," says Tim Biggs, "is when we're really challenged, when people throw us a curve, something we haven't done before."

Photo: Peter Clemens

It's appropriate that Tim and Andrea Biggs appreciate a challenge, because their murals, painted walls, non-imagery wall textures and ceilings—found worldwide—have included a little bit of everything. Still, a few projects really stand out.

One case in point: a bedroom. "The client wanted it to look like a room in an old castle, with crumbling walls and a view of a medieval landscape and a brick ceiling that's partially fallen away. A lot of sky shows and the view on one wall is of the rest of the castle."

On a similar theme, the Biggs were asked to paint from the memories of an older Italian aristocrat. "He had grown up in Italy and had to hide with his family during the war," Tim recalls. "He wanted us to replicate memories of his youth, memories that were sometimes dim, sometimes specific. He wanted us to include a fountain where his grandmother had taken him and maidens gathered water; he described their clothing to us in great detail."

This mural, completed in time for his daughter's wedding, still graces the huge main wall of the gentleman's Long Island estate. "The family was so pleased, they invited us to the wedding," says Tim. "It was really challenging, but so is every job. It's a challenge to create something that looks right and is still an illusion."

See these GUILD publications:
THE GUILD: 2, 3, 4, 5
Architect's Edition: 6, 7, 8, 9, 10
Designer's Edition: 7, 9, 10

FURNITURE

Ted Box
Jeff Entner

Ocean Art
PO Box 1764
Edgartown, MA 02539
TEL 508-696-6126

The driftwood pieces of designer Ted Box and colorist Jeff Entner are sculpted on Martha's Vineyard and reflect the relationship of sea, sand and weathering which is so much the spirit of coastal New England.

These pieces have been successfully marketed to major galleries and private collections throughtout Canada, the United States and Japan. A rolltop desk of Box's design is currently in the White House.

The works' versatility and functional durability, and the close collaboration between artist and client, combine to create the heirloom quality of these pieces.

Pieces shown range in price from $2,800 to $3,900.

Photos: Bob Schellhammer

John Clark

John Clark Furniture
Penland Road
Penland, NC 28765
(704) 765-7510
FAX (704) 765-7510

John Clark blends traditional furniture forms with historical architectural references to create modern pieces that are fresh yet familiar. The pieces are primarily constructed from domestic and imported woods, both solid and fine veneers. The surfaces are often detailed with inlays of exotic woods, stone, pearl and even unusual industrial materials.

He has been recognized for his many successful commissions and collaborations with prominent architects and designers. His work has appeared in *Fine Woodworking*, *The New York Times* and *American Craft*.

John earned his MFA in Furniture Design from the Program in Artisanry at Boston University. He further developed his work during his tenure as an artist-in-residence at the Penland School of Crafts.

Conference table, wenge, coachwoood, quilted maple, ebony, mother of pearl, 4' x 10'

Corner china cabinet, mahogany, curly maple, ebony, 36" x 80"

Conference table (detail)

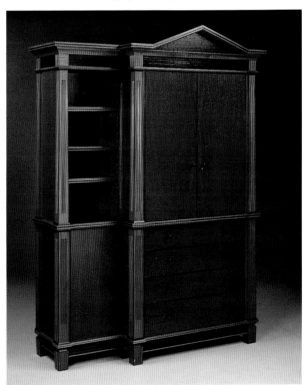

Armoire, quilted mahogany, ebony, for video equipment, 24" x 64" x 84"

Concepts By J, Inc.

Jay Meepos
834 E. 108th Street
Los Angeles, CA 90059
FAX 213-564-4332
TEL 213-564-9988

Concepts By J has been designing, manufacturing and finishing high-end custom cabinetry, furniture, millwork and architectural woodwork since 1978. Designs cover virtually all styles and periods, traditional and contemporary, and have been installed locally, nationally and internationally.

In addition, Concepts By J has completed several projects for home theaters and entertainment units of all sizes and complexity. The president, Jay Meepos, has done extensive design work in all areas of cabinet and furniture design.

We pride ourselves on producing fine cabinetry for a wide variety of job conditions.

Printed in Hong Kong ©1995 THE GUILD: Designer's Edition

Glenn Elvig

Glenn Elvig Sculpture/Furniture Design
7716 Lakeview Lane NE
Minneapolis, MN 55432
FAX 612-780-1212
TEL 612-780-2028

The Big Bopper
"The most daring seat at the 1994 International Contemporary Furniture Fair."

Sonia Rykiel
Eastern Express, Hong Kong

Honey, We're Not Moving!
"Imaginative...outrageous..."

Barbara Garet
Custom Woodworking Business

Heavy Metal Rocker
"...transforming craft into art..."
Al Morch, *San Francisco Examiner*

Table With Red Ball
"The one to see at the ICFF in New York in May."
CASA VOGUE, Italy

"American designer Glenn Elvig's work raises questions about his identity. Poet or cartoonist? Sculptor or furniture designer? The answer is he practices a bit of everything."
Pace Interior Architecture, Hong Kong

Commissions accepted; portfolio available.

All images ©1995 Glenn S. Elvig.

Also see these GUILD publications:
THE GUILD: 4, 5
Designer's Edition: 7

The Big Bopper   Paul Crosby

Honey, We're Not Moving!   Paul Crosby

Heavy Metal Rocker   George Post

Table With Red Ball   George Post

Off The Wall
Design Studios, Inc.

10479 Ditch Road
Carmel, IN 46032
FAX 317-844-3648
TEL 317-846-3702

James David Lee
Designer

At Off The Wall, superior artisans specialize in eloquently expressive works. Whether displaying craftsmanship in metal or wood, traditional and contemporary creations portray grace and functionality. Off The Wall's creative applications encompass original furniture designs in a variety of mediums, as well as decorative ironwork.

Taking a commission from conception through implementation, experts at Off The Wall enter a collaborative process that fosters a partnership with the client to assure the preservation of conceptual and visual intent.

A versatile company, Off The Wall creates works of wood, metal, plastics, laminates and fabric to enhance corporate, private and municipal arenas.

A weaver's organizer, walnut, maple, glass, laminate, 72"H x 120"L x 24"D

B ladderback chair, formed walnut, 48"H x 22"D x 22"W

C piano bar, birch plywood, laminate, 46"H x 74"L x 36"D

A

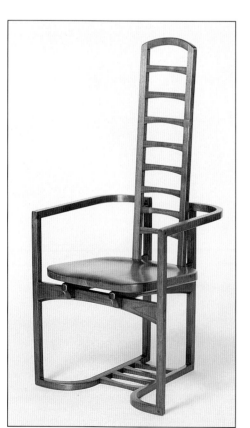

B

C

Paul Reiber

43861 Road 409
Mendocino, CA 95460
TEL 707-964-7151

Drawing on visual images of diverse origin, Paul Reiber creates wooden seating furniture, beds, and carved panels using traditional techniques and finishes. He augments the traditional with a very nontraditional use of naturalistic carving, dyes, and gold and silver leaf. While most of his work incorporates the use of leather or fabric upholstery, commissions calling for cane or other materials are welcomed.

During the 12 years Mr. Reiber has maintained his studio he has developed a reputation for high-quality work done to contracted price and time schedules.

Individual one-of-a-kind pieces or sets available by commission or from inventory. Collaboration with client or design professional on all aspects of a project is welcomed.

Please call or write for more information.

Also see this GUILD publication:
Designer's Edition: 9

Photos: Jess Shirley

Bill Rix

Old Time Woods
4296 Waconda Road N.E.
Salem, OR 97303
TEL 503-390-2482

Bill Rix established Old Time Woods in 1983, constructing furniture using both modern and traditional techniques. Mortise-and-tenon and frame-and-panel are used throughout his case pieces. Many of the woods he uses come from the Willamette Valley in Oregon.

Detailed information, photographs, prices and schedules are available on request.

A lectern desk, Oregon black walnut, 33"W x 42"H x 22"D

B stereo cabinet, cherry, 46"H x 24"W x 18"D, CDs stored in the drawer

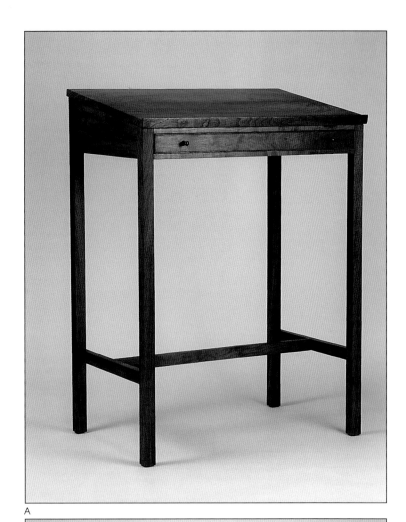

A

B

Photos: Don Vallereux

Ryerson Designs

Mitch Ryerson
12 Upton Street
Cambridge, MA 02139
FAX 617-391-4551
TEL 617-391-1231

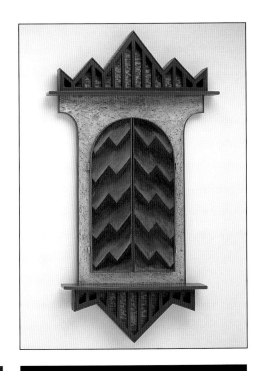

For the past 12 years, Mitch Ryerson has been building unique pieces of furniture on a limited-production and one-of-a-kind basis. He has established a national reputation for his whimsical and colorful interpretations of traditional forms and his inventive use of found objects in his work.

His pieces are in major public and private collections and have toured nationally and internationally. He is experienced in working with clients and designers to meet the specific needs of each commission.

Claude Terrell

Claude G. Terrell III
PO Box 906
Saratoga Springs, NY 12866-0891
TEL 518-584-1057

Artist/craftsman for 22 years. BFA, School for American Craftsman, RIT.

Designer and fabricator of one-of-a-kind furniture and limited editions for the individual and corporate client.

Claude has exhibited in numerous galleries and shown work in regional and national magazines. His furniture incorporates the environment and utilitarian needs of the client, creating pleasing ambience of form and function.

Peter Tischler

P. Tischler Chair & Cabinetmaker, Inc.
4 Barnet Road
Pine Brook, NJ 07058
FAX 201-244-0703
TEL   201-244-0654

With formal training as a cabinetmaker, Pete Tischler produces contemporary furniture based on traditional techniques and ideals. His work is custom tailored to fit his clients' needs in creating a unique piece of furniture. His designs showcase the natural beauty inherent within the grain. He has a vast inventory of highly figured wide boards in stock, both common and less-utilized species indigenous to the hardwood forests of the Northeast.

Pete Tischler's work has been widely exhibited throughout the country in galleries and museums, and has been published extensively in *Fine Woodworking* magazine.

Portfolio available upon request.

A settee, flame birch, 38½" x 44" x 20½"

B *Wood Comes From Trees*, display stand, honey locust, 36" x 44" x 16"

C dining table, cherry, 28½" x 70" x 38"

D showcase, white oak, figured white oak, 81" x 28" x 16"

A

B

C

D

Photos: Peter Jacobs

THE STUDIO FURNITURE MOVEMENT

*Editor's note: In this article, the term "studio" differentiates the furniture created
by artists in their studios from that made by factories. Jorge Arango provides this historical overview.*

Since the late 1940s, something momentous has been brewing in the universe of American studio furniture makers. It started haphazardly, just a few individual woodworkers setting up shops where they could produce furniture completely by hand that transcended the genre's functional goals. They used furniture to explore the nature of their materials, the techniques that would help them achieve new kinds of designs and, finally, to explore the ability of furniture to powerfully convey emotion and ideas the way painting and sculpture have for centuries. Over the years, their one-of-a-kind works have caused a massive accretion, drawing new talents to the field from areas as disparate as architecture and jewelry making. The gathering momentum has reached its climax in this decade. It is clear today that the American studio furniture movement has arrived at its Big Bang.

Without a doubt, contemporary studio furniture enjoys the cultural status of being a bona fide artistic movement. Its history was carved out by the movement's progenitors; seminal figures like Wharton Esherick, George Nakashima, Wendell Castle and Tage Frid became

respected and well-known in the 1960s. Since then the movement has spawned a sophisticated body of writings and criticism. And it has demanded attention as an independent art form in the art departments of American colleges and universities.

At the center of this movement is the artist/craftsperson whose creativity and imagination have been able to summon new concepts out of the aesthetic and philosophical repertoire of fine and decorative art history. What most sets today's studio furniture artists apart from the early practitioners is formal education. Some of today's best-known furniture makers were students of the college programs established first by Tage Frid in the '50s, then later by Jere Osgood, Dan Jackson, Alphonse Mattia, Wendell Castle and others. They have been dubbed the "second generation" furniture makers by Edward S. Cooke Jr. in his influential essay for the *New American Furniture* exhibition at the Museum of Fine Arts, Boston (1989). The new academic environment, as well as the liberal social and political climate during which it took root (in the '60s and '70s), resulted in work that was daring and confrontational.

Yet much of the early furniture from this period was primarily concerned with technical bravura and the exploration of artistic ideas. It was esoteric and inaccessible to many and had little to do with function and comfort. "I knew many woodworkers who would throw everything they knew into one piece," recalls the metal artist Peter Handler. "It showed their virtuosity, almost to a baroque extent. But it often went beyond good taste and comfort."

Gradually, however, these artists matured and moved away from shock value toward more livable designs. As they left this early period of experimentation, they became, in the words of woodworker Kevin Earley, "ready to explore the functional aspects of furniture, to look at it as furniture first, and secondarily as sculpture." What's more, he adds, "Over the last ten years, we've seen the functional aspects of furniture being accepted, in and of themselves, as artistic."

The ascendance of Post Modernism during the '80s also had a huge impact on the second generation furniture makers. It not only brought a renewed appreciation of classical proportion and

THE ARTS AND CRAFTS MOVEMENT AROSE AS A WELL-DEFINED SOCIAL AND PHILOSOPHICAL FORCE. IN CONTRAST, THE MODERN STUDIO FURNITURE MOVEMENT IS HIGHLY IDIOSYNCRATIC— FOR MOST, A VERY PERSONAL SOLITARY PURSUIT.

form to their work, but it opened up the whole vocabulary of art and design history to the modern artist/craftperson's interpretation.

This is not to say that the avant-garde impulse among furniture makers is dead. But, as Cooke states in his essay, by the early '80s in the worlds of art, architecture, design, music and literature, "The need to constantly invent an avant-garde position had become self-absorbed, circular, and, therefore, alienated from normal activity." The most successful work today fuses the rigorous technique of craft with the functional problem-solving approach of design and the intellectual and creative conceptualization of art.

When artists like George Nakashima, Art Carpenter and Sam Maloof began exhibiting their designs in the late '40s and early '50s, the buying public was not thinking about furniture as art. The importance of the academic landscape during the '60s and '70s cannot be overstated. Places like Boston University's Program in Artistry, the Rochester Institute of Technology, and the Rhode Island School of Design changed the conceptual development of studio furni-

ture in America. Also in the 1970s, museums began acquiring and exhibiting studio furniture, and galleries began to specialize in it as the commercial value of the work became apparent. Places like Workbench Gallery (New York), Pritam & Eames (East Hampton, NY) and Snyderman Gallery (Philadelphia) can be credited with vigorously promoting the furniture of the emerging movement among the art-buying public and with adding momentum to the movement's growth.

The prosperity of the 1980s brought a new dimension to studio furniture. People began to travel and see the work of Italian, Scandinavian and Japanese furniture designers, making the mature American work—with its clean, classic lines and solid construction—seem comfortable and familiar. The sophistication of American studio furniture appealed to what these consumers perceived to be their own newly acquired sophistication and worldliness.

Marianne McNamara, director of the International Contemporary Furniture Fair (ICFF), which has become one of the most influential commercial venues

for furniture makers who seek larger markets, admits, "One of the things that made it easier for us to set up ICFF in 1989 is that more and more Americans were going to the fairs in Europe and were being exposed to the type of furniture that they couldn't see here because there was no commercial arena to see it in." And Ilene Shaw, a design consultant who was instrumental in creating the concept behind ICFF, points out that one of the main reasons for the creation of the show was to give these emerging furniture makers a voice to effect change in the sedentary world of American commercial furniture design. (ICFF, now in its seventh year, showcases work that is about 40 percent one-of-a-kind or limited-production.)

Visibility—in museum exhibitions, design magazines, galleries—gave the American furniture-buying public a new way to see the work of the second, and by now an emerging third, generation of American furniture makers. But there were several other social factors that conspired to enhance the allure of American studio furniture. Primarily, the materialism and excess of the '80s made it clear that Americans

THESE ARE THE ANTIQUES OF TOMORROW, AS PRIZED FOR THEIR BEAUTY AS THEY ARE FOR THE WAY THEY CHANGED CULTURAL AND AESTHETIC ATTITUDES AT EVERY LEVEL OF ART AND DESIGN.

had lost their connection to what was really important. Even worse, the belief that technology would improve our quality of life suddenly seemed more the cause for the erosion of that quality than its betterment.

This manifested itself in a desire to reconnect with the earth and with products that did not exploit it. A rejection of industrialism gave way to a yearning for something machines could not offer—beautifully detailed handwork. Like the initiators of the Arts and Crafts movement at the turn of the century, many modern furniture makers believe in the virtue of the craftsperson's lifestyle. But there the similarity ends. Whereas the Arts and Crafts movement arose as a well-defined social and philiosophical force, the modern studio furniture movement is highly idiosyncratic—for most, a very personal, solitary pursuit. And collectors buy the work precisely because of its individualism.

"People are looking for a product that's not just functional, but that also hits an emotional chord," explains Shaw. Studio furniture "gives us a sense of humanity because it is handmade. But, also, you're buying a piece of an artist —that person's craft, that person's touch, that artist's vision, point of view and expression. And that's what you get from art. You get an emotional, as well as an aesthetic, punch."

The present political climate holds great promise for studio furniture makers. As the society continues to reassess the 'traditional values' that were touted as idyllic in the '80s, its aesthetic appreciation is bound to evolve as well.

"Socially, I think on a global scale there's a lot of change taking place," adds Gary Upton, another furniture maker. "People are taking a look again at their perceptions. They're questioning those perceptions politically, environmentally, and in terms of design."

Whatever the future holds in terms of new designers, however, it seems clear that studio furniture has definitely passed a point of no return. It is evident not only in the prices it commands, but also in the general acknowledgment that it is an art form unto itself. It does not need to be compared in any way to painting and sculpture or even to other traditional craft media like clay and glass. And now that it has reached aesthetic independence, studio furniture's place as an art historical movement will continue to fuel the market, increasing the work's monetary and emotional value. These are the antiques of tomorrow, as prized for their beauty as they are for the way they changed cultural and aesthetic attitudes at every level of art and design.

YOU'RE BUYING A PIECE OF AN ARTIST—
THAT PERSON'S CRAFT, THAT PERSON'S TOUCH,
THAT ARTIST'S VISION, POINT OF VIEW AND
EXPRESSION. AND THAT'S WHAT YOU GET
FROM ART.

Sean Calyer

200 Anderson Street
Rochester, NY 14607
TEL 716-271-3520

Sean Calyer, a nationally shown artist, creates impressive, bold—yet affordable—pieces with exceptional craftsmanship and resolution. Using references to historic forms, Sean creates award-winning contemporary steel furniture with an enduring integrity of design.

A side table, 36"L x 12"W x 26"H

B reception desk, 96"L x 60"W x 30"H

C table, 32"L x 32"W x 30"H

D candle holders, 6"L x 4"W x 18"H

E sofa, 88"L x 36"W x 35"H

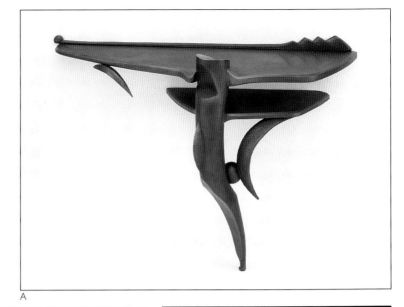

A

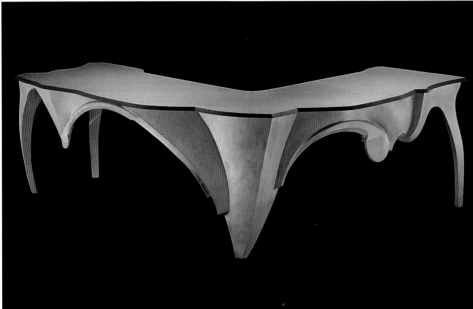

B

D

C

E

Photos: Bruce Miller

Christopher Thomson Ironworks

Christopher Thomson
PO Box 578
Ribera, NM 87560
FAX 505-421-2618
TEL 505-421-2645

"Sitting on water-smoothed rocks, welcoming the dampness, and listening to the interplay and echoes of teeming life and splashing riffles, I designed this *Vessel Bed* in a state of wonder, identifying with the stylized vessel, offering its contents to the horizons."

Christopher's furnishings enhance private and public spaces with their original designs and exceptionally high-quality craftsmanship. All of his functional pieces, including beds, benches, floor and table lamps, wall sconces, chairs, dining and occasional tables, fireplace tools, and candlesticks, add elegance to rustic, classical, western, oriental, or contemporary interiors.

A catalog and sample finishes are available for $15.

Larger architectural projects considered.

Make a gallery appointment for your next trip to New Mexico.

Also see these GUILD publications:
Designer's Edition: 8, 9

Herb Lotz

Craig Kaviar

Kaviar Forge
147 Stevenson Avenue
Louisville, KY 40206
FAX 502-561-0377
TEL 800-500-3890
TEL 502-561-0377

Kaviar Forge is a sculpture studio that specializes in hand-forged metal work. The work is distinguished by a natural ambiance, with extreme attention to fine craftsmanship and, in the case of furniture, comfort and utility. Craig Kaviar really enjoys working with designers and is able to customize projects, not only through his design and forging skills, but also by providing a large assortment of metals and finishes.

Work is delivered on time and within budget.

A *Perelmuter Memorial Gates*, 8'H x 8'W, forged iron with gold leaf menorah, located at the Jewish Community Center, Louisville, KY

B *Dining Ensemble*, grand chair #505-K, 48"H x 25"W x 27"L; dining table #525A, with glass top, 42" x 66" x 30"H; dining chair #504-K, 36"H x 20"W x 20"L; all pieces of forged iron with leaves and birds.

A

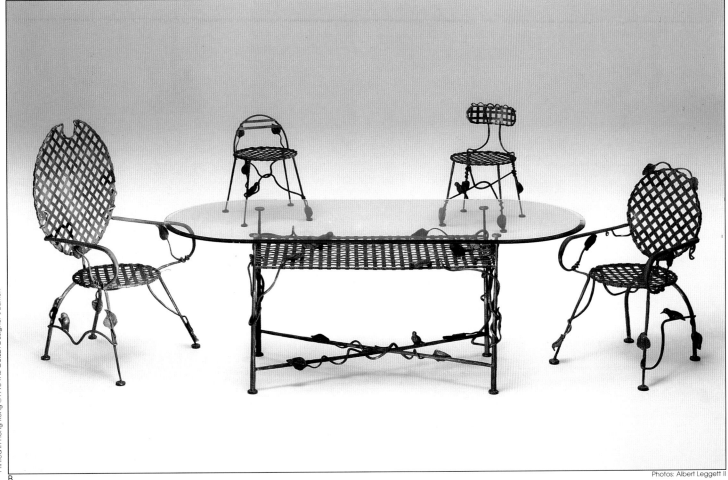

B

Photos: Albert Leggett II

Paul Knoblauch

45 Beacon Street
Rochester, NY 14607
TEL 716-442-3381

Paul creates functional art utilizing metal, glass and wood. While constantly involved with producing new work, he also enjoys the challenges commissions bring.

A   bench, 72"L

B   floor lamp, 91"H

C   containers, 12"H; 17"H

D   candleholder, 28"H

E   table with chairs, 42" square

C

A

D

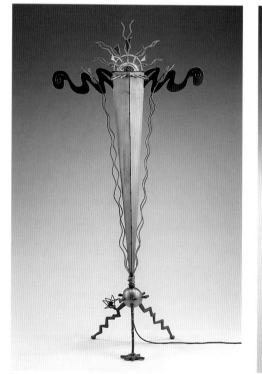

B

E

Photos: Bruce Miller

Printed in Hong Kong ©1995 THE GUILD: Designer's Edition

Konried Muench Designs

Konried Muench
2222 East Hawthorne Street
Tucson, AZ 85719
TEL 520-325-6767

Konried Muench has a 20-year foundation in sculpture (BFA, School of the Art Institute of Chicago; MFA, University of Arizona) that blends into the steel and multi-media compositions he has created for numerous private and public environments. Giving new definition to post-industrial steel and new materials characterizes his line, form and final product. Multi-faceted productions have included single tables to collaborative residential and corporate interiors.

Ongoing collaboration with clients, architects and designers through time-sensitive professional communication typifies past and present commissions.

Portfolio sample available to the industry or individual clients by phone request.

A end table, 1993, train steel, 18" x 18" x 24", collection: Dr. Thornburg

B *Plow Wall Sconce*, 1994, steel, 24" x 12" x 6"

C coffee table, 1993, train steel, 20" x 22" x 36", collection: Coppola Architects

D dining table, 1994, steel, 30" x 36" x 60", collection: Dr. Giuliano

E *The Stone Gate*, 1993, used ¼" plate steel, 8' x 13' x 6", collection: Mr. and Mrs. Stone

A

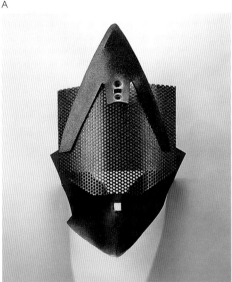

B

C

D

E

Photos: Mary Findysz Studios, Tucson, AZ

Doug Weigel

Steel Sculptures by Doug Weigel
PO Box 92408
Albuquerque, NM 87199-2408
FAX 505-821-9696
TEL 505-821-6600

Weigel designs and produces two- and three-dimensional sculptures and furniture in steel. Styles include Southwestern, Western, Art Deco and client-commissioned ideas.

Allow four to eight weeks from design approval and contract to completion. Shipping and handling, FOB Albuquerque.

Selected commissions include the collection of President George Bush, Petrified National Forest, Scottsdale Airport, Sandia Laboratories and the Hyatt Aruba.

A steel petroglyph framed mirror, 36"H x 24"W and *Corn Maiden* steel sculpture, 3'H

B queen-sized four-poster steel petroglyph bed and steel *Day's End* table lamp

GLENN ELVIG *wood*

The medium is wood, says sculptor and furniture designer Glenn Elvig, but the essential elements are humor and music. "I like art that creates a further interaction," he says. "I create things that poke and prod a bit."

Elvig incorporates a lot of puns into his work, which uses some interesting secondary media. Examples are his *Lawn Chair*, which has a seat of sod, and a chair titled *Sit Down!* which incorporates duck feathers into its composition. A chair with a Handel sonata screen-printed on the back is called *Sonata Chair*.

The sound and dynamic of music are a joy to Elvig, but he's also enchanted with the beauty of music on the printed page. This, too, is reflected in his work. In a current commission, he's writing a musical score that will be represented on a large sheet-music sculpture. As the viewer reads it left to right, it hits a perpendicular wall. At that point, the music blows up, scattering notes randomly over the wall. The piece is titled *And the Music Went On Forever*, and it satisfies a client's desire for a sculpture that would work in a narrow, horizontal space in a dining room.

Photo: Andrea Biosberg

But if music is important, humor is the driving force. "A beautiful object has universal appeal, but you can keep beauty to yourself," Elvig says. "Humor is different, it's something you want to share, and in fact, have to share.

"Ideally, my work brings a sense of joy and fulfillment at four levels: when I'm thinking about it, when I'm creating it, when I present it to a client and see that they appreciate it, and when they share the humor with their friends."

See these GUILD publications:
THE GUILD: 4, 5
Designer's Edition: 7, 10

Brigitte Benzakin

7201 Keystone Street, Loft 109
Philadelphia, PA 19135
TEL 215-331-1636

Brigitte Benzakin's distinctive hand-painted folding screens are derived from a combination of old themes like folklore, children's stories and natural settings, and recast with fanciful innovation. The screens are made of solid wood and are sealed with polyurethane. Her work has appeared in Bloomindale's and selective art shows and can be commissioned. Other pieces include panels and decorative boxes.

A *The Garden*, three panels, 72" x 51"

B *The Four Seasons*, four panels, 72" x 68"

A

B

Photos: Jeff Reeder

Printed in Hong Kong ©1995 THE GUILD: Designer's Edition

Lynn DiNino

1632 17th Avenue
Seattle, WA 98122
TEL 206-325-9392

Twenty-one years and hundreds of commissions later, Lynn DiNino continues creating novel animals for decorative and functional use. Her creations are sold regularly in selected galleries, both nationally and in Japan. Many public and private collections include her work. Successful experience includes collaborating with architects and designers on site-specific projects, as well as working with corporations.

Ms. DiNino is experienced in many media; her current work includes steel skeletons finished with specialized concrete skins formulated for thin applications. Surfaces can be prepared for interior and exterior use. Inventory is available for viewing or purchase.

A *Twiggy* table, painted concrete over steel, 28"H x 40"L x 16"D

B *Three Ring Circus*, cabinet embellishments of sculpted and low-relief stained concrete, 36"H x 5'L x 22"D

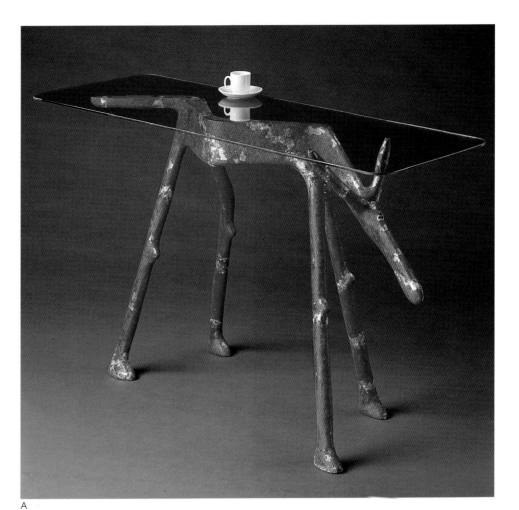

A

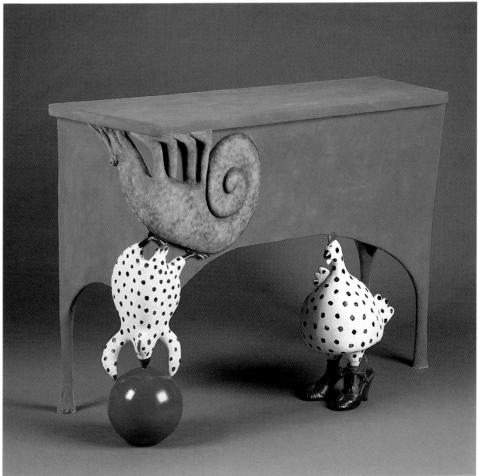

B

Photos: Tom Holt

furnARTure etc.

Charly Stockl
152 Fairmount Avenue
Philadelphia, PA 19123
TEL 215-592-9669

Self-taught artist Charly Stockl specializes in transforming old furniture into new works of art that are functional, pleasing to the eye and valued collecter's pieces.

Starting with found pieces or with the client's existing furniture, and using a wide range of visual references and design influences, he creates one-of-a-kind contemporary, yet nostalgic furniture and accessories.

Each piece is protected with several coats of extremely durable acrylic polymer, requiring minimal care.

A *The Hot Line*, 1993, hand-painted phone bench

B *Chest of Verneuil*, 1994, hand-painted high boy

A

B

Photos: Robert Batey

Igor Naskalov

Roslyn Manor House, Inc.
87-B Cutter Mill Road
Great Neck, NY 11021
FAX 516-466-7403
TEL 516-621-8824

A combination of the Old Masters' traditions and techniques with his personal talents and creativity makes Igor Naskalov an outstanding and unique artist, capable of creating high-quality works in different decorative styles, genres and techniques.

His deep knowledge of world art and his versatility helped him to acquire the reputation of a world-class artist for whom each image is unique.

Please call for additional information.

A four-panel room screen, French baroque style, two-sided, oil paint, 6'W x 6½'H

B headboard, Pompeii style, oil paint

C four-panel room screen (reverse side)

A

B

C

Toni Putnam

Rt. 9D, RR2
Garrison, NY 10524
TEL 914-424-3416

Sculptor Toni Putnam creates furniture employing plant and animal forms and images. These evocative yet practical works can be used out of doors or in. The bronzes are created directly in wax and cast by the lost-wax process. The pieces are beautifully crafted and colorfully patinated, sometimes using touches of gold and silver leaf. The griffin bench is plastic sprayed over foam, making it extremely light and durable.

Putnam is represented in collections and prestigious exhibitions across America and overseas. Prices range from $1,500 to $4,000.

FRANK COLSON
clay

When an architect approached sculptor Frank Colson to create a large wall relief for a nursing home—but offered only a vague notion of what the client wanted—Colson considered the psychological elements that would make sense in such a setting.

"The sun is a soothing focal point," he says, "but usually when we talk about the sun, it's about a sunset. That seemed inappropriate for a nursing home, so I suggested a sunrise instead."

By keeping the lighter colors at the horizon, with darker colors above as they would be in a sunrise, Colson created a strong, inviting sense of dawn on a clay wall relief 16 feet high by 10 feet wide. It was a subtle example of collaboration, Colson says. "The client didn't know what they wanted, they weren't even sure they liked my work, but they were very open to the idea of a customized piece."

In a different kind of collaboration, Colson worked with a client who had a very clear vision of what she wanted at the entry to her upscale condo development: She liked the design of the Emmy Award statue and wanted something that resembled it. Colson and his client refined the design to the point that she was happy with the representation and he was confident he hadn't violated copyright restrictions.

"My primary goal is to satisfy the client," he says. "That might mean working with someone who is very knowledgeable about the kind of art I create and has very specific ideas about the outcome, or it can mean guiding the client into understanding how to appreciate and enjoy the artistic value of something he or she may have no knowledge or awareness of."

See these GUILD publications:
THE GUILD: 1, 3, 4, 5
Architect's Edition: 6
Designer's Edition: 7, 8, 9, 10

ACCESSORIES

Peter M. Fillerup

Wild West Designs
PO Box 286
Heber, UT 84032
FAX 801-654-1653
TEL 801-654-4151

Having grown up in Cody, Wyoming, Peter M. Fillerup was greatly influenced by the romance and adventure of the West. Trained and educated in sculpture, Fillerup apprenticed with renowned artist Dr. Avard Fairbanks.

Known throughout the country for his sculpture, Fillerup makes each creation a work of art, specializing in unique custom designs for distinctive homes and businesses. With timeless materials such as relief-cast bronze, rawhide and stained glass, each piece becomes both distinctive and functional.

Versatile and talented, Fillerup designs bronze sculpture, chandeliers, sconces, lanterns, fireplace screens and hardware, all with his unique vision and style.

LIGHTSPANN
Illumination Design

Christina Spann
5753 Landregan Street
Emeryville, CA 94608
FAX 510-601-8500
TEL 510-601-8500

Christina Spann designs and creates illuminated fixtures for restaurant, residential and corporate clients. Each project is a one-of-a-kind creation, designed in collaboration with interior designers, architects and owners. Lightspann produces everything from whimsical restaurant lights to classic boardroom pendants.

The work empasizes glass but also incorporates metals and painted surfaces. Glass treatments include: cast, slumped, blown, fused and painted. Metal and painted surfaces include: hammered, forged, brushed, patinas and distressed surfaces.

Call for a complete profile and representative projects listing.

Studio visits are welcome. Prices begin at $350.

A *Cuckoo's Nest* pendant, brushed steel, glass and custom oxide patina

B *Sapphire Mynx* pendants, bar railing and sconces, fused and slumped glass with forged iron

C *Sapphire Mynx* (detail)

A

B

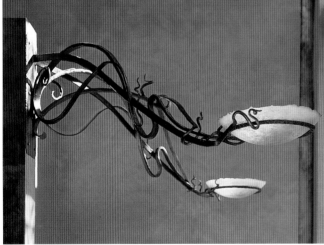

C

Pam Morris

Exciting Lighting
14 East Sir Francis Drake Boulevard
Larkspur, CA 94939
FAX 415-925-1305
TEL 415-925-0840

Pam Morris, owner of EXCITING LIGHTING, studied at the Art Student's League in New York City and has a degree in Fine Arts. Her clients encompass top restaurants, hotels, and private residences, including Wolfgang Puck, Sugar Ray Leonard, Georgio Armani, and The Hong Kong Regent Hotel. She was honored in General Electric's Edison Awards and was selected as an Outstanding Designer in San Francisco. She has spoken and been published nationally.

She is a creative force, distinguished as an innovator of avant-garde design, using formed and cast metal with blown, slumped, and cast glass to create highly original and evocative lit sculptures and luminaires.

As you stand before a lit piece ... you are involved; color and light energy are transmitted to you ... even a Rembrandt cannot do that ....

This is EXCITING!

Call to discuss commission work.

A kiln-slumped glass with metal inclusions

B Postrio restaurant, San Francisco, CA

C artist in her studio

D blown glass cone and cast bronze pendant

A

C

B

D

William C. Richards

Clay Canvas Designs
P.O. Box 361
Underwood, WA 98651
(509) 493-3928
FAX (509) 493-2732

Will Richards received his BFA in ceramics and glass from the University of Minnesota in 1978, and an MFA from the University of Washington in 1981.

His ceramic work can be found in numerous corporate collections, as well as residential environments (see Work for the Wall: Ceramics). Will has created a new and unique approach to commercial and residential lighting. Stoneware bases mix with parchment-like shades for a one-of-a-kind lamp. Custom shades have already been installed in restaurants and other public settings.

He welcomes commissions and custom orders.

Below: ceramic lamps

Angelika Traylor

100 Poinciana Drive
Indian Harbour Beach, FL 32937
FAX 407-779-3612
TEL 407-773-7640

Featuring one-of-a-kind lamps, autonomous panels and architectural installations, Traylor's award-winning work can be recognized by its intricate, jewel-like composition.

Often referred to as having painterly qualities, the exquisite lamp and charming autonomous panel (shown) reflect an original and intensive design process, implemented with meticulous craftsmanship and an unusually beautiful selection of glass.

Traylor's attention to detail and vibrant colors have resulted in her work being eagerly sought by collectors.

Her work can be found in many publications. Traylor is listed in *Who's Who in America*, *Who's Who in American Art*, *Who's Who in American Crafts* and *Who's Who in Contemporary Glass Art*.

Please inquire for more specific information on available work, commissions and pricing.

Also see these GUILD publications:
THE GUILD: 2, 3, 4, 5
Architect's Edition: 6
Designer's Edition: 7, 8, 9

Ron Constantino

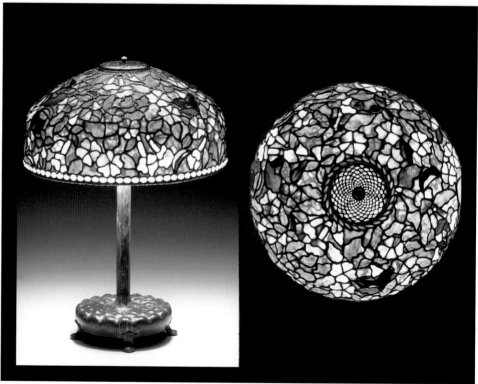

Randall Smith

NANCY J. YOUNG

paper

Hand-cast paper artist Nancy Young strives to create art with a universal appeal while striking a personal chord.

Young creates and molds paper into shapes and figures, and then treats the surface to achieve the effect of bronze or wood or some other finish—sometimes even paper. Young often collaborates with her husband, Allen Young, who works primarily in wood carving.

An example is a commission she completed for the U.S. Embassy in New Guinea: a large plate, three large wall panels, the biggest vessel she could make, and three five-to-six-foot-tall spirit guides. She was working in a time-frame of just seven weeks, so collaboration with her husband was essential to meet the client's deadline.

For Young, it was an opportunity to stretch herself in her personal goal of sharing the meaning in her art. "I don't want to create pieces that are mine alone, I want people to experience an inner response," she explains. "I want something positive, a reaching for something viewers remember, something they want to bring up and work out within themselves."

New Guinea has a very expressive type of art, Young says, so she had strong cultural traditions to guide her. At the same time she could lend a more personal interpretation. "It was an opportunity to push myself in new ways," she says, "both in my own work and in my expanding collaborations with my husband."

Photo: Allan Green

See these GUILD publications:
THE GUILD: 3, 4, 5
Designer's Edition: 6, 7, 8, 9, 10
Gallery Edition: 1

Natalie Darmohraj

Natalka Designs
P.O. Box 40309
Providence, RI 02940
(401) 351-8841

From luxurious hand-dyed, handwoven
blankets to sophisticated upholstery and
drapery, Natalie Darmohraj's unique fabrics
enrich any interior space.

Using the finest fibers, including wool, silk and
mohair, the artist creates abstract images
and patterns through the juxtaposition of
textures and colors. Fabrics are suitable for
both functional use or hanging on the wall.
They are designed for both durability and
aesthetic appeal, appropriate for residential
as well as commercial spaces. Commissions
of all sizes are welcome.

Natalie Darmohraj holds a B.F.A. in Textile
Design from Rhode Island School of Design.

For further information please contact
the artist.

Photography: Cathy Carver

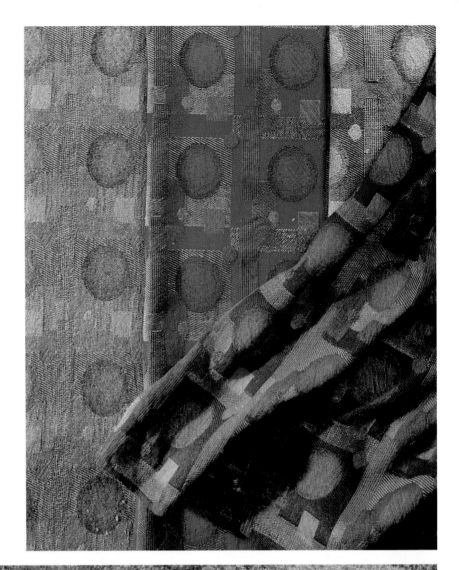

Diann Parrott

Diann Parrott Yardage Art
875 St. Clair Avenue #4
St. Paul, MN 55105
FAX 612-222-4149
TEL 612-222-4149

Parrott is a unique printmaker/designer who orchestrates your specified color palette with images to create custom, hand-printed yardage on natural fibers. Through an impeccable combination of appliqué, piecing and hand fringing, she creates one-of-a-kind, functional accessories: wall art, throw pillows, table and bed linens, lampshades, window treatments, and upholstery. All art may be dry-cleaned; zippered enclosures allow for easy removal.

Parrott is a recipient of the Surface Design Association's Award of Excellence. She exhibits locally in galleries and design showrooms.

A *Being*, 16" x 13", unframed wall art, $150/sq. ft.

B *Domesticating*, 45" wide muslin, $140/yd; lampshade, $130; pillow, $90

C *Azulejos*, $1,200

D *African Queen*, $1,400

A

B

C

D

Photos: Petronella Ytsma

J.E. JASEN

enamel

The delight in her art, says enamelist J.E. Jasen, lies in the exploration of her medium. "Enamel can be such a painstaking material," she says. "And the process can be trying and time-consuming. The fun is in pushing the material to the max and doing things others say you can't do with it."

But flexibility, she believes, is born of intimacy. "When you have an understanding of the material based on familiarity and intuition, you become intimate with the medium, and then you can anticipate and predict what's going to happen." Enameling involves fusing oxides and silica onto a metal surface; for Jasen, that surface is typically steel or copper. "When heat bathes the enamel, it becomes liquid or fluid glass," Jasen explains. "My work is fired repeatedly at high temperatures to enhance the intensity and deliciousness of the colors." The medium never compromises, she says, but she herself is willing to compromise with her clients. "There's a personal aspect when I work with people, and I don't ignore that," she explains. "I get feelings about people when I talk with them, and that guides me in how I approach a commission." Jasen also appreciates the insight she gains from other artists. "Sometimes a commission may lead you in a new direction, or sometimes a friend will show you a new material and you'll say, 'Hey, I can do something with that!' Then you push that material with your kind of imagery, and that's how you grow as an artist."

See these GUILD publications:
THE GUILD: 3, 4, 5
Designer's Edition: 6, 7, 8, 9, 10
Architect's Edition: 7, 10

Shawn Athari

Shawn Athari's, Inc.
14332 Mulholland Drive
Los Angeles, CA 90077
FAX 818-787-MASK
TEL 310-476-0066

Shawn Athari's 20 years of experience in her field has given her the opportunity to perfect a variety of glass techniques. The combination of these techniques allows her to create glass sculptures unique in her field. Most pieces are inspired by images from history.

See additional work in the Work for the Wall section of this book.

Galleries include:
The Art of Disney, Walt Disney World, FL
Little Switzerland, AK and Caribbean
Symmetry, Saratoga Springs, NY
Mindscape, Evanston, IL

Also see these GUILD publications:
THE GUILD: 5
Designer's Edition: 6, 7, 8, 9
Gallery Edition: 1

A *Spirit Post*, Snoqualmie Tribe, Pacific Northwest, 15" x 33" x 5"

B *Peruvian Post*, from the Inca period, 15th century, 15" x 33" x 5"

C *Wolf*, Kwakuitl, Pacific Northwest, 21" x 24" x 4"

D *Soul Spirit Mask*, Vancouver Island, 10" x 18" x 2"

E *Swirl Bowl*, contemporary, 18"Dia

A

B

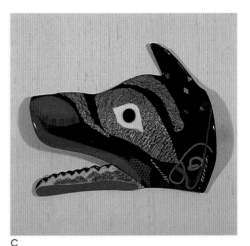

C

D

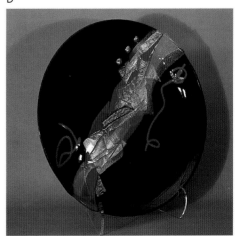

E

Photos: Robert Baumbach

Frank Colson

Colson School of Art/Colson Studio
1666 Hillview Street
Sarasota, FL 34239
FAX 813-953-5892
TEL 813-953-5892

Frank Colson and the Colson Studio offer original one-of-a-kind and limited-edition sculptures and reliefs in clay and bronze. Editions of THE GUILD, one through nine, include visual expressions from this established studio. Since 1963, the artist has placed work in both private and public places of note.

In addition to the *Painted Horse* (16" x 12" x 4") at top right, Colson's *Han Horses* (10" x 10½" x 3") are based on Chinese ceramic sculptures from 206 B.C. Each is unique and individually refired several times using techniques ranging from organic smoke firing to low-fired chrome infusion application.

A portfolio and price list are available upon serious intent of commission or acquisition.

Also see these GUILD publications:
THE GUILD: 1, 3, 4, 5
Architect's Edition: 8
Designer's Edition: 6, 7, 8, 9
Gallery Edition: 1

Printed in Hong Kong ©1995 THE GUILD: Designer's Edition

Carole Alden Doubek

Doubek & Doubek Studios
2030 South 300 East
Salt Lake City, UT 84115
TEL 801-487-1410

Ms. Doubek's creatures have been seen at the National Museum for Women in the Arts and the Royal Museum in Brussels, Belgium. Whether based in nature or the imagination, each fiber sculpture has its own distinct personality. In addition to individual pieces, Ms. Doubek enjoys creating complete environments. She is currently building a rainforest from recycled polyester double knits for the Red Butte Garden Arboretum at the University of Utah. Custom work includes freestanding sculptures, wall hangings, and educational exhibits. All work is primarily fabric, hand sewn, painted, and airbrushed.

Additional information available upon request.

A *Canyon Treefrog* and *Desert Tortoise*, 1994, recycled poly double knit, dimensional fabric paint, Utah Museum of Natural History

B *Gila & Beavertail Cactus*, 1994, fiber, dimensional fabric paint, 2' x 1'

C *Gaboon Viper*, 1994, fiber, dimensional fabric paint, 2' x 3'

A

B

C

Photos: Gary Ott

Mari Marks Fleming

1431 Glendale Avenue
Berkeley, CA 94708-2027
TEL 510-548-3121

Mari Marks Fleming creates highly evocative mixed-media work by incorporating natural materials and subtle, rich texture and coloration. In an ongoing dialog between subject and material, sculptural objects, wall pieces and installations incorporate fiber work, laminating, and embedding material in beeswax and pigment.

Since 1970, Fleming has exhibited nationally and is represented in university and private collections. She will design work for custom installation.

A *Childhood's Shrine*, 1990, mixed-media sculpture, 15" x 12" x18"

B *Reliquary*, 1994, mixed media with encaustic and fiber, 18" x 18" x 3"

C *Childhood's Shrine V*, 1990, mixed-media sculpture, 15" x 12" x 18".

A

B

C

Photos: Kim Harrington

Shuji Ikeda

3012 King Street
Berkeley, CA 94703
FAX 510-845-1634
TEL 510-845-1634

Handbuilt woven ceramic baskets, inspired by traditional Japanese hanakago (flower-arranging baskets).

Shuji Ikeda's work was featured in *Ceramic Arts of Japan*, an exhibition of contemporary and traditional Japanese ceramic artists presented by the Consul General of Japan in San Francisco. His work was also included in a show of California artists at the Renwick Gallery of the Smithsonian Institution, Washington, DC. He has received two Niche awards.

A black clay basket, 11½" x 11½" x 10"H

B black and red clay nerikomi basket, 6" x 6" x 17"H

A

B

Johanna Okovic Goodman

Goodman Associates, Inc.
718 South 22nd Street
Philadelphia, PA 19146
TEL 800-445-1448
TEL 215-546-8048

Known for her innovative sculptural chairs, Goodman's newest work includes portraits. The Clinton chair was on display in the National Portrait Gallery at the Smithsonian Museum from December 1993 to September 1994, on loan from the White House.

These chairs can be either functional or non-functional. The soft sculpted portraits are formed from clothing, fabric and acrylic built directly on the chair. Goodman works from photographs. Clients are encouraged to choose their favorite person, famous or not.

Goodman's work has been exhibited throughout the country and is in many fine collections.

Also see these GUILD publications:
THE GUILD: 5
Designer's Edition: 6, 7, 8

A *Marie Antoinette, President Clinton*

B *Queen Victoria*

C *The Duke*

A

B

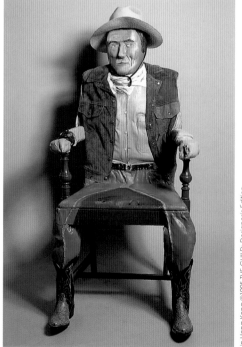

C

Photos: Robert M. Goodman

J. E. Jasen

36 East 10th Street
New York City, NY 10003-6219
FAX 212-777-6375
TEL 212-674-6113

Recognized nationally and internationally for unique, investment-quality, lead-free vitrified enameled artworks, Jasen produces dynamically designed pieces made to the specifications desired by the clients, whether a large mural or an accent to spruce up a small niche.

Enameling is the art of fusing glass particles onto a base metal. The colors are always permanent. Jasen pushes the traditional boundaries by enameling on curved, angled and flat surfaces, while experimenting with integrating compatible pyro-technical materials.

ENAMEL ART IS PERFECT FOR ALL ENVIRONMENTS!

More information available upon request.

Also see these GUILD publications:
THE GUILD: 3, 4, 5
Architect's Edition: 6, 10
Designer's Edition: 6, 7, 8, 9

Printed in Hong Kong © 1995 THE GUILD: Designer's Edition

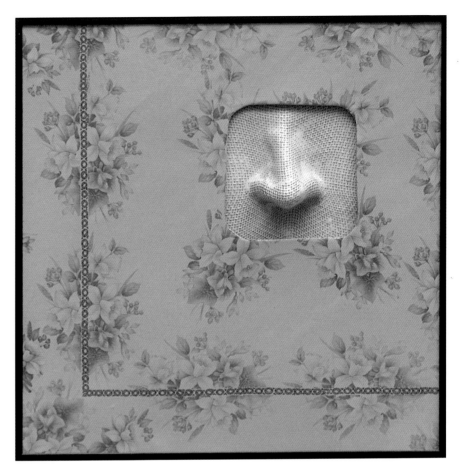

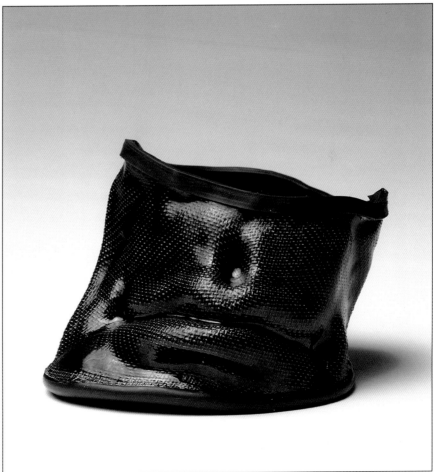

Anne Mayer Meier

Creative Textures
169 Sandalwood Way
Longwood, FL 32750
TEL 407-332-6713

Anne Mayer Meier has been creating a broad range of contemporary art to complement residential and corporate settings since 1979. Meier's *Ancestors©* and *Old Souls©* are mixed-media figures that evoke man's primitive past, using original design and fabrication. Often, found objects are included to enhance the magical qualities of the pieces. At times, Meier will complete the *Ancestor* with one of her unusual story baskets. Although fictional in nature, each one-of-a-kind *Ancestor* or *Old Soul* explores cultural, spiritual and folkloric concepts.

Contact artist for further information.

Also see these GUILD publications:
THE GUILD: 4, 5
Designer's Edition: 6, 7, 8
Gallery Edition: 1

A *Ancestors*, clay, fabric, leather, fur, beads, 28"

B *Offering*, clay, wood, fabric, leather, feathers, glass and clay beads, ting, lucite base, 4'

A

David Powell

B

Jerry Anthony

National Sculptors' Guild

2683 N. Taft Avenue
Loveland, CO 80538
FAX 970-667-2068
TEL 970-667-2015
TEL 800-606-2015

Sharles
Sculptor

Nationally known bronze sculptor with works in fine art museums, public art collections, corporate art collections, fine art galleries and botanical gardens.

"Official Wildlife Sculptor" for the American Endangered Species Foundation.

See *Southwest Art, Wildlife Arts News, Landscape Architecture, Artists of Colorado, Art & Antiques.*

- Small tabletop reliefs
- Large botanical, medicinal plant reliefs for hospitals, medical schools and botanical gardens
- Endangered desert flora and fauna
- Tropical birds, plants, lizards and insects
- Fountains
- Bronze vases of irises and popular flowers

Videos and slides sheets available. Collaborations with designers, architects, corporate art consultants and art galleries welcome.

Also see these GUILD publications:
Architect's Edition: 9, 10

SHOWN (clockwise from top): *Sandy's Iris Garden*, vase; *Kyoto Koi and Iris*, circular relief; *Sunflowers, Snowbirds*, relief, from the Palm Desert Public Art Collection

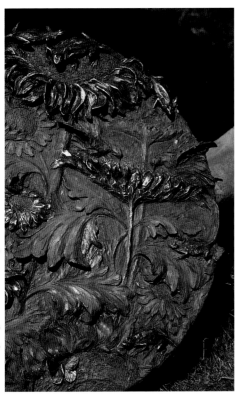

Nourot Glass Studio

Micheal Nourot, Ann Corcoran, David Lindsay
675 East H Street
Benicia, CA 94510
FAX 707-745-2181
TEL 707-745-1463

Working together for nearly 20 years, these artists employ a variety of styles. Corporate commissions include work for the Bechtel Corporation, Bently Inc., and the World Figure Skater's Federation.

Other recent projects include lighting fixtures for Mustard's Restaurant, CA; brick casting for the Southern California Gas Co.; and a commemorative dish for the San Jose Archdiocese.

Brochure, video, film, and price list available.

A *Satin Cane Bowl* by Micheal Nourot,
6¼"H x 10"Dia

B *Rocking Void Vase* by Ann Concoran,
10"H x 7¾"W x 4"D

C *Peak Weight* by David Lindsay,
7"H, faceted by Denali Crystal

A

B

C

170   Sculpture and Objects

Charles Pearson
Timothy Roeder

Whitehead Street Pottery
1011 Whitehead Street
Key West, FL 33040
TEL 305-294-5067

Charles Pearson and Timothy Roeder collaborate to produce large hand-thrown and slab-built raku-fired vessels.

The forms have a visual strength that demands a response while maintaining the traditional subtleties of color by reduction in a post-firing of seaweed.

Commissions include the Southern Progress Corporation; Rath Manufacturing Co., Inc; Demille Corporation; and various public sites.

Slides ($3 refundable) and additional information can be obtained by writing directly to the Whitehead Street Pottery.

Represented by:
The Signature Shop and Gallery, Atlanta, GA
Acropolis Now, Santa Monica, CA
The Red Lion Gallery, Vero Beach, FL
The Bell Gallery of Fine Art, Memphis, TN

A *Fish Head Bowl* (profile and inside view), 16" x 6"

B *Soul Keeper*, 14"W x 17"H

D *Soul Keeper 2*, 13"W x 6"D x 19"H

A

B

C

Martin Sturman

M. Sturman Steel Sculptures
20412 Roca Chica Drive
Malibu, CA 90265
FAX 818-905-7173
TEL 310-456-5716

Martin Sturman creates original steel sculptures in floral, figurative and abstract designs.

His sculptures range from tabletop to free-standing indoor and outdoor pieces, including sculpted tables and entry gates. These beautiful sculptures are executed in stainless steel, weathered (rusted) steel, powder-coated carbon steel and acrylic-painted carbon steel.

Martin frequently has sculptures available for immediate delivery, but encourages site-specific and collaborative efforts. Depending upon complexity, most sculptures can be shipped within 10 to 12 weeks of commission.

Sizes range from 12 inches to 10 feet high. Prices upon request.

Also see these GUILD publications:
Designer's Edition: 7, 8, 9

A *Standing Flowers*, 1994, stainless steel,
   59" x 47" x 14"

B *The Pose*, 1994, enamel/steel, 47" x 31" x 17";
   Dreamer, 1994, enamel/steel, 47" x 26" x 24"

A

B

Photos: Barry Michlin

Tim Walker

Pop Cat Studio
28277 Townley
Madison Heights, MI 48071-2846
FAX 810-543-1942
TEL 810-543-1942

Artist Tim Walker creates extraordinary two- and three-dimensional mixed media sculptures that are humorous and refreshing in attitude. Sophisticated in style, satirical in content, and clever in approach, Tim's sculptures express his unique perception of the human condition.

Tim incorporates many technical innovations to achieve archival longevity, internal and external strength, and surface smoothness, and has chosen to draw inspiration from many different sculptural mediums. The result is a hybrid approach to his craft.

The goal is to redefine the medium and to put a whimsical spin on life.

Commissions are accepted.

Portfolio available upon request.

A *Billionaire's Prayer*, 1994, mixed media, 40" x 33" x 19½"

B *The Healthy Jogger*, 1994, mixed media, 47" x 47" x 7"

C *Luciano Pavarotti*, 1994, mixed media, 55" x 60" x 9"

A

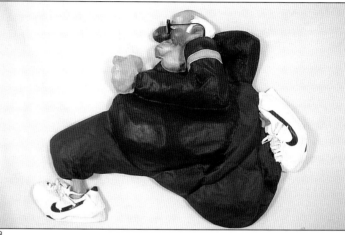

B

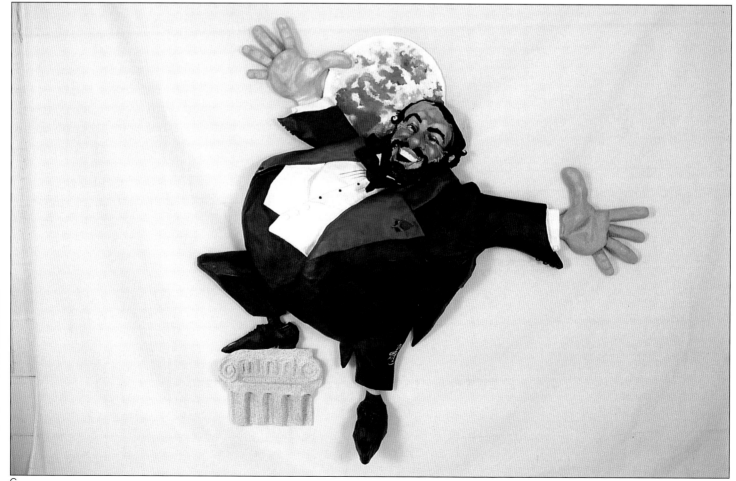

C

Printed in Hong Kong ©1995 THE GUILD: Designer's Edition

Sculpture and Objects 173

Jonathan Winfisky

Potter Road/Legate Hill
Charlemont, MA 01339
TEL 413-339-8319

Jonathan Winfisky has been designing and
producing unique and original blown and
cast sculptural glass vessel forms since 1975.

Forms in the *Cast Design Series* are designed to
work collectively or individually when displayed
in private residences and public spaces.

Larger pieces are available by commission
and all designs can be produced in a wide
variety of sizes and colors. Please call or write
for further information.

A *Cast Design Series,* ©1995, bowl, 15"; vase, 14";
   vial, 6"; bud vase, 8"; Ming vessel, 9"

B cast bowl form on pedestal base, 16" x 9"

A

B

Nancy J. Young
Allen Young

11416 Brussels NE
Albuquerque, NM 87111
FAX 505-299-2238
TEL 505-299-6108

The Youngs create original two- and three-dimensional free-standing sculptures and mixed-media wall art. Color preferences and commissions accepted.

Prices depend on size and complexity. Allow four to eight weeks from design approval and contract to completion. Shipping and handling FOB Albuquerque.

Selected commissions include the U.S. State Department, IBM, AT&T, and American Express.

A bronze patinated hand-cast paper,
   54"H x 11"W x 3"D

B hand-cast panel, 20"H x 4"W x 2½"D;
   mixed-media figures, 4'6" to 5'6"H x 4½" to
   6"W x 2½"D; vessel, 16"H x 13"W; plate, 30" Dia

A

B

Photos: Pat Berrett

ANGELIKA TRAYLOR
stained glass

Angelika Traylor approaches her Tiffany glass work from a painter's perspective. "It's full of detail and color," she says. "I create like a painter would, then I translate the color and detail into glass."

Her work is executed on a small scale and is known for its intricate, jewel-like composition. "Most people think of the function of stained glass," she adds. " I create for those who fall in love its artistry."

Traylor uses texture, as well as color, in her work, which has primitive overtones. "My work has an unskilled look," she says. "I have no formal art training, so my work doesn't look perfect, and that has a distinctive appeal."

Her clients, she says, open her eyes to what is most appealing about her glass. " I've learned from them that there is almost a sensual quality to my work," she explains. "People immediately want to touch it. I had to learn from people who buy my work that when they see it, they just have to float their fingers over it and feel the ripples and bumps and textures."

Most of Traylor's clients have eclectic homes, and many come to her for multiple pieces. "They're not looking for a certain size or function, but for a certain piece," she says. " It might be something I've already done, or it might be something I create for them, but once they find it, they make it fit into their environment.

" I want people to be more than happy with my work," she adds. "I want them to be ecstatic. That's the most rewarding part of being an artist."

Photo: Ron Constantino

See these GUILD publications:
THE GUILD: 2, 3, 4, 5
Designer's Edition: 7, 8, 9, 10
Architect's Edition: 6
Gallery Edition: 2

GALLERY LISTINGS
A State-by-State Directory

All of the 1,500 galleries included in our listing carry the work of craft artists. Some specialize in media, others have a regional or thematic focus, and many can facilitate special orders and projects. The listing is a great travel companion and may reveal some unfamiliar galleries in your own backyard.

ALABAMA

HOLLAND SMITH GALLERY
301 JEFFERSON ST N
HUNTSVILLE, AL 35801-4853
205-534-1982

JEFFERSON STREET GALLERY
313 E JEFFERSON ST
MONTGOMERY, AL 36104-3645
205-263-5703

MARALYN WILSON GALLERY
2010 CAHABA RD
BIRMINGHAM, AL 35223-1110
205-879-0582

THE KENTUCK MUSEUM
3500 MCFARLAND BLVD
NORTHPORT, AL 35476-3183
205-333-1252

ALASKA

KIKO B FIBERARTS
108 CARLYLE WAY
FAIRBANKS, AK 99709-2930
907-456-2202

OBJECTS OF BRIGHT PRIDE
165 S FRANKLIN ST
JUNEAU, AK 99801-1321
907-586-4969

STONINGTON GALLERY
415 F ST
ANCHORAGE, AK 99501-2218
907-272-1489

ARIZONA

AGUAJITO DEL SOL
TLAQUEPAQUE 103A
PO BOX 1607
SEDONA, AZ 86336
602-282-5258

ARTAMERICA GALLERY OF ART
9301 E SHEA BLVD
SCOTTSDALE, AZ 85260-6733
602-661-8772

ARTISTIC GALLERIES
7077 E MAIN ST
SCOTTSDALE, AZ 85251-4325
602-945-6766

AUSI GALLERY
38 CAMINO OTERO
TUBAC, AZ 85646
602-398-3193

BENTLEY TOMLINSON GALLERY
4161 N MARSHALL WAY
SCOTTSDALE, AZ 85251-3809
602-941-0078

BERTA WRIGHT GALLERY
260 E CONGRESS ST
TUCSON, AZ 85701-1829
602-742-4134

DESERT MOON
2785 WEST 89A
SEDONA, AZ 86336
602-204-1195

EL PRADO GALLERIES, INC
PO BOX 1849
SEDONA, AZ 86339-1849
602-282-7390

ERTCO
PO BOX 1970
SEDONA, AZ 86339-1970
602-282-4945

ES POSIBLE GALLERY
34505 N SCOTTSDALE RD
SCOTTSDALE, AZ 85262-1202
602-488-3770

EVERY BLOOMING THING, INC
2010 E UNIVERSITY DR
TEMPE, AZ 85281-4681
602-921-1196

GALERIA MESA
155 N CENTER
MESA, AZ 85201-6626
602-644-2242

GALLERY TEN
7045 E 3RD AVE
SCOTTSDALE, AZ 85251-3801
602-994-0405

GALLERY THREE
3819 N 3RD ST
PHOENIX, AZ 85012-2074
602-277-9540

GIFTED HANDS
PO BOX 1388
SEDONA, AZ 86339-1388
602-282-4822

IMAGINE GALLERY
CONRAD LEATHER BOUTIQUE
34505 N SCOTTSDALE ROAD E8
SCOTTSDALE, AZ 85262
602-488-2190

JOANNE RAPP GALLERY
THE HAND AND THE SPIRIT
4222 N MARSHALL WAY
SCOTTSDALE, AZ 85251
602-949-1262

LA FUENTE GALLERY
B123 TLAQUEPAUE
PO BOX 2169
SEDONA, AZ 86339-2169
602-282-5276

OBSIDIAN GALLERY
4340 N CAMPBELL AVE STE 90
TUCSON, AZ 85718-6582
602-577-3598

PEARSON & COMPANY
7022 E MAIN ST
SCOTTSDALE, AZ 85251-4314
602-840-6447

PINK ADOBE GALLERY
222 E CONGRESS ST
TUCSON, AZ 85701-1810
602-623-2828

RAKU GALLERY
GENERAL DELIVERY
PO BOX 965
JEROME, AZ 86331-9999
602-639-0239

SUN WEST GALLERY
152 S MONTEZUMA ST
PRESCOTT, AZ 86303-4718
602-778-1204

SUZANNE BROWN GALLERIES
7160 E MAIN ST
SCOTTSDALE, AZ 85251-4316
602-945-8475

GALLERY LISTINGS

THE MIND'S EYE CRAFT GALLERY
4200 N MARSHALL WAY
SCOTTSDALE, AZ 85251-3204
302-941-2494

TOTALLY SOUTHWESTERN GALLERY
5575 E RIVER RD STE 131
TUCSON, AZ 85715-6737
602-577-2295

ARKANSAS

CONTEMPORANEA GALLERY
516 CENTRAL AVE
HOT SPRINGS, AR 71901-3556
501-624-0516

CRAZY BONE GALLERY
37 SPRING ST
EUREKA SPRINGS, AR 72632-3147
501-253-6600

CALIFORNIA

A GALLERY OF FINE ART
73580 EL PASEO
PALM DESERT, CA 92260-4306
619-346-8885

A NEW LEAF GALLERY
1286 GILMAN ST
BERKELEY, CA 94706-2353
510-525-7621

A PASSING GLIMPSE
9219 W PICO BLVD
LOS ANGELES, CA 90035-1318

AESTHETIC COLLECTION, INC
1060 17TH ST
SAN DIEGO, CA 92101-5707
619-238-1860

AGNES BOURNE, INC
2 HENRY ADAMS ST STE 220
SAN FRANCISCO, CA 94103-5024
415-626-6883

ALLEN FINE ART GALLERY
37656 BANKSIDE DR
CATHEDRAL CITY, CA 92234-7827
619-341-8655

AMBIANCE GALLERY
405 2ND ST
EUREKA, CA 95501-0405
707-445-8950

AMERICAN MUSEUM OF QUILTS
776 S 2ND ST
SAN JOSE, CA 95112-5859
408-971-0323

AMERICAN PANACHE
31430 BROADBEACH RD
MALIBU, CA 90265-2669

ANGIE & COMPANY
360 TITLEIST CT
SAN JOSE, CA 95127-5439

ART OPTIONS
319 S ROBERTSON BLVD
LOS ANGELES, CA 90048-3805
310-392-9099

ART OPTIONS
372 HAYES ST
SAN FRANCISCO, CA 94102-4420
415-567-8535

ART WORLD DESIGN
18337 SHERMAN WAY
RESEDA, CA 91335-4425
818-774-3620

ARTIFACT
17 STOCKTON ST
SAN FRANCISCO, CA 94108-5805
415-788-9375

ARTIFACTS GALLERY
3024 FILLMORE ST
SAN FRANCISCO, CA 94123-4010
415-922-8465

ARTIFAX INT'L GALLERY & GIFTS
450 1ST ST E STE C
SONOMA, CA 95476-6760
707-996-9494

ARTISANCE
278 BEACH ST
LAGUNA BEACH, CA 92651-2105
714-494-0687

ARTISTS COLLABORATIVE GALLERY
1007 SECOND ST, OLD TOWN
SACRAMENTO, CA 95814
916-444-3764

BANAKER GALLERY
CONTEMPORARY ART & FINE ART
251 POST ST
SAN FRANCISCO, CA 94108
415-397-1397

BAY ARTS
1847 INDIAN VALLEY RD
NOVATO, CA 94947-4226
415-399-9925

BAYSIDE GALLERY
4555 N PERSHING AVE STE 33153
STOCKTON, CA 95207-6740
619-233-4350

BAZAR DEL MUNDO
2754 CALHOUN ST
SAN DIEGO, CA 92110-2706

BELL'OCCHIO
8 BRADY ST
SAN FRANCISCO, CA 94103-1211
415-864-4048

BENDICE GALLERY
380 1ST ST W
SONOMA, CA 95476-5631
707-938-2775

BETH CHRISTENSEN FINE ART
538 SILVERADO DR
TIBURON, CA 94920-1321
415-435-2314

BOB LEONARD, INC
2727 MAIN ST
SANTA MONICA, CA 90405-4052
310-399-3251

BRAVO GALLERY
535 4TH AVE
SAN DIEGO, CA 92101-6904

BRENDAN WALTER GALLERY
1001 COLORADO AVE
SANTA MONICA, CA 90401-2809
310-395-1155

BRONZE PLUS, INC
6790 DEPOT ST
SEBASTOPOL, CA 95472-3452
707-829-5480

CA CONTEMPORARY CRAFTS ASSOC.
PO BOX 2060
SAUSALITO, CA 94966-2060
415-927-3158

CALIFORNIA ART GALLERY
305 N COAST HWY STE A
LAGUNA BEACH, CA 92651-1681

CALIFORNIA CONTEMPORARY CRAFT
109 CORTE MADERA AVE
TOWN CENTER
CORTE MADERA, CA 94925-1304
415-927-3158

CALIFORNIA CRAFT MUSEUM
GHIRADELLI SQUARE
900 N POINT ST
SAN FRANCISCO, CA 94109
415-774-1919

CALIFORNIA PACIFIC DESIGNS
2060 LINCOLN AVE
ALAMEDA, CA 94501-2713

CARD DE A
1570 Q ROSECRANS AVE
MANHATTAN BEACH, CA 90266

CARR & ASSOCIATES
2 HENRY ADAMS ST STE 333
SAN FRANCISCO, CA 94103-5025
415-861-1021

CASKEY LEES GALLERY
PO BOX 1409
TOPANGA, CA 90290-1409
310-455-2886

CAVANAUGH GALLERY
415 MAIN ST
HALF MOON BAY, CA 94019-1749
415-726-7771

CECILE MOOCHNEK GALLERY
1809D 4TH ST
BERKELEY, CA 94710-1910
510-549-1018

CEDANNA GALLERY
400 MAIN ST
HALF MOON BAY, CA 94019-1725
415-726-6776

CEDANNA GALLERY & STORE
1925 FILLMORE ST
SAN FRANCISCO, CA 94115-2744
415-474-7152

CELEBRATE LIFE
28 E COLORADO BLVD
PASADENA, CA 91105-1956
818-585-0690

CHAN SCHATZ
626 E HALEY ST # 630
SANTA BARBARA, CA 93103-3110
805-962-3720

CHAPSON ARTSVISION
1750 UNION ST
SAN FRANCISCO, CA 94123-4407
415-292-6560

CHAPSON ARTSVISION, LTD
2 HENRY ADAMS ST STE 489
SAN FRANCISCO, CA 94103-5026
415-863-2117

CHEZ MAC
812 POST ST
SAN FRANCISCO, CA 94109-6013
415-775-2515

CHRISTINE OF SANTA FE
220 FOREST AVE
LAGUNA BEACH, CA 92651-2114
714-494-3610

CLAUDIA CHAPLINE GALLERY
3445 SHORELINE HWY
PO BOX 946
STINSON BEACH, CA 94970
415-868-2308

CLOSETS & CLOTHS
617 BLUE SPRUCE DR
DANVILLE, CA 94506-4524

CLYDE STREET GALLERY
34 CLYDE ST
SAN FRANCISCO, CA 94107-1718
415-546-5185

COAST GALLERY
HIGHWAY 1
BIG SUR, CA 93920
408-667-2301

CODA GALLERY
73151 EL PASEO
PALM DESERT, CA 92260-4217
619-346-4661

COLLAGE STUDIO GALLERY
1345 18TH ST
SAN FRANCISCO, CA 94107-2822
415-282-4401

COMPOSITIONS GALLERY
317 SUTTER ST
SAN FRANCISCO, CA 94108-4301
415-693-9111

CONTEMPORARY CRAFTS ASSOCIATION GALLERY
109 CORTE MADERA TOWN CENTER
CORTE MADERA, CA 94925
415-331-8520

COONLEY GALLERY
325 STANFORD SHOPPING CTR
PALO ALTO, CA 94304-1413
415-327-4000

COUTURIER GALLERY
166 N LA BREA AVE
LOS ANGELES, CA 90036-2912
213-933-5557

CRAFTSMAN'S GUILD
300 DE HARO ST STE 342
SAN FRANCISCO, CA 94103-5144
415-431-5425

CROCK-R-BOX
EL PASEO VILLAGE
73-425 EL PASEO
PALM DESERT, CA 92260
619-568-6688

DAVID AUSTIN CONTEMPORARY ART
355 W EL PORTAL
PALM SPRINGS, CA 92264-8908
619-322-7709

DE NOVO
250 UNIVERSITY AVE
PALO ALTO, CA 94301-1713
415-327-1256

DEL MANO GALLERY
11981 SAN VICENTE BLVD
LOS ANGELES, CA 90049-5003
310-476-8508

DEL MANO GALLERY
33 E COLORADO BLVD
PASADENA, CA 91105-1901
818-793-6648

DEVERA GALLERY
334 HAYES ST
SAN FRANCISCO, CA 94102-4421
415-861-8480

DISCOVERIES CONTEMPORARY CRAFT
17350 17TH ST STE E
TUSTIN, CA 92680-1956
714-544-6206

DOLCE VITA
2907 PASATIEMPO LN
SACRAMENTO, CA 95821-4911

DOROTHY WEISS GALLERY
256 SUTTER ST
SAN FRANCISCO, CA 94108-4409
415-397-3611

ECLECTIC GALLERY
KASTEN & UKIAH ST
MENDOCINO, CA 95460
707-937-5951

EDITIONS LIMITED GALLERY
625 2ND ST # 400
SAN FRANCISCO, CA 94107-2050
415-543-9811

EILEEN KREMEN GALLERY
619 N HARBOR BLVD
FULLERTON, CA 92632-1517
714-879-1391

ELEGANT EARTH GALLERY
13101 HIGHWAY 9
BOULDER CREEK, CA 95006-9120
408-338-3646

ELIZABETH FORTNER GALLERY
100 W MICHELTORENA ST
SANTA BARBARA, CA 93101-3019
805-969-9984

FEINGARTEN GALLERIES
PO BOX 5383
BEVERLY HILLS, CA 90209-5383
310-274-7042

FERRARI OF CARMEL
SAN CARLOS 5TH & 6TH
PO BOX 3273
CARMEL, CA 93921
408-624-9677

FINE GALLERY
PO BOX 1494
SUTTER CREEK, CA 95685-1494
209-267-0571

FINE WOODWORKING GALLERY
1201C BRIDGEWAY
SAUSALITO, CA 94965-1916
415-332-5770

FINE WOODWORKING OF CARMEL
SAN CARLOS & MISSION
6TH & 5TH
CARMEL, CA 93921
408-622-9663

FOLLOWING SEA
8522 BEVERLY BLVD
LOS ANGELES, CA 90048-6204
213-659-0592

FOX ON THE GREEN
254 MAIN ST
SALINAS, CA 93901-2704

FREDERICK SPRATT GALLERY
920 S 1ST ST
SAN JOSE, CA 95110-3125
408-294-1135

FREEHAND GALLERY
8413 W 3RD ST
LOS ANGELES, CA 90048-4111
213-655-2607

FRESNO ART MUSEUM SHOP
2233 N 1ST ST
FRESNO, CA 93703-2364
209-485-4810

GALLERI ORREFORS KOSTA BODA
3333 BEAR ST S COAST PLAZA
COSTA MESA, CA 92626
714-549-1959

GALLERY ALEXANDER
7850 GIRARD AVE
LA JOLLA, CA 92037-4230
619-459-9433

GALLERY EIGHT
7464 GIRARD AVE
LA JOLLA, CA 92037-5142
619-454-9781

GALLERY FAIR
PO BOX 263
MENDOCINO, CA 95460-0263
707-937-5121

GALLERY FOURTEEN
300 NAPA ST SLIP 21
SAUSALITO, CA 94965-1971
510-547-7608

GALLERY JAPONESQUE
824 MONTGOMERY ST
SAN FRANCISCO, CA 94133
415-398-8577

GALLERY OF FUNCTIONAL ART
2429 MAIN ST
SANTA MONICA, CA 90405-3539
310-450-2827

GALLERY ONE
32 LIBERTY ST
PETALUMA, CA 94952-2901
707-778-8277

GARRETT WHITE GALLERY
664 S COAST HWY
LAGUNA BEACH, CA 92651-2416
714-494-4117

GALLERY LISTINGS

GEORGEO'S COLLECTION
1139 PROSPECT ST
LA JOLLA, CA 92037-4534
619-551-8664

GEORGEO'S COLLECTION
269 FOREST AVE
LAGUNA BEACH, CA 92651-2113
714-497-0907

GEORGEO'S COLLECTION
416 N RODEO DR
BEVERLY HILLS, CA 90210-4502
310-275-7967

GOLDEN TULIP
464 1ST ST
SUITE E
SONOMA, CA 95476
707-938-3624

GOOD DAY SUNSHINE
29 E NAPA ST
SONOMA, CA 95476-6708
707-938-4001

GRAYSTONE
SECOND & F STS
EUREKA, CA 95501

GUMP'S GALLERY
250 POST ST
SAN FRANCISCO, CA 94108-5101
415-982-1616

HANDWORKS
DOLORES & 6TH AVE
CARMEL, CA 93921
408-624-6000

HANK BAUM GALLERY
2842 PIERCE ST
SAN FRANCISCO, CA 94123-3819
415-752-4336

HARLEEN ALLEN FINE ARTS
427 BRYANT ST
SAN FRANCISCO, CA 94107-1302
415-777-0920

HENLEY'S GALLERY
ON THE SEA RANCH
1000 ANNAPOLIS RD
THE SEA RANCH, CA 95497
707-785-2951

HIGHLANDS SCULPTURE GALLERY
DOLORES BETWEEN 5TH & 6TH
CARMEL, CA 93921
408-624-0535

HIGHLIGHT GALLERY
45052 MAIN ST
MENDOCINO, CA 95460-
707-937-3132

HUMBOLDT'S FINEST
417 2ND ST
EUREKA, CA 95501-0405
707-443-1258

ICAAN GALLERIES
228 MANHATTAN BEACH
  BLVD # 107
MANHATTAN BEACH, CA 90266.
310-376-6171

IMAGES OF THE NORTH
1782 UNION ST
SAN FRANCISCO, CA 94123-4407
415-673-1273

INTERIA
11404 SORRENTO VALLEY RD
SAN DIEGO, CA 92121-1315
619-455-7177

INTERNATIONAL GALLERY
643 G ST
SAN DIEGO, CA 92101-7028
619-235-8255

IRA WOLK GALLERY
1235 MAIN ST
SAINT HELENA, CA 94574-1902
707-963-8801

JOAN ROBEY GALLERY
2912 4TH ST
SANTA MONICA, CA 90405-5504

JOANNE CHAPPEL GALLERY
625 SECOND ST
SAN FRANCISCO, CA 94107
415-777-5711

JOHN NATSOULAS GALLERY
140 F ST
DAVIS, CA 95616-4628
916-756-3938

JOSLYN STUDIO & ART GALLERY
GENERAL DELIVERY
PO BOX 596
COLOMA, CA 95613-9999
916-621-2049

JUDITH LITVICH CONTEMP. ARTS
2 HENRY ADAMS ST # M-69
SAN FRANCISCO, CA 94103-5016
415-863-3329

KALEIDOSCOPE GALLERY
3273 ROGERS AVE
WALNUT CREEK, CA 94596-1846
510-210-1336

KIMBERLEY'S
25601 PINE CREEK LN
WILMINGTON, CA 90744-1827
310-835-4169

KIYO HIGASHI GALLERY
8332 MELROSE AVE
LOS ANGELES, CA 90069-5420
213-655-2482

LH SELMAN, LTD
761 CHESTNUT ST
SANTA CRUZ, CA 95060-3751
800-538-0766

LA QUINTA SCULPTURE PARK
57325 MADISON ST
PO BOX 1566
LA QUINTA, CA 92253
619-564-6464

LA VAE GALLERY
4703 SPRING ST
LA MESA, CA 91941-5207

LEGENDS GALLERY
483 1ST ST W
SONOMA, CA 95476-6608
707-939-8100

LEONE NII GALLERY
198 CASTRO ST
MOUNTAIN VIEW, CA 94041-1202

LORI'S ART GALLERY
20929 VENTURA BLVD
WOODLAND HILLS, CA 91364-2334
818-884-1110

LOS GATOS COMPANY
17½ N SANTA CRUZ AVE
LOS GATOS, CA 95030-5916
408-354-2433

MADE IN MENDOCINO
PO BOX 510
HOPLAND, CA 95449-0510
707-744-1300

MAIN STREET JEWELERS
125 N MAIN ST
LAKEPORT, CA 95453-4814

MANDEL & COMPANY
8687 MELROSE AVE
LOS ANGELES, CA 90069-5701
310-652-5025

MANY HANDS CRAFT GALLERY
655 G ST
SAN DIEGO, CA 92101-7028

MANY HANDS GALLERY
1510 PACIFIC AVE
SANTA CRUZ, CA 95060-3903
408-429-8696

MARCELLA NOON IMPORTS
101 HENRY ADAMS ST STE 423
SAN FRANCISCO, CA 94103-5214
415-255-8485

MARTIN LAWRENCE GALLERIES
2855 STEVENS CREEK BLVD
SANTA CLARA, CA 95050-6709
408-985-8885

MASTER'S MARK GALLERY
3228 SACRAMENTO ST
SAN FRANCISCO, CA 94115-2007
415-885-6700

MATRIX GALLERY
1725 I ST
SACRAMENTO, CA 95814-3001
916-441-4818

MICHAEL HIMOVITZ GALLERY
1020 10TH ST
SACRAMENTO, CA 95814-3502
916-448-8723

MODERN LIVING
8125 MELROSE AVE
LOS ANGELES, CA 90046-7011
213-655-3898

NADEL PHELAN GALLERY
1245 EL SOLYO HEIGHTS DR
FELTON, CA 95018-9336
408-426-4980

NATURESQUE
PIER 39, SPACE H-3
SAN FRANCISCO, CA 94133

NEW PIECES GALLERY
1597 SOLANO AVE
BERKELEY, CA 94707-2116
510-527-6779

OFF YOUR DOT
2241 MARKET ST
SAN FRANCISCO, CA 94114-1612
415-252-5642

OUT OF HAND GALLERY
1303 CASTRO ST
SAN FRANCISCO, CA 94114-3620
415-826-3885

GALLERY LISTINGS

P.R. COONLEY
325 STANFORD SHOPPING CTR
PALO ALTO, CA 94304-1413
508-546-6200

PACIFIC GALLERY
228 FOREST AVE
LAGUNA BEACH, CA 92651-2114
714-494-8732

PAINTED LADY GALLERY
1407 JACKSON GATE RD
JACKSON, CA 95642-9575
209-223-1754

**PALM SPRINGS
DESERT MUSEUM**
101 N MUSEUM DR
PALM SPRINGS, CA 92262-5659
619-325-7186

PAZAR GALLERY
23561 MALIBU COLONY RD
MALIBU, CA 90265-4626
310-456-1142

PERIWINKLE PRINTS & GIFTS
88 EUREKA SQ
PACIFICA, CA 94044-2653
415-359-4236

PETRI'S
675 BRIDGEWAY
SAUSALITO, CA 94965-2218
415-332-2225

PIECEMAKERS
1720 ADAMS AVE
COSTA MESA, CA 92626-4890

PINNACLE GROUSE
127 FOREST ST
BOULDER CREEK, CA 95006-8900

PLUMS CONTEMPORARY ART
5096 N PALM AVE
FRESNO, CA 93704-2201
209-227-5389

POT-POURRI GALLERY
4100 REDWOOD RD
OAKLAND, CA 94619-2363
510-531-1503

POWER SEWING
185 5TH AVE
SAN FRANCISCO, CA 94118-1309
415-386-0400

PRIMAVERA GALLERY
214 E OJAI AVE
OJAI, CA 93023-2737
805-646-7133

PUBLIC ART SERVICES
1242 CRESCENT HEIGHTS #20
WEST HOLLYWOOD, CA 90046
213-650-3709

RANDOLPH & HEIN
101 HENRY ADAMS ST STE 101
SAN FRANCISCO, CA 94103-5211
415-864-3550

RANDOLPH & HEIN, INC
8687 MELROSE AVE STE 310
LOS ANGELES, CA 90069-5701
310-855-1222

RED ROSE GALLERY
2251 CHESTNUT ST
SAN FRANCISCO, CA 94123-2607
415-776-6871

**RITAMARIE SUSTEK
& ASSOCIATES**
712 BANROFT ROAD STE 197
WALNUT CREEK, CA 94598
510-944-4711

ROBERGE GALLERY
73520 EL PASEO
PALM DESERT, CA 92260-4338
619-340-5045

ROOKIE-TO GALLERY
PO BOX 606
14300 HWY 128
BOONVILLE, CA 95415-0606
707-895-2204

RUTH BACHOFNER GALLERY
2046 BROADWAY
SANTA MONICA, CA 90404-2910
310-458-8007

**SANTA BARBARA STYLE
& DESIGN**
137 E DE LA GUERRA ST
SANTA BARBARA, CA 93101-2228
805-965-6291

SCHWARTZ CIERLAK GALLERY
26106 PAOLINO PL
VALENCIA, CA 91355-2039
213-396-3814

SCULPTURE TO WEAR
9638 BRIGHTON WAY
BEVERLY HILLS, CA 90210-5110
310-277-2542

**SEEKERS COLLECTION &
GALLERY**
2450 MAIN ST
CAMBRIA, CA 93428-3420
805-927-8626

SHADY LANE CRAFT GALLERY
441 UNIVERSITY AVE
PALO ALTO, CA 94301-1813

SHARON PARK GALLERY
325 SHARON PARK DR
MENLO PARK, CA 94025-6848
415-854-6878

SHERWOOD GALLERY
460 S COAST HWY
LAGUNA BEACH, CA 92651-2404
714-497-3185

SHIBUI HOUSE
630 CLIFF DR
APTOS, CA 95003-5312
408-688-7195

SIGNATURE GALLERY
3693 5TH AVE
SAN DIEGO, CA 92103-4218
619-297-0430

SIMPSON HELLER GALLERY
2289 MAIN ST
CAMBRIA, CA 93428-3017
805-927-1800

SOFT TOUCH ARTISTS
COLLECTIVE GALLERY
1580 HAIGHT ST
SAN FRANCISCO, CA 94117

SOPHIA/CHIARA DESIGNER
80 THROCKMORTON
MILL VALLEY, CA 94941

SOUTH BAY BRONZE
PO BOX 3254
SAN JOSE, CA 95156-3254

**STARY SHEETS FINE ART
GALLERY**
14988 SAND CANYON AVE
IRVINE, CA 92718-2107
714-733-0445

STEVE STEIN GALLERY
13934 VENTURA BLVD
SHERMAN OAKS, CA 91423-3564
818-990-0777

STILLWATER'S
1228 MAIN ST
SAINT HELENA, CA 94574-1901
707-963-1782

STUDIO 41
739 1ST ST
BENICIA, CA 94510-3213
707-745-0254

STUDIO FORTY-TWO
23 N SANTA CRUZ AVE
LOS GATOS, CA 95030-5916
408-395-3191

SUMMER HOUSE GALLERY
14 MILLER AVE
MILL VALLEY, CA 94941-1904
415-383-6695

SUSAN CUMMINS GALLERY
12 MILLER AVE
MILL VALLEY, CA 94941-1904
415-383-1512

TAFOYA GALLERY
LINCOLN COURT BLDG #110
2105 S BASCOM ST
CAMPBELL, CA 95008
408-559-6161

TAKADA FINE ARTS GALLERY
251 POST ST SIXTH FLOOR
SAN FRANCISCO, CA 94108-5004
415-956-5288

TARBOX GALLERY
1202 KETTNER BLVD
SAN DIEGO, CA 92101-3338
619-234-5020

TAYLOR-GRATZER GALLERY
8667 W SUNSET BLVD
WEST HOLLYWOOD, CA 90069
213-659-6422

TEN DIRECTIONS GALLERY
723 SANTA YSABEL AVE
LOS OSOS, CA 93402-1137
805-528-4574

TERCERA GALLERY
24 N SANTA CRUZ AVE
LOS GATOS, CA 95030-5917
408-354-9482

TERRAIN
165 JESSIE ST STE 2
SAN FRANCISCO, CA 94105-4008
415-543-0656

TESORI GALLERY
30 E 3RD AVE
SAN MATEO, CA 94401-4011
415-344-4731

TESORI GALLERY
319 S ROBERTSON BLVD
LOS ANGELES, CA 90048-3805
213-273-9890

GALLERY LISTINGS

TEXTURES GALLERY
550 DEEP VALLEY DR STE 135
RLLNG HLS EST, CA 90274-3620
213-541-1943

THE ARCHITECT'S INTERIOR
1300 N SANTA CRUZ AVE
LOS GATOS, CA 95030
408-354-1020

THE ART COLLECTOR'S GALLERY
4151 TAYLOR ST
SAN DIEGO, CA 92110-2740
619-299-3232

THE ART COMPANY
25 W GUTIERREZ ST
SANTA BARBARA, CA 93101-3449
805-963-1157

THE ART WORKS
340 WESTBOURNE ST
LA JOLLA, CA 92037-5345
619-459-7688

THE ARTFUL EYE
1333A LINCOLN AVE
CALISTOGA, CA 94515-1701
707-942-4743

THE BRAUNSTEIN QUAY GALLERY
250 SUTTER ST
SAN FRANCISCO, CA 94108-4403
415-392-5532

THE COURTYARD GALLERY
1349 PARK ST
ALAMEDA, CA 94501-4533
415-521-1521

THE CRAFT & FOLK ART MUSEUM
5800 WILSHIRE BLVD
LOS ANGELES, CA 90036-4500
213-937-9099

THE CRATE: AMERICAN HANDCRAFTS
#9 HYATT REGENCY PLAZA
1200 K ST
SACRAMENTO, CA 95814
916-441-4136

THE DEVORZON GALLERY
8687 MELROSE AVE # B188
LOS ANGELES, CA 90069-5701
310-659-0555

THE GALLERY
329 PRIMROSE RD
BURLINGAME, CA 94010-4037
415-347-9392

THE GALLERY AT VENTANA
BIG SUR, CA 93920
408-667-2787

THE LIMN COMPANY
457 PACIFIC AVE
SAN FRANCISCO, CA 94133-4613
415-986-3884

THE LOS ANGELES ART EXCHANGE
2451 BROADWAY
SANTA MONICA, CA 90404-3046
310-828-6866

THE MEADOWLARK GALLERY
317 CORTE MADERA AVE
TOWN CENTER
CORTE MADERA, CA 94925-1308
415-924-2210

THE MUSEUM OF CONTEMPORARY ART
250 S GRAND AVE
LOS ANGELES, CA 90012-3021
213-621-2766

THE OAK TREE
546 OLD MAMMOTH RD
MAMMOTH LAKES, CA 93546
619-935-4032

THE OUTSIDE-IN GALLERY
6909 MELROSE AVE
LOS ANGELES, CA 90038-3305
213-933-4096

THE PACIFIC GALLERY
PO BOX 844
DANA POINT, CA 92629-0844
714-240-9099

THE PALUMBO GALLERY
DOLORES ST (AT SIXTH)
PO BOX 5727
CARMEL, CA 93921
408-625-5727

THE PLAZA GALLERY
746 HIGUERA ST STE 8
SAN LUIS OBISPO, CA 93401-3501
805-543-5681

THE QUEST
777 BRIDGEWAY
SAUSALITO, CA 94965-2174
415-332-6832

THE SOCO GALLERY
101 S COOMBS ST
NAPA, CA 94559-4500
707-255-5954

THE TROVE GALLERY
73700 EL PASEO
PALM DESERT, CA 92260-4323
619-346-1999

THE VIEWPOINT GALLERY
224 THE CROSSROADS
CARMEL, CA 93923-8648
408-624-3369

THE WILD BLUE GALLERY
7220 MELROSE AVE
LOS ANGELES, CA 90046-7620
213-939-8434

TOPS MALIBU GALLERY
23410 CIVIC CENTER WAY
MALIBU, CA 90265-4857
213-456-8677

ULRICH CREATIVE ARTS
PO BOX 684
VENTURA, CA 93002-0684
805-643-4160

VALERIE MILLER FINE ART
73100 EL PASEO
PALM DESERT, CA 92260-4263
619-773-4483

VALERIE MILLER FINE ARTS
611 S MUIRFIELD RD
LOS ANGELES, CA 90005-3832
213-467-1511

VARIOUS & SUNDRIES
411 SAN ANSELMO AVE
SAN ANSELMO, CA 94960-2611
415-454-1442

VERDI
723 BRIDGEWAY
SAUSALITO, CA 94965-2102
415-331-3009

VICTOR FISCHER GALLERIES
1300 CLAY ST STE 510
OAKLAND, CA 94612-1427
510-464-8044

VICTOR FISCHER GALLERIES
1525 SANTANELLA TER
CORONA DEL MAR, CA 92625-1746
714-644-9655

VIDEOLA
2110 VINE ST #A
BERKELEY, CA 94709-1524
510-549-3373

VIEWPOINTS ART GALLERY
315 STATE ST
LOS ALTOS, CA 94022-2816
415-941-5789

VIEWPOINTS GALLERY
11315 HWY 1
PO BOX 670
POINT REYES STATION, CA 94956
415-663-8861

VILLAGE ART
121 W BRANCH ST
ARROYO GRANDE, CA 93420-2601
805-489-3587

VILLAGE ARTISTRY GALLERY
DOLORES (BETWEEN OCEAN
  & 7TH)
PO BOX 5493
CARMEL, CA 93921
408-624-7628

VIRGINIA BREIER GALLERY
3091 SACRAMENTO ST
SAN FRANCISCO, CA 94115-2016
415-929-7173

WALTER WHITE FINE ARTS
107 CAPITOLA AVE
CAPITOLA, CA 95010-3202
408-476-7001

WELLSPRING GALLERY
120 BROADWAY STE 105
SANTA MONICA, CA 90401-2385
310-451-1924

Z GALLERY
5500 W 83RD ST
LOS ANGELES, CA 90045-3309
310-410-6655

COLORADO

21ST CENTURY GALLERY
235 FILLMORE ST
DENVER, CO 80206-5023
303-320-0926

A SHOW OF HANDS GALLERY
2440 E 3RD AVE
DENVER, CO 80206-4704
303-920-3071

ANN HYDE ART & ANTIQUES

302 E HOPKINS AVE
ASPEN, CO 81611-1906
303-925-7904

ART WEST DESIGNS LTD

8743 W FLOYD AVE
DENVER, CO 80227-4729
303-986-1439

ART YARD

1251 S PEARL ST # A
DENVER, CO 80210-1537
303-777-3219

ARTISAN CENTER

2757 E 3RD AVE
DENVER, CO 80206-4802
303-333-1201

ASPEN MOUNTAIN GALLERY

555 EAST DURANT
ASPEN, CO 81611
303-925-5083

CANYON ROAD GALLERY

257 FILLMORE ST
DENVER, CO 80206-5003
303-321-4139

COMMONWHEEL ARTIST CO-OP

102 CANON AVE
MANITOU SPRINGS, CO 80829-1708
719-685-1008

DAVID FLORIA GALLERY

6 WOOD CREEK PL
WOOD CREEK, CO 81656
303-923-5705

FINE LINE GALLERY & STUDIO

GENERAL DELIVERY
BRECKENRIDGE, CO 80424-9999

FOUR DIRECTIONS GALLERY

117 8TH ST
STEAMBOAT SPRINGS, CO 80487
303-870-9188

**GINGERBREAD SQUARE
GALLERY**

649 QUINCE CIR
BOULDER, CO 80304-1030
303-443-3180

GOTTHELFF GALLERY

122 E MEADOW DR
VAIL, CO 81657-5330
303-476-1777

HABATAT GALLERIES

213 S MILL ST
ASPEN, CO 81611-1926
303-920-9098

HEATHER GALLERY

555 E DURANT AVE
ASPEN, CO 81611-1856
303-925-6641

HIBBERD MCGRATH GALLERY

GENERAL DELIVERY
PO BOX 7638
BRECKENRIDGE, CO 80424-9999
303-453-6391

HOWELL GALLERY

1420 LARIMER ST
DENVER, CO 80202-1705
303-820-3925

J COTTER GALLERY

234 WALL ST
PO BOX 385
VAIL, CO 81657-4538
303-476-3131

MAXIMS ART GALLERY

818 9TH ST
GREELEY, CO 80631-1104

MILL STREET GALLERY

112 S MILL ST
ASPEN, CO 81611-1976
303-925-4988

NANCY LEE, LTD

DENVER MERCHANDISE MART
#1508
DENVER, CO 80216
303-295-1283

NATIONAL SCULPTORS' GUILD

2683 N TAFT AVE
LOVELAND, CO 80538
800-606-2015

PISMO

2727 E 3RD AVE
DENVER, CO 80206-4802
303-333-7724

SANDY CARSON GALLERY

1734 WAZEE ST
DENVER, CO 80202-1232
303-297-8585

SHANAHAN COLLECTIONS

595 S BROADWAY STE 100S
DENVER, CO 80209-4072
303-778-7088

SKILLED HANDS GALLERY

GENERAL DELIVERY
PO BOX 5048
BRECKENRIDGE, CO 80424-9999
303-453-7818

SQUASHBLOSSOM

198 GORE CREEK DR
VAIL, CO 81657-4511

STEAMBOAT ART COMPANY

903 LINCOLN AVE
STEAMBOAT SPRINGS, CO 80487

SUSAN DUVAL GALLERY

525 E COOPER ST
ASPEN, CO 81611-1860
303-925-9044

TAPESTRY, LTD

2859 E 3RD AVE
DENVER, CO 80206-4905
303-393-0535

TAVELLI GALLERY

555 N MILL ST
ASPEN, CO 81611-1509
303-920-3071

**TELLURIDE GALLERY
OF FINE ART**

GENERAL DELIVERY
PO BOX 1900
TELLURIDE, CO 81435-9999
303-728-3300

THE PANACHE CRAFT GALLERY

315 COLUMBINE ST
DENVER, CO 80206-4223
303-321-8069

THE RACHAEL COLLECTION

433 E COOPER ST
ASPEN, CO 81611-1831
303-920-1313

THE UNIQUE GALLERY

11 E BIJOU ST
COLORADO SPRINGS, CO 80903
719-473-9406

THE UPPEREDGE GALLERY

SNOWMASS VILLAGE - UPPER LEVEL
PO BOX 5294
SNOWMASS VILLAGE, CO 81615
303-923-5373

THE WHITE HART GALLERY

843 LINCOLN AVE
STEAMBOAT SPRINGS, CO 80487
303-879-1015

TOH-ATIN GALLERY

145 W 9TH ST
DURANGO, CO 81301-5431
800-525-0384

CONNECTICUT

A TOUCH OF GLASS

PO BOX 433
N MOODUS RD
MOODUS, CT 06469-0433
203-873-9709

AMERICA WORKS INC

29 SANDY BEACH RD
MIDDLEBURY, CT 06762-1322

AMERICAN HAND

125 POST RD E
WESTPORT, CT 06880-3410
203-226-8883

ARTISTIC SURROUNDINGS

40 ½ PADANARAM RD
DANBURY, CT 06811-4840
203-798-0361

ATELIER STUDIO GALLERY

27 EAST ST
NEW MILFORD, CT 06776-3028
203-354-7792

BROWN GROTTA GALLERY

39 GRUMMAN HILL RD
WILTON, CT 06897-4504
203-834-0623

COMPANY OF CRAFTSMEN

43 W MAIN ST
MYSTIC, CT 06355-2545
203-536-4189

ENDLEMAN GALLERY

1014 CHAPEL ST
NEW HAVEN, CT 06510-2402
203-776-2517

FISHER GALLERY

25 BUNKER LN
AVON, CT 06001
203-678-1867

**HERON AMERICAN
CRAFT GALLERY**

MAIN ST
P.O. BOX 535
KENT, CT 06757
203-927-4804

MENDELSON GALLERY

TITUS SQUARE
WASHINGTON DEPOT, CT 06794
203-868-0307

GALLERY LISTINGS

NEW HORIZONS GALLERY
122 GARWOOD RD
TRUMBULL, CT 06611-2220
203-261-6767

STARSHINE GALLERY
319 HORSE HILL RD
WESTBROOK, CT 06498-1402
203-399-5149

THE ELEMENTS
14 LIBERTY WAY
GREENWICH, CT 06830-5509
203-661-0014

THE RED PEPPER GALLERY
41 MAIN ST
CHESTER, CT 06412-1311
203-526-4460

THE SILO GALLERY
44 UPLAND RD
NEW MILFORD, CT 06776-2104
203-355-0300

VARIATIONS GALLERY
PO BOX 246
RT 20
RIVERTON, CT 06065-0246
203-379-2964

WHITNEY MUSEUM OF ART
FAIRFIELD COUNTY
ONE CHAMPION PLAZA
STAMFORD, CT 06921-0001
203-358-7652

WOODEN LEATHER
760 MAIN ST
PLANTSVILLE, CT 06479-1536

DELAWARE

BLUE STREAK GALLERY
1723 DELAWARE AVE
WILMINGTON, DE 19806-2342
302-429-0506

CRAFT COLLECTION
129D REHOBOTH AVE
REHOBOTH BEACH, DE 19971-2138
302-227-3640

THE STATION GALLERY
3922 KENNETT PIKE
GREENVILLE, DE 19807-2304
302-654-8638

DISTRICT OF COLUMBIA

AMERICAN HAND PLUS
2906 M ST NW
WASHINGTON, DC 20007-3713
202-965-3273

ANNE O'BRIEN GALLERY
4829 BENDING LN NW
WASHINGTON, DC 20007-1527
202-265-9697

COLLECTORS CABINET
1023 CONNECTICUT AVE NW
WASHINGTON, DC 20036-5403

GAZELLE GALLERY
5335 WISCONSIN AVE NW
WASHINGTON, DC 20015-2030
202-686-5656

INDIAN CRAFT SHOP
1050 WISCONSIN AVE NW
WASHINGTON, DC 20007-3633
202-342-3918

INDIAN CRAFT SHOP
DEPT OF THE INTERIOR
1849 C ST NW #1023
WASHINGTON, DC 20240-0001
202-737-4381

JACKIE CHALKLEY GALLERY
1455 PENNSYLVANIA AVE NW
WASHINGTON, DC 20004-1008
202-683-3060

JACKIE CHALKLEY GALLERY
3301 NEW MEXICO AVE NW
WASHINGTON, DC 20016-3622
202-686-8882

JACKIE CHALKLEY GALLERY
5301 WISCONSIN AVE NW
WASHINGTON, DC 20015-2015
212-537-6100

MAUREEN LITTLETON GALLERY
1667 WISCONSIN AVE NW
WASHINGTON, DC 20007-2721
202-333-9307

NATIONAL BUILDING MUSEUM
401 F ST NW
WASHINGTON, DC 20001-2728
202-272-2448

RENWICK GALLERY
PENNSYLVANIA AVE AT 17 ST NW
WASHINGTON, DC 20006

SANSAR GALLERY
4200 WISCONSIN AVE NW
WASHINGTON, DC 20016-2143
202-244-4448

STUDIO DESIGN INC
1508 19TH ST NW
WASHINGTON, DC 20036-1102
202-667-6133

THE COLLECTOR ART GALLERY
DUPONT PLAZA HOTEL
1500 NEW HAMPSHIRE AVE NW
WASHINGTON, DC 20036
202-797-0160

THE FARRELL COLLECTION
2633 CONNECTICUT AVE NW
WASHINGTON, DC 20008-1522
202-483-8334

THE KELLOGG COLLECTION
3424 WISCONSIN AVE NW
WASHINGTON, DC 20016-3009
202-363-6878

THE TOUCHSTONE GALLERY
2009 R ST NW
WASHINGTON, DC 20009-1011
202-797-7278

UPTOWN ARTS
3236 P ST NW
WASHINGTON, DC 20007-2755
202-337-0600

FLORIDA

5G COLLECTION, ART PLUS
4534 COCOPLUM WAY
DELRAY BEACH, FL 33445-4304
407-637-8899

A STEP ABOVE GALLERY
500 N TAMIAMI TRL
SARASOTA, FL 34236-4823
813-955-4477

AHAVA
MIZNER PARK
414 PLAZA REAL
BOCA RATON, FL 33433
407-395-5001

ALBERTSON PETERSON GALLERY
329 S PARK AVE
WINTER PARK, FL 32789-4390
407-628-1258

ALEXANDERS A FINE ART SHOWCASE
3225 S MACDILL AVE STE 107
TAMPA, FL 33629-8171
813-839-6088

ANITA L. LOUIS PICKREN GALLERY
33 S PALM AVE
SARASOTA, FL 34236-5610
813-954-0180

ART GLASS ENVIRONMENTS, INC
174 NW 13TH ST
BOCA RATON, FL 33432-1605
407-391-7310

ARTCETERA
640 E ATLANTIC AVE
DELRAY BEACH, FL 33483-5353

BARBARA GILLMAN GALLERY
939 LINCOLN RD
MIAMI BEACH, FL 33139-2601

BAYFRONT GALLERY
713 S PALAFOX ST
PENSACOLA, FL 32501-5935
904-438-7556

BELVETRO GLASS GALLERY
934 LINCOLN RD
MIAMI BEACH, FL 33139-2602
305-673-6677

CENTER STREET GALLERY
136 S PARK AVE
WINTER PARK, FL 32789-4396
407-644-1545

CHRISTY TAYLOR ART GALLERY
MIZNER PARK
410 PLAZA REAL
BOCA RATON, FL 33433
407-394-6387

CLAY SPACE GALLERY
924 LINCOLN RD
MIAMI BEACH, FL 33139-2609
305-534-3339

CLAYTON GALLERIES
4105 S MACDILL AVE
TAMPA, FL 33611-1936
813-831-3753

COLLECTORS GALLERY
213 W VENICE AVE
VENICE, FL 34285-2002
813-488-3029

CONCEPTS 3 INTERNATIONAL
1133 LOUISIANA AVE STE 105
WINTER PARK, FL 32789-2350
407-740-0645

EG CODY GALLERY
80 NE 40TH ST
MIAMI, FL 33137-3510
305-374-4777

EXIT ART
THE CENTRE
5380 GULF OF MEXICO DR
LONGBOAT KEY, FL 34228-
813-383-4099

FLORIDA CRAFTSMEN GALLERY
237 2ND AVE S
SAINT PETERSBURG, FL 33701-4312
813-821-7391

**FLORIDA GLOBAL
GALLERY, INC**
3020 PENMAR DR
CLEARWATER, FL 34619-4331
813-276-3957

GALERIA OF SCULPTURE, INC.
VIA PARIGI #11 WORTH AVE
PALM BEACH, FL 33480
407-659-7557

GALLERY CAMINO REAL
GALLERY CENTER
608 BANYAN TR
BOCA RATON, FL 33428
407-241-1606

GALLERY CONTEMPORANEA
526 LANCASTER ST
JACKSONVILLE, FL 32204-4138
904-359-0016

GALLERY FIVE
363 TEQUESTA DR
TEQUESTA, FL 33469-3027
407-747-5555

GALLERY ONE
1301 3RD ST S
NAPLES, FL 33940-7203
813-263-0835

GRAND CENTRAL GALLERY
442 W GRAND CENTRAL AVE # 100
TAMPA, FL 33606-1926
813-254-4977

GREEN GALLERY
1541 BRICKELL AVE # 1503
MIAMI, FL 33129-1213
305-858-7868

GREYWOLF GALLERY
3044 SCHERER DR N
SAINT PETERSBURG, FL 33716-1027

HB BRICKELL GALLERY
905 S BAYSHORE DR
MIAMI, FL 33131-2935
305-358-2088

HABITAT GALLERIES
GALLERY CENTER
608 BANYAN TR
BOCA RATON, FL 33428
407-241-4544

HARPER COMPANY
4 VIA PARIGI
PALM BEACH, FL 33480-4613

HEARTWORKS
820 LOMAX ST
JACKSONVILLE, FL 32204-3902
904-355-6210

HELIUM
760 OCEAN DR
MIAMI, FL 33139-6273
305-538-4111

HELLER GALLERY PALM BEACH
203 WORTH AVE
PALM BEACH, FL 33480-4614
407-833-4457

HODGELL GALLERY
46 S PALM AVE
SARASOTA, FL 34236-5609
813-366-1146

HOFFMAN GALLERY
4070 NE 15TH TER
FORT LAUDERDALE, FL 33334-4647
305-561-7300

IMAGES ART GALLERY
7400 TAMIAMI TRL N STE 101
NAPLES, FL 33963-2855
813-598-3455

J LAWRENCE GALLERY
535 W EAU GALLIE BLVD
MELBOURNE, FL 32935-6506
407-728-7051

LEWIS CHARLES GALLERY
1627 W SNOW CIR
TAMPA, FL 33606-2562
813-254-8700

LUCKY STREET GALLERY
919 DUVAL ST
KEY WEST, FL 33040-7407
305-294-3976

MARGEAUX
2808 BIRD AVE
MIAMI, FL 33133-4605
305-444-8343

MARIE FERRER GALLERY
309 N PARK AVE
WINTER PARK, FL 32789-3815
407-647-7680

MASTERPIECE GALLERY
449 PLAZA REAL
BOCA RATON, FL 33432-3942
407-394-0070

NANCY KAYE GALLERY
201 E PALMETTO PARK RD
BOCA RATON, FL 33432-5013
407-392-8220

NEWBILL COLLECTION
309 RUSKIN PLACE
SEASIDE, FL 32459
904-231-4500

OEHLSCHLAEGER GALLERY II
253 BIRD KEY DR
SARASOTA, FL 34236-1601
813-366-0652

OVERWHELMED
445 PLAZA REAL
MIZNER PARK
BOCA RATON, FL 33432-3942
407-368-0078

**PASSAGE WEST
FINE ART GALLERY**
3020 N FEDERAL HWY
FORT LAUDERDALE, FL 33306-1417
305-565-8009

PLANTATION POTTERS
521 FLEMING ST
KEY WEST, FL 33040-6824
305-294-3143

PRESIDIO GALLERY
36 SPANISH ST
SAINT AUGUSTINE, FL 32084-3612
904-826-1758

PRODIGY GALLERY
4320 GULF SHORE BLVD N STE 206
NAPLES, FL 33940-2662
813-263-5881

RALEIGH GALLERY
1855 GRIFFIN RD
DANIA, FL 33004-2242
305-922-3330

**RICK MOORE
FINE ART GALLERY**
5455 TAMIAMI TRL N
NAPLES, FL 33963-2870
813-592-5455

RICK SANDERS GALLERIES
1310 BAY RD
SARASOTA, FL 34239-6801
813-364-9911

ROBERT WINDSOR GALLERY
1855 GRIFFIN RD
DANIA, FL 33004-2200
305-923-9100

**SOKOLSKY GALLERY
FOR FINE ARTS**
942 LINCOLN RD
SOUTH FLORIDA ART CTR
MIAMI BEACH, FL 33139-2602
305-674-8278

**SPECTRUM OF AMERICAN
ARTISTS**
3101 PGA BLVD #B117
PALM BEACH GARDENS, FL 33410
407-622-2527

STATE STREET GALLERY
1517 STATE ST
SARASOTA, FL 34236-5808
813-362-3767

TEQUESTA GALLERIES, INC
361 TEQUESTA DR
TEQUESTA, FL 33469-3027
407-744-2534

THE PARK SHORE GALLERIES
501 GOODLETTE RD N # 8-204
NAPLES, FL 33940-5661
813-434-0833

THE RAIN BARREL
86700 OVERSEAS HWY
ISLAMORADA, FL 33036-3138
305-852-3084

THE RAIN FOREST GALLERY
5535 TAMIAMI TRL N STE 811
NAPLES, FL 33963-2863

THE TURNBERRY ART GALLERY
19707 TURNBERRY WAY
MIAMI, FL 33180-2566
305-931-5272

VISUAL ARTS CENTER
19 E 4TH ST
PANAMA CITY, FL 32401-3106
904-769-4454

ZOO GALLERY
1209 AIRPORT RD STE 3
DESTIN, FL 32541-2933

GEORGIA

ADVENTURES
2626 AUBURN AVE STE G
COLUMBUS, GA 31906-1330

**ALIYA, GALLERY
AT MORNINGSIDE**
1402 N HIGHLAND AVE NE STE 6
ATLANTA, GA 30306-3301
404-892-2835

BY HAND SOUTH
W PONCE PLACE
308 W PONCE DE LEON AVE #E
DECATUR, GA 30030
404-378-0118

CONNELL GALLERY
333 BUCKHEAD AVE NE
ATLANTA, GA 30305-2305
404-261-1712

EVE MANNES GALLERY
116 BENNETT ST NW STE A
ATLANTA, GA 30309-1267
404-351-6651

FAY GOLD GALLERY
247 BUCKHEAD AVE NE
ATLANTA, GA 30305-2237
404-233-3843

HEATH GALLERY, INC
416 E PACES FERRY RD NE
ATLANTA, GA 30305-3307
404-262-6407

ILLUMINA
3500 PEACHTREE RD NE STE A24
ATLANTA, GA 30326-1251

LAGERQUIST GALLERY INC
3235 PACES FERRY PL NW
ATLANTA, GA 30305-1308
404-261-8273

SOUTHERN ACCESSORIES TODAY
ATLANTA MERCHANDISE MART
  #12A2
ATLANTA, GA 30303
404-581-0811

THE CREATIVE MARK
130 W WASHINGTON ST
MADISON, GA 30650-1216
404-342-2153

THE LOWE GALLERY
75 BENNETT ST NW STE A-7
ATLANTA, GA 30309-1275
404-352-8114

THE MAIN STREET GALLERY
MAIN ST
CLAYTON, GA 30525
404-782-2440

THE MCINTOSH GALLERY
ONE VIRGINIA HILL
587 VIRGINIA AVE
ATLANTA, GA 30306
404-892-4023

**THE SIGNATURE SHOP
& GALLERY**
3267 ROSWELL RD NE
ATLANTA, GA 30305-1840
404-237-4426

THE TULA GALLERIES
75 BENNETT ST NW STE D1
ATLANTA, GA 30309-1275
404-351-6724

TRINITY GALLERY
940 MYRTLE ST NE APT 8
ATLANTA, GA 30309-4144
404-525-7546

UP THE CREEK GALLERY
HWYS 115 & 105
DEMOREST, GA 30535
404-754-4130

VESPERMANN GLASS GALLERY
2140 PEACHTREE ST NW
ATLANTA, GA 30309-1314
404-350-9698

WINN/REGENCY GALLERY
2344 LAWRENCEVILLE HWY
ATLANTA, GA 30033
404-633-1789

HAWAII

COAST GALLERY
PO BOX 565
HANA, HI 96713-0565
808-248-8636

DREAMS OF PARADISE
308 KAMEHAMEHA AVE STE 106
HILO, HI 96720-2960
808-935-5670

**FINE ART ASSOC.
THE ART LOFT**
1020 AUAHI ST STE 4
HONOLULU, HI 96814-4133
808-523-0489

MADALINE MICHAELS GALLERY
108 LOPAKA PL
KULA, HI 96790-9504
800-635-9369

RAKU INTERNATIONAL
917 HALEKAUWILA ST
HONOLULU, HI 96814-4002
808-537-4181

THE FOLLOWING SEA
4211 WAIALAE AVE
HONOLULU, HI 96816-5311
808-734-4425

THE VILLAGE GALLERY
120 DICKENSON ST
LAHAINA, HI 96761-1203
808-669-0585

VOLCANO ART CENTER
PO BOX 104
HAWAII NATIONAL PARK, HI 96718
808-967-8222

IDAHO

ANNE REED GALLERY
620 SUN VALLEY RD
PO BOX 597
KETCHUM, ID 83340
208-726-3036

GAIL SEVERN GALLERY
620 SUN VALLEY RD
PO BOX 1679
KETCHUM, ID 83340
208-726-5079

RICHARD KAVESH GALLERY
PO BOX 6080
KETCHUM, ID 83340-6080
208-726-2523

ILLINOIS

A UNIQUE PRESENCE
2121 N CLYBOURN AVE
CHICAGO, IL 60614-4031
312-929-4292

ANN NATHAN GALLERY
210 W SUPERIOR ST
CHICAGO, IL 60610-3508
312-664-6622

ART & INTERIOR DESIGN
4826 5TH AVE
MOLINE, IL 61265-1962
309-762-1135

ART CONCEPTS
2411 S MACARTHUR BLVD
SPRINGFIELD, IL 62704-4505
217-793-1600

ART EFFECT
641 W ARTMITAGE
CHICAGO, IL 60614
312-664-0997

ART SCAPE
1625 N ALPINE RD
ROCKFORD, IL 61107-1414
815-397-1223

ATLAS GALLERIES
549 N MICHIGAN AVE
CHICAGO, IL 60611-1201
800-423-8702

BETSY ROSENFIELD GALLERY
212 W SUPERIOR ST
CHICAGO, IL 60610-3533
312-787-8020

BILLY HORK GALLERY
272 E GOLF RD
ARLINGTON HEIGHTS, IL 60005-4006
708-640-7272

CALLARD & OSGOOD
1611 MERCHANDISE MART
CHICAGO, IL 60654
312-670-3640

CAREY GALLERY
1062 W CHICAGO AVE
CHICAGO, IL 60622-5416
312-942-1884

CARL HAMMER GALLERY
200 W SUPERIOR ST
CHICAGO, IL 60610-3532
312-226-8512

**CENTER FOR
CONTEMPORARY ART**
325 W HURON ST
CHICAGO, IL 60610-3617
312-944-0094

CHICAGO STREET GALLERY
204 S CHICAGO ST
LINCOLN, IL 62656-2701
217-732-5937

CITY WOODS
659 CENTRAL AVE
HIGHLAND PARK, IL 60035-3227
708-432-9393

DOUGLAS DAWSON GALLERY
222 W HURON ST
CHICAGO, IL 60610-3613
312-751-1961

DREAM FAST GALLERY
2035 W WABANSIA AVE
CHICAGO, IL 60647-5501
312-235-4779

EVA COHON GALLERY
301 W SUPERIOR 2ND FLR
CHICAGO, IL 60610
312-664-3669

FUMIE GALLERY
126 S FRANKLIN ST
CHICAGO, IL 60606-4606
312-726-0080

GALLERY MOYA
835 N MICHIGAN AVE
CHICAGO, IL 60611-2203
312-337-2900

GWENDA JAY GALLERY
301 W SUPERIOR ST FL 2
CHICAGO, IL 60610-3515
312-664-3406

HELTZER DESIGN
4853 N RAVENSWOOD AVE
CHICAGO, IL 60640-4409
312-561-5612

HOKIN KAUFMAN GALLERY
PO BOX 14761
CHICAGO, IL 60614-0761
312-266-1212

ILLINOIS ARTISANS GALLERY
100 W RANDOLPH ST
CHICAGO, IL 60601-3218
312-814-5321

**JACQUELINE LIPPITZ
ART TO WEAR**
431 LAKESIDE TER
GLENCOE, IL 60022-1760
312-835-2666

JAYSON GALLERY
1915 N CLYBOURN AVE
CHICAGO, IL 60614-4903
312-525-3100

JEAN ALBANO GALLERY
311 W SUPERIOR ST
CHICAGO, IL 60610-3537
312-440-0770

JOY HORWICH GALLERY
226 E ONTARIO ST
CHICAGO, IL 60611-3205
312-787-0171

KALEIDOSCOPE GALLERY
205 S COOK ST
BARRINGTON, IL 60010-4313
708-381-4840

KLEIN ART WORKS
400 N MORGAN ST
CHICAGO, IL 60622-6538
312-243-0400

LILL STREET GALLERY
1021 W LILL AVE
CHICAGO, IL 60614-2205
312-477-6185

LINDSEY GALLERY
146 N OAK PARK AVE
OAK PARK, IL 60301-1321
708-386-5272

LOVELY FINE ARTS, INC
18 W 10022ND ST
OAKBROOK TERRACE, IL 60181
708-369-2999

LYMAN HEIZER ASSOCIATES
325 W HURON ST STE 407
CHICAGO, IL 60610-3617
312-751-2985

MANDEL & COMPANY
1600 MERCHANDISE MART
CHICAGO, IL 60654
312-644-8242

MARX GALLERY
230 W SUPERIOR ST
CHICAGO, IL 60610-3536
312-573-1400

MERRILL CHASE GALLERIES
1090 JOHNSON DR
BUFFALO GROVE, IL 60089-6918
708-215-4900

MINDSCAPE
1506 SHERMAN AVE
EVANSTON, IL 60201-4407
708-864-2660

PEARLMAN GALLERY
474 N LAKE SHORE DR # 5806
CHICAGO, IL 60611-3400
312-467-0144

PERIMETER GALLERY
750 N ORLEANS ST
CHICAGO, IL 60610-3540
312-266-9473

PERLMAN FINE JEWELRY
1322 SPRINGHILL MALL
DUNDEE, IL 60118-1262

PIECES
644 CENTRAL AVE
HIGHLAND PARK, IL 60035-3222
708-432-2137

PORTIA GALLERY
1702 N DAMEN AVE
CHICAGO, IL 60647-5509
312-862-1700

PRESTIGE ART GALLERIES
3909 HOWARD ST
SKOKIE, IL 60076-3793
708-679-2555

PRESTIGE ART PLUS
8800 GROSS POINT RD
SKOKIE, IL 60077-1809
708-966-4020

PRINCETON ART GALLERY
1844 1ST ST
HIGHLAND PARK, IL 60035-3102
708-432-1930

R.C. DANON GALLERY
1224 W LUNT AVE # 1
CHICAGO, IL 60626-3030
312-262-9222

SCHNEIDER GALLERY
230 W SUPERIOR ST
CHICAGO, IL 60610-3536
312-988-4033

SPECIAL EFFECTS INTERIORS
405 LAKE COOK RD
DEERFIELD, IL 60015-4918
708-480-1973

**STUDIO OF LONG GROVE
GALLERY**
360 N OLD MCHENRY RD
LONG GROVE, IL 60047-8077
708-634-4244

SUNRISE ART GALLERY
227 S 3RD ST
GENEVA, IL 60134-2778
708-232-0730

SWANK
401 N MILWAUKEE AVE
CHICAGO, IL 60610-3914
312-942-0444

TEXTILE ARTS CENTRE
916 W DIVERSEY PKY
CHICAGO, IL 60614-1429
312-929-5655

THE ARTISAN SHOP & GALLERY
1515 SHERIDAN RD
PLAZA DEL LAGO
WILMETTE, IL 60091-1822
312-251-3775

THE PLUM LINE GALLERY
1511 CHICAGO AVE
EVANSTON, IL 60201-4405
708-328-7586

UNIQUE ACCENTS
3137 DUNDEE RD
NORTHBROOK, IL 60062-2402
708-205-9400

VALE CRAFT GALLERY
207 W SUPERIOR ST
CHICAGO, IL 60610-3507
312-337-3525

WENTWORTH GALLERY
835 N MICHIGAN AVE
FIFTH LEVEL
CHICAGO, IL 60611-2203
312-944-0079

WHIMSY
3234 N SOUTHPORT AVE
CHICAGO, IL 60657-3227
312-665-1760

WOOD STREET GALLERY
1239 N WOOD ST
CHICAGO, IL 60622-3252
312-227-3306

INDIANA

ARTIFACTS
6327 GUILFORD AVE
INDIANAPOLIS, IN 46220-1709
317-255-1178

GALLERY LISTINGS

ARTISANS
721 W MULBERRY ST
P.O. BOX 1222
KOKOMO, IN 46901-4482
317-452-5505

BY HAND GALLERY
104 E KIRKWOOD AVE
BLOOMINGTON, IN 47408-3330
812-334-3255

CENTRE ART GALLERY
301B E CARMEL DR
CARMEL, IN 46032-2809
317-844-6421

CHESTERTON ART GALLERY
115 FOURTH ST
CHESTERTON, IN 46304
219-926-4711

CORNERSTONE GALLERY
176 W MAIN ST
GREENWOOD, IN 46142-3126
317-887-2778

EARTHLY DESIGNS
8701 KEYSTONE XING
INDIANAPOLIS, IN 46240-4626
372-580-1861

FABLES GALLERY
317 LINCOLN WAY E
MISHAWAKA, IN 46544-2012
219-255-9191

JM MALLON GALLERIES
EDITIONS LIMITED
4040 E 82ND ST
INDIANAPOLIS, IN 46250-
317-253-7800

JUBILEE GALLERY
121 W COURT AVE
JEFFERSONVILLE, IN 47130-3527
812-282-9997

KATHERINE TODD FINE ARTS
5356 HILLSIDE AVE
INDIANAPOLIS, IN 46220-3446
317-253-0250

PATRICK KING
CONTEMPORARY ART
1726 E 86TH ST
INDIANAPOLIS, IN 46240-2360
317-634-4101

SIGMAN'S GALLERY
930 BROAD RIPPLE AVE
INDIANAPOLIS, IN 46220-1938
317-253-9953

THE GALLERY
109 E 6TH ST
BLOOMINGTON, IN 47408-3363
912-336-0564

TRILOGY GALLERY
120 E MAIN ST, BOX 200
NASHVILLE, IN 47448
812-988-4030

IOWA

AGORA ARTISANS MARKETPLACE
308 W WATER ST
DECORAH, IA 52101-1730
319-382-8786

ARTISTS CONCEPTS, LTD
7 LONGVIEW KNLS NE
IOWA CITY, IA 52240-9148
319-337-2361

CORNERHOUSE GALLERY
& FRAME
2753 1ST AVE SE
CEDAR RAPIDS, IA 52402-4804
319-365-4348

FROM GIFTED HANDS
400 MAIN (ON THE PARK)
AMES, IA 50010
515-232-5656

IOWA ARTISANS GALLERY
117 E COLLEGE ST
IOWA CITY, IA 52240-4002
319-351-8686

JEAN SAMPLE STUDIO GALLERY
3111 INGERSOLL AVE
DES MOINES, IA 50312-3909

THE LAGNIAPPE
114 5TH ST
WEST DES MOINES, IA 50265-4716
515-277-0047

KANSAS

GALLERY AT HAWTHORNE
4833 W 119TH ST
OVERLAND PARK, KS 66209-1560
913-469-8001

SANTA FE CONNECTION
4563 INDIAN CREEK PKY
SHAWNEE MISSION, KS 66207-4004
913-897-2275

THE SILVER WORKS & MORE
715 MASSACHUSETTS ST
LAWRENCE, KS 66044-2345
913-842-1460

KENTUCKY

AFFINITY
2030 TYLER LN
LOUISVILLE, KY 40205-2904

APPALACHIAN FIRESIDE
182 MAIN ST
BEREA, KY 40403-1763
606-986-9013

ART BIZ GALLERY
414 BAXTER AVE
LOUISVILLE, KY 40204-1160
502-585-2809

ARTIQUE GALLERY
410 W VINE ST
FIRST LEVEL
LEXINGTON, KY 40507-1616
606-233-1774

BENCHMARK GALLERY
I-75 INTERCHANGE
BEREA, KY 40403
606-986-9413

CHESTNUT STREET GALLERY
3409 NICHOLASVILLE RD
LEXINGTON, KY 40503-3605

COMMON WEALTH GALLERY
313 S 4TH AVE
LOUISVILLE, KY 40202-3001
502-589-4747

COMPLETELY KENTUCKY
235 W BROADWAY ST
FRANKFORT, KY 40601-1956
502-223-5240

CONTEMPORARY ARTIFACTS
128 N BROADWAY ST
BEREA, KY 40403-1504
606-986-1096

EDENSIDE GALLERY
1422 BARDSTOWN RD
LOUISVILLE, KY 40204-1419
502-459-2787

KENTUCKY ART & CRAFT
609 W MAIN ST
LOUISVILLE, KY 40202-2951
502-589-0102

PROMENADE GALLERY
204 CENTER ST
BEREA, KY 40403-1733
606-986-1609

THE LIBERTY GALLERY
416 W JEFFERSON ST
LOUISVILLE, KY 40202-3202
502-566-2081

THE NASH COLLECTION
843 LANE ALLEN RD
LEXINGTON, KY 40504-3605
606-276-0161

THE ZEPHYR GALLERY
812 W MAIN ST
LOUISVILLE, KY 40202-2620
502-585-5646

LOUISIANA

ARIODANTE:
CONTEMPORARY CRAFT
535 JULIA ST
NEW ORLEANS, LA 70130-3623
604-524-3233

ARTISTS ALLIANCE
125 W VERMILION ST
LAFAYETTE, LA 70501-6915
318-233-7518

BATON ROUGE GALLERY
1442 CITY PARK AVE
BATON ROUGE, LA 70808-1037
504-383-1470

CAROL ROBINSON GALLERY
4537 MAGAZINE ST
NEW ORLEANS, LA 70115-1542
504-895-6130

GALLERIE I/O
1812 MAGAZINE ST
NEW ORLEANS, LA 70130-5014
800-875-2113

HILDERBRAND GALLERIES
4524 MAGAZINE ST
NEW ORLEANS, LA 70115
504-895-3313

MAGGIO GALLERY
941 RUE ROYAL
NEW ORLEANS, LA 70116
504-523-4093

MOREHEAD FINE ARTS
GALLERY
603 JULIA ST
NEW ORLEANS, LA 70130-3709
504-568-5470

STONER ARTS CENTER
614 EDWARDS ST
SHREVEPORT, LA 71101-3641
318-222-1780

MAINE

ABACUS HANDCRAFTERS GALLERY
8 MCKOWN ST
BOOTHBAY HARBOR, ME 04538
207-633-2166

BENSON'S FIBER & WOOD, ETC
59 MOUNTAIN ST
CAMDEN, ME 04843-1635
207-236-6564

COMPLIMENTS GALLERY
PO BOX 567
KENNEBUNKPORT, ME 04046-0567
207-967-2269

EARTHLY DELIGHTS
81 WATER ST
HALLOWELL, ME 04347-1411
207-622-9801

EDGECOMB POTTERS
RT 27, BOX 2104
EDGECOMB, ME 04556
207-882-6802

ELEMENTS GALLERY
190 DANFORTH ST
PORTLAND, ME 04102-3828
207-729-1108

ETIENNE & CO
20 MAIN ST
CAMDEN, ME 04843-1704
207-236-9696

FRICK GALLERY
139 HIGH ST
BELFAST, ME 04915-1539
207-338-3671

GREEN HEAD FORGE
OLD QUARRY RD
STONINGTON, ME 04681
207-367-2632

MAINE COTTAGE FURNITURE
LOWER FALLS LANDING
YARMOUTH, ME 04046
207-846-0602

NANCY MARGOLIS GALLERY
367 FORE ST
PORTLAND, ME 04101-5010
207-775-3822

PHILIP STEIN GALLERY
20 MILK ST
PORTLAND, ME 04101-5024
207-772-9072

PLUM DANDY GALLERY
21 DOCK SQ
KENNEBUNKPORT, ME 04046-6012
207-967-4013

THE BLUE HERON GALLERY
CHURCH ST
DEER ISLE, ME 04627
207-348-6051

THE SHORE ROAD GALLERY
112 SHORE RD
OGUNQUIT, ME 03907
207-646-5046

THE VICTORIAN STABLE GALLERY
WATER ST
P.O. BOX 728
DAMARISCOTTA, ME 04543
207-563-1991

TURTLE GALLERY
39 MORNING ST
PORTLAND, ME 04101-4481
207-774-0621

MARYLAND

APPALACHIANA
10400 OLD GEORGETOWN RD
BETHESDA, MD 20814-1914

ART INSTITUTE & GALLERY
RTE 50 & LEMMON HILL LN
SALISBURY, MD 21801
301-546-4748

ARTISANS COLLECTION, LTD
11216 OLD CARRIAGE RD
GLEN ARM, MD 21057-9415
301-661-1118

AURORA GALLERY
67 MARYLAND AVE
ANNAPOLIS, MD 21401-1629
301-263-9150

BARBARA FENDRICK GALLERY
4104 LELAND ST
BETHESDA, MD 20815-5034
212-226-3881

CATHY HART POTTERY STUDIO
MILL CENTRE STUDIO #221
BALITMORE, MD 21211
301-467-4911

CHESAPEAKE EAST
GENERAL DELIVERY
UPPER FAIRMOUNT, MD 21867-9999
301-543-8175

DISCOVERIES
COLUMBIA MALL
COLUMBIA, MD 21044
410-740-5800

GAZELLE GALLERY
5100 FALLS RD
BALTIMORE, MD 21210-1935
301-433-3305

JURUS, LTD
5618 NEWBURY ST
BALTIMORE, MD 21209-3604
410-542-5227

MARGARET SMITH GALLERY
8090 MAIN ST
ELLICOTT CITY, MD 21043-4617
410-461-0870

MEREDITH GALLERY
805 N CHARLES ST
BALTIMORE, MD 21201-5307
301-837-3575

PIECES OF OLDE
716 W 36TH ST
BALTIMORE, MD 21211-2505
301-366-4949

RUBY BLAKENEY GALLERY
SAVAGE MILL
8600 FOUNDRY ST
SAVAGE, MD 20763
410-880-4935

THE BRASSWORKS COMPANY, INC
1641 THAMES ST
BALTIMORE, MD 21231-3430
301-327-7280

THE FINER SIDE
209B NORTH BLVD
SALISBURY, MD 21801-6252
410-749-4081

THE GLASS GALLERY
4720 HAMPDEN LN
BETHESDA, MD 20814-2910
301-657-3478

TOMLINSON CRAFT COLLECTION
711 W 40TH ST
BALTIMORE, MD 21211-2120
410-338-1572

ZYZYX
1809 REISTERSTOWN RD
BALTIMORE, MD 21208-6329
410-486-9785

MASSACHUSETTS

ALIANZA CONTEMPORARY CRAFTS
154 NEWBURY ST
BOSTON, MA 02116-2838
617-262-2385

ANDREA MARQUIT FINE ARTS
38 NEWBURY ST
BOSTON, MA 02116-3210
617-859-0190

ARTFUL HAN GALLERIES
MAIN ST SQUARE
P.O. BOX 131
ORLEANS, MA 02653
617-255-2969

ARTIQUE GALLERY
400 COCHITUATE RD
FARMINGHAM MALL
FRAMINGHAM, MA 01701-4655
508-872-3373

ARTISTS & CRAFTSMEN GALLERY
72 MAIN ST
WEST HARWICH, MA 02671-1115
508-432-7604

ARTWORK GALLERY
261 PARK AVE
WORCESTER, MA 01609-1919
508-755-7808

ATELIER GALLERY
200 BOYLSTON ST STE 405
CHESTNUT HILL, MA 02167-2008
617-965-5757

BARACCA GALLERY
PO BOX 85
NORTH HATFIELD, MA 01066-0085
413-247-5262

BARBARAS TWO GALLERY
58 GREENLAWN AVE
NEWTON CENTER, MA 02159-1714

BLACKS HANDWEAVING SHOP
597 MAIN ST
WEST BARNSTABLE, MA 02668-1128
508-362-3955

BOSTON CORPORATE ART
470 ATLANTIC AVE
BOSTON, MA 02210-2208
617-426-8880

GALLERY LISTINGS

BRAMHALL & DUNN
BOX 923 MAIN ST
VINEYARD HAVEN, MA 02568
508-693-6437

BRAMHALL & DUNN GALLERY
16 FEDERAL ST
NANTUCKET, MA 02554-3568
508-228-4688

CLARK GALLERY
PO BOX 339
LINCOLN STATION
LINCOLN, MA 01773-0339
617-259-8303

CRAFTY YANKEE
1838 MASSACHUSETTS AVE
LEXINGTON, MA 02173-5303
617-863-1219

CROMA GALLERY
94 CENTRAL ST
WELLESLEY, MA 02181-5714
617-235-6230

DANCO FURNITURE
ROUTES 5 & 10
WEST HATFIELD, MA 01088
413-247-5681

DECOR INTERNATIONAL, INC
141 NEWBURY ST
BOSTON, MA 02116-2906
617-262-1529

DESIGNERS GALLERY LTD
1 DESIGN CENTER PL STE 329
BOSTON, MA 02210-2313
617-426-5511

FIRE OPAL
7 POND ST
JAMAICA PLAIN, MA 02130-2502
617-524-0262

FULLER MUSUEM OF ART
MUSEUM SHOP
455 OAK ST
BROCKTON, MA 02401
508-588-6000

GALLERIE OCEANNA
18 N SUMMER ST
EDGARTOWN, MA 02539
508-627-3121

GALLERY NAGA
67 NEWBURY ST
BOSTON, MA 02116-3010
617-267-9060

GIFTED HAND GALLERY
32 CHURCH ST
WELLESLEY, MA 02181-6322
617-235-7171

GM GALLERIES
MAIN ST
WEST STOCKBRIDGE, MA 01266
413-232-8519

HALF MOON HARRY
19 BEARSKIN NCK
ROCKPORT, MA 01966-1666
508-546-6601

HAND OF MAN CRAFT GALLERY
29 WENDELL AVE
PITTSFIELD, MA 01201-6311
413-443-6033

HAND OF MAN CRAFT GALLERY
THE CURTIS SHOPS
WALKER ST
LENOX, MA 01240
413-637-0632

HANDWORKS INC
157 GREAT RD # 2A
ACTON, MA 01720-5712
508-263-7107

HOLSTEN GALLERIES
GENERAL DELIVERY
STOCKBRIDGE, MA 01262-9999
413-298-3044

HOORN ASHBY GALLERY
10 FEDERAL ST
NANTUCKET, MA 02554-3514
508-228-9314

IMPULSE
188 COMMERCIAL ST
PROVINCETOWN, MA 02657-2117
508-487-1154

JOHN LEWIS, INC
97 NEWBURY ST
BOSTON, MA 02116-3086
617-266-6665

JUBILATION
91 UNION ST
PICADILLY STATION
NEWTON, MA 02159-2224
617-965-0488

LACOSTE GALLERY
39 THOREAU ST
CONCORD, MA 01742-2410
508-369-0278

LIMITED EDITIONS, INC
1176 WALNUT ST
NEWTON HIGHLANDS, MA 02161
617-965-5474

MDF
19 BRATTLE ST
CAMBRIDGE, MA 02138-3709
617-491-2789

MOBILIA
358 HURON AVE
CAMBRIDGE, MA 02138-6828
617-876-2109

NEAL ROSENBLUM GOLDSMITHS
287 PARK AVE
WORCESTER, MA 01609-1846
508-755-4244

NORTHSIDE CRAFT GALLERY
933 MAIN ST
YARMOUTH PORT, MA 02675-2124
508-362-5291

NOTHING TOO COMMON
1502 HIGHLAND AVE
NEEDHAM, MA 02192-2607

ORIEL
17 COLLEGE ST
SOUTH HADLEY, MA 01075-1403
413-532-6469

QUADRUM
THE MALL AT CHESTNUT HILL
CHESTNUT HILL, MA 02167
617-262-9601

RICE POLAK GALLERY
432 COMMERCIAL ST
PROVINCETOWN, MA 02657-2426
508-487-1052

SALMON FALLS ARTISANS SHOWROOM
PO BOX 17
ASHFIELD RD
SHELBURNE FALLS, MA 01370-0017
413-625-9833

SIGNATURE GALLERY
10 STEEPLE ST
MASHPEE, MA 02649
508-539-0029

SIGNATURE GALLERY
DOCK SQUARE
24 NORTH ST
BOSTON, MA 02109
617-227-4885

SILVERSCAPE DESIGNS
1 KING ST
NORTHAMPTON, MA 01060-3221
413-253-3324

SILVERSCAPE DESIGNS
264 N PLEASANT ST
AMHERST, MA 01002-1725
413-253-3324

SKERA GALLERY
221 MAIN ST
NORTHAMPTON, MA 01060-3122
413-586-4563

SPECTRUM OF AMERICAN ARTISTS
26 MAIN ST
NANTUCKET, MA 02554-3531
508-228-4606

SPECTRUM OF AMERICAN ARTISTS
369 MAIN ST
BREWSTER, MA 02631-1036
508-385-3322

THE ARTFUL HAND GALLERY
36 COPLEY PL
100 HUNTINGTON AVE
BOSTON, MA 02116-6514
617-262-9601

THE ARTISAN GALLERY
150 MAIN ST
NORTHAMPTON, MA 01060-3131
413-586-1942

THE ARTS & CRAFTS GALLERY
27 WHITEHAVEN WAY
SOUTH DENNIS, MA 02660-2681
508-385-4414

THE BALCONY
PO BOX 489
VINEYARD HAVEN, MA 02568-0489
508-693-5127

WHIPPOORWILL CRAFTS GALLERY
126 S MARKET ST
FANEUIL HALL MARKET
BOSTON, MA 02109-1626
617-523-5149

WOLOV GALLERY
4 LONGFELLOW PL APT 1806
BOSTON, MA 02114-2815
617-426-5511

MICHIGAN

ACKERMAN GALLERY
327 ABBOTT RD
EAST LANSING, MI 48823-4309
517-332-6818

ALICE SIMSAR GALLERY
PO BOX 7089
ANN ARBOR, MI 48107-7089
313-665-4883

ANIMALIA GALLERY
403 WATER ST
P.O. BOX 613
SAUGATUCK, MI 49453
616-857-3227

ANN ARBOR ART ASSOCIATION
117 W LIBERTY ST
ANN ARBOR, MI 48104-1380
313-994-8004

ARIANA GALLERY
119 S MAIN ST
ROYAL OAK, MI 48067-2610
810-546-8810

ART LEADERS GALLERY
26111 NOVI RD
NOVI, MI 48375-1140
810-348-5540

ARTISANS GALLERY
2666 CHARLEVOIX AVE
PETOSKEY, MI 49770-9707
616-347-6466

BOYER GLASSWORKS
207 N STATE ST
HARBOR SPRINGS, MI 49740
616-526-6359

CAROL HOOBERMAN GALLERY
124 S WOODWARD AVE STE 12
BIRMINGHAM, MI 48009-6119
313-647-3666

CAROL JAMES GALLERY
301 S MAIN ST
ROYAL OAK, MI 48067-2613
313-541-6216

COURTYARD GALLERY
813 E BUFFALO ST
NEW BUFFALO, MI 49117-1522
616-469-4110

DECO ART
815 1ST ST
MENOMINEE, MI 49858-3231
906-863-3300

DETROIT GALLERY OF CONTEMPORARY CRAFTS
104 FISHER BLDG
DETROIT, MI 48202
313-873-7888

DONNA JACOBS GALLERY, LTD
574 N WOODWARD AVE
SECOND FLOOR
BIRMINGHAM, MI 48009-5375
313-540-1600

FOR LOVE NOR MONEY
314 E LAKE ST
PETOSKEY, MI 49770-2418
616-348-5533

FRIENDS FURNISHINGS & DESIGN
126 MAINCENTRE
NORTHVILLE, MI 48167-1562
313-380-6930

GALLERIE 454
15105 KERCHEVAL ST
GROSSE POINTE, MI 48230-1389
313-822-4454

GALLERY FOUR FOURTEEN
414 DETROIT ST
ANN ARBOR, MI 48104-1118
313-747-7004

GALLERY ON THE ALLEY
611 BROAD ST
SAINT JOSEPH, MI 49085-1257
616-983-6161

GARDEN HOUSE INTERIORS
9426 BIRCH RUN RD
BIRCH RUN, MI 48415-9442
517-624-9649

GLEN ARBOR CITY LIMITS
PO BOX 444
GLEN ARBOR, MI 49636-0444

GOOD GOODS
106 MASON ST
SAUGATUCK, MI 49453
616-857-1557

HABITAT GALLERIES
TRIATRIA BLDG #45
32255 NORTHWESTERN HWY
FARMINGTON HILLS, MI 48334
313-851-9090

HANDIWORKS, LTD
5260 HELENA ST
ALDEN, MI 49612
616-331-6787

HOOVER HOUSE GALLERY
8730 CURTIS LN
PETOSKEY, MI 49770-9789
616-526-9819

HUZZA
136 E MAIN ST
HARBOR SPRINGS, MI 49740-1510
616-526-2128

JOYCE PETTER GALLERY
134 BUTLER ST
DOUGLAS/SAUGATUCK, MI 49453
616-857-7861

JUDITH RACHT GALLERY, INC
GENERAL DELIVERY
HARBERT, MI 49115-9999
517-469-1080

KENNEDY'S
661 CROSWELL AVE SE
GRAND RAPIDS, MI 49506-3003

KOUCKY GALLERY
319 BRIDGE ST
CHARLEVOIX, MI 49720-1414
616-547-2228

LAKESIDE STUDIO
15251 LAKESHORE RD
LAKESIDE, MI 49116-9712
616-469-1377

LINDA HAYMAN GALLERY
5 PINE GATE CT
BLOOMFIELD HILLS, MI 48304-2111
810-433-3430

MATTIE FLYNN
1033 E FULTON ST
GRAND RAPIDS, MI 49503-3608
616-454-8775

MESA ARTS GALLERY
32800 FRANKLIN RD
FRANKLIN, MI 48025-1111
313-851-9949

NICOL STUDIO & GALLERY
2531 CHARLEVOIX AVE
PETOSKEY, MI 49770-8524
616-347-0227

NORTHERN POSSESSIONS
222 PARK AVE
PETOSKEY, MI 49770
616-348-3344

PDA ASSOCIATES
1019 W KILGORE RD
KALAMAZOO, MI 49008-3615
616-342-0103

PELLETIER GALLERY
414 DETROIT ST
ANN ARBOR, MI 48104-1118
313-741-0571

PRESTON BURKE GALLERY
37622 W 12 MILE RD
FARMINGTON HILLS, MI 48331-3074
313-963-2350

PRIVATE COLLECTION GALLERY
6736A ORCHARD LAKE RD
WEST BLOOMFIELD, MI 48322-3411
313-737-4050

REVOLUTION
23257 WOODWARD AVE
FERNDALE, MI 48220-1361

ROBERT KIDD GALLERY
107 TOWNSEND ST
BIRMINGHAM, MI 48009-6001
313-642-3909

RUSSELL KLATT GALLERY
1467 S WOODWARD AVE
BIRMINGHAM, MI 48009-5125
313-647-6655

SANDRA COLLINS, INC
470 N WOODWARD AVE
BIRMINGHAM, MI 48009-5372
313-642-4795

SAPER GALLERY
433 ALBERT AVE
EAST LANSING, MI 48823-4406
517-351-0815

SELO SHEVEL GALLERY
301 S MAIN ST
ANN ARBOR, MI 48104-2107
313-761-4620

SPITLER GALLERY
2007 PAULINE CT
ANN ARBOR, MI 48103-5185
313-662-8914

SUZIE VIGLAND GALLERY
1047 MICHIGAN AVE
BENZONIA, MI 49616
616-882-7203

SYBARIS GALLERY
202 E 3RD ST
ROYAL OAK, MI 48067-2620
313-544-3388

T'MARRA GALLERY
111 N 1ST ST
ANN ARBOR, MI 48104-1301
313-769-3223

GALLERY LISTINGS

TAMARACK CRAFTSMEN
GENERAL DELIVERY
OMENA, MI 49674-9999
616-386-5529

TEWLEWS GALLERY
54 E 8TH ST
HOLLAND, MI 49423-3502
616-396-2653

THE BELL GALLERY
257 E MAIN ST
HARBOR SPRINGS, MI 49740-1511
616-526-9855

THE GREAT FRAME UP
2876 WASHTENAW RD
YPSILANTI, MI 48197-1507
313-434-8556

THE PEACEABLE KINGDOM
210 S MAIN ST
ANN ARBOR, MI 48104-2106

THE PENNIMAN SHOWCASE
827 PENNIMAN AVE
PLYMOUTH, MI 48170-1621
313-455-5531

THE PINE TREE GALLERY
824 E CLOVERLAND DR
US HWY 2
IRONWOOD, MI 49938-1502
906-932-5120

THE POSNER GALLERY
32407 N WESTERN HWY
FARMINGTON HILLS, MI 48332
313-626-6450

THE SAJON-MAY GALLERY
6251 ISLAND LAKE DR
EAST LANSING, MI 48823-9733

THE WETSMAN COLLECTION
132 N WOODWARD AVE
BIRMINGHAM, MI 48009-3375
810-645-6212

THE YAW GALLERY
550 N WOODWARD AVE
BIRMINGHAM, MI 48009-5375
313-747-5470

TOUCH OF LIGHT GALLERY
23426 WOODWARD AVE
FERNDALE, MI 48220-1344
313-543-1868

TRULY GIFTED
515 S WASHINGTON AVE
ROYAL OAK, MI 48067-3825

URBAN ARCHITECTUR INC
15 E KIRBY ST
DETROIT, MI 48202-4047
313-873-2707

MINNESOTA

ANDERSON & ANDERSON GALLERY
414 1ST AVE N
MINNEAPOLIS, MN 55401-1702
612-332-4889

ART LENDING GALLERY
25 GROVELAND TER
MINNEAPOLIS, MN 55403-1104
612-377-7800

ART RESOURCES GALLERY
494 JACKSON ST
SAINT PAUL, MN 55101-2320
612-222-4431

BOIS FORT GALLERY
130 E SHERIDAN ST
ELY, MN 55731-1215
218-365-5066

CELEBRATION DESIGNS
1089 GRAND AVE
SAINT PAUL, MN 55105-3002
612-690-4344

FORUM GALLERY
1235 YALE PL APT 1308
MINNEAPOLIS, MN 55403-1947
612-333-1825

GLASSPECTACLE
402 MAIN ST N
STILLWATER, MN 55082-5051
612-439-0757

GOLDSTEIN GALLERY
250 MCNEAL HALL
1985 BUFORD AVE
SAINT PAUL, MN 55108
612-624-7434

GRAND AVENUE FRAME & GALLERY
964 GRAND AVE
SAINT PAUL, MN 55105-3014
612-224-9716

MC GALLERY
400 1ST AVE N STE 336
THIRD FLOOR
MINNEAPOLIS, MN 55401-1721
612-339-1480

MADE IN THE SHADE GALLERY
600 E SUPERIOR ST
DULUTH, MN 55802-2230
218-722-1929

NORTHERN CLAY CENTER
2375 UNIVERSITY AVE W
SAINT PAUL, MN 55114-1603
612-642-1735

OUT OF THE ORDINARY
8800 HIGHWAY 7
SAINT LOUIS PARK, MN 55426-3908

PETER M DAVID GALLERY
3351 SAINT LOUIS AVE
MINNEAPOLIS, MN 55416-4394
612-339-1825

RAYMOND AVENUE GALLERY
761 RAYMOND AVE
SAINT PAUL, MN 55114-1522
612-644-9200

ROURKE'S GALLERY
523 4TH ST S
MOORHEAD, MN 56560-2620
218-236-8861

SAYER STRAND GALLERY
275 MARKET ST STE 222
MINNEAPOLIS, MN 55405-1623
612-375-0838

SONIA'S GALLERY, INC
400 1ST AVE N STE 318
MINNEAPOLIS, MN 55401-1721
612-338-0350

SUPERIOR LAKE - N AMERICA, INC
716 E SUPERIOR ST
DULUTH, MN 55802-2210
218-722-6998

SUZANNE KOHN GALLERY
1690 GRAND AVE
SAINT PAUL, MN 55105-1806
612-699-0417

TECHNIC GALLERY
1055 GRAND AVE
SAINT PAUL, MN 55105-3002
612-222-0188

TEXTILE ARTS INTERNATIONAL
PO BOX 52063
MINNEAPOLIS, MN 55402-5063
612-338-6776

THE ROOMERS GALLERY
5632 SANIBEL DR
MINNETONKA, MN 55343-9428
612-822-9490

THE WHITE OAK GALLERY
3939 W 50TH ST
EDINA, MN 55424-1244
614-927-3575

THOMAS BARRY FINE ARTS
400 1ST AVE N STE 304
MINNEAPOLIS, MN 55401-1721
612-338-3656

MISSISSIPPI

BRYANT GALLERIES
2845 LAKELAND DR
JACKSON, MS 39208-8831
601-932-1993

CHIMNEYVILLE CRAFTS
1150 LAKELAND DR
JACKSON, MS 39216-4701
601-988-9253

EARTH TRADERS INC
1060 E COUNTY LINE RD
RIDGELAND, MS 39157-1900

HILLYER HOUSE
207 E SCENIC DR
PASS CHRISTIAN, MS 39571-4417
601-452-4810

SERENITY GALLERY
126½ MAIN ST
BAY SAINT LOUIS, MS 39520-4526
601-467-3061

THE OLD TRACE GALLERY, LTD
120 E JEFFERSON ST
P.O. BOX 307
KOSCIUSKO, MS 39090-3736
601-289-9170

THE THIRD DIMENSION GALLERY
201 BANNER HALL
4465 I-55 N
JACKSON, MS 39206
601-366-3371

MISSOURI

ART ATTACK GALLERY
420 W 7TH ST
KANSAS CITY, MO 64105-1407
816-474-7482

AUSTRAL GALLERY
2115 PARK AVE
SAINT LOUIS, MO 63104-2539
314-776-0300

BARUCCI GALLERY
8101 MARYLAND AVE
CLAYTON, MO 63105-3720
314-727-2020

CENTRAL PARK GALLERY
1644 WYANDOTTE ST
KANSAS CITY, MO 64108-1224
816-471-7711

GLYNN BROWN DESIGN GALLERY
420 W 7TH ST
KANSAS CITY, MO 64105-1407
816-842-2115

HELLA'S ART TO WEAR & FIBERS
9769 CLAYTON RD
SAINT LOUIS, MO 63124-1503
314-997-9696

INTERWOVEN DESIGNS
4400 LACLEDE AVE
SAINT LOUIS, MO 63108-2204
314-531-6200

LEEDY VOULKOS GALLERY
2012 BALTIMORE AVE
KANSAS CITY, MO 64108-1914
816-474-1919

NANCY SACHS GALLERY
7700 FORSYTH BLVD
SAINT LOUIS, MO 63105-1810
314-727-7770

PORTFOLIO GALLERY
3514 DELMAR BLVD
SAINT LOUIS, MO 63103-1003
314-533-3323

PRIVATE STOCK GALLERY
4550 WARWICK BLVD
KANSAS CITY, MO 64111-7725
816-561-1191

PRO ART GALLERY
625 S SKINKER BLVD # 503
SAINT LOUIS, MO 63105-2301
314-231-5848

RANDALL GALLERY
999 N 13TH ST
SAINT LOUIS, MO 63106-3836
314-231-4808

STYLE WORKS
6934 DARTMOUTH AVE
SAINT LOUIS, MO 63130-3132
314-531-3900

THE CRAFT ALLIANCE GALLERY
6640 DELMAR BLVD
SAINT LOUIS, MO 63130-4503
214-725-1151

THE MORGAN GALLERY
412 DELAWARE ST STE A
KANSAS CITY, MO 64105-1269
816-842-8755

UNION HILL ARTS GALLERY
3013 MAIN ST
KANSAS CITY, MO 64108-3323
816-561-3020

MONTANA

ARTISTIC TOUCH
209 CENTRAL AVE
WHITEFISH, MT 59937-2661
406-862-4813

CHANDLER GALLERY
FRONT ST
MISSOULA, MT 59802
406-721-5555

FURNITURE, ETC.
17 MAIN ST
KALISPELL, MT 59901-4449
406-756-8555

THE SQUIRREL NEST
1332 LEWIS AVE
BILLINGS, MT 59102-4238
406-259-5461

NEBRASKA

ADAM WHITNEY GALLERY
8725 SHAMROCK RD
OMAHA, NE 68114-5238
402-393-1051

ANDERSON O'BRIEN GALLERY
8724 PACIFIC ST
OMAHA, NE 68114-5232
402-390-0717

HAYMARKET GALLERY
119 S 9TH ST
LINCOLN, NE 68508-2212
402-475-1061

LEWIS ART GALLERY
8025 W DODGE RD
OMAHA, NE 68114-3413
402-391-7733

UNIVERSITY PLACE ART CENTER
2601 N 48TH ST
LINCOLN, NE 68504-3632
402-466-8692

NEVADA

MARK MASUOKA GALLERY
1149 S MARYLAND PKY
LAS VEGAS, NV 89104-1738
702-366-0377

MINOTAUR FINE ARTS
3500 LAS VEGAS BLVD S
LAS VEGAS, NV 89109-8900
702-737-1400

MOONSTRUCK GALLERY
6368 W SAHARA AVE
LAS VEGAS, NV 89102-3050
702-364-0531

SHUTLER-ZIV ART GROUP
3119 W POST RD
LAS VEGAS, NV 89118-3840
702-896-2218

STREMMEL GALLERY
1400 S VIRGINIA ST
RENO, NV 89502-2889
702-786-0558

NEW HAMPSHIRE

ART 3 GALLERY
44 WEST BROOK ST
MANCHESTER, NH 03101-1215
603-668-6650

ARTISANS GROUP
GENERAL DELIVERY
DUBLIN, NH 03444-9999
603-563-8782

AVA GALLERY
4 BANK ST
LEBANON, NH 03766-1730
603-448-3117

CRAFTINGS
72 HANOVER ST
MANCHESTER, NH 03101-2212
603-623-4108

GALLERY THIRTY-THREE
111 MARKET ST
PORTSMOUTH, NH 03801-3703
603-431-7403

JEWELRY CREATIONS
388 CENTRAL AVE
DOVER, NH 03820-3411
603-749-3129

LEAGUE OF NH CRAFT CENTER
36 N MAIN ST
CONCORD, NH 03301-4912
603-228-8171

LEAGUE OF NH CRAFTS CENTER
13 LEBANON ST
HANOVER, NH 03755-2124
603-643-5050

MCGOWAN FINE ART, INC
10 HILLS AVE
CONCORD, NH 03301-4803
603-225-2515

THE ARTISANS GROUP
GENERAL DELIVERY
P.O. BOX 1039
DUBLIN, NH 03444-9999
603-563-8782

NEW JERSEY

ALICE WHITE GALLERY
105 PULIS AVE
FRANKLIN LAKES, NJ 07417-2710
201-848-1855

ART DIRECTIONS
38 WILCOX DR
MOUNTAIN LAKES, NJ 07046-1148
201-263-1420

ARTFORMS
16 MONMOUTH ST
RED BANK, NJ 07701-1614
908-530-4330

CBL FINE ART
459 PLEASANT VALLEY WAY
WEST ORANGE, NJ 07052-2919
201-736-7776

CONTRASTS
49 BROAD ST
RED BANK, NJ 07701-1902
908-741-9177

DESIGN QUEST LTD.
3 GRAND AVE
ENGLEWOOD, NJ 07631-3508
201-568-7001

DEXTERITY, LTD
26 CHURCH ST
MONTCLAIR, NJ 07042-2702
201-746-5370

GALLERY LISTINGS

EAST WEST CONNECTION
1274 ROUTE 31
LEBANON, NJ 08833
908-713-9655

ELVID GALLERY
PO BOX 5267
ENGLEWOOD, NJ 07631-5267
201-871-8747

GALERIE ATELIER
347 KINGS HWY W
HADDONFIELD, NJ 08033-2103
215-627-3624

GALLERY AT BRISTOL-MEYERS
PO BOX 4000
PRINCETON, NJ 08543-4000
609-921-5896

GOLDSMITHS
26 N UNION ST
LAMBERTVILLE, NJ 08530-2140
609-398-4590

KIMBERLY DESIGNS
1111 PARK AVE
PLAINFIELD, NJ 07060-3006
201-561-5344

LA GALLERIE DU VITRAIL
70 TANNER ST # 2
HADDONFIELD, NJ 08033-2419
609-428-6712

LIMITED EDITIONS, INC
2200 LONG BEACH BLVD
SURF CITY, NJ 08008-5555
609-494-0527

MARGARET'S CRAFT SHOP
413 RARITAN AVE
HIGHLAND PARK, NJ 08904-2739
908-247-2210

MATREX DALTON
485 BERGEN BLVD
RIDGEFIELD, NJ 07657-2803
201-945-8077

MELME GALLERY
BRIDGEWATER COMMONS
400 COMMONS WAY #256
BRIDGEWATER, NJ 08807
908-722-0933

NK THAINE GALLERY
150 KINGS HWY E
HADDONFIELD, NJ 08033-2004
609-428-6961

NATHANS GALLERY
1205 MCBRIDE AVE
WEST PATERSON, NJ 07424-2540
201-785-9119

PETERS VALLEY CRAFT GALLERY
RT 615
LAYTON, NJ 07851
201-948-5202

POTTERY INTERNATIONAL
28 PARK PL ON THE GREEN
MORRSTOWN, NJ 07960
201-538-1919

SCHERER GALLERY
93 SCHOOL RD W
MARLBORO, NJ 07746-1572
201-536-9465

SHEILA NUSSBAUM GALLERY
341 MILLBURN AVE
MILLBURN, NJ 07041-1609
201-467-1720

SIGNATURE DESIGNS
5 W MAIN ST
MOORESTOWN, NJ 08057-2429
609-778-8657

STRAND GALLERY
9209 VENTNOR AVE
MARGATE CITY, NJ 08402-2447
609-822-8800

THE QUEST
38 MAIN ST
CHESTER, NJ 07930-2535
908-879-8144

WALKER-KORNBLUTH ART GALLERY
7-21 FAIR LAWN AVE
FAIR LAWN, NJ 07410-1823
201-791-3374

WILLIAMS GALLERY
8 CHAMBERS ST
PRINCETON, NJ 08542-3708
609-921-1142

NEW MEXICO

ANDREWS PUEBLO GALLERY
400 SAN FELIPE ST NW
ALBUQUERQUE, NM 87104-1462
505-243-0414

BAREISS CONTEMPORARY ART
PO BOX 2739
TAOS, NM 87571-2739
505-776-2284

BELLAS ARTES
653 CANYON RD
SANTA FE, NM 87501-2762
212-274-1115

CLAY & FIBER GALLERY
126 W PLAZA
TAOS, NM 87571-5923
505-758-8093

CONTEMPORARY SOUTHWEST GALLERY
123 W PALACE AVE
SANTA FE, NM 87501-2045
800-283-0440

EL PRADO GALLERY
112 W SAN FRANCISCO ST
SANTA FE, NM 87501-2068
505-988-2906

FORM & FUNCTION
328 GUADALUPE ST
SANTA FE, NM 87501
505-984-8226

GARLAND GALLERY
125 LINCOLN AVE # 113
SANTA FE, NM 87501-2005
505-984-1555

GERALD PETERS GALLERY
PO BOX 908
SANTA FE, NM 87504-0908
505-988-8961

HANDSEL GALLERY
306 CAMINO DEL MONTE SOL
SANTA FE, NM 87501-2824
505-988-4030

HANDWOVEN ORIGINALS
211 OLD SANTA FE TRL
SANTA FE, NM 87501-2160
505-982-4118

JOAN CAWLEY GALLERY
133 W SAN FRANCISCO ST
SANTA FE, NM 87501-2111
505-984-1464

JOHNSON BENKERT
128 W WATER ST
SANTA FE, NM 87501-2137
505-984-2768

KENT GALLERIES
130 LINCOLN AVE
SANTA FE, NM 87501-2069
505-988-1001

LA MESA OF SANTA FE
225 CANYON RD
SANTA FE, NM 87501-2755
505-984-1688

LAURA CARPENTER FINE ART
309 READ ST
SANTA FE, NM 87501-2628
505-986-9090

LEW ALLEN GALLERY
225 GALISTEO ST
SANTA FE, NM 87501-2125
505-988-5387

LIGHTSIDE GALLERY
225 CANYON RD
SANTA FE, NM 87501
505-982-5501

MABEL'S WEST
201 CANYON RD
SANTA FE, NM 87501-2714
505-986-9105

MADE IN THE USA GALLERY
110 W SAN FRANCISCO ST
SANTA FE, NM 87501-2189
505-982-3232

MARIPOSA GALLERY
225 CANYON RD
SANTA FE, NM 87501-2755
505-982-3032

MICHAEL WIGLEY GALLERIES, LTD
1111 PASEO DE PERALTA
SANTA FE, NM 87501-2737
505-984-8986

MISI LAKIA-BI KISI GALLERY
312 READ ST
SANTA FE, NM 87501-2629
505-984-0119

NEW TRENDS GALLERY
225 CANYON RD
SANTA FE, NM 87501-2755
505-988-1199

OFF THE WALL GALLERY
616 CANYON RD
SANTA FE, NM 87501-2722
505-983-8337

OKUN GALLERY
301 N GUADALUPE ST
SANTA FE, NM 87501-5502
505-989-4300

OOT'I GALLERY
708 CANYON RD
SANTA FE, NM 87501-2751
505-984-1676

ORNAMENT GALLERY
209 W SAN FRANCISCO ST
SANTA FE, NM 87501-2128

POST WESTERN
201 GALISTEO ST
SANTA FE, NM 87501-2125
505-984-9195

QUILTS, LTD
625 CANYON RD
SANTA FE, NM 87501-2721
505-988-5888

SANTA FE EAST
200 OLD SANTA FE TRL
SANTA FE, NM 87501-2107
505-988-3103

SANTA FE WEAVING GALLERY
124½ GALISTEO ST
SANTA FE, NM 87501-2124
505-982-1737

SHIDONI CONTEMPORARY GALLERY
GENERAL DELIVERY
PO BOX 250
TESUQUE, NM 87574-9999
505-988-8001

SKY'S THE LIMIT
1031 MECHEM DR
RUIDOSO, NM 88345-7064

TEXTILE ARTS, INC
1571 CANYON RD
SANTA FE, NM 87501-6135

THE LIGHTSIDE GALLERY
225 CANYON RD
SANTA FE, NM 87501-2755
505-982-5501

THE RUNNING RIDGE GALLERY
640 CANYON RD
SANTA FE, NM 87501-2722
505-988-2515

WEAVING SOUTHWEST GALLERY
216B PASEO DEL PUEBLO SUR
TAOS, NM 87571-5960
505-758-0433

WEEMS GALLERY
2801 M EUBANK BLVD NE
ALBUQUERQUE, NM 87112-1300
505-293-6133

WEYRICH GALLERY
2935D LOUISIANA BLVD NE
ALBUQUERQUE, NM 87110-3537
505-883-7410

WORTH GALLERY
112A CAMINO DE LA PLACITA
TAOS, NM 87571-5939
505-751-0816

NEW YORK

15 STEPS
CENTER ITHACA
171 E STATE ST
ITHACA, NY 14850
607-272-4902

AARON FABER GALLERY
666 5TH AVE
NEW YORK, NY 10103-0001
212-586-8411

ADIRONDACK ARTWORK
RT 3, MAIN ST
NATURAL BRIDGE, NY 13665

AFTER THE RAIN
149 MERCER ST
NEW YORK, NY 10012-3240
212-431-1044

AMERICA HOUSE
466 PIERMONT AVE
PIERMONT, NY 10968-1038
914-359-0106

AMERICAN CRAFT MUSEUM GIFTSHOP
40 W 53RD ST
NEW YORK, NY 10019
212-956-3535

AN AMERICAN CRAFTSMAN
PO BOX 480
SLATE HILL, NY 10973-0480

ANTHONY GARDEN BOUTIQUE LTD
1190 LEXINGTON AVE
NEW YORK, NY 10028-1405

ARCHETYPE
115 MERCER ST
NEW YORK, NY 10012-3805
212-334-0100

ARRANGEMENTS
172 MERRICK RD
MERRICK, NY 11566-4532
516-378-4820

ARTISANS GALLERY
6 BOND ST
GREAT NECK, NY 11021-2409
516-829-6747

ARTISANS INTERNATIONAL
89 MAIN ST
WESTHAMPTON BEACH, NY 11978
516-288-2222

ARTIUM
730 5TH AVE STE 1710
NEW YORK, NY 10019-4105
212-333-5800

ASHLEY COLLECTION
322 W 57TH ST APT 19S
NEW YORK, NY 10019-3716
212-247-7294

AUSTIN HARVARD GALLERY
NORTHFIELD COMMON
50 STATE ST
PITTSFORD, NY 14534
716-383-1472

BABCOCK GALLERIES
724 5TH AVE
NEW YORK, NY 10019-4106
212-767-1852

BALAMAN CRAFT GALLERY
1031 LEXINGTON AVE
NEW YORK, NY 10021-3504
212-472-8366

BARRY PALUM GALLERY
21 PRINCE ST
ROCHESTER, NY 14607-1405
716-244-9407

BELLARDO, LTD
100 CHRISTOPHER ST
NEW YORK, NY 10014-4201
212-675-2668

BEN JANE ARTS
PO BOX 298
WEST HEMPSTEAD, NY 11552-0298
516-483-1330

BERNICE STEINBAUM GALLERY
132 GREENE ST
NEW YORK, NY 10012-3242
212-431-4224

CARRIAGE HOUSE STUDIO
79 GUERNSEY ST
BROOKLYN, NY 11222-3111
617-629-2337

CERAMICS & MORE
197 HAWKINS ST
BRONX, NY 10464-1443
718-885-0319

CHARLES COWLES GALLERY
420 W BROADWAY
NEW YORK, NY 10012-3764
212-925-3500

CIMARRON
64 S BROADWAY
NYACK, NY 10960-3837

COE KERR GALLERY
49 E 82ND ST
NEW YORK, NY 10028-0387
212-628-1340

CONTEMPORARY PORCELAIN GALLERY
105 SULLIVAN ST
NEW YORK, NY 10012-3669
212-219-2172

COUNTRY GEAR, LTD
GENERAL DELIVERY
BRIDGEHAMPTON, NY 11932-9999
516-537-1032

CRAFTS PEOPLE
424 SPILLWAY RD
WEST HURLEY, NY 12491-5114

DAWSON GALLERY
17 SELDEN ST
ROCHESTER, NY 14605-2921
716-454-6966

DESIGNERS' STUDIO
492 BROADWAY
SARATOGA SPRINGS, NY 12866-2207
518-584-0987

DESIGNERS, TOO
8037 JERICHO TNPK
WOODBURY, NY 11797
516-921-8080

DISTANT ORIGIN GALLERY
150 MERCER ST
NEW YORK, NY 10012-3212
212-941-0024

ELAINE BENSON GALLERY
PO BOX 3034
2317 MONTAUK HWY
BRIDGEHAMPTON, NY 11932-3034
516-537-3233

GALLERY LISTINGS

ENCHANTED FOREST
85 MERCER ST
NEW YORK, NY 10012-4438
212-431-1045

ENGEL GALLERY
51 MAIN ST
EAST HAMPTON, NY 11937-2701
516-324-6462

ENTREE LIBRE
GALERIE CONTEMPORAINE
110 WOOSTER ST
NEW YORK, NY 10012
212-431-5279

ERIC ZETTERQUIST GALLERY
24 E 81ST ST APT 5C
NEW YORK, NY 10028-0227
212-988-3399

EUREKA CRAFTS
210 WALTON ST
SYRACUSE, NY 13202-1227
315-471-4601

FABULOUS FURNITURE, INC
RTE 28
BOICEVILE, NY 12412
914-657-6317

FAST FORWARD GALLERY
580 5TH AVE
PENTHOUSE
NEW YORK, NY 10036-4701
212-302-5518

FIRSTHAND GALLERY
MAIN ST
SAG HARBOR, NY 11963
516-725-3648

FRANKLIN PARRASCH GALLERY
584 BROADWAY
NEW YORK, NY 10012-3229
212-925-7090

GALLERY 514, LTD
98 WHEATLEY RD
OLD WESTBURY, NY 11568-1212
516-626-0387

GALLERY AT THE COURTYARD
223 KATONAH AVE
KATONAH, NY 10536-2139
914-232-9511

GALLERY AUTHENTIQUE
1499 OLD NORTHERN BLVD
ROSLYN, NY 11576-2146
516-484-7238

GALLERY MUHR
PO BOX 572
PORT WASHINGTON, NY 11050
516-883-0571

GALLERY NINETY ONE
91 GRAND ST
NEW YORK, NY 10013-2612
212-966-3072

GALLERY NORTH
90 N COUNTRY RD
SETAUKET, NY 11733-1345
516-751-2676

GALLERY TEN
7 GREENWICH AVE
NEW YORK, NY 10014-3512
212-206-1058

GARGOYLES, LTD
138 W 25TH ST
NEW YORK, NY 10001-7405
212-255-0135

GARTH CLARK GALLERY
24 W 57TH ST
NEW YORK, NY 10019-3918
212-246-2205

GAYLE WILLSON GALLERY
16 JOBS LN
SOUTHAMPTON, NY 11968-4807
516-283-7430

GIFT GALLERY
6584 NASH RD
NORTH TONAWANDA, NY 14120

GIMPEL WEITZENHOFFER GALLERY
PO BOX 20006
NEW YORK, NY 10011-0001
212-925-9060

GLORIA PLEVIN GALLERY
PO BOX 188
CHAUTAUQUA, NY 14722-0188

GRAHAM GALLERY
1014 MADISON AVE
MAIN FLOOR
NEW YORK, NY 10021-0103
212-535-5767

HAMMER GALLERY
33 W 57TH ST
NEW YORK, NY 10019-3499
212-644-4400

HAND OF THE CRAFTSMAN
5 S BROADWAY
NYACK, NY 10960-3117
914-358-3366

HELLER GALLERY
71 GREENE ST
NEW YORK, NY 10012-4338
212-966-5948

HENOCH GALLERY
80 WOOSTER ST
NEW YORK, NY 10012-4347
212-966-0303

HUDSON RIVER GALLERY
217 MAIN ST
OSSINING, NY 10562-4704
914-762-5300

HUDSON RIVER MUSEUM
GIFT SHOP
511 WARBURTON AVE
YONKERS, NY 10701
914-963-4550

HUMMINGBIRD DESIGNS
29 3RD ST
TROY, NY 12180-3205
518-272-1807

HUMMINGBIRD JEWELERS
14 E MARKET ST
RHINEBECK, NY 12572-1606
914-876-4585

HYACINTH CONTEMPORARY CRAFTS
4004 BELL BLVD
BAYSIDE, NY 11361-2063
718-224-9228

IMAGES ART GALLERY
1157 PLEASANTVILLE RD
BRIARCLIFF MANOR, NY 10510-1603
914-762-3000

IMPORTANT AMERICAN CRAFT
70 RIVERSIDE DR
NEW YORK, NY 10024-5714
212-496-1804

IMPRESSIVE INTERIOR GALLERY
14 OLD INDIAN TRL
MILTON, NY 12547-5114
914-795-5101

JARO ART GALLERIES
955 MADISON AVE
NEW YORK, NY 10021-2702
212-734-5475

JEWELRY 10
11625 UNION TPKE
FOREST HILLS, NY 11375-6058
718-793-4225

JOHN CHRISTOPHER GALLERY
131 MAIN ST
STONY BROOK, NY 11790-1911
516-689-1601

JOHN CHRISTOPHER GALLERY
43 MAIN ST
COLD SPRING HARBOR, NY 11724
516-367-3978

JULIE ARTISANS GALLERY
687 MADISON AVE
NEW YORK, NY 10021-8042
212-688-2345

KELMSCOTT GALLERY
131 MAIN ST
COLD SPRING, NY 10516-2813
914-265-2379

LEE GALLERY
83 MAIN ST
SOUTHAMPTON, NY 11968-4808
516-287-2361

LEO KAPLAN MODERN
965 MADISON AVE
NEW YORK, NY 10021-2702
212-535-0240

LEWIS DOLIN GALLERY, INC
PO BOX 239
KATONAH, NY 10536-0239
212-941-8130

LIMESTONE GALLERY
205 THOMPSON ST
FAYETTEVILLE, NY 13066-1911
315-637-0460

MARI GALLERIES OF WESTCHESTER
133 E PROSPECT AVE
MAMARONECK, NY 10543-3710
914-698-0008

MARK MILLIKEN GALLERY
1200 MADISON AVE
NEW YORK, NY 10128-0507
212-534-8802

MAX PROTECH GALLERY
560 BROADWAY
NEW YORK, NY 10012-3938
212-966-5454

MELE GALLERY
6 TERRACE CT
OLD WESTBURY, NY 11568-1302
212-486-8304

**MICHAEL INGBAR
GALLERY OF ART**
568 BROADWAY
NEW YORK, NY 10012-3225
212-334-1100

MILLER GALLERY
560 BROADWAY (AT PRINCE ST)
FOURTH FLOOR
NEW YORK, NY 10012
212-226-0702

MODERN STONE AGE, LTD
111 GREENE ST
NEW YORK, NY 10012-3803
212-966-2570

**MOOSE RIVER
TRADING COMPANY**
419 MANDEVILLE ST
UTICA, NY 13502-4609

NAN MILLER GALLERY
3450 WINTON PL
ROCHESTER, NY 14623-2805
716-292-1430

NANCY MARGOLIS GALLERY
251 W 21ST ST
NEW YORK, NY 10011-3101
212-255-0386

NEIL ISMAN GALLERY
1100 MADISON AVE
NEW YORK, NY 10028-0310
212-628-3688

NEW GLASS GALLERY
345 W BROADWAY
NEW YORK, NY 10013-2238
212-431-0050

NOHO GALLERY
168 MERCER ST
NEW YORK, NY 10012-3284
212-219-2210

OBJECTS OF BRIGHT PRIDE
455A COLUMBUS AVE
NEW YORK, NY 10024-5129
212-721-4579

OF CABBAGES & KINGS
587 E BOSTON POST RD
MAMARONECK, NY 10543-3740
914-698-0445

ONE OF A KIND, LTD
978 BROADWAY
THORNWOOD, NY 10594-1139
914-769-5777

PEOPLE'S POTTERY
150 ITHACA COMMONS
ITHACA, NY 14850
607-277-3597

PETER JOSEPH GALLERY
745 5TH AVE
NEW YORK, NY 10151-0407
212-751-5500

PRITAM & EAMES GALLERY
29 RACE LN
EAST HAMPTON, NY 11937-2445
516-324-7111

PRODIGY
126 W MAIN ST
ENDICOTT, NY 13760-4772
607-748-0190

RAKU GALLERY
171 SPRING ST
NEW YORK, NY 10012-3843
212-226-6636

RANDOLPH & HEIN INC
232 E 59TH ST # 234
NEW YORK, NY 10022-1464
212-826-9878

ROBERTA WOOD GALLERY
6907 E GENESEE ST
LYNDON PLAZA
FAYETTEVILLE, NY 13066-1012
315-445-0423

**ROCHESTER MEMORIAL
GALLERY**
500 UNIVERSITY AVE
ROCHESTER, NY 14607-1415
716-473-7720

RUTH RAIBLE GALLERY
41 FOREST AVE
HASTINGS ON HUDSON, NY 10706
914-478-0585

SCULPTURE FIELDS GALLERY
PO BOX 94
KENOZA LAKE, NY 12750-0094
914-482-3669

SEDONI GALLERY
304 A NEW YORK AVE
HUNTINGTON, NY 11743
516-547-4811

SHOWCASE GALLERY
246 SOUTHDOWN RD
HUNTINGTON, NY 11743-1719
516-367-3037

SILVER FOX GIFT GALLERY
7935 BOSTON STATE RD
HAMBURG, NY 14075-7306
716-649-0300

**SOUTHWEST STUDIO
CONNECTION**
65 MAIN ST
SOUTHAMPTON, NY 11968-4808
516-283-9649

STEINHARDT GALLERY
370 NEW YORK AVE
HUNTINGTON, NY 11743-3316
516-549-4430

SWEETHEART GALLERY
34C TINKER ST
WOODSTOCK, NY 12498-1233
914-679-2622

SYMMETRY GALLERY
348 BROADWAY
SARATOGA SPRINGS, NY 12866-3110
518-584-5090

TERRACOTTA GALLERY
259 W 4TH ST
NEW YORK, NY 10014-3205
212-243-1952

THE CLAY POT
162 7TH AVE
BROOKLYN, NY 11215-2243
718-788-6564

THE CRAFTSMEN
RT 9 SOUTH RD
POUGHKEEPSIE, NY 12601
914-454-2336

THE DAVID COLLECTION
161 W 15TH ST
NEW YORK, NY 10011-6720
212-929-4602

THE INTERART CENTER
167 SPRING ST
SECOND FLOOR
NEW YORK, NY 10012-3842
212-431-7500

THE JEWELRY PROJECT
9A 59 WEST 71ST ST
NEW YORK, NY 10023
212-877-0573

THE LANDING GALLERY
7956 JERICHO TPKE
WOODBURY, NY 11797-1204
516-364-2787

THE RICE GALLERY
135 WASHINGTON AVE
ALBANY, NY 12210-2202
518-463-4478

THE UNIQUE GALLERY
5701 TRANSIT RD
EAST AMHERST, NY 14051-1805
716-689-2160

THE WEST END GALLERY
87 W MARKET ST
CORNING, NY 14830-2526
607-962-8692

THE WHITE BUFFALO GALLERY
13 MILL RD
WOODSTOCK, NY 12498
800-724-2113

THE WHITE TREE GALLERY
140 KING ST
CHAPPAQUA, NY 10514-3433
914-238-4601

TRACKSIDE EMPORIUM LTD
14 E BROADWAY
PORT JEFFERSON, NY 11777-1400

TURBULENCE
812 BROADWAY
NEW YORK, NY 10003-4804

VICTRIX GALLERY
77 W MARKET ST
CORNING, NY 14830-2526

VISUAL JAPAN
860 BROADWAY FL 5
NEW YORK, NY 10003-1228
212-254-1229

WARD MASSE GALLERY
178 PRINCE ST
NEW YORK, NY 10012-2905
212-925-6951

WARES FOR ART
421 HUDSON ST APT 220
NEW YORK, NY 10014-3647
212-989-7845

WHEELER-SEIDEL GALLERY
606 3RD ST
BROOKLYN, NY 11215-3004
212-533-0319

GALLERY LISTINGS

WILLIAM BARTHMAN GALLERY
174 BROADWAY
NEW YORK, NY 10038-2503
212-227-3524

WINSTON & COMPANY
97A 7TH AVE
BROOKLYN, NY 11215-1305
718-638-7942

WINTER TREE GALLERY
147 SPRING ST
NEW YORK, NY 10012-3860
212-343-2220

**WOODSTOCK GUILD
CRAFT SHOP**
34 TINKER ST
WOODSTOCK, NY 12498-1233
914-679-2079

NORTH CAROLINA

AMERICAN CRAFT SHOWROOM
DESIGN CNTR D-408
INT'L HOME FURNITURE
HIGH POINT, NC 27260
301-889-2933

ART
502 POLLOCK ST
NEW BERN, NC 28562-5612
919-636-2120

ART ON THE WALL
16 WALL ST
ASHEVILLE, NC 28801-2710

BELLAGIO
5 BILTMORE PLZ
ASHEVILLE, NC 28803-2628
704-277-8100

BIZARRE DUCK BAZAAR
16 WALL ST
ASHEVILLE, NC 28801-2710

BLUE SPIRAL 1
38 BILTMORE AVE
ASHEVILLE, NC 28801-3625
704-251-0202

BROADHURST GALLERY
800 MIDLAND RD
PINEHURST, NC 28374-8215
910-295-2296

BROWNING ARTWORK
PO BOX 275
HWY 12
FRISCO, NC 27936-0275
919-995-5538

CEDAR CREEK GALLERY
RR 2 BOX 420
1150 FLEMING RD
CREEDMOOR, NC 27522-9641
919-528-1041

COMPTON ART GALLERY
409 W FISHER AVE
GREENSBORO, NC 27401-2039
919-370-9147

CONTINUITY, INC
PO BOX 999
US HWY 19
MAGGIE VALLEY, NC 28751-0999
704-926-0333

FINE LINE
304 S STRATFORD RD
WINSTON SALEM, NC 27103-1820
919-723-8066

FIRST LIGHT GALLERY
8508 PARK RD # 123
CHARLOTTE, NC 28210-5803
704-543-9939

FOLK ART CENTER
MILEPOST 382
BLUE RIDGE PKWY
ASHEVILLE, NC 28805
704-298-7928

GALLERY OF THE MOUNTAINS
290 MACON AVE
ASHEVILLE, NC 28804-3711
714-254-2068

HAYDEN GALLERY
7 S MAIN ST
BURNSVILLE, NC 28714-2928
704-682-7998

HEARTWOOD GALLERY
PO BOX 546
SALUDA, NC 28773-0546

HODGES TAYLOR GALLERY
227 N TRYON ST
CHARLOTTE, NC 28202-2136
704-334-3799

HORIZON GALLERY
905 W MAIN ST
DURHAM, NC 27701-2054
919-688-0313

ISLAND ART GALLERY
PO BOX 265
HWY 64
MANTEO, NC 27954-0265
919-473-2838

JULIA RUSH GALLERY
216 UNION SQ NW
HICKORY, NC 28601-6111
714-324-0409

JULIA RUSH GALLERY
SOUTHERN NATIONAL CTR
CHARLOTTE, NC 28202
704-324-0409

LICK LOG MILL STORE
DILLARD RD
HIGHLANDS, NC 28741
704-526-3934

LITTLE ART GALLERY
NORTH HILLS MALL
RALEIGH, NC 27609
919-787-6317

LITTLE MOUNTAIN POTTERY
PENIEL RD
RT. 2 BOX 60
TRYON, NC 28782
704-894-8091

MAKADO GALLERY
307 N FRONT ST
THE COTTON EXCHANGE
WILMINGTON, NC 28401-3955
919-762-8922

MASTER WORKS GALLERY
WRIGHT SQUARE
MAIN ST
HIGHLANDS, NC 28741
704-526-2633

MOUNTAIN POTTERY
GENERAL DELIVERY
DILLSBORO, NC 28725-9999
704-586-9183

NEW ELEMENTS GALLERY
216 N FRONT ST
WILMINGTON, NC 28401-3920
919-343-8997

NEW MORNING GALLERY
7 BOSTON WAY
BILTMORE VILLAGE
ASHEVILLE, NC 28803-2681
704-274-2831

PEDEN GALLERY II
132 E HARGETT ST
RALEIGH, NC 27601-1440
919-834-9800

PIEDMONT CRAFTSMEN, INC
1204 REYNOLDA RD
WINSTON SALEM, NC 27104-1121
919-725-1516

POTTERS GALLERY
RR 1 BOX 283
BANNER ELK, NC 28604-9736
704-963-4258

**RALEIGH CONTEMPORARY
GALLERY**
134 E HARGETT ST
RALEIGH, NC 27601-1440
919-828-6500

SECCA, CENTER SHOP
750 MARGUERITE DR
WINSTON SALEM, NC 27106-5861

SKILLBECK GALLERY
238 S SHARON AMITY RD
CHARLOTTE, NC 28211-2801
704-366-9613

**SOUTHERN
EXPRESSIONS GALLERY**
2157 NEW HENDERSONVILLE HWY
PISGAH FOREST, NC 28768-8600
704-884-6242

THE MORNING STAR GALLERY
RR 1 BOX 292-10
BANNER ELK, NC 28604-9752
704-963-6902

THE PICTURE HOUSE, INC
1520 E 4TH ST
CHARLOTTE, NC 28204-3224
704-333-8235

THE SOMERHILL GALLERY
3 EASTGATE SHOPPING CTR
E FRANKLIN ST
CHAPEL HILL, NC 27514
919-868-8868

NORTH DAKOTA

BROWNING ARTS
22 N 4TH ST
GRAND FORKS, ND 58203-3720
701-746-5090

THE ART CONNECTION
624 MAIN AVE
FARGO, ND 58103-1966
701-237-6655

OHIO

AMERICAN CRAFTS GALLERY
13101 LARCHMERE BLVD
CLEVELAND, OH 44120-1148
216-231-2008

ART AT THE POWERHOUSE
2000 SYCAMORE ST
NAUTICA COMPLEX
CLEVELAND, OH 44113-2340
216-696-1942

ARTERNATIVE GALLERY
2034 MADISON RD
CINCINNATI, OH 45208-3238
513-871-2218

ARTSPACE CENTER FOR CONTEMPORY ART
8501 CARNEGIE AVE
CLEVELAND, OH 44106
216-421-8671

AVANTE GALLERY
2094 MURRAY HILL RD
CLEVELAND, OH 44106-2359
216-791-1622

BENCHWORKS
2563 N HIGH ST
COLUMBUS, OH 43202-2555
614-263-2111

BONFOEY COMPANY
1710 EUCLID AVE
CLEVELAND, OH 44115-2106
216-621-0178

BRENDA KROOS GALLERY
1360 W 9TH ST
CLEVELAND, OH 44113-1254
216-621-1164

CARGO NET, INC
GENERAL DELIVERY
P.O. BOX 369
PUT IN BAY, OH 43456-9999
419-285-4231

CHELSEA GALLERIES
23225 MERCANTILE RD
BEACHWOOD, OH 44122-5911
216-591-1066

DAYTON ART INSTITUTE
PO BOX 941
DAYTON, OH 45401-0941
513-223-5277

DESIGNS OF ALL TIMES
28001 CHAGRIN BLVD
CLEVELAND, OH 44122-4543
216-831-3010

DRUMM STUDIOS & GALLERY
437 CROUSE ST
AKRON, OH 44311-1220
216-253-6268

FACE IT
110 W ASH ST
PIQUA, OH 45356-2304
513-773-1838

FIORI-OMNI GALLERY, INC
2072 MURRAY HILL RD
CLEVELAND, OH 44106-2359
216-721-5319

GALLERY 400
4659 DRESSLER RD NW
CANTON, OH 44718-2535
216-492-2600

GALLERY AT STUDIO B
140 W MAIN ST
LANCASTER, OH 43130-3718
614-653-8424

HELIOTROPE ART GALLERY
3001 CALTALPA DR
DAYTON, OH 45405
513-275-1071

IMAGES GALLERY
3154 MARKWAY RD
TOLEDO, OH 43606-2925

KUSSMAUL GALLERY
103 N PROSPECT ST
GRANVILLE, OH 43023-1336
614-587-4640

MILLER GALLERY
2715 ERIE AVE
CINCINNATI, OH 45208-2103
513-871-4420

MURIEL MERAY STUDIO SHOP
537 E MAPLE ST
NORTH CANTON, OH 44720-2603
216-494-3736

MURRAY HILL ART & CRAFTS
2181 MURRAY HILL RD
CLEVELAND, OH 44106-2338
216-231-2012

OH DESIGNER CRAFTSMEN GALLERY
1665 W 5TH AVE
COLUMBUS, OH 43212-2315
614-486-7119

OSHER OSHER GALLERY
5662 MAYFIELD RD
LYNDHURST, OH 44124-2916
216-646-9191

RAINBOWERS
7720 OLDE EIGHT RD
HUDSON, OH 44236-1055
216-467-0259

RILEY HAWK GLASS GALLERY
2026 MURRAY HILL RD # 103
CLEVELAND, OH 44106-2337
216-421-1445

RILEY HAWK GLASS GALLERY
642 N HIGH ST
COLUMBUS, OH 43215-2010
614-228-6554

SANDUSKY CULTURAL CENTER
2130 HAYES AVE
SANDUSKY, OH 44870-4740
419-625-8097

SANTA CLARA GALLERY
1942 N MAIN ST
DAYTON, OH 45405-3801
513-279-9100

SOMETHING DIFFERENT
3427 MEMPHIS AVE
CLEVELAND, OH 44109-3264
216-398-0472

STANLEY KAUFMAN GALLERY
GENERAL DELIVERY
BERLIN, OH 44610-9999
216-893-2842

THE ART BANK GALLERY
317 W 4TH ST
CINCINNATI, OH 45202-2605
513-621-7779

THE GALLERY
24 S GAMBLE ST # 10
SHELBY, OH 44875-1541
419-347-4206

THE MALTON GALLERY
2709 OBSERVATORY AVE
CINCINNATI, OH 45208-2107
513-321-8014

THE PUMP HOUSE ART GALLERY
ENDERLIN CIRCLE
P.O. BOX 1613
CHILLICOTHE, OH 45601
614-772-5783

THE SCULPTURE CENTER
12206 EUCLID AVE
CLEVELAND, OH 44106-4311
216-229-6527

TONI BIRCKHEAD GALLERY
342 W 4TH ST
CINCINNATI, OH 45202-2603
513-241-0212

VILLAGE ARTISANS COOPERATIVE
220 XENIA AVE
YELLOW SPRINGS, OH 45387-1831
513-767-1209

WILLIAM BUSTA GALLERY
2021 MURRAY HILL RD
CLEVELAND, OH 44106-2348
216-231-7363

WOODBOURNE GALLERY
9885 MONTGOMERY RD
CINCINNATI, OH 45242-6424
513-793-1888

WOODBOURNE GALLEY
175 E ALEX BELL RD STE 208
DAYTON, OH 45459-2794
513-434-3565

OKLAHOMA

DORAN GALLERY
3509 S PEORIA AVE
TULSA, OK 74105-2517
918-748-8700

OREGON

ALDER GALLERY & ART SERVICE
160 E BROADWAY
EUGENE, OR 97401-3140
503-342-6411

ART DECOR GALLERY
136 HIGH ST SE
SALEM, OR 97301-3608
503-378-0876

CONTEMPORARY CRAFTS GALLERY
3934 SW CORBETT AVE
PORTLAND, OR 97201-4304
503-223-2654

EARTHWORKS GALLERY
2222 HIGHWAY 101 N
YACHATS, OR 97498-9435
503-547-4300

GANGO GALLERY
205 SW 1ST AVE
PORTLAND, OR 97204-3502
503-222-3850

GALLERY LISTINGS

GRAYSTONE GALLERY
3279 SE HAWTHORNE BLVD
PORTLAND, OR 97214-5044
503-238-0651

ITCHY FINGERS
513 NW 23RD AVE
PORTLAND, OR 97210-3206
503-222-5237

LAURA RUSSO GALLERY
805 NW 21ST AVE
PORTLAND, OR 97209-1408
503-635-7419

LAWRENCE GALLERY
PO BOX 187
SHERIDAN, OR 97378-0187
503-843-3633

MAVEETY GALLERY
PO BOX 148
GLENEDEN BEACH, OR 97388-0148
503-764-2318

MONTAGE GALLERY
5875 SW ELM AVE
BEAVERTON, OR 97005-4222
503-643-7513

PORTLAND ART MUSEUM
RENTAL SALES GALLERY
1219 SW PARK AVE
PORTLAND, OR 97205
503-274-4121

SAXONS
3138 N HIGHWAY 97
BEND, OR 97701-7514
503-389-6655

SKYLARK GALLERY
130 SPAULDING AVE
BROWNSVILLE, OR 97327-2258
503-466-5221

SUNBIRD GALLERY
916 NW WALL ST
BEND, OR 97701-2022
503-389-9196

THE INDIGO GALLERY
311 AVE B #B
LAKE OSWEGO, OR 97034
503-636-3454

THE REAL MOTHER GOOSE GALLERY
927 SW YAMHILL ST
PORTLAND, OR 97205-2532
503-223-3737

THE WHITE BIRD GALLERY
N HEMLOCK RD
P.O. BOX 502
CANNON BEACH, OR 97145
503-436-2681

THE WOOD GALLERY, INC
818 SW BAY BLVD
NEWPORT, OR 97365-4838

TOAD HALL
237 W 3RD ST
YACHATZ, OR 97498
503-547-4044

TWIST
30 NW 23 PL
PORTLAND, OR 97210-3533
503-224-0334

PENNSYLVANIA

479 GALLERY
55 N 2ND ST
PHILADELPHIA, PA 19106-2229
215-922-1444

A-MANO
128 S MAIN ST
NEW HOPE, PA 18938-1202
215-862-5122

AART VARK GALLERY
17TH AT LOCUST
PHILADELPHIA, PA 19103
215-735-5600

ACCENTS & IMAGES
GENERAL DELIVERY
P.O. BOX 18931
LAHASKA, PA 18931-9999
215-794-7660

ART AC'CENTS
350 MONTGOMERY AVE
MERION STATION, PA 19066-1202
215-664-4444

ARTISANS GALLERY
PEDDLERS VILLAGE
P.O. BOX 133
LAHASKA, PA 18931
215-794-3112

ARTISANS THREE
THE VILLAGE CENTER
SPRING HOUSE, PA 19477
215-643-4504

BACH & COMPANY
447 CHESTNUT ST
EMMAUS, PA 18049-2401

BEST FRIENDS
4329 MAIN ST
PHILADELPHIA, PA 19127-1516
215-487-1250

CALICO CAT GALLERY
36 W KING ST
LANCASTER, PA 17603-3809
717-397-6372

CAT'S PAW GALLERY
31 RACE ST
JIM THORPE, PA 18229-2003
717-325-4041

CATHERINE STARR GALLERY
4235 MAIN ST
PHILADELPHIA, PA 19127-1602
215-482-7755

CHADDS FORD GALLERY
US HWY 1 & 100
PO BOX 179
CHADDS FORD, PA 19317
610-459-5510

CLAY PLACE GALLERY
MINEO BLDG
5416 WALNUT ST
PITTSBURG, PA 15232
412-682-3737

CREATIVE HANDS
PEDDLERS VILLAGE
LAHASKA, PA 18931
215-794-7012

DESIGN ARTS GALLERY
NESBITT COLLEGE OF DESIGN ARTS
33RD & MARKET STS
PHILADELPHIA, PA 19104
215-895-2386

DINA PORTER GALLERY
1655 HAUSMAN RD
ALLENTOWN, PA 18104-9345
215-434-7363

DISCOVERIES
221 CHERRY ST
READING, PA 19602
215-372-2595

DOWNINGTOWN ART GALLERY
305 MANOR AVE
DOWNINGTOWN, PA 19335-2542

EARTHWORKS GALLERY
227 HAVERFORD AVE
NARBERTH, PA 19072-2216
215-667-1143

FAN GALLERY
311 CHERRY ST
PHILADELPHIA, PA 19106-1803
215-922-5155

GALLERIA TRICIA
102 HARRISON DR
NEW CUMBERLAND, PA 17070-1718
717-691-0263

GALLERIE NADEAU
118 N 3RD ST
PHILADELPHIA, PA 19106-1802
215-574-0202

GALLERY 500
CHURCH & OLD YORK RDS
ELKINS PARK, PA 19117
215-572-1203

GALLERY G
211 9TH ST
PITTSBURGH, PA 15222-3501
412-562-0912

GALLERY OF 1ST IMPRESSIONS
4 E LANCASTER AVE
PAOLI, PA 19301-1402

GALLERY RIGGIONE- FINE CRAFTS
130 ALMSHOUSE RD
RICHBORO, PA 18954
215-322-5035

GLASS GROWERS GALLERY
701 HOLLAND ST
ERIE, PA 16501-1216
814-453-3758

GREENE & GREENE GALLERY
88 S MAIN ST
NEW HOPE, PA 18938-1232
215-862-9620

GUNLEFINGERS
303 W STATE ST
MEDIA, PA 19063-2615

HAHN GALLERY
8439 GERMANTOWN AVE
PHILADELPHIA, PA 19188-0001
215-247-8439

HELEN DRUTT GALLERY
1721 WALNUT ST
PHILADELPHIA, PA 19103
215-735-1625

HONEY BROOK WOODS
102 TELEGRAPH RD
HONEY BROOK, PA 19344
215-273-2680

IMAGINE GALLERY & GIFTS
3330 W 26TH ST
ERIE, PA 16506-2449
814-858-8077

JAB GALLERY
225 RACE ST
PHILADELPHIA, PA 19106-1909
215-923-8122

JAMES A. MICHENER
ART MUSEUM
128 S PINE ST
DOYLESTOWN, PA 18901-4931
215-340-9800

JAMES GALLERY
2892 W LIBERTY AVE
PITTSBURGH, PA 15216-2621
412-343-1366

JESSICA BERWIND GALLERY
301 CHERRY ST
PHILADELPHIA, PA 19106-1803
215-574-1645

JUN GALLERY
114 MARKET ST
PHILADELPHIA, PA 19106-3006
215-627-5020

KAISER NEWMAN GALLERY
134 N 3RD ST
PHILADELPHIA, PA 19106-1814
215-923-7438

LANGMAN GALLERY
WILLOW GROVE PARK
2500 MORELAND RD
WILLOW GROVE, PA 19090
215-657-8333

LANNON'S
1007 LANCASTER AVE
BRYN MAWR, PA 19010
215-525-4526

LARIMORE FURNITURE
160 N 3RD ST
PHILADELPHIA, PA 19106-1814
215-440-7136

LATITUDES GALLERY
4325 MAIN ST
PHILADELPHIA, PA 19127-1516
215-482-0417

LOCKS GALLERY
600 S WASHINGTON SQ
PHILADELPHIA, PA 19106-4155
215-629-1000

LOST ARTS
2556 EASTERN BLVD
YORK, PA 17402-2914

MADE BY HAND GALLERY
303 S CRAIG ST
PITTSBURGH, PA 15213-3706
412-681-8346

MARSHA CHILD CONTEMPORARY
PO BOX 0364
SOLEBURY, PA 18963-9999
215-297-0414

MEDIA POTTERY
303 W STATE ST
MEDIA, PA 19063-2615

MEDICI CORPORATION
68 N 2ND ST
PHILADELPHIA, PA 19106-4505
215-627-8109

MOSER SHOWROOM & GALLERY
210 W WASHINGTON SQ
PHILADELPHIA, PA 19106-3514
215-922-6440

NEXUS GALLERY
137 N 2ND ST
PHILADELPHIA, PA 19106-2009
215-629-1103

OLC GALLERY
152 N 3RD ST # 154
PHILADELPHIA, PA 19106-1814
215-923-6085

OWEN PATRICK GALLERY
4345 MAIN ST
PHILADELPHIA, PA 19127-1415
215-482-9395

PITTSBURGH CENTER
FOR THE ARTS
6300 5TH AVE
PITTSBURGH, PA 15232-2922
412-361-0873

REISBORD GALLERY
4313 MAIN ST # 17
PHILADELPHIA, PA 19127-1525
215-483-3232

ROCHE BOBOIS
MARKET PLACE DESIGN CENTER
2400 MARKET ST
PHILADELPHIA, PA 19103
215-972-0168

RODGER LAPELLE GALLERY
122 N 3RD ST
PHILADELPHIA, PA 19106-1802
215-592-0232

RUTH ZAFIR GALLERY
13 S 2ND ST
PHILADELPHIA, PA 19106-3003
215-627-7098

SANDE WEBSTER GALLERY
2018 LOCUST ST
PHILADELPHIA, PA 19103-5614
215-732-8850

SAVOIR-FAIRE
837 W ROLLING RD
SPRINGFIELD, PA 19064-1133
215-544-8998

SHOW OF HANDS
1006 PINE ST
PHILADELPHIA, PA 19107-6007
215-592-4010

SIMCOE GALLERY
1925 MAIN ST
NORTHAMPTON, PA 18067-1313
215-262-8154

SNYDERMAN GALLERY
303 CHERRY ST
PHILADELPHIA, PA 19106-1803
215-238-9576

SOCIETY FOR CONTEMPORARY
CRAFT
2100 SMALLMAN ST
PITTSBURGH, PA 15222-4430
412-261-7003

SOMETHING SPECIAL
153 MAIN ST
BRADFORD, PA 16701-2171
814-368-6011

STARR POTTERY
754 ABBOTTSTOWN PIKE
HANOVER, PA 17331-8801
717-632-0027

STRAWBERRY & COMPANY
79 W KING ST
LANCASTER, PA 17603-3842
717-392-5345

STUDIO IN SWARTHMORE
GALLERY
14 PARK AVE
SWARTHMORE, PA 19081-1723
215-543-5779

STYLE & SUBSTANCE GALLERY
GREENGATE MALL
GREENSBURG, PA 15601
412-834-9299

SUNDANCE
PEDDLER'S VILLAGE
P.O. BOX 311
LAHASKA, PA 18931
215-794-8871

THE CLAY STUDIO
139 N 2ND ST
PHILADELPHIA, PA 19106-2009
215-925-3453

THE COUNTRY STUDIO
590 GEORGETOWN RD
HADLEY, PA 16130-1098
412-253-2493

THE FABRIC WORKSHOP
1100 VINE ST
THIRTEENTH FLOOR
PHILADELPHIA, PA 19107-1717
215-922-7303

THE GALLERY
AT CEDAR HOLLOW
2447 YELLOW SPRINGS RD
MALVERN, PA 19355-1411
610-640-2787

THE GALLERY
AT THE CLAY LADY
GENERAL DELIVERY
UWCHLAND, PA 19480-9999
610-458-8262

THE PAINTED BRIDE GALLERY
230 VINE ST
PHILADELPHIA, PA 19106-1213
215-925-9914

THE WORKS GALLERY
319 SOUTH ST
PHILADELPHIA, PA 19147-1518
215-922-7775

TOPEO GALLERY
35 N MAIN ST
NEW HOPE, PA 18938-1339
215-862-2750

TURTLEDOVE
4373 MAIN ST
PHILADELPHIA, PA 19127-1415
215-487-7350

GALLERY LISTINGS

RHODE ISLAND

RAMSON HOUSE ANTIQUES
36 FRANKLIN ST
NEWPORT, RI 02840-3013
401-847-0555

SPECTRUM OF AMERICAN ARTISTS
306 THAMES ST
NEWPORT, RI 02840-6610
401-847-4477

TROPER-PUERINI
391 THAMES ST
NEWPORT, RI 02840-6603
401-846-3344

VIRGINIA LYNCH GALLERY
4 CORNELL RD
3883 MAIN RD
TIVERTON, RI 02878-3202
401-624-3392

SOUTH CAROLINA

ARTISTS PARLOR
126 LAURENS ST NW
AIKEN, SC 29801-3846
803-648-4639

BLUE HERON GALLERY
D2 LAGOON ROAD COLIGNY
  PLAZA
HILTON HEAD, SC 29928
803-785-3788

BOHEMIAN
2112 DEVINE ST
COLUMBIA, SC 29205-2414
803-256-0629

CAROL SAUNDERS GALLERY
922 GERVAIS ST
COLUMBIA, SC 29201-3128
803-256-3046

CHECKERED MOON GALLERY
208 WEST ST
BEAUFORT, SC 29902-5559
802-522-3466

CRAFTSELLER GALLERY
818 BAY ST
P.O. BOX 1968
BEAUFORT, SC 29902-5566
803-525-6104

DUKE STREET GALLERY
109 DUKE ST
PENDLETON, SC 29670
803-646-3469

HARBOUR TOWN CRAFTS
#7 HARBOUR HOUSE PO BOX 306
HILTON HEAD, SC 29928
803-671-3643

NINA LIU & FRIENDS
24 STATE ST
CHARLESTON, SC 29401-2815
803-722-2724

SMITH GALLERIES OF FINE CRAFTS
THE VILLAGE AT WEXFORD #J-11
HILTON HEAD ISLAND, SC 29928
803-842-2280

SOUTHERN GALLERIES
402 SE MAIN ST
SIMPSONVILLE, SC 29681-2652
803-963-4893

TENNESSEE

AMERICAN ARTISAN, INC
4231 HARDING RD
NASHVILLE, TN 37205-2076
615-298-4691

ARTIFACTS GALLERY
1007 OAKHAVEN RD
MEMPHIS, TN 38119-3811
901-767-5236

BOONES CREEK POTTER'S GALLERY
4903 KINGSPORT HWY 36
JOHNSON CITY, TN 37615
615-282-2801

CUMBERLAND GALLERY
4107 HILLSBORO CIR
NASHVILLE, TN 37215-2742
615-297-0296

HANSON ARTSOURCE
5607 KINGSTON PIKE
KNOXVILLE, TN 37919-6347
615-584-6097

HOVANEC GALLERY
408 10TH ST
KNOXVILLE, TN 37916-1613
615-624-5312

KURTS BINGHAM GALLERY
766 S WHITE STATION RD
MEMPHIS, TN 38117-4579
901-683-6200

ROBERT TINO GALLERY
812 OLD DOUGLAS DAM RD
SEVIERVILLE, TN 37876-1676
615-428-6519

THE BELL GALLERY OF FINE ART
6150 POPLAR AVE #118
MEMPHIS, TN 38119
901-682-2189

THE BROWSERY
424 RIVERMONT DR
CLARKSVILLE, TN 37043-5991
615-552-2733

THE RIVER GALLERY
400 E 2ND ST
BLUFF VIEW
CHATTANOOGA, TN 37403-1105
615-267-7353

TEXAS

ACQUISATORY
3016 GREENVILLE AVE
DALLAS, TX 75206-6030

ADELLE M. GALLERY
3317 MCKINNEY AVE # 203
DALLAS, TX 75204-2336
214-220-0300

APPLE CORPS
2324 UNIVERSITY BLVD
HOUSTON, TX 77005-2642
713-524-2221

ART GROUP
1119 N WINDOMERE AVE
DALLAS, TX 75208-3506
214-942-0258

ARTISANS FINE CRAFTS GALLERY
10000 RESEARCH BLVD
AUSTIN, TX 78759-5801
512-345-3001

BANKS FINE ART
3316 ROYAL LN
DALLAS, TX 75229-5061
214-352-1811

BLAIRE CARNAHAN FINE ART
418 LA VILLITA ST
SAN ANTONIO, TX 78205-2906
201-227-6313

BLUE HAND
2323 UNIVERSITY BLVD
HOUSTON, TX 77005-2641

BOWDEN GALLERY
6981 BLANCO RD
SAN ANTONIO, TX 78216-6164
512-341-4367

CARLYN GALERIE
6137 LUTHER LN
DALLAS, TX 75225-6202
214-368-2828

CARSON ART
1444 OAK LAWN AVE STE 610
DALLAS, TX 75207-3613
214-747-3055

CIRCA NOW GALLERY
2162 PORTSMOUTH ST
HOUSTON, TX 77098-4057
713-529-8234

CLARKSVILLE POTTERY
1013 W LYNN ST
AUSTIN, TX 78703-3996
512-478-9079

CLARKSVILLE POTTERY 2
ARBORETUM MARKET
9722 GREAT HILLS
AUSTIN, TX 78759
512-794-8580

CREATIVE ARTS GALLERY
836 NORTH STAR MALL
SAN ANTONIO, TX 78216
210-342-8659

CULLER CONCEPTS
1347 CEDAR HILL AVE
DALLAS, TX 75208-2404
214-942-1646

DALE STRYKER
3425 W 7TH ST
FORT WORTH, TX 76107
817-336-8042

DEBUSK GALLERIES
3813 N COMMERCE ST
FORT WORTH, TX 76106-2713
817-625-8476

FINE ART CONSULTANTS/SOUTHWEST
1744 NORFOLK ST
HOUSTON, TX 77098-4408
713-526-5628

FREE FLIGHT GALLERY
603 MUNGER AVE STE 309
DALLAS, TX 75202-2003
214-720-9147

GOLDEN EYE GALLERY
20035 KATY FWY
KATY, TX 77450-2238
713-678-2820

GREGORY'S
2 MAIN ST
SALADO, TX 76571
817-947-5703

HANSON GALLERIES
800 W SAM HOUSTON PKY N
HOUSTON, TX 77024-3900
713-984-1242

HEARTLAND GALLERY
4006 S LAMAR BLVD STE 950
AUSTIN, TX 78704-7971
512-447-1171

HUMMINGBIRD ORIGINALS
4319 CAMP BOWIE BLVD
FORT WORTH, TX 76107-3833

JACK MEIER GALLERY
2310 BISSONNET ST
HOUSTON, TX 77005-1512
713-526-2983

JUDY YOUENS GALLERY
3115 DAMICO ST
HOUSTON, TX 77019-1901

KEENE GALLERY
242 LOSOYA ST
SAN ANTONIO, TX 78205-2610
210-299-1999

LEGACY'S
1846 ROSE MEAD PKWY, STE 148
CARROLLTON, TX 75007

LYONS MATRIX GALLERY
1712 LAVACA ST
AUSTIN, TX 78701-1316
512-479-0068

POSITIVE IMAGES
1118 W 6TH ST
AUSTIN, TX 78703-5304
512-472-1831

SABLE V FINE ART GALLERY
PO BOX 1792
WIMBERLEY, TX 78676-1792
512-847-8975

SOL DEL RIO GALLERY
1020 TOWNSEND AVE
SAN ANTONIO, TX 78209-5144
210-828-5555

SOUTHWEST CRAFT CENTER
300 AUGUSTA ST
SAN ANTONIO, TX 78205-1296
210-224-1848

THE ARRANGEMENT
2605 ELM ST
DALLAS, TX 75226-1423
214-748-4540

THE GALLERY AT LOS PATIOS
2015 NE LOOP #410
SAN ANTONIO, TX 78217
210-655-0538

THE NEW GALLERY
2639 COLQUITT ST
HOUSTON, TX 77098-2117
713-520-1753

THE OLE MOON
3016 GREENVILLE AVE
DALLAS, TX 75206-6030
214-827-9921

THE PRESTON COLLECTION
305 PRESTON ROYAL
DALLAS, TX 75230
214-373-6065

THE ROCK HOUSE GALLERY
1311 W ABRAM ST
ARLINGTON, TX 76013-1704
817-265-5874

THE SPICEWOOD GALLERY
1206 W 38TH ST
AUSTIN, TX 78705-1018
512-458-6575

THE TWO FRIENDS GALLERY
2301 STRAND ST
GALVESTON, TX 77550-1546
409-765-7477

THE URSULINE GALLERY
300 AUGUSTA ST
SAN ANTONIO, TX 78205-1216
210-224-1848

THE VILLAGE WEAVERS
418 LA VILLITA ST
SAN ANTONIO, TX 78205-2906
210-222-0776

WEST BANK GALLERY
4201 BEE CAVES RD STE A100
AUSTIN, TX 78746-6458
512-329-8514

**WM CAMPBELL
CONTEMPORARY ART**
4935 BYERS AVE
FORT WORTH, TX 76107-4198
817-737-9566

PHILLIPS GALLERY
444 E 200 S
SALT LAKE CITY, UT 84111-2103
801-364-8284

**UTAH DESIGNER CRAFTS
GALLERY**
38W W 200 S
SALT LAKE CITY, UT 84101-1603
801-359-2770

F.J. PRESTON
17 CHURCH ST
BURLINGTON, VT 05401-4417
802-864-4591

FROG HOLLOW CRAFT CENTER
1 MILL ST
MIDDLEBURY, VT 05753-1144
802-388-3177

HAWKINS HOUSE
262 NORTH ST
BENNINGTON, VT 05201-1828
802-447-1171

**MOUNTAIN HIGH
AMERICAN CRAFT**
THE MARKET PL
LUDLOW, VT 05149
802-228-5216

**NORTH WIND
ARTISAN GALLERY**
81 CENTRAL ST
WOODSTOCK, VT 05091-1145
802-457-4587

SIMON PEARCE GLASS
GENERAL DELIVERY
QUECHEE, VT 05059-9999
802-295-2711

THE SPIRAL GALLERY
PO BOX 29
MARLBORO, VT 05344-0029
802-257-5696

VERMONT ARTISAN DESIGNS
115 MAIN ST
BRATTLEBORO, VT 05301-3061
802-257-7044

VERMONT STATE CRAFT CENTER
MAIN ST
P.O. BOX 1777
WINDSOR, VT 05089
802-674-6729

WINDHAM ART GALLERY
75 MAIN ST
BRATTLEBORO, VT 05301-3257
802-257-1881

WOODSTOCK GALLERY OF ART
GALLERY PL
RT 4 EAST
WOODSTOCK, VT 05091
802-457-1900

A TOUCH OF EARTH
6580 RICHMOND RD
WILLIAMSBURG, VA 23188-7200
804-565-0425

AMERICAN ARTISAN INC
201 KING ST
ALEXANDRIA, VA 22314-3209
703-548-3431

ART & SOUL
1127 KING ST
ALEXANDRIA, VA 22314-2924
703-549-4881

ARTISAN'S STUDIO
105 HANOVER AVE
ASHLAND, VA 23005-1813

BLUE SKIES GALLERY
120 W QUEENS WAY # 201
HAMPTON, VA 23669-4014
804-727-0028

BREIT FUNCTIONAL CRAFTS
1701 COLLEY AVE
NORFOLK, VA 23517-1610
804-640-1012

BROADWAY GALLERY
11213J LEE HWY
FAIRFAX, VA 22030-5608
703-273-2388

CAVE HOUSE CRAFT SHOP
279 E MAIN ST
ABINGDON, VA 24210-2903
703-628-7721

**COUNTRY HERITAGE
ANTIQUES & CRAFTS**
PO BOX 148
WASHINGTON, VA 22747
703-675-3738

CRAFTERS' GALLERY
RR 12 BOX 97
CHARLOTTESVILLE, VA 22901-9501
804-295-7006

GALLERY LISTINGS

CUDAHY'S GALLERY
1314 E CARY ST
RICHMOND, VA 23219-4118
804-782-1776

D'ART CENTER
125 COLLEGE PL
NORFOLK, VA 23510-1907
804-625-4211

EBASHAE GALLERY
GENERAL DELIVERY
OCCOQUAN, VA 22125-9999
703-491-5984

ELECTRIC GLASS GALLERY
823 W PEMBROKE AVE
HAMPTON, VA 23669-3326
804-722-6300

FENTON GALLERY
110 S HENRY ST
WILLIAMSBURG, VA 23185-4153
804-253-8700

FIBER WORKS
105 N UNION ST
ALEXANDRIA, VA 22314-3217
703-836-5807

GALLERY FOUR
115 S COLUMBUS ST
ALEXANDRIA, VA 22314-3003
703-548-4600

GALLERY OF MOUNTAIN SECRETS
RT 250
MAIN ST
MONTEREY, VA 24465
703-468-2020

GALLERY THREE
213 MARKET ST SE
ROANOKE, VA 24011-1800
703-343-9698

HARRIET'S ART & ANTIQUES
7306 LANGSFORD CT
SPRINGFIELD, VA 22153-1536
703-644-1121

MARINA SHORES GALLERY
2100 MARINA SHORES DR
VIRGINIA BEACH, VA 23451-6819
804-496-7000

MCMANN MCDADE FINE ART
364 WALNUT AVE SW
ROANOKE, VA 24016-4621
703-345-5123

MELLOWOOD
4313 35TH ST N
ARLINGTON, VA 22207-4470
703-528-3037

METALLUM
105 N UNION ST
ALEXANDRIA, VA 22314-3217
703-548-4600

ON THE HILL CREATIVE ARTS CTR
121 ALEXANDER HAMILTON BLVD
PO BOX 222
YORKTOWN, VA 23690-3800
804-898-3076

PALMER RAE GALLERY, INC
112 GRANBY ST
NORFOLK, VA 23510-1656
804-627-0081

PAULA LEWIS GALLERY
COURT SQUARE
216 FOURTH ST NE
CHARLOTTESVILLE, VA 22902
804-295-6244

POTOMAC CRAFTSMEN
105 N UNION ST # 18
ALEXANDRIA, VA 22314-3217
703-548-0935

PRIMAVERA GALLERY
4216 VIRGINIA BEACH BLVD
VIRGINIA BEACH, VA 23452-1233
804-431-9393

QUILTS UNLIMITED
THE HOMESTEAD RESORT
HOT SPRINGS, VA 24445
708-839-5955

SIGNET GALLERY
212 5TH ST NE
PO BOX 753
CHARLOTTESVILLE, VA 22902-5208
804-296-6463

STARDUST
1774 U INTERNATIONAL DR
MCLEAN, VA 22102

THE OLD MILL CRAFT GALLERY
EVANS FARM INN
RT 123
MCLEAN, VA 22101
703-893-2736

THE RUSH RIVER COMPANY
PO BOX 74 GAY ST
WASHINGTON, VA 22747-0074
703-675-1136

VINCENT'S FINE ART
4429 SHORE DR
VIRGINIA BEACH, VA 23455-2821
804-464-9380

VISTA FINE CRAFTS GALLERY
5 W WASHINGTON ST
PO BOX 2034
MIDDLEBURG, VA 22117
703-687-3317

WHISTLE WALK CRAFTS GALLERY
7 S KING ST
LEESBURG, VA 22075-2903
703-777-4017

YORKTOWN ARTS FOUNDATION
121 ALEXANDER HAMILTON BLVD
PO BOX 244
YORKTOWN, VA 23690-3800
804-898-3076

WASHINGTON

AMERICAN ART GALLERY
1126 BROADWAY
TACOMA, WA 98402-3503
206-272-4327

ARTWOOD
1000 HARRIS AVE
BELLINGHAM, WA 98225-7035
206-647-1628

ARTWORKS GALLERY
155 S MAIN ST
SEATTLE, WA 98104-2571
206-625-0932

CARNEGIE ART CENTER, INC
109 S PALOUSE ST
WALLA WALLA, WA 99362-3006
509-525-4270

CHILDERS/PROCTOR GALLERY
302 1ST ST
PO BOX 458
LANGLEY, WA 98260-8802
206-221-2978

CHILDHOOD'S END GALLERY
222 4TH AVE W
OLYMPIA, WA 98501-1004
206-943-3724

CORPORATE ART WEST, INC
12360 NE 8TH ST
BELLEVUE, WA 98005-3188
206-454-2595

CREATIONS GALLERY
7651 COAL CREEK PKY SE
RENTON, WA 98059-3212
206-624-5578

EARTHENWORKS
1015 WATER ST
PORT TOWNSEND, WA 98368-6705
206-385-0328

EARTHENWORKS
713 FIRST ST
PO BOX 702
LA CONNER, WA 98257
206-466-4422

ELEMENTS GALLERY
113 SEAFIRST BLDG
10500 NE EIGHTH ST
BELLEVUE, WA 98004
206-454-8242

ELLIOTT BROWN GALLERY
619 N 35TH ST STE 101
SEATTLE, WA 98103-8639
206-547-9740

EMERALD CITY GALLERY
17508 VASHON HWY SW
VASHON ISLAND, WA 98070
206-292-8932

FIRE WORKS GALLERIES
210 1ST AVE S
SEATTLE, WA 98104-2504
206-682-8707

FLYING SHUTTLE GALLERY
607 1ST AVE
SEATTLE, WA 98104-2209
206-343-9762

FOLK ART GALLERY
LA TIENDA
4138 UNIVERSITY WAY NE
SEATTLE, WA 98105
206-634-1795

FOSTER WHITE GALLERY
126 CENTRAL WAY
KIRKLAND, WA 98033-6106
206-822-2305

FOSTER WHITE GALLERY
311½ OCCIDENTAL AVE S
SEATTLE, WA 98104-2839
206-622-2833

FRANK DUNYA GALLERY
3418 FREMONT AVE N
SEATTLE, WA 98103-8812
206-547-6760

FRIESEN GALLERY
1210 2ND AVE
SEATTLE, WA 98101-2926
206-628-9502

GALLERY ONE
408½ N PEARL ST
ELLENSBURG, WA 98926-3112
509-925-2670

GARDENS OF ART
2900 SYLVAN ST
BELLINGHAM, WA 98226-4372
206-671-1069

GLASS EYE GALLERY
1902 POST ALY
SEATTLE, WA 98101-1015
206-441-3221

GLASSHOUSE ART GLASS
PIONEER SQUARE
311 OCCIDENTAL AVE S
SEATTLE, WA 98104
206-682-9939

GROVER/THURSTON GALLERY
532 1ST AVE S
SEATTLE, WA 98104-2804
206-223-0816

HICKS DESIGN LINE
3406 N BRISTOL ST
TACOMA, WA 98407-1508
206-759-4917

HIGHLY STRUNG
4222 E MADISON ST
SEATTLE, WA 98112-3237
206-328-1045

JANET HUSTON GALLERY
PO BOX 845
LA CONNER, WA 98257-0845
206-466-5001

LYNN MCALLISTER GALLERY
1028 LAKEVIEW BLVD E APT 5
SEATTLE, WA 98102-4400
206-624-6864

MELANGE
120 LAKESIDE AVE
SEATTLE, WA 98122-6548
206-322-1341

MESOLINI & AMICI
77½ S MAIN ST
SEATTLE, WA 98104-2513
206-587-0275

MIA GALLERY
512 1ST AVE S
SEATTLE, WA 98104-2804
206-467-8283

NORTHWEST DISCOVERY
142 BELLEVUE SQ
BELLEVUE, WA 98004-5021
206-454-1676

NW GALLERY OF FINE WOODWORKING
202 1ST AVE S
SEATTLE, WA 98104-2504
206-625-0542

NW GALLERY OF FINE WOODWORKING
317 NW GILMAN BLVD
ISSAQUAH, WA 98027-2485
206-391-4221

PETERSON ART FURNITURE GALLERY
122 CENTRAL WAY
KIRKLAND, WA 98033-6106
206-827-8053

PHOENIX RISING GALLERY
2030 WESTERN AVE
SEATTLE, WA 98121-2124
206-728-2332

RON SEGAL GALLERY
1420 5TH AVE STE 208
SEATTLE, WA 98101-2333
800-688-2788

SERENDIPITY
909 COMMERCIAL AVE
ANACORTES, WA 98221-4114

STONINGTON GALLERY
2030 1ST AVE
SEATTLE, WA 98121-2112
206-443-1108

THE COLLECTION
118 S WASHINGTON ST
PIONEER SQUARE
SEATTLE, WA 98104-2522
206-682-6184

THE PANACA GALLERY
133 BELLEVUE SQ
BELLEVUE, WA 98004-5021
206-454-0234

TOPPERS
1260 CARILLON PT
KIRKLAND, WA 98033-7351
206-889-9311

WILLIAM TRAVER GALLERY
110 UNION ST
SEATTLE, WA 98101-2028
206-448-4234

WEST VIRGINIA

QUILTS UNLIMITED
203 E WASHINGTON ST
LEWISBURG, WV 24901-1423
304-647-4208

SANGUINE GRYPHON GALLERY
PO BOX 3120
SHEPHERDSTOWN, WV 25443-3120
304-876-6569

THE ART STORE
1013 BRIDGE RD
CHARLESTON, WV 25314-1305
304-345-1038

WISCONSIN

ARGOSY
18900 W BLUE MOUND RD
WAUKASHA, WI 53188
414-821-6900

ART ELEMENTS GALLERY
1400 W MEQUON RD
MEQUON, WI 53092-3226
414-241-7040

ART INDEPENDENT GALLERY
623 W MAIN ST
LAKE GENEVA, WI 53147-1907
414-248-3612

ARTISTRY STUDIO GALLERY
833 E CENTER ST
MILWAUKEE, WI 53212-3047
414-372-3372

ARTSPACE
725 G WOODLAKE ROAD
KOHLER, WI 53044
414-452-8602

AVENUE ART
10 COLLEGE AVE
APPLETON, WI 54911-5756
414-734-7710

BERGSTROM MAHLER MUSEUM
165 N PARK AVE
NEENAH, WI 54956-2956
414-751-4658

BRODEN GALLERY, LTD
114 STATE ST
MADISON, WI 53703-2560
608-256-6100

BY JAMES
115 N 4TH
LA CROSSE, WI 54601
608-785-2637

CEDAR CREEK POTTERY
N70 W6340 BRIDGE RD
CEDARBURG, WI 53012
414-375-1226

DELIND FINE ART
801 N JEFFERSON ST
MILWAUKEE, WI 53202-3709
414-271-8525

EDGEWOOD ORCHARD GALLERIES
W 4140 PENINSULA PLAYERS RD
FISH CREEK, WI 54212
414-868-3579

FANNY GARVER GALLERY
230 STATE ST
MADISON, WI 53703-2215
608-256-6755

FANNY GARVER GALLERY
7432 MINERAL POINT RD
MADISON, WI 53717
608-833-8000

GALLERY 323 AT RUBINS
323 E WILSON ST
MADISON, WI 53703-3426
608-255-8998

GALLERY OF WISCONSIN ART
931 E OGDEN AVE
MILWAUKEE, WI 53202-2830
414-278-8088

GRACE CHOSY GALLERY
218 N HENRY ST
MADISON, WI 53703-2204
608-255-1211

HARDWARE DESIGN
438 W NATIONAL AVE
MILWAUKEE, WI 53204-1744
414-647-8089

JM KOHLER ART CENTER
608 NEW YORK AVE
SHEBOYGAN, WI 53081-4507
414-458-6144

JOHNSTON GALLERY
245 HIGH ST
MINERAL POINT, WI 53565-1209
608-987-3787

GALLERY LISTINGS

JULIE STATZ
6508 TOTTENHAM RD
MADISON, WI 53711-4014
608-274-0528

JURA SILVERMAN GALLERY
143 S WASHINGTON ST
SPRING GREEN, WI 53588
608-588-7049

KARLA JORDAN INTERNATIONAL
3505 N 124TH ST
BROOKFIELD, WI 53005-2409
414-783-5575

KATIE GINGRISS GALLERY
241 N BROADWAY
MILWAUKEE, WI 53202-5819
414-289-0855

MCMILLAN GALLERY
AT KNICKERBOCKER PLACE
2701 MONROE ST
MADISON, WI 53711
608-238-6501

METRO ONE GALLERY
7821 EGG HARBOR RD
EGG HARBOR, WI 54209-9624
414-868-3399

MINKOFF FINE ART, LTD
10004 N KIRKLAND CT
MEQUON, WI 53092-5444
414-242-5900

MOYER GALLERY
2351 S WEBSTER AVE
GREEN BAY, WI 54301-2123
414-435-3388

NEW VISIONS GALLERY, INC
1000 N OAK AVE
MARSHFIELD, WI 54449-5703
715-387-5562

OCONOMOWOC GALLERY LTD
157 E WISCONSIN AVE
OCONOMOWOC, WI 53066-3033
414-567-8123

PEDESTRIAN ARTS
11 MERRITT AVE
OSHKOSH, WI 54901-4926
414-231-9790

SCHRAGER'S
2837 N SHERMAN BLVD
MILWAUKEE, WI 53210-1702

SEEBECK GALLERY
5601 6TH AVE
KENOSHA, WI 53140-4101
414-657-7172

STONEHILL CRAFTS
GENERAL DELIVERY
EPHRAIM, WI 54211-9999
414-854-4749

STUDIO ON HIGH
154 HIGH ST
MINERAL POINT, WI 53565-1208
608-987-2834

THE GREAT MIDWEST CRAFTMARKET
7700-120 AVE
KENOSHA, WI 53142
414-857-9448

THE HANG UP GALLERY
204 W WISCONSIN AVE
NEENAH, WI 54956-2502
414-722-0481

THE PUMP HOUSE
REGIONAL CENTER FOR THE ARTS
119 KING ST
LA CROSSE, WI 54601
608-785-1434

THE RED BALLOON GALLERY
HWY 35
P.O. BOX 606
STOCKHOLM, WI 54769
715-442-2504

THE WOODLOT GALLERY
5215 N EVERGREEN DR
SHEBOYGAN, WI 53081-8213
414-458-4798

TORY FOLLIARD GALLERY
233 N MILWAUKEE ST
MILWAUKEE, WI 53202-5811
414-273-7311

VALPARINE GALLERY
1719 MONROE ST
MADISON, WI 53711-2022
608-256-4040

WEST BEND GALLERY OF FINE ARTS
300 S 6TH AVE
WEST BEND, WI 53095-3312
414-334-1151

WISCONSIN ARTISAN GALLERY
6858 PAOLI RD
BELLEVILLE, WI 53508-9223
608-845-6600

WYOMING

ART WEST GALLERY
PO BOX 1248
JACKSON, WY 83001-1248
307-733-6379

MARGO'S POTTERY & FINE CRAFTS
457 N MAIN ST
BUFFALO, WY 82834-1732
307-684-9406

CANADA
ALBERTA

ALICAT GALLERY
MAIN ST
BRAGG CREEK, AB T0L-0K0
CANADA
403-949-3777

CABBAGES & KING
710 NINTH ST
CANMORE, AB T0L-0M0
CANADA
403-678-6915

CANADIAN ART GALLERIES
901 10TH AVE SW
CALGARY, AB T2R-0B4
CANADA
403-290-0203

CREDO
309 10TH ST NW
CALGARY, AB T2N-1V5
CANADA
614-283-4743

MOUNTAIN AVENS GALLERY
709 EIGHTH ST PO BOX 47
CANMORE, AB T0L-0M0
CANADA
403-678-4471

MOUNTAIN CRAFT GALLERY
4050 WHISTLER WAY BOX 1234
WHISTLER, AB V0N-1B0
CANADA
604-932-5001

NIJINSKA'S GALLERY
CAIRBOU ST
BANFF, AB T0L-0C0
CANADA
403-762-5006

ROWLES & PARHAM DESIGN GALLERY
MEZZ LEVEL
10130 103RD ST
EDMONTON, AB T6E-3X8
CANADA
403-426-4035

THE ALICAT GALLERY
BOX 463 WHITE AVE
BRAGG CREEK, AB T0L-0K0
CANADA
403-949-3777

THE QUEST
105 BANFF AVE
BANFF, AB T0L-0C0
CANADA
403-762-2722

VIRGINIA CHRISTOPHER GALLERIES
1134 8TH AVE SW
CALGARY, AB T2P-1S5
CANADA
403-263-4346

WEST END GALLERY
12308 JASPER AVE
EDMONTON, AB T5N-3K5
CANADA
403-488-4892

BRITISH COLUMBIA

CRAFT HOUSE
1386 CARTWRIGHT ST
GRANVILLE ISLAND, BC V6H-3R8
CANADA

DIANE FARRIS GALLERY
1565 WEST 7TH
VANCOUVER, BC V6J-1S1
CANADA
604-737-2629

EQUINOX GALLERY
2321 GRANVILLE ST
VANCOUVER, BC V7C-1C8
CANADA
604-736-2405

GALLERY OF BC, CERAMICS
1359 CARTWRIGT ST
VANCOUVER, BC V6H-3R7
CANADA
604-609-5545

INUIT GALLERY
345 WATER ST
VANCOUVER, BC V6B-1B8
CANADA
608-688-7323

NEWSMALL & STERLING STUDIO
1440 OLD BRIDGE
VANCOUVER, BC V6H-3S6
CANADA
614-681-6730

SYLVAN CRAFTS & POTTERY
3080 EDGEMONT BLVD
N VANCOUVER, BC V7R-2N5
CANADA
416-986-4863

MANITOBA

UPSTAIRS GALLERY
266 EDMONTON ST
WINNEPEG, MB R3C-1R9
CANADA
204-943-2734

NEW BRUNSWICK

GALLEY 78
796 QUEEN ST
FREDERICTON, NB E3B-1C6
CANADA
506-454-5192

NB CRAFT GALLERY
103 CHURCH ST
FREDERICTON, NB E3B-4C8
CANADA
506-450-8989

NEWFOUNDLAND

CHRISTINE PARKER GALLERY
7 PLANK RD
ST JOHN'S, NF A1E-1H3
CANADA
709-753-0580

DEVON HOUSE CRAFT GALLERY
59 DUCKWORTH ST
ST JOHN'S, NF A1C-1E6
CANADA
709-753-2749

NOVA SCOTIA

ZWICKERS GALLERY
5415 DOYLE ST
HALIFAX, NS B3J-1H9
CANADA
902-423-7662

ONTARIO

A SHOW OF HANDS GALLERY
1947 AVE RD
TORONTO, ON M5M-4AZ
CANADA
416-782-1696

A VERY SPECIAL PLACE
463 SUSSEX DR
OTTAWA, ON K1N-6Z4
CANADA
613-235-0394

ASHTON'S
267 QUEEN ST E
TORONTO, ON M5A-1S6
CANADA
416-366-6846

ATELIER CERAMIQUE
709 QUEEN ST W
TORONTO, ON M6J-1E6
CANADA
416-366-2467

BECKETT GALLERY LIMITED
142 JAMES ST S
HAMILTON, ON L8P-3A2
CANADA
416-525-4266

BOUNTY, YORK QUAY CENTRE
235 QUEEN'S QUAY W
TORONTO, ON M5J-2G8
CANADA
416-973-4993

CANADA'S FOUR CORNER'S
93 SPARKS ST
OTTAWA, ON K1P-5B5
CANADA
613-233-2322

CRAFTWORKS
35 MCCAUL ST CHALMERS BLDG
TORONTO, ON M5T-1V7
CANADA
416-977-3487

DEXTERITY
173 KING ST E
TORONTO, ON M5A-1J4
CANADA
416-367-4775

GALLERY LYNDA GREENBERG
13 MURRAY ST
OTTAWA, ON K1N-9M5
CANADA
613-236-2767

GALLERY MOOS LTD.
622 RICHMOND W
TORONTO, ON M5V-1Y9
CANADA
416-777-0707

GALLERY ONE
121 SCOLLARD ST
TORONTO, ON M5R-1C4
CANADA
416-929-3103

MARBEL ARCH GALLERY
3329 YONGE ST
TORONTO, ON M4N-2L9
CANADA
416-440-1995

MARIPOSA GALLERY
312 COLLEGE ST
TORONTO, ON M5T-1S3
CANADA
416-923-2085

MIRA GODARD GALLERY
22 HAZELTON AVE
TORONTO, ON M5R-2E2
CANADA
416-964-8197

NANCY POOLE'S STUDIO
16 HAZELTON AVE
TORONTO, ON M5R-2E2
CANADA
416-964-9050

SANDRA AINSLEY GALLERY
2 FIRST CANADIAN PLAZA
TORONTO, ON M5X-1G8
CANADA
416-362-4480

SNOW GOOSE HANDICRAFTS
83 SPARKS ST
OTTAWA, ON K1P-5A5
CANADA
613-232-2213

THE ART GLASS GALLERY
21 HAZLETON AVE
TORONTO, ON M5R-2E1
CANADA
416-968-1823

THE ART ZONE
592 MARKHAM ST
TORONTO, ON M6G-2L8
CANADA
416-534-1892

THE PRIME GALLERY
52 MCCAUL ST
TORONTO, ON M5T-1V9
CANADA
416-593-5750

UNFUNDI GALLERY
541 SUSSEX DR
OTTAWA, ON K1N-6Z6
CANADA
613-232-3975

YDESSA HENDELES ART FOUNDATION
778 KING W
TORONTO, ON M5V-1N6
CANADA
416-941-9400

PRINCE EDWARD ISLAND

CONFEDERATION OF THE ARTS GALLERY
PO BOX 848
CHARLOTTETOWN, PE C1A-7M1
CANADA
902-628-6131

SASKATCHEWAN

HUMANUM ART GALLERY
123 2ND AVE S
SASKATOON, SK S7K-7E6
CANADA
306-665-9912

LAKELAND ART GALLERY
BOX 180
CHRISTOPHER LAKE, SK S0J-0N0
CANADA
306-982-2223

MENDEL ART GALLERY
PO BOX 569
SASKATOON, SK S7K-3L6
CANADA
306-975-7610

SUSAN WHITNEY GALLERY
2220 LORNE ST
REGINA, SK S4P-2M7
CANADA
306-569-9279

THE HAND WAVE GALLERY
BOX 145
MECHAM, SK S0K-2V0
CANADA
306-376-2211

ACKNOWLEDGMENTS

Be forewarned. A cast of thousands has participated in this process called 'making a business.' So many have encouraged, supported and contributed along the way that any attempt at acknowledgments seems doomed from the beginning. So many will be left out. And the words are oh, so inadequate to express the gratitude in my heart. Nevertheless, here goes:

Bill Kraus, who put his considerable skills, experience, knowledge, and money to work on behalf of artists, and, in the process, taught me the meaning of the word 'partner' in business and in life, and who brings his unparalleled spirit, heart and good sense to every project he comes to, from in-house newsletter to international marketing scheme.

Jim Black and **Ray Goydon,** the best kind of partners one could ask for, offering advice out of experience, pushing me to expand my thinking, and changing the business in the process.

Naomi Rhodes, dear friend and advisor who taught me the meaning of the power breakfast; **Romalyn Tilghman,** who worked with me on early plots and plans; **Christilyn Biek, Catharine Hiersoux, Susan McLeod, Sylvia White,** our first team of sales representatives, who bought into this dream and somehow managed to convince others to buy into it as well, and who, through their friendship and wonderful spirit, kept me going in those difficult first years; **Dan Mack, Rita Cherubini, Diane** and **Barry Eigen, John Venekamp, Lyn Waring, Ellen Schiffman, Claudia Bloom, Liz Fisher, Cynthia Snook, Lois Gilligan, Andrea Moriarty, Kelly Rude, Rachel Degenhardt,** sales reps extraordinaire who were our eyes and ears in the field, telling our story to large numbers of artists and befriending them all in the process; **Sharon Marquis, Bastien Atterbury, Martha Johnson, Diane Nelson, Karen Brown, Kimberly McKnight,** a powerful group of women who continue to propel us forward, and who make it fun to go to work every day, and **Susan Evans,** partner and fellow plotter, who listens to all the crazy ideas and then helps me figure out how to turn them into reality.

Laura Quick, Gretchen Wohlgemuth, Vicki Finke, Kris Firchow, Jill Steinle, production staff over the years, all dedicated to producing beautiful books on schedule within budget, often requiring herculean effort and devotion beyond the call of duty; **Kyle Hanson-Hanslien,** for her friendship and immense generosity of spirit; **Fiona L'Estrange,** wise and experienced consultant who told us to print in Japan, and then proceeded to show us how; **Robb Besteman,** who provided the basic page designs that we still use ten years later; **Dana Lytle** and **Kevin Wade,** of Planet Design, who have been tangled up with us for six years now, all the while marrying good design with good marketing; **Susan Troller** and **John Anderson,** wordsmiths who understand what I want to say, and manage to say it better.

Ursula Abrams, Gina Roose, Linda Eglin, Shirley Ricketts, Jo Anne Schlesinger, Rose Noone, Pat Rahm, Karen Stocker, Darin Edington, previous staff members, individually and collectively contributing to a growing company and tutoring me in the process about the business of management.

The world's greatest management team, the ones who do all the work and gracefully allow me to get all the glory—**Yvonne Cooley,** for taking care of business in her own caring way; **Theresa Ace,** the master of the numbers; **Katie Kazan,** for caring about words that have meaning; **Deb Lovelace,** whose cool head and sense of humor keep us all on track; **Lillian Sizemore** and **Kathlyn Williams,** who give me and our books inspiration.

The late **Robert Jensen,** for his early vision that artists and architects should be talking to one another, and his very good thinking on our first two Review Committees; **Sue Wiggins,** another strong Southern woman, for being there; and **Malcolm Holzman, Beverly Russell, Paula Rice Jackson, Charles Morris Mount, Diana Calamari, Larry Shattuck, Peter Mistretta, Dorothy Solomon, Mark Simon, David Philippart, Janet Schirn, Bob Shipley**, all wise Review Committee members who have made the toughest of decisions over the years.

Mike Strohl and **Betty Vaughn**, who took me in hand and introduced me to the world of publishing and public relations; **Donna Warner, Dorothy Kalins, Joe Ruggiero, Roscoe Smith**, and many other big-time, real-life editors and publishers who believed, and in doing so, moved our credibility up by leaps and bounds; **Arnie Feldman**, for his all-important market research.

Ira Shapiro, generous advisor, sharing fountains of knowledge and experience, and encouraging this foolish idea; **Hidetoshi Gohara, George Dick, John Hanley**, representing the world's finest printers—they know how to make dreams come true; **Roland Algrant**, from Hearst, the first to recognize that the whole world would be interested in American crafts; **Don Traynor**, who then took the books out into the world, with affection and enthusiasm; **Bonnie Burke**, who watches out for us; **Stan Patey**, who made my life miserable but taught me one or two things about cash flow; **Bill Koehne**, our banker, who puts his money where his mouth is (thank goodness!).

Carol Sedestrom Ross, who wrote our first press release and sent it to her friends, gave us our first two sales reps, helped with that first (most important) party and in so many other ways since then; the late **Michael Scott**, for his early, generous support; **Lloyd Herman**, who let me drag my first set of color proofs into his office to show off, for his warmth and kindness over the years; **JoAnn Brown**, who extended her hand in friendship at the very beginning; **Leslie Ferrin**, gallery owner with a vision, for her energy and enthusiasm; **Josh Simpson** and **Lois Ahrens**, CERF soldiers who exalt in helping others; **Jeanne Fleming** and **Sheila O'Hara**, the best party organizers in the western world, who understood that dancing was the best means of communicating.

Jim Carley, who believed and invested in the abortive book that ended up launching a business; **David Rockefeller, Jr.**, for his psychic sustenance from day one; **Carew Hartwig**, who gave our book a name during a long evening of wine and talk; **Marsha Lindsay**, clear and stalwart friend, whose company helped us with the major marketing decisions; **Diane Everson**, who kept whispering encouragement when encouragement was sorely needed; **Susan King**, the attorney and confidant everyone should be so lucky to have; **Bob Horowitz**, who handles copyrights and trademarks, and makes me laugh; **Stephanie Jutt**, for being there; and **Claire** and **Len Tow**, for their sustaining friendship and blind faith that I could really pull this off.

My family, whose pride in what we have accomplished is only exceeded by their deep love, from which I benefit every day.

And lastly, the artists, the people who have overwhelmed me with blessings, making me rich with friendships, filling my life with laughter and dancing. There are too many to name, but you know who you are.

This book is dedicated to **Bill Dawson**, former employer and mentor, who has passed on his passion for marketing the arts to me and many others. This business is one of his footprints.

—*Toni Fountain Sikes*

SELECTED PUBLICATIONS & ORGANIZATIONS

PUBLICATIONS

AMERICAN CERAMICS

9 EAST 45 ST #603
NEW YORK, NY 10017
FAX 212-661-2389
TEL 212-661-4397

$28/year

American Ceramics, an art quarterly, was founded to enhance the preservation of ceramics' rich heritage and to document contemporary developments in the field. Articles feature the best and brightest ceramists: rising stars and established luminaries, as well as those early pioneers who transformed ceramics into a genuine art form.

AMERICAN CRAFT

AMERICAN CRAFT COUNCIL
72 SPRING ST
NEW YORK, NY 10012-4019
FAX 212-274-0650
TEL 212-274-0630

$40/year

American Craft, a bimonthly magazine, focuses on contemporary craft through artist profiles, reviews of major shows, a portfolio of emerging artists, a national calendar and news section, book reviews, as well as illustrated columns reporting on commissions, acquisitions and exhibitions.

CERAMICS MONTHLY

PROFESSIONAL PUBLICATIONS, INC.
1609 NORTHWEST BLVD
PO BOX 12788
COLUMBUS, OH 43212-0788
FAX 614-488-4561
TEL 614-488-8236

$22/year

Ceramics Monthly offers a broad range of articles—including artist profiles, reviews of exhibitions, historical features, and business and technical information—for potters, ceramic sculptors, collectors, gallery and museum personnel, and interested observers.

FIBERARTS

50 COLLEGE ST
ASHEVILLE, NC 28801
FAX 704-253-7952
TEL 704-253-0467
TEL 800-284-3388

$21/year

Five annual issues of *FIBERARTS* focus on contemporary textile art, including clothing, quilts, baskets, paper, tapestry, needlework and surface design. Features include artist profiles, critical essays, book reviews, and extensive listings of opportunities, events and resources.

FINE WOODWORKING

THE TAUNTON PRESS, INC.
PO BOX 5506
NEWTOWN, CT 06470-5506
FAX 203-426-3434
TEL 203-426-8171

$29/year

Fine Woodworking is a bimonthly magazine for all those who strive for and appreciate excellence in woodworking—veteran professional and weekend hobbyist alike. Articles by skilled woodworkers focus on basics of tool use, stock preparation and joinery, as well as specialized techniques and finishing.

GLASS MAGAZINE

THE GLASS WORKSHOP
647 FULTON ST
BROOKLYN, NY 11217
TEL 718-625-3685

$28/year

Glass Magazine, a full-color quarterly for design professionals, artists and collectors, features profiles of contemporary artists, an educational directory, and critical reviews of national and international exhibitions.

GLASS ART

TRAVIN INC.
PO BOX 260377
HIGHLANDS RANCH, CO 80126
FAX 303-791-7739
TEL 303-791-8998

$24/year U.S.

Glass Art, published bimonthly, includes business articles geared towards glass retailers and professional studios, as well as features on hot and cold glass techniques and artist profiles.

HOME FURNITURE

THE TAUNTON PRESS, INC.
63 S. MAIN ST
NEWTOWN, CT 06470-5506
FAX 203-426-3434
TEL 203-426-8171
TEL 800-888-8286

$20/year

Home Furniture, a new, full-color quarterly magazine, is both a 'how-to' and a portfolio of top contemporary furniture-makers. Articles include illustrated design features and artist profiles.

METALSMITH

5009 LONDONDERRY DR
TAMPA, FL 33647
FAX 813-977-8462
TEL 813-977-5326

$26/year

Metalsmith, a four-color quarterly, includes artist profiles, critical essays and reviews. Its focus is on contemporary metal artists producing jewelry, small sculpture and objects. *Metalsmith* is published by the Society of North American Goldsmiths.

PSG'S GLASS ARTIST

28 S STATE ST
NEWTOWN, PA 18940
FAX 215-860-1812
TEL 215-860-9947

$25/year

PSG's Glass Artist is a full-color bimonthly publication featuring articles on the creative use of the glass arts and crafts. In addition to how-to information and artist and studio profiles, each issue contains book reviews, career tips, a home-studio section, and a complete calendar of glass-related events.

SCULPTURE

INTERNATIONAL SCULPTURE CENTER
1050 17TH ST NW #250
WASHINGTON, DC 20036
FAX 202-785-0810
TEL 202-785-1144

$32/year

Sculpture, a bimonthly, four-color journal, focuses on established and emerging sculptors from the United States and abroad through profiles, interviews and critical reviews. Each issue also highlights collectors, commissions, opinion pieces, site-specific works and a calendar of exhibitions.

WOODSHOP NEWS

SOUNDINGS PUBLICATIONS, INC.
PRATT ST
ESSEX, CT 06426
FAX 203-767-1048
TEL 203-767-8227

$14.97/year

Woodshop News, published monthly, includes features and descriptions about new technology, artists and their techniques, trade news and source information.

SELECTED PUBLICATIONS & ORGANIZATIONS

ORGANIZATIONS

AMERICAN ASSOCIATION OF WOODTURNERS

667 HARRIET AVE
SHOREVIEW, MN 55126-4085
FAX 612-484-1724
TEL 612-484-9094

Mary Redig, Administrator

The American Association of Woodturners (AAW) is a non-profit organization dedicated to the advancement of woodturning. Sixty-seven chapters throughout the United States provide education and information for those interested in woodturning. Members include hobbyists, professionals, gallery owners, collectors, and wood and equipment suppliers.

AMERICAN CRAFT COUNCIL

72 SPRING ST
NEW YORK, NY 10012-4006
FAX 212-274-0650
TEL 212-274-0630

Hunter Kariher, Executive Director

The American Craft Council (ACC) stimulates public awareness and appreciation of the work of American craftspeople through museum exhibitions and educational programs, visual aids and publications. The American Craft Museum is an affiliate of the ACC; membership is shared.

The ACC consists of four operating units:

1. American Craft Enterprises produces exhibitions of handmade objects made by America's most talented craftspeople to enhance the awareness of American crafts and to provide the opportunity for the public to acquire such crafts;

2. American Craft Publishing produces a bimonthly magazine to enhance the understanding and appreciation of American crafts;

3. American Craft Association produces educational seminars and audio-visual materials to educate craftspeople, and provides support services for craftspeople;

4. American Craft Information Center provides information on American crafts through a book/exhibit catalog collection and unique files on American craftspeople.

AMERICAN SOCIETY OF FURNITURE ARTISTS

PO BOX 7491
HOUSTON, TX 77248-7491
FAX 713-556-5444
TEL 713-556-5444

Adam St. John, Executive Director

The American Society of Furniture Artists (ASOFA) is a non-profit organization dedicated to the field of 'art furniture' and to the artists who create it. Organized in 1989, ASOFA is the only national organization of such artists. The society's nationwide scope promotes the highest professional standards and provide its members with significant avenues for continued artistic and professional development.

AMERICAN TAPESTRY ALLIANCE

128 MONTICELLO RD
OAK RIDGE, TN 37830
TEL 615-483-0772

Marti Fleischer, Director

The American Tapestry Alliance was founded in 1982 to: (1) promote an awareness of and an appreciation for tapestries designed and woven in America; (2) establish, perpetrate and recognize superior quality tapestries by American tapestry artists; (3) encourage greater use of tapestries by corporate and private collectors; (4) educate the public about tapestry; and (5) coordinate national and international juried tapestry shows, exhibiting the finest quality American-made works.

CREATIVE GLASS CENTER OF AMERICA

1501 GLASSTOWN ROAD
PO BOX 646
MILLVILLE, NJ 08332-1566
FAX 609-825-2410
TEL 609-825-6800

The Creative Glass Center is a public attraction devoted to increasing know-how of glass works. The Creative Glass Center of America offers insight to glass arts through the Museum of American Glass, an informational resource center providing fellowships; demonstrations in the T.C. Wheaton Glass Factory; and various tours throughout Wheaton Village.

THE EMBROIDERERS' GUILD OF AMERICA, INC.

335 W. BROADWAY #100
LOUISVILLE, KY 40202
FAX 502-584-7900
TEL 502-589-6956

Jeanette Lovensheimer, President

The Embroiderer's Guild of America (EGA) seeks to set and maintain high standards of design, color and workmanship in all kinds of embroidery and canvas work. EGA sponsors lectures, exhibitions, competitions and field trips; offers examinations for teaching certification; and serves as an information source for needlework in the United States. EGA also maintains a comprehensive reference library for research and study, and publishes *Needle Arts*, a quarterly magazine.

GLASS ART SOCIETY

1305 FOURTH AVE #711
SEATTLE, WA 98101-2401
FAX 206-382-2630
TEL 206-382-1305

Alice Rooney, Executive Director

The Glass Art Society (GAS), an international non-profit organization, was founded in 1971 to encourage excellence and advance appreciation, understanding and development of the glass arts worldwide. GAS promotes communication among artists, educators, students, collectors, gallery and museum personnel, art critics, manufacturers and others through an annual conference and through the *Glass Art Society Journal* and newsletters.

HANDWEAVERS GUILD OF AMERICA, INC.

2402 UNIVERSITY AVE W #702
ST. PAUL, MN 55114-1701
FAX 612-646-0806
TEL 612-646-0802
E-MAIL to Compuserve 73744.202

Joan Cass Wells, Executive Director

The Handweavers Guild of America, Inc. (HGA) is an international non-profit organization dedicated to upholding excellence, promoting the textile arts, and preserving our textile heritage. HGA provides a forum for education, opportunities for networking, and inspiration and encouragement for handweavers, handspinners and related fiber artists. HGA publishes a quarterly journal for members, *Shuttle, Spindle & Dyepot*.

SELECTED PUBLICATIONS & ORGANIZATIONS

ORGANIZATIONS cont.

INTERNATIONAL SCULPTURE CENTER

1050 17TH ST NW #250
WASHINGTON, DC 20036
FAX 202-785-0810
TEL 202-785-1144

David Furchgott, Executive Director

The International Sculpture Center (ISC) is a not-for-profit membership organization devoted to the advancement of contemporary sculpture. The ISC publishes *Sculpture* magazine, *Maquette*, and *InSite*. Activities include conferences; workshops; Sculpture Source, a computerized referral service and registry; exhibitions; and various other member benefits.

INTERNATIONAL TAPESTRY NETWORK

PO BOX 203228
ANCHORAGE, AK 99520-3228
FAX 907-346-3316
TEL 907-346-2392

Helga Berry, President

International Tapestry Network (ITNET) is a not-for-profit global network of tapestry artists, teachers, curators and collectors. ITNET works to develop greater awareness of contemporary tapestry as an art form by sponsoring international tapestry exhibitions and by educating the public and encouraging dialogue about tapestry on an international level. ITNET publishes a quarterly newsletter, distributed worldwide. Newsletter correspondents and advisory board members search for and share news of exhibitions, educational opportunities and other tapestry events.

NATIONAL COUNCIL ON EDUCATION FOR THE CERAMIC ARTS

PO BOX 158
BANDON, OR 97411
TEL 503-347-4394

Regina Brown, Executive Secretary

The National Council on Education for the Ceramic Arts (NCECA) is a professional organization of individuals whose interests, talents, or careers are primarily focused on the ceramic arts. NCECA strives to stimulate, promote and improve education in the ceramic arts, and to gather and disseminate information and ideas that are vital and stimulating to teachers, studio artists and others throughout the creative studies community.

NATIONAL WOODCARVERS ASSOCIATION

PO BOX 43218
CINCINNATI, OH 45243
TEL 513-561-0627

Edward F. Gallenstein, President

The National Woodcarvers Association (NWCA) promotes woodcarving and fellowship among its members; encourages exhibitions and area get-togethers; and assists members in finding tool and wood suppliers, as well as markets for their work. Many distinguished professional woodcarvers in the United States and abroad share their know-how with fellow members.

SOCIETY OF AMERICAN SILVERSMITHS

PO BOX 3599
CRANSTON, RI 02910-0599
FAX 401-461-3196
TEL 401-461-3156

Jeffrey Herman, Executive Director

The Society of American Silversmiths (SAS) was founded in 1989 to preserve the art and history of contemporary handcrafted holloware, flatware and sculpture. SAS also provides its juried artisan members with support, networking and greater access to the market, partly through its annual traveling exhibitions. The public is welcome to consult SAS with all silver-related questions, including those regarding silversmithing techniques, history and restoration. A unique referral service commissions work from artisan members for collectors, corporations and museums.

SURFACE DESIGN ASSOCIATION

PO BOX 20799
OAKLAND, CA 94620
FAX 707-829-3285
TEL 510-841-2008

Joy Stocksdale, Administrator

The Surface Design Association promotes surface design through education; encouragement of individual artists; communication of technical information and information concerning professional opportunities; and the exchange of ideas through conferences and publications.

INDEX OF ARTISTS BY STATE

ARIZONA
Konreid Muench Designs   141
Lindstrom, Rachel   38
Peterson, Jewell   40

ARKANSAS
Cade, Barbara   31

CALIFORNIA
Adachi, Karen   20
Allebes, Emma   10
Athari, Shawn   89, 93, 161
Bailey, Sally   29
Brotherton, Barbara   96
Burg, Myra   97
Buskirk, Mary Balzer   47
Chatelain, Martha   22
Concepts By J, Inc.   126
Davis, Alonzo   101
Finch, Doris   33
Fleming, Mari Marks   164
Hayashi, Yoshi   117
Ikeda, Shuji   165
Ilie, Marie-Laurie   37
Jacobson-May, Carrie   56
Jacoby, Victor   5
Klein, M.A.   12
Lightspann Illumination
  Design   153
Ling, Cal   59
May, Therese   14
Mordak, Edward   61
Morris, Pam   154
Neblett, Jean   15
Nelson, Keiko   24
Nourot Glass Studio   170
O'Hara, Sheila   8
Ratcliff, Mary Curtis   41
Reiber, Paul   129
Schulze, Joan   xiv, 43
Sharp, Kathleen   18
Sturman, Martin   172, 108
Todaro, Daniele   67
Torrance, Ama   79
Venable, Susan   109
Zeitlin, Harriet   69

COLORADO
Carlson, Deborah   98
National Sculptors' Guild   169

CONNECTICUT
Cunningham, Beth   100, 111
Friedman, Alexandra   53
MacDonald, Elizabeth   76, 86, 88
Masaryk, Thomas   xi, 118
Thomchuk, Marjorie   25

DISTRICT OF COLUMBIA
Adams, B.J.   27, 28
Levine, Verena   13

FLORIDA
Bryant, Laura Militzer   4
Colson, Frank   149, 162
Fishman, George F.   83
Meier, Anne Mayer   168
Pearson, Charles   171
Roeder, Timothy   171
Traylor, Angelika   156, 176

GEORGIA
Lahtinen, Silja   103

ILLINOIS
Langmar, Itala   58
Lopez, Joyce P.   19, 39

INDIANA
Miller, Dianna Thornhill   104
Miller, Jim   104
Off The Wall Design
  Studios, Inc.   128

KENTUCKY
Kaviar, Craig   139

LOUISIANA
Soper, Celia   107

MARYLAND
Blakeslee, Carolyn   94

MASSACHUSETTS
Box, Ted   95, 124
Entner, Jeff   95, 124
Perry, Linda S.   xiii, 16
Ryerson Designs   131
Winfisky, Jonathan   xvi, 174

MICHIGAN
Walker, Tim   173

MINNESOTA
Elvig, Glenn   127, 143
Parrott, Diann   159

NEVADA
Pellman, Kathryn Alison   63

NEW JERSEY
Cloisonné Enamels by
  M. Slepian   99
Lenker, Marlene   23
Tischler, Peter   133

NEW MEXICO
Alexander, George   81
Christopher Thomson
  Ironworks   138
Dozier, Pat   51
Weigel, Doug   xiii, 142
Young, Allen   157, 175
Young, Nancy J.   157, 175

NEW YORK
Art on Tiles   82
Biggs, Andrea M.   113, 121
Biggs, Timothy G.   113, 121
Bill Gibbons Studio   114
Calyer, Sean   137
Farley, Marsha   102
Forth, Marilyn   x, 34
Griffin, Joan   54
Heithmar, J. Louis   84
Hio, Bill   36
Jasen, J.E.   160, 167
Kimber, Susan   57
Knoblauch, Paul   140
Koenigsberg, Nancy   58
Naskalov, Igor   147
Plotner, Judith   63
Putnam, Toni   148
Terrell, Claude   132
Uehling, Judith   26

NORTH CAROLINA
Clark, John   xv, 125
Grenell, Barbara   9, 35
Owen, Carol   63

OHIO
Burnes, Susan Eileen   30
Cohen, Elaine Albers   21
Stubbins, Joan   66

OKLAHOMA
Atwood, Marjorie A.   112

OREGON
Rix, Bill   130
Van Leunen, Alice   110

PENNSYLVANIA
Benzakin, Brigitte   144
FurnARTure etc.   146
Goodman, Johanna
  Okovic   166

RHODE ISLAND
Lehr, Beverlee   85
Mossman, Loretta   7
Shaw, Kurt   106

Darmohraj, Natalie   158

TENNESSEE
Leander, Ulrika   xiv, 6
Rowell, Bernie   105
Whatley, Anita Joan   69

TEXAS
Eyecon, Inc.   115
Murphy, Melissa A.   119

UTAH
Doubek, Carole Alden   163
Fillerup, Peter M.   152

VERMONT
Sawyer, Susan   17

VIRGINIA
Mason, Toby   92

WASHINGTON
Cassidy, Beth   11
DiNino, Lynn   145
Evans, Phyllis 'Ceratto'   32
Holzknecht, Katherine   55
Perrine, Karen   63
Richards, William C.   87, 155
Richardson, Amanda   xvi, 42
Stonington, Nancy Taylor   44
Vigini & Associates   120

WEST VIRGINIA
Hutchinson, Janet M.   55

WISCONSIN
Eggert, Dale R.   91
Neff, Laurel   77

CANADA
Brathwaite, Stephen   90
Fehr, Dale B.   116
King, Chris   57

INDEX OF ARTISTS AND COMPANIES

A

Acord, James 65
Adachi, Karen 20
Adair, Sandy 46
Adams, B.J. 27, 28
Alberetti, Mary Lou 70
Albert, Donna 46
Alexander, George 81
Alexander, Robert W. 46
Alfredo Ratinoff Studio 70
Allebes, Emma 10
Armstrong, Carol 46
Amundson, Marta 46
Anansa-Puruo Designs 46
Andrew Leicester & Associates 70
Antichità Moderna 70
Architectural Ceramics 70
Arnold, Chris 115
Art Quilts 46
Art in Fiber 28
Art on Tiles 82
Artfocus, Ltd. 22
Artistic License 71
Asato, Mimi 71
Ashley, Melinda 71
Askew, Sandy 46
Aten, Cathy Phillips 46
Athari, Shawn 89, 93, 161
Athens, Ellen 46
Atleson, Carol 46
Atwood, Marjorie A. 112

B

Bachelder, Joann 46
Bahnsen, Shirley Roese 46
Bailey, Sally 29
Baker, Martin K. 46
Bally, Doris 46
Barbara Farrell Arts 46
Barbro Designs 96
Barker-Schwartz Designs 46
Barkley, Teresa 46
Barrington, Sonya Lee 47
Barron, Barbara, Ruth & Steven 47
Bartel, Marvin 71
Bartels, Marlo 71
Beck, Doreen 47
Becker, Judy 47
Becker, Pamela E. 47
Bedessem, Barbara 71
Benedikt Strebel Ceramics 71
Benner, Sue 47
Bennett, Astrid Hilger 47
Benson-Vos, Christina 47
Benzakin, Brigitte 144
Berkowitz, Lynn 47
Berman, Simi 71
Berner, Julie 47
Bernie Rowell Studio 105
Bérubé, Louise Lemieux 47

Big Sur Handwovens 47
Biggs, Andrea M. 113, 121
Biggs, Timothy G. 113, 121
Bill Gibbons Studio 114
Billings, Elizabeth 47
Blakeslee, Carolyn 94
Bliss, Susan O. 71
Bluestone, Rebecca 47
Bobin, Chris 47
Boney, Nancy 47
Boozer, Margaret 71
Boussard, Dana 47
Bowers, George-Ann 47
Box, Ted 95, 124
Brabec, Odette 47
Braen, Jeanne 48
Brathwaite, Stephen 90
Brauer, Ann 48
Breckenridge, Bruce 71
Bringle, Cynthia 71
Brisson Studio 71
Bromberg, Ann Sherwin 48
Brothers, Lynda 48
Brotherton, Barbara 96
Brown, Tafi 48
Bryant, Laura Militzer 4
Bryant, Lois 48
Burg, Myra 97
Burling, Patricia 48
Burnes, Susan Eileen 30
Buskirk Studios 48
Buskirk, Mary Balzer 48

C

Cade, Barbara 31
Cal Ling Paperworks 58
Calvert, Moneca 48
Calyer, Sean 137
Card, Karen 71
Carlson, Deborah 98
Carlson, Robert 71
Carlstrom, Lucinda 48
Carter, Erika 48
Cassidy, Beth 11
Chaisson, Mary Allen 49
Chatelain, Martha 22
Christopher Thomson Ironworks 138
Clark, Jill Nordfors 49
Clark, John xv, 125
Clawson, Susanne 49
Clay Canvas Designs 87, 155
Claymania 71
Cloisonné Enamels by M. Slepian 99
Cocilovo, Antonio 49
Coelho Studios 71
Cohen, Elaine Albers 21
Colson School of Art/Colson Studio 162
Colson, Frank 162, 149
Concepts By J, Inc. 126

Contemporary Tapestry Weaving 6
Content, Judith 49
Cooper, Debbi 49
Cooper, Stephanie Randall 49
Corcoran, Ann 170
Cornett, Barbara 49
Crain, Diana 72
Crain, Joyce 49
Crane, Barbara Lydecker 49
Creative Textures 168
Crouse, Gloria E. 49
Cunningham, Beth 100, 111
Curtis, Lynda 72
Cusack, Margaret 50

D

D. Benjamin Fehr Design 116
Dabbert Studio 72
Dabinett, Diana 50
Dale Allison-Hartley Studio Gallery 72
Dales, Judy B. 50
Dalton, Suzanne 50
Darmohraj, Natalie 158
Darr-Hope, Heidi 50
Dauzig, Phillip 72
Davidson, Karen 50
Davies, D. Joyce 50
Davis Tile Techniques, Inc. 72
Davis, Alonzo 101
Davis, Ardyth 50
Davis, Lenore 50
Davis, Nancy Stanford 50
Davis-Shaklho, Nanette 50
DeYoung, Nancy 51
Deconstructed Designs Ltd 50
Deemer, Jean 50
Deimel, Andrea 50
DelZoppo, E. 50
Denier, Linda 51
Denton, Lynn B. 72
Design Tiles of Mifflinburg 72
Devitt, Nell 72
DiNino, Lynn 145
Diann Parrott Yardage Art 159
Dillon, Sally 51
Dimension Designs 72
Dingle, Judith 51
Dioszegi, Judy 51
Doctors, Eric 72
Donegan, Steven 72
Donneson, Seena 51
Doris Finch Fabric Art 33
Doubek & Doubek Studios 163
Doubek, Carole Alden 163
Dow, Arnelle A. 51
Dozier, Pat 51
Drawn Thread Designs 51
Dudchenko, Nancy Weeks 72
Dunshee, Susan 51
Durbin, Donna 51

E

Eaton Designs 51
Echols, Margit 52
Edzard, Lore 52
Efrem Weitzman Art Works 52
Egen, Su 52
Eggert Glass 91
Eggert, Dale R. 91
Einstein, Sylvia H. 52
Ellis, Andra 72
Ellis, Maureen 72
Elvig, Glenn 127, 143
Entner, Jeff 95, 124
Erickson, Nancy N. 52
Eubel, Karen 52
Evans, Phyllis 'Ceratto' 32
Evart, Eleanor J. 73
Exciting Lighting 154
Eyecon, Inc. 115

F

Fallert, Caryl Bryer 52
Farley, Marsha 102
Fawkes, Judith Poxson 52
Fehr, Dale B. 116
Fein, Randy 73
Fiber Design Studio 50
Fillerup, Peter M. 152
Finch, Doris 33
Fireclay Tile 73
Fishman, George F. 83
Flanders, Pamela 52
Fleisher, Marti 52
Fleming, Carol 73
Fleming, Mari Marks 164
Fleming, Penelope 73
Fletcher, Barbara 52
Forbes-deSoule, Steven 73
Forman, Mark W. 73
Forman, Robert 52
Forth, Marilyn x, 34
Foster, Jim 73
Fountain, Roberta A. 53
Fowler and Thelen Studio 53
Frederick, Sarah 73
Friedman, Alexandra 53
Friedman, Jan 53
Fuerst, Wayne A.O. 53
Fulper Tile 73
FurnARTure etc. 146

G

Gardels, Susan 53
Garrison, Jeff 115
Geiger, Judith 53
Gersen, Carol H. 53
Gilbert, James R. 53
Gilmour, Susan 53
Glashausser, Suellen 53
Glenn Elvig Sculpture/Furniture Design 127
Goldsmith, Layne 53

Golub, Ina   53
Goodman Associates, Inc.   166
Goodman, Johanna Okovic   166
Gooseneck Designs   73
Gowell, Ruth   53
Gray, Charles   53
Gray, Elise   73
Grebow, Marion   73
Green, Laura Elizabeth   53
Gregor, Michelle   73
Grenell, Barbara   9, 35
Griffin, Don   53
Griffin, Joan   54
Grisham, Marilyn   54
Gunderman, Karen, M.   73

H

Haberfeld, Claire Fay   54
Hall, Marilee   71
Halvorsen, Larry   73
Hammond, Marcia   54
Handsel Gallery   81
Hanson, Harriet   54
Harding, Tim   54
Harris, Lisa   74
Harris, Peter   54
Harris, Renee   54
Hartley, Ann L.   54
Haskell, Sarah D.   54
Hayashi, Yoshi   117
Hecht, Deborah   74
Heidingsfelder, Sharon   54
Heimann, Mark   74
Heine, Martha   54
Heithmar, J. Louis   84
Held, Marion E.   74
Held, Sheila A.   54
Helio Graphics   54
Heller, Barbara   54
Henegar, Susan Hart   54
Henrion, Marilyn   54
Hernmarck, Helena   54
Herrick, Jane   55
Hill, Pamela   55
Hio, Bill   36
Hogan Young   74
Holden, Dorothy   55
Holland, Bonnie Lee   55
Hollister, Claudia   74
Hollister, Jeri   74
Holster, Elizabeth   55
Holzknecht, Katherine   51
Hooked on Art   29
Houston, Richard   74
Hsiung, Dora   55
Hubbard, John D.   55
Hughes, Dorothy   55
Huhn, Wendy C.   55
Hunt Keiser Studio Tile   74
Hunt, Constance   55
Hutchinson, Janet M.   55

I

Ikeda, Shuji   165
Ilie, Marie-Laurie   37
Intaglia   84
Ira Ono Designs   55
Ireland, Elaine   55
Irene R. De Gair Tapestries   56
Irish, Peg   56
Irving, Carol Kasmer   56
Irwin, Jeff   74
Island Silk   52
Iverson, Susan   56

J

J K Design   56
Jacobson, Shellie   74
Jacobson-May, Carrie   56
Jacoby, Victor   5
Jaffe, Amanda   74
Jahns, Lucy A.   56
James, Lois   56
James, Michael   56
Jansen, Catherine   56
Jasen, J.E.   160, 167
Jensen, B.J.   74
Jeroski, Anthony J.   74
Jocelyn Studio   56, 75
Joell Mileo - Papermaker   56
Johansen, Tove B.   75
Johanson, Rosita   56
John Clark Furniture   125
Johnson, Vicki L.   56
Johnston, Ann   56
Jolly, Olgalyn   56
Joyce Hulber Tapestry & Textile
   Restoration   56
Joyce Lopez Studio   39
Judith H. Perry Designs   57
Judith Plotner Art Quilts/L'Atelier
   Plotner   63
Juniper Tree Tileworks   75

K

Kaida Originals   57
Kamstra, Hendrika   57
Kanter, Janis   57
Karesh, Anna   57
Karlin, Marcia   57
Kasper, Mary Luce   57
Katsiaficas, Diane   75
Katz, Donna J.   57
Kaviar Forge   139
Kaviar, Craig   139
Keen, Judi   57
Keer, Ira A.   xv
Kemenyffy, Steven & Susan   75
Kennedy, Janet   57
Kenney, Douglas   75
Kenny, Anne Marie   57
Kimber, Susan   57
King, Chris   57
King, Glenda   57

King, Sara Newberg   58
Klein, Kimberly Haldeman   58
Klein, M.A.   12
Knapp, Stephen   75
Knoblauch, Paul   140
Koblitz, Karen   75
Kochansky, Ellen   58
Koenigsberg, Nancy   58
Konreid Muench Designs   141
Kopchik, Joan   58
Korwin, Laurence   58
Kowalski, Libby   58
Kraft, Grace   58
Kreitlow, Candace   58
Krysia   75
Kuchma, Lialia   58
Kuemmerlein, Janet   58

L

LaLuz Canyon Studio Tiles   75
Ladochy, Peter   75
Lahtinen, Silja   103
Laico, Colette   58
Lane, Mary   58
Langmar, Itala   58
Larned, Gail   58
Larochette, Jean Pierre   60
Larsen, Karen   59
Larsen, Suzanne   59
Larzelere, Judith   59
Latka Studios   75
Lawrence, Iran   59
Lay, Patricia   75
Leander, Ulrika   xiv, 6
Lee, Deirdre   75
Lee, James David   128
Lee, Susan Webb   59
Lehman, Connie   59
Lehr, Beverlee   85
Lenker Fine Arts   23
Lenker, Marlene   23
Lester, Michelle   59
Levine, Judy Zoelzer   59
Levine, Verena   13
Lhotka, Bonny   59
Lightspann Illumination
   Design   153
Lilienthal, Wendy   59
Lindsay, David   170
Lindstrom, Rachel   38
Ling, Cal   59
Lintault, M. Joan   59
Lollar, Thomas W.   75
Lopez, Joyce P.   19, 39
LorArt Ceramics   76
Lowden, Antonia   60
Lubin, Nancy   60
Lumpkins, Peggy Clark   60
Lurie, Yael   60
Lykins, Jere   76
Lyon, Nancy   60

M

M. Sturman Steel Sculptures
   108, 172
M.A. Klein Design   12
MacDonald, Elizabeth   76, 86, 88
MacDonald, Margo   60
MacEachern, Ann   60
MacKay, Jackie   60
Maginniss, Irene   60
Maher, Jan   60
Malarcher, Patricia   60
Maltbie, Thomas   76
Manning, Ruth   60
Marcus, Sharon   60
Marie, Jane Golding   60
Marilor Art Studio   37
Mark Lawrence Associates   102
Mary Kay Colling Contemporary
   Paper Art   60
Masaryk, Thomas   xi, 118
Mason, Toby   92
Matiosian, Pamela   61
Matthews, Martha   61
Maureen R. Weiss   76
May, Therese   14
McAfee, Phoebe   61
McGee, Donna   76
McGinnis, Julie   61
McKenzie, Dianne   61
Meepos, Jay   126
Meier, Anne Mayer   168
Merriman, Christine   76
Miller, Dianna Thornhill   104
Miller, Jim   104
Millham, Geraldine   61
Minear, Beth   61
Minisa, Brenda   76
Minkowitz, Norma   61
Mitchell, Julia   61
Mollohan, Kathleen   61
Montana Art Works   77
Moonelis, Judy   77
Moore, Dottie   61
Mordak, Edward   59
Morris, Pam   154
Mossman, Loretta   7
Muench, Konried   141
Murphy, Melissa A.   119

N

N. Taylor Stonington, Inc.   44
Nadolski, Stephanie   62
Nash, Dominie   62
Naskalov, Igor   147
Natalka Designs   158
Nathan-Roberts, Miriam   62
National Sculptors' Guild   169
Navarrete, Juan & Patricia   77
Naylor, Patricia   77
Neblett, Jean   15
Neff, Laurel   77
Nelson, Dana H.   62

INDEX OF ARTISTS AND COMPANIES

Nelson, Keiko   24
Nesbitt, Anna   62
Newman, Rochelle   62
Newman, Velda E.   62
Nickolson, Anne McKenzie   62
Nigrosh, Leon   77
Nixon, Cynthia   62
Nørdgren, Elizabeth   62
Norgaard, Inge   62
Nourot Glass Studio   170
Nourot, Michael   170

O

O'Hara, Sheila   8
Oaks, Susan M.   62
Ocean Art   95, 124
Off The Wall Design
   Studios, Inc.   128
Old Time Woods   130
Omni Art Design   104
One Off Studio   77
Oppenheimer, Ellen   62
Ort, Alena   77
Owen, Carol   63

P

P. Tischler Chair & Cabinetmaker,
   Inc.   133
Page, Karen S.   63
Park, Soyoo Hyunjoo   63
Parker, Sharron   63
Parrott, Diann   159
Parsley, Jacque   63
Paul, Rita   82
Payne, Carolyn   77
Peace Valley Tile   77
Pearce, Eve S.   63
Pearson, Charles   171
Pellman, Kathryn Alison   63
Penny, Donald C.   77
Perrine, Karen   63
Perry, Linda S.   xiii, 16
Peterson, Jewell   40
Piepenburg, Gail   78
Pierce, Sue   63
Pipsissewa   63
Pleur Air Studios   79
Plotner, Judith   63
Pollack, Junco Sato   63
Pollen, Jason   63
Pop Cat Studio   173
Powers, Kristin & Stephen   78
Powning Designs Ltd.   78
Pretty, Suzanne   63
Prichard, Nancy   64
Putnam, Toni   148

Q

Quint-Rose   64

R

Randall, Jud   78
Ratcliff, Mary Curtis   41
Redman, Collins   64
Reed, Fran   64
Reflective Glass Mosaics   92
Reiber, Paul   129
Reichel, Myra   64
Reider, Robin   64
Revor, Sister Remy   64
Rice, Paula   78
Richards, William C.   87, 155
Richardson, Amanda   xvi, 42
Rix, Bill   130
Robarge, Nanilee S.   64
Robbins, Eva R.   64
Rococo Studio Of Fiber, Color
   & Design   64
Roeder, Timothy   171
Rogers, John Winston   78
Romey-Tanzer, Gretchen   64
Roslyn Manor House, Inc.   147
Ross, Gloria F.   64
Rowell, Bernie   105
Russell, Joan   64
Russell, Jude   64
Ryerson Designs   131
Ryerson, Mitch   131

S

Sandoval, Arturo Alonzo   64
Santmyers, Stephanie   64
Sattler, Lois S.   78
Saville, Joy   64
Sawyer, Susan   17
Scherbak, Loren   78
Scherer, Deidre   64
Schloss, Julia   64
Schulze, Joan   xiv, 43
Sears, Amanda   65
Sebastian, Barbara   78
Sellers, Sally A.   65
Sharles   169
Sharp, Kathleen   18
Shaw, Ericka Clark   78
Shaw, Kurt   106
Shawcroft, Barbara   65
Shawn Athari's, Inc.   89, 161
Sheba, Michael   78
Shie, Susan   65
Shore, Sally   65
Shusta, Ane   65
Siegel, Dink   47
Siegel, Laura Lazar   65
Silja's Fine Art Studio   103
Silk, Louise   65
Sinclair, Mary Jo   65
Singleton, Susan   65
Sires, J. Paul   78
Skarl Ceramics   78
Slepian, Marian   99
Sloane, Julie   65

Sly, Mary E.   65
Smathers, C. Elizabeth   65
Smith, Barbara Lee   65
Smith, Elly   66
Smith, Gloria Zmolek   66
Smith, Pat   78
Soper, Celia   107
Soriero, Margaret   78
Southworth, Lyn   66
Spann, Christina   153
Specially For Chidren   119
Spoering, Kathy   66
Springflower   66
Standley, Care   66
Steel Sculptures by Doug
   Weigel   142
Steel, Hillary   66
Steele, Elinor   66
Steinberg, Alan   79
Stockl, Charly   146
Stocksdale, Joy   66
Stoll, Glenne   66
Stonington, Nancy Taylor   44
Story, Harriet   79
Stubbins, Joan   66
Sturman, Martin   108, 172
Sullivan, Janice M.   67
Surving, Natalie & Richard   79
Susan Starr & Co.   67
Sward, Lynne   67
Sylwester, Laurie   79

T

Tactile Impressions   40
Tangier Sound Studios   94
Taube, Terry   67
Taylor-Brown, Cameron   67
Tennen, Denise S.   79
Terra Designs   79
Terrell, Claude   132
Tetkowski, Neil   79
Textile Studio   67
Thomchuk, Marjorie   25
Thomson, Christopher   138
Tischler, Peter   133
Todaro & Associates   66
Todaro, Daniele   66
Tolpo, Carolyn & Vincent   67
Tomasso, Raymond D.   67
Topham, Pamela   67
Torrance, Ama   79
Touchstone Ceramics   77
Traylor, Angelika   156, 176
Trenshaw, Katheryn M.   79
Trompe L'Oeil and Painted
   Finishes   118
Tuegel, Michele   67
Tunick, Susan   79
Tustin, Gayle L.   79
Twinrocker Handmade Paper   67
Tyni-Rautiainen, Kaija   67

U

Uehling, Judith   26
Utterback, Connie   67

V

Vaccaro Studio   79
Van Gelder, Lydia   67
Van Leunen, Alice   110
Vaslow, Aase   67
Venable Studio   109
Venable, Susan   109
Vera, Betty   68
Verena Levine Pictorial and
   Narrative Quilts   13
Vierow, Judith   68
Vigini & Associates   120
Vigini, Nicola   120

W

Wagner, Barbara Allen   68
Walker, David   68
Walker, Tim   173
Walsh, Julia   68
Warn, GraceAnn   68
Wasilowske, Laura   68
Weaving/Southwest   68
Webber, Helen   69
Weigel, Doug   xiii, 142
Weissler, Leanne   69
Weissman, Joan   80
Westfall, Carol D.   69
Whatley, Anita Joan   69
White, Judi Maureen   69
Whitehead Street Pottery   171
Whittington, Nancy   69
Wild West Designs   152
Wiley, Elizabeth   69
Williams, Jody   69
Wilson, Jay   69
Windlines   69
Wines-DeWan, Nancy   69
Winfisky, Jonathan   xvi, 174
Winokur, Paula   80

Y

Yankowitz, Nina   80
Young, Allen   157, 175
Young, Nancy J.   157, 175

Z

Zale, Maureen   69
Zeitlin, Harriet   69
Zen Again Productions   69
Zheutlin, Dale   80
Zicafoose, Mary   69
Ziebarth, Charlotte   69
Ziek, Bhakti   69
Zigulis, A. Jeffrey   80
Zimmerman, Arnold   80